Commentary on the Treatise on the True Devotion to the Blessed Virgin

by

Fr. Armand Plessis
(Montfort Father)

Copyright © 2014 Casimir Valla
All rights reserved.

This book, in whole or in part, may not be reproduced or transmitted in any form or by any means, electronic or mechanical, including, but not limited to, audio recordings, facsimiles, photocopying, email, floppy disk, network, or information storage and retrieval systems without explicit written permission, dated and signed from the publisher.

"God wishes that His holy Mother should be at present more known, more loved, more honoured, than she has ever been" (St. Louis-Marie Grignion de Montfort, *Treatise on the True Devotion to Mary*, n° 55).

For more excellent Marian books, please visit:

BlessedMaryMotherofGod.com/books.html

Visit us here also:
pinterest.com/ephesus431
holymarymotherofgod.wordpress.com

To the Reader

This commentary is the seventh book in the only series ever published on the "True Devotion to Mary".

The other books are:
(1) **The Holy Slavery of the Admirable Mother of God** – The book which made the Marian devotion of St. Louis-Marie de Montfort "go viral". Reading this book led to his starting the group 'the Slaves of Jesus in Mary'.
(2) **Consecration to Mary according to St. Louis de Montfort** – Two books in one. These two books explain very clearly the reasons for consecrating ourselves to Mary, and they refute any objections to doing so.
(3) **Preparation for Consecration to the Most Blessed Virgin** – A unique book in preparing for the consecration, because it includes examples from the life of St. Louis-Marie at the end of each meditation, showing you how he himself lived the Marian devotion that he taught.
(4) **To Jesus through Mary** – This book goes beyond any preparation for consecration book, because it shows you how to live the True Devotion at every moment of your life. Very enlightening.
(5) **Holy Communion in Union with Mary according to Blessed de Montfort** – A thorough explanation of the teaching of St. Louis-Marie in the last part of the "True Devotion to Mary" on how to receive and profit from Holy Communion made in union with Mary.
(6) **The Virgin Mary and the Apostles of the Last Times** – St. Louis-Marie de Montfort said: "At the end of the world, the Most High with His holy Mother has to form for Himself great saints, who shall surpass most of the other saints in sanctity." This is the only book solely devoted to explaining this particular teaching of St. Louis-Marie.

You may also be interested in:
The Marian Writings of St. Robert Bellarmine – This book contains the Marian writings and previously untranslated biographical material about the Saint of whom Pope Clement VIII said "the Church of God has not his equal in learning."

All of these Marian books are available through Amazon.

Table of Contents

Preface..1
Historical Introduction to the Study of the True Devotion........6

Commentary on the Treatise on the True Devotion
Introduction..40

First Part
The True Devotion in General

Chapter I..53
Necessity of the True Devotion

Chapter II..185
Nature of the True Devotion to Mary

Second Part
The Perfect Devotion to Mary

Chapter I..270
The Nature of the Perfect Devotion

Chapter II...291
The Motives of the Perfect Devotion

Chapter III..361
The Effects of the Perfect Devotion

Chapter IV...384
The Practices of the Perfect Devotion

Supplement to Chapter 4..455

PREFACE

The public gave a favorable reception to the first literal Commentary on the Treatise on the True Devotion. *Five thousand copies were quickly snatched up. Proof that people ardently wish to fathom the teachings of St. Louis-Marie de Montfort.*

The second edition that we present today has been carefully revised, and, in this work, we took into account the wishes expressed by our readers. If, however, certain strongly doctrinal pages could neither be eliminated nor totally clarified, this is due to the very nature of the work. We had undertaken to comment on the Treatise on the True Devotion. *We have to explain all that it contains. And it would be impossible to accomplish that without ever touching on philosophical or theological notions.*

Nevertheless, let the reader who is unfamiliar with these lofty sciences not become discouraged. His persevering efforts will perhaps triumph over the difficulty. But, certainly, the momentary obscurity which he will sometimes run into will by no means harm his full understanding of the following pages.

*
* *

Let us recall the works of our predecessors which we specially utilized.

There is, first of all, **La vie spirituelle à l'école du Bienheureux Louis-Marie de Montfort** (The spiritual life at the school of Blessed Louis-Marie de Montfort), *by the Very Rev. Fr. Antonin Lhoumeau, S.M.M. (1852-1920). This book was and still is a very great success. He expresses the Marian spirituality of the Treatise, and he explains it fully, by situating it in its traditional dogmatic and ascetic context. It will* *gain from being read or read again after this Commentary, whose logical sequel it is henceforth.*

There is also the Italian magazine "Regina dei cuori," founded in Rome, in 1914, by Rev. Fr. Hubert-Marie Gebhard, S.M.M. (1876-1939). Every month, from 1914 to 1925 and from 1932 to 1934, this magazine contained a part of a vast commentary, begun by the editor. But a man's lifetime would not have been enough to bring to a conclusion a work of these proportions, because, over the course of thirteen years, Father Gebhard succeeded in commenting only on the first 42 numbers of the Treatise.

It is a work of the same kind that we wanted to start again, on a smaller scale, and to continue until the end. But by no means do we claim to have exhausted the matter. Successors will come who will fill the gaps of those who will have opened the path. Would it not already be a good excuse for those whom our work would have disappointed?

*
* *

Others will say perhaps: Why this project? Is not the book of Father de Montfort sufficiently clear by itself? What good is it to overload it with all this cumbersome apparatus?

Now, the **Treatise on the True Devotion** *condenses in one small volume a considerable sum of dogmatic truths and spiritual counsels. Several times, the author shows his intention of only saying things briefly, and he avoids lingering over proofs. Benedict XV himself notes this character: If the book is of great authority and great unction, it is also "little by volume."*

Doctrinal density, included in a brief text! The same conciseness naturally calls for explanations. Otherwise many readers will be confused, and will declare themselves incapable of enjoying the Monfortian spirituality.

Thus is justified the idea of commenting on such a work. We tried to reconstitute on the one hand the theological argumentation of which Montfort most often gives only the conclusion; on the other hand, the most obvious authorities on which he relies, in order to oblige the text to deliver to us its splendors. Sometimes this text will be taken, taken up again, dissected, in order to show all the richness of it. On the other hand, when it is sufficiently detailed or when it repeats itself, the Commentary will make itself more useful by singling out the main ideas and accentuating them.

At any rate, it will be indispensable to have the True Devotion *at hand. It is by comparing the Commentary and the Treatise that we shall understand both, and derive the desired fruit from it.*

*
* *

Overall and in its details, the **plan** *of the Commentary is that of the* Treatise *itself. We shall point this out farther on. Before that, however, we saw fit to retrace the historic blossoming of the Marian Montfortian devotion. This will be the object of our introduction.*

To whomever would wish to acquire, first of all, or to summarize afterward the precise and detailed notion of the Holy Slavery, we would recommend reading in the 2nd part, Chapter I (Nature of the Perfect Devotion, nn. 120-133) and Chapter IV (Practices of the Perfect Devotion, nn. 226-265), with the supplement to this chapter (Communion with Mary, nn. 266-273) and the general conclusion. This extract provides a complete presentation of the form of Marian devotion preached by Father de Montfort.

*
* *

Everything which relates to theology was of use to us as moral support.

From dogmatic Mariology, we briefly recall all that is necessary for the understanding of the Treatise. *But, in general, the proofs of our assertions are supplied by our* **Manuel de Mariologie dogmatique**. *We frequently refer to it by its initials the M.M.D.*

The authors whom we have used are quoted at the foot of the page. They are relatively few. On the rather restricted platform on which we had to move, the ideas were supplied to us exclusively by the Treatise *itself. Encounters with other authors, especially modern, were in that case more difficult. We give, however, a rather extensive bibliography; the readers who would wish to do so can draw from it, on one point or another, for more ample information.*

Conversely, we were happy to find in some recent books, such as that of Rev. Fr. Poupon, the echo of our explanations touching certain particularly difficult problems of Montfortian Mariology.

*
* *

On the solemn feasts which were organized almost everywhere in honor of the new Saint, people were fond of proclaiming Montfort "Marian Doctor." It is quite so, indeed, that he reveals himself in the Treatise *on the True Devotion. All agree in considering his work "as one of the most beautiful books written about the Most Blessed Virgin."*

When he published his translation of the Treatise, *Fr. Faber announced that the spiritual writings of Montfort were called to have a remarkable influence on the Church. Under the breath of the Holy Ghost, we see, indeed, a movement, which goes on increasing, to urge souls towards the Perfect Devotion.*

May our modest work contribute to the accentuating of this movement, to spread the reign of Mary in hearts, and to glorify the great apostle whom the Church has just proclaimed: **"Saint Louis-Marie Grignion de Montfort."** *This is our whole purpose in writing these pages.*

Montfort-sur-Meu (I.-et-V.)
December 8, 1947
On the Feast of Mary Immaculate

HISTORICAL INTRODUCTION
to the study
OF THE TRUE DEVOTION

I. – Devotion to the Virgin before St. Louis-Marie Grignion de Montfort

Mary is truly the knot of the history of Redemption. It is in her that the Old Testament ends, as in the masterpiece of which it is legitimately proud. It is in her that the New Testament begins, by the miraculous conception of the Savior. Even before knowing her, men put all their hope in her. Is she not this mysterious woman predicted by God from the beginning of the world, who herself is to repair the work of the first woman, and whose almighty Son will crush the head of the infernal serpent? Is it not this Virgin, who, without any damage to her virginity, is to conceive and give birth to the Emmanuel?

But the illusions, raised on all sides by the messianic hope, prevented His contemporaries from recognizing in such a simple personage as Jesus the Messiah promised under such magnificent figures. They also prevented them from recognizing in Mary, wife of the carpenter Joseph, outwardly merged in the crowd of her fellow men, this extraordinary woman, this fertile Virgin, expected as a true prodigy.

This obscurity was providential. Willed by God, accepted, or better, requested by Mary, it entered into the execution of the plan of Redemption. It is necessary to think about it in order to explain this anomaly: the woman for whom all previous generations had sighed; the one that all the following generations were to proclaim blessed, was absolutely unknown to the generation in the midst of which she lived. Even when her divine Son revealed to the crowds the supreme dignity in which He was clothed, these same crowds did not draw the spontaneous conclusion which ensued from His words: the glory of the woman who had brought Him into the world. And if a woman, one day, lifted up her voice to exalt the merit of this Mother, is it indeed her true grandeur that she wanted to exalt? Did she not proclaim rather the pride which she attributed to the one who had given birth to such a prestigious orator?

Father de Montfort finely analyzes, in his **Treatise on the True Devotion to the Blessed Virgin** (nn. 2, 5 and 49), the reasons for this obscurity. We shall find them again in the course of the *Commentary*. For the moment, we only want to point out one of the effects of this obscurity, namely the relative slowness with which devotion to Mary developed in the world.

Let us retrace the main lines of its evolution century by century.

1º **FROM THE 1ST TO THE 5TH CENTURY**. – The veneration of Mary exists rather under a speculative and theological form. Her privileges are attacked by heresies and defended by Christians.

Her *perpetual Virginity* was honored first of all. On one hand, indeed, the virginal conception of Christ was then considered as the supreme proof of His divinity. Everything had been said on the subject when it had been asserted in the *Creed*: "*Born of the Virgin Mary.*" On the other hand, the first forms of Christian asceticism quickly evolved towards the practice of continence. Mary had been the first one to make profession of and even a vow of virginity. She was proposed naturally as an example for chaste souls. To destroy its influence, heresy and the human mind tried to decrease the virginal halo surrounding the person of the Mother of Christ. But this was in vain. The blasphemies of Helvidius and Jovinian served only to arouse the forceful replies of St. Ambrose and especially of St. Jerome, and to bring more to light Mary's perpetual virginity.

In the time of St. Justin, St. Irenaeus and Tertullian, attention was drawn to the role of Mary in our Redemption, and the famous *parallel between Eve and Mary* was established. If mankind was drawn into ruin by a woman, it began to be raised up again by a woman. The devil used Eve to ruin us, God, to overthrow the plans of Satan, uses Mary to redeem us. Mary is thus our liberator, and our advocate with God. From this doctrine ensues all the Mediation of Mary in the acquisition and distribution of graces. For the same reason St. Augustine greets Mary as the spiritual Mother of all the members of Christ.

Finally, devotion to Mary advanced considerably, when the dogma of the divine Maternity was proclaimed at the Council of Ephesus, in 431. The outburst of joy that this definition caused in the people is sufficient proof of how much the aspirations of Christian piety were satisfied. From this moment especially, the greatness of the Mother of God, her incomparable holiness, her exquisite purity, the wealth of the supernatural gifts which had been bestowed on her, were exalted by all Christians. "Mary as Mother of God, is venerated in the whole universe," said St. Nilus.

2° **FROM THE 5TH TO THE 17TH CENTURY**. – During this period, the devotion of the faithful to the Most Blessed Virgin manifested itself in every field of art and thought.

LITURGICAL MANIFESTATIONS. – Previously, the veneration of Mary was mixed with the worship of Jesus. For example, the feast of the Purification of Mary, celebrated in Jerusalem since the 4th century, was combined with the feast of the Presentation of Jesus.

From the 5th century, the distinction becomes established. *In the East*, three feasts of the Virgin (5th or 6th century) are known: the one at Christmastime; the second in May, and the third in August. During the 6th century, the Annunciation is removed from the cycle of Christmas and becomes a properly Marian feast. The Dormition of the Virgin is celebrated at this point, and the Purification (alone) was celebrated at Antioch in 526.

The *western* Liturgy also makes room for Mary extensively. In the 6th century, in Gaul, Spain, and perhaps in Rome, a commemoration of the Virgin at Christmastime is reported. In the 7th century the Annunciation appears, fixed on March 25, except in Spain where it falls on March 18. The Nativity of Mary is celebrated in Reims and Rome; however its diffusion is slow. The Assumption is more widespread. But the Purification will spread only later.

Besides these general feasts, certain churches have particular feasts. Byzantium for example, celebrates each year the anniversary of its deliverance from the Avars, obtained through Mary's intercession.

These ceremonies sometimes include processions, often homilies and a very rich hymnography.

Furthermore, in the 6th century the name of Mary is introduced into the "Communicantes" of the Canon of the Mass.

Later, the liturgical calendar will be further enriched with several Marian feasts: the Visitation (13th century), the Presentation of Mary (14th century), the Espousals (14th century), the Conception (from the 12th to the 15th century, depending on the country).

ARTISTIC MANIFESTATIONS. – In this realm, the first importance belongs to churches dedicated to Mary, then to Marian iconography.

The churches consecrated to Mary. According to Grisar (disputed, however, by Mgr. Duchesne), St. Sylvester is said to have built a church in Rome in honor of Mary, in the neighborhood of the temple of Vesta. It is possible as well that the Basilica where the Council of Ephesus was held is dedicated to the Blessed Virgin. Be that as it may, the 5th century saw this custom become widespread in

Constantinople, Jerusalem and Rome. In this last city Sixtus III (432-440) dedicated to Mary the reconstructed Liberian Basilica, the one which is since called Saint-Mary-Major. Boniface I (608-615) dedicated the ancient Pantheon to Saint-Mary of the Martyrs, and John VII (705-707) had a chapel of the Virgin constructed in Saint-Peter's which was destroyed in the Renaissance, and engraved on the ambo of *Santa Maria antiqua* a famous inscription, about which we shall speak several times.

In the Middle Ages, several wonderful cathedrals were dedicated to Mary: thirty in France, eighteen in England.

Marian iconography is inaugurated in the Catacombs of Saint Priscilla by a fresco going back to the middle of the 2nd century representing the Virgin and Child. This mode of representation is fixed at about the 6th century. The Virgin sits, in the posture of a Queen. Around the forehead shines the nimbus. Some images even claim to go back to the contemporaries of Mary and to give us her true features: for example the Madonna said to be by St. Luke, copies of which spread everywhere. They are inspired rather by the apocryphal Gospels and show us more exactly the popular side of devotion to Mary.

The *Iconoclasm* controversy (8th-9th centuries) provides the Church the occasion to clarify the veneration of images and to distinguish the various sorts of veneration: the veneration of dulia common to all the saints and the veneration of hyperdulia reserved for the Blessed Virgin Mary. Besides, iconoclasm did not attack Marian devotion, even if it disapproved of images of Mary.

Later, painting and sculpture multiplied their masterpieces. The Virgin Queen, seated, carrying the scepter becomes little by little, under the influence of the mystics, more of a woman, more mother, and more poignant. Or rather perhaps it was her sorrows which most happily inspired artists.

THEOLOGICAL AND LITERARY WORKS. – Since the teachings of the Fathers of the Church appeared most often in the form of homilies adapted to the feast day, these homilies will discuss Mary in the same proportion as the Marian feasts will be multiplied (6th-8th centuries). Marian theology properly so-called begins with St. John Damascene (+754). It is clarified in the Middle Ages: relying on scriptural and traditional data, it accentuates the power, purity and dignity of Mary.

Contemporary literature dedicates works of all sorts to the Marian question: poets, playwrights (mystery plays), orators, and mystics diligently vied with one another in singing the glory of Mary.

MANIFESTATIONS OF THE PRACTICES OF MARIAN PIETY. – Any true devotion longs to be expressed in multiple practices involved with ordinary life.

Among these practices we find:

The Little Office (10th century), – The Little Office of Mary Immaculate (15th century), – The devotion to the seven joys and seven sorrows of Mary (14th century), – The consecration of Saturday to Mary and the *Missa de Beata* this day (9th century).

The *Ave Maria* is completed in the 13th century and becomes widespread in the 15th. Sometimes five psalms are recited in honor of Mary whose connected initials compose her name: *Magnificat, Ad Dominum cum tribularer clamavi, Retribue, In convertendo, Ad te levavi.*

The ringing of the *Angelus* goes back to the 14th and 15th centuries.

Tradition attributes the institution of the Rosary to St. Dominic. Its organization in decades is due to a Carthusian monk of Cologne (late 15th century). The meditation on the main mysteries was added by another Carthusian monk of Trier (early 15th century). At the end of the 15th century, Blessed Alain de la Roche generalized the practice.

The Carmelites, especially St. Simon Stock (13th century), spread the scapular of Mount-Carmel.

In the Middle Ages religious Orders and Confraternities in honor of Mary are multiplied. At the same time famous and very popular places of pilgrimage are established in the cities which possess either relics of Mary (robes, belts, etc.), or more often a miraculous image: Loreto in Italy, Chartres, Notre Dame des Ardilliers, Rocamadour in France, Walsingham in England, and Our Lady of Montserrat in Spain are the most famous Marian places of pilgrimage.

Some, imitating Pope John VII, and Blessed Marin, the brother of St. Peter Damian, consecrate themselves to Mary as slaves, and voluntarily wear little chains, symbolizing this slavery.

3° **17TH CENTURY**. During this century we find the most vigorous effort to bring devotion to the Most Blessed Virgin to its most perfect form.

In the previous century, Protestantism had violently attacked this devotion, accusing it of relegating Christ to obscurity, in order to direct hearts to Mary, and make of this creature a kind of helping divinity.

In view of these attacks, Catholics had not remained sluggish. St. Peter Canisius, St. Robert Bellarmine, Suarez, Pétau, and St. Francis de Sales had triumphantly explained the Catholic Marian theology and avenged the honor of the Mother of God. St. Francis de Sales even used a formula which was to point the way for the major authors of the 17th century. He said: "We go to Mary through God Himself." The worship of Our Lord infallibly gives rise to the veneration of His

Most Holy Mother. To know the Mother completely, it would be necessary to know the Son first.

This is the point from which what H. Brémond quite correctly called "the French school", started. **Cardinal de Bérulle**, the first and chief representative of this school, is above all the apostle of the Incarnate Word. Better than any other, he sang this adorable mystery in all his writings, but especially in his chief work: "The discourse about the state and grandeurs of Jesus by the ineffable union of His Divinity with His Humanity and the dependence of servitude which is due to Him and to His Most Holy Mother as a result of this admirable state."

For him, the Incarnate Word is the supreme model to which we have to conform. The state of servitude in which His humanity was established in regard to His divinity, as a result of the mystery of the Incarnation, will show to us to what point we ourselves must submit ourselves to God. But, as the connection between the Mother and the Son is very close, it is impossible to belong to one without belonging to the other.

In return for what His Mother gave Him, Jesus gave her part of His own greatness and royalty. It is not, then, our devotion which subjects us to this great Queen. She is "Our Lady" independently of our will. We do not belong to her because we give ourselves to her, but because Jesus Christ, to Whom we belong, gave us to her.

To help us, on one hand to acquire this resemblance with Jesus, and on the other to express perfectly our relations with Mary, Bérulle recommends the state of voluntary *servitude* to Jesus and Mary. This state is not repugnant to the adoptive sonship which was granted to us. But just as Jesus was at the same time Son and servant of His Father, Son by nature, servant by mercy for us, similarly we are at the same time servants and children of God, servants by nature and children by mercy. And just as Jesus lived in an admirable dependence on His Mother by virtue of His sonship in her regard, so too we are in a relation of servitude towards Mary by virtue of her Maternity over us.

This state of servitude is solemnly inaugurated by an *act of oblation and offering*, which is nothing else than a *renewal of the vows of baptism*. A complete donation, which lets nothing escape, and which embraces time and eternity. It addresses Jesus Christ and Mary at the same time in honor of the mutual, ineffable and unknown relations of the Son of God and the Virgin.

Bérulle, however, is not the creator of this form of devotion. He was very probably put in touch with it during a journey which he made in Spain. There, he admired the flourishing confraternities of the holy slavery which had been established by Father Simon de Rojas, of the Trinitarian Order. From there, they were transported into the Netherlands, then under Spanish dominion, by Father Bartholomew de los Rios, of the Order of St. Augustine, and to India, by the zeal of the missionaries. The Theatines spread it in the kingdom of Naples, in Sicily and in Savoy.

On his return to France, Bérulle became the defender and propagator of this slavery of love, especially with the consecrated souls under his direction. And it is precisely while defending himself against the innumerable attacks on him which this apostolate inspired that he had the opportunity to explain his Marian doctrine.

If we turn from Bérulle to some other representatives of the French school, we find at first **Fr. Olier**, founder of the Seminary of Saint-Sulpice. The Sulpician spirituality is summed up in one phrase: *Jesus living in Mary*. It is again the imitation of the Incarnate Word, but especially bearing on the dispositions which Jesus showed during the very first months of His earthly existence. Absolute dependence on Mary, in everything which concerns the preservation and development of His temporal life; but a fully conscious and perfectly voluntary dependence. To realize this dependence, the seminarians were invited to carry out all their actions with Mary, in Mary and for Mary, as they were reminded by an inscription in the chapel, surrounding a picture of the Virgin in the mystery of Pentecost: *Cum ipsa, et in ipsa, et per ipsam.*

St. John Eudes practices and teaches the Holy Slavery of Jesus and Mary, and he proclaims their reign over all hearts. But he mainly stresses the affectionate character of Marian devotion, by drawing the attention of souls to "*The Admirable Heart of the Most Holy Mother of God.*"

A great number of still other authors come to offer to Mary the tribute of their works and talents. Some will be mentioned one time or another in the course of the *Commentary*. For the moment, it is enough to have indicated briefly the principal currents of Marian thought in the 17th century.

II. – The Devotion to the Virgin preached by St. Louis-Marie Grignion de Montfort

If we recall in broad outline the origin and development of devotion to Mary till the beginning of the 18th century, it is not for the purpose of redoing a work, carried out by so many others and in greater detail. It is to show that Father de Montfort really belongs to the Church and to his time.

Joyful, indeed, for the rich prize which he found in the Christian Tradition, and especially in the French School, Montfort prepares himself to draw a whole new advantage from it.

"Now," says Rev. Fr. Lhoumeau, "if for having composed a bouquet of flowers picked here and there, someone is justly considered as the author, we can thus attribute to our Blessed this doctrine which forms a marvelous whole of truths and practices borrowed from various schools. Especially since his work was not limited to grouping them; he also clarified, developed or perfected them at several points. How many in the sciences and arts have become heads of Schools on that score." And Fr. Lhoumeau cites St. Thérèse as an example in spirituality and Palestrina in polyphony, thus justifying the title of his book: *La vie spirituelle à l'école du Bienheureux Louis-Marie Grignion de Montfort* (*The Spiritual Life at the School of Blessed Louis-Marie Grignion de Montfort*).

We too hope to show in this book that Montfort really is a head of a school, by his powerful individuality and by the high value of his Marian doctrine. Before entering, however, the heart of the *Commentary*, it is indispensable to present to our readers the author and the work on which we propose to comment. But to be complete, and to note more clearly our Montfortian references, before confining ourselves to the study of the *Treatise*, we shall speak very briefly about the other writings of the Holy Missionary.

*
* *

§ I. – SAINT LOUIS-MARIE GRIGNION DE MONTFORT

When God destines a man for an especially difficult and important task, He takes care, says St. Thomas, to assure him all the graces needed to acquit himself of it worthily (III, qu. XXVII; art. 5, ad I).

This rule applies to St. Louis-Marie de Montfort. He was born in Montfort-sur-Meu, then Montfort-la-Cane, on January 31, 1673, in the full literary and Marian glory of the 17th century. He received the first name of Louis at baptism, to which he spontaneously added, at Confirmation, that of Mary. Later, he renounced his familial title, "de la Bachelleraie," and even his surname "Grignion", and called himself, in gratitude for the grace of baptism, the most beautiful title of nobility of the Christian: "Louis-Marie de Montfort."

God had given him a mother who was a model of Christian patience and resignation in the midst of the most painful domestic difficulties. Perhaps, in the mysterious series of divine graces which constitute predestination, this filial piety was not foreign to his Marian piety.

From his earliest years he gave obvious signs of his precocious and extraordinary devotion to Mary. He persuaded his younger sister Louise to recite rosaries with him by saying: "My dear sister, you will be quite beautiful, and everybody will love you, if you love the good God." Like her brother, the latter persuaded her companions. He was already the apostle and head of a school who allows us to catch a glimpse of himself.

"Everything which can contribute to the glory of Mary", says Father de Clorivière, "was the particular object of his care. It was always a new pleasure for him to hear talk about her grandeurs and mysteries. He visited her chapels, decorated her images, and did not pass a day without reciting her rosary."

*
* *

At the age of twelve, in 1685, he came to study in Rennes in the middle school of St. Thomas, run by the Jesuit Fathers, and which has since become the secondary school of the state. This middle school, which had been famous for its teachers and students, gave to an elite, of which our Saint was soon a member, a good Marian formation. The means was the Congregation of the Blessed Virgin, established within the middle school. This Congregation was then directed by the Rev. Fr. Prévost, professor of philosophy. Fr. Blain, speaking about the devotion of Father Prévost to the Blessed Virgin and of his influence on Louis-Marie, gives assurance: "I would say that Louis Grignion would have taken it (this devotion) from him (Fr. Prévost) if he had not shown signs of it from the cradle."

During this period, the Saint especially revealed his Marian piety by a daily and prolonged visit to the shrines dedicated to Mary: Our Lady of Peace, in the chapel of the Carmelites; Our Lady of Good News, in the convent of the Dominicans; especially *Our Lady of Miracles*, in the church Holy Savior. He entrusted all his concerns to his good Mother, particularly those which concerned his future, and, one day, Mary revealed to him clearly his priestly vocation: "You will be a priest."

*
* *

By a combination of providential circumstances, he was brought to Paris, to take the course of theology there, at the Sorbonne first, then at Saint-Sulpice. It is during this stay in the capital that he read almost all the books discussing devotion to the Most Blessed Virgin, as he asserts in n° 118 of his *Treatise*. He had been chosen as librarian at Saint-Sulpice. This supplied him the wonderful opportunity to study Mary. In any case, he diligently read the Holy Fathers, as the public defense of a thesis on grace proves, in which he quoted long passages of St. Augustine from memory, to refute his opponents.

It is at Saint-Sulpice also that he composed an "ample collection" of the Fathers and Doctors. For he already specialized in devotion to the Blessed Virgin. His heart inclined him to it, and the thoroughly Marian doctrine bequeathed to the Seminary by Fr. Olier uncovered new horizons for him. He read Bérulle and became imbued with his ideas (n° 162). Furthermore, we know by the witnesses of his life that he studied the works of **Canon Boudon**, archdeacon of Evreux, particularly *Les saintes voies de la Croix* (The Holy Ways of the Cross) and *Dieu seul, ou le Saint Esclavage de l'admirable Mère de Dieu* (God alone, or the

Holy Slavery of the admirable Mother of God) (n°s 159 and 163). The manuscript of **Baron de Renty** on *Marie des Vallées* (Mary of the Valleys) was found at Saint-Sulpice. The Saint was acquainted with it and quotes it in n° 47.

He also took advantage of his stay at Saint-Sulpice to consult other famous authors, either of the Society of Jesus, like **Father Poiré**, in his work: *La triple couronne de la Sainte Vierge* (The Triple Crown of the Blessed Virgin) (n° 26), which was for him a real arsenal; **Father Paul Barry**, in his book *Le ciel ouvert à Philagie* (Heaven opened to Philagie) (number 117); **Suarez**, whom he calls "the learned and pious Suarez" (n° 40), and **Cornelius a Lapide** (n° 61); or of other Congregations, like **Fr. Simon de Rojas** and **Fr. Bartholomew de Los Rios**. The latter had proved, in his book "**Hierarchia Mariana**," "*the antiquity, excellence and solidity of this devotion*" (n° 160). He also relies on, in n° 244, on the authority of **Fr. Tronson**, Superior General of the Seminary of Saint-Sulpice.

At this time, Montfort testified to his Marian zeal by carefully decorating the chapel of the Virgin in the church of Saint-Sulpice, and by greeting devoutly, on passing by, the images or statuettes placed over doors, sometimes in imperceptible niches.

He also asserts (n° 118) that he conversed with the holiest and learned personages of his time. Which ones exactly? It is difficult to say. His relations, however, with the Benedictines of the Blessed Sacrament of Paris and Rouen, with the Jesuits of Nantes and with Saint-Sulpice enabled him to have very useful meetings that were to increase or communicate his love for Mary.

Thus prepared, sure of himself and his doctrine, Montfort taught, in public and in private, in the pulpit and in the confessional, his admirable secret of holiness. Finally, so that it might have a wider diffusion, he resigned himself to put it down in writing, by composing his *Treatise on the True Devotion*.

§ II. – THE WORKS OF FATHER DE MONTFORT

The works of Fr. de Montfort are inspired by the necessities of his personal studies or his apostolate. He thus drafted a large number of summaries, collections, etc., to which we have already alluded, and which all remained unpublished if not lost. He composed numerous sketches of sermons, also unpublished. His printed works are nevertheless rather numerous. We shall indicate here only the most important, those which will sometimes serve us in understanding the *Treatise* itself.

*
* *

The first of these works chronologically seems to be **L'Amour de la Sagesse éternelle** (The Love of eternal Wisdom), a short work of approximately 250 pages, which, in all probability, would have been composed between September 1703 and March 1704, almost at the beginning of the Saint's priestly life. He was then in Paris, in a dark small room in the street of Pot-de-Fer, savoring the contempt of which he was universally the object. In several letters, he requests special prayers to obtain divine Wisdom for him.

"This thought of Wisdom obsessed Montfort: the subject, first of all, of his meditations, it soon became the great object of his loves, the divine center toward which all his labors converged.

"For him, *Christ-Wisdom*, and Wisdom-Crucified, dominates everything. Prepared by the Old Testament, and especially by the Wisdom books, Christ-Wisdom blossoms in the Gospel preaching and the epistles. He thus dominates the activity of the Church and her Saints.

"If man is created, it is by this Wisdom and for this Wisdom. If Wisdom became incarnate and was crucified, it is so that man might become wise with Eternal Wisdom, and foolish with the holy folly of the Cross.

"Everything has to give way, in order to make room for the *unique* search for the Unique Wisdom, Jesus Christ. No sacrifice is too much for the acquisition of so great a treasure.

"But, alas, how few men know Wisdom. How many are mistaken about its nature. How few seek for it. How many are especially wrong about the great means of acquiring it, which is a "*True Devotion*" to the Most Blessed Virgin.

"It is an immense misfortune thus to miss the unique and magnificent destiny which God prepared for us in His love, because the one who, by his own fault, does not find Wisdom Incarnate, Jesus Christ, what he could find except eternal death and hell?

"Now, Montfort notes it with sorrow: this subject of Wisdom had not yet been treated as it deserved, and he could not allow his tongue to be silent. He meditated, he prayed, he spoke; finally, he wrote."

He himself gives us, in n° 14, the summary plan of his work:

"We shall contemplate it (Wisdom) from His origin, in *eternity*, living in the bosom of His Father, as the object of His pleasure. We shall see Him *in time* shining in the creation of the universe. We shall look at Him then completely humbled in His *Incarnation* and in His *mortal life*, and then we shall find Him glorious and triumphant *in Heaven*.

"Finally, we shall see what the means are to acquire and preserve it."

It is with good reason that people regarded this *Treatise* as a "powerful synthesis of Montfortian spirituality." The doctrine of the holy missionary is discovered in it in embryonic form. The *Treatise on the True Devotion* is included in chapter XVII: the fourth and most powerful means to acquire Wisdom and the only means to preserve it, namely: "*A tender and true devotion to the Blessed Virgin.*" All the divisions and subdivisions of the *Treatise on the True Devotion* are found in this chapter: the first and second parts, the necessity and nature of the True Devotion, the nature, qualities and the efficacy of the Holy Slavery. The *Letter to the Friends of the Cross* is sketched in the magnificent passages in which the author sings the triumph of eternal Wisdom in the Cross and by the Cross (Ch. XIV). Finally, the missionary speaks there enthusiastically about the *Rosary* (Ch. XV, n° 193).

*
* *

The Letter to the Friends of the Cross was written by Father de Montfort in 1714, at the end of a fervent retreat which he made at Rennes, under the direction of the Jesuit Fathers. It addresses the Confraternity of the Friends of the Cross, organized by him in Nantes and elsewhere. It expresses the elevated thoughts which he meditated on during his retreat.

After having described the Friend of the Cross, he outlines the program which he must carry out: "All evangelical perfection consists in: 1° wanting to become a saint; 2° abstinence: *let him renounce himself*; 3° suffering: *let him carry his cross*; 4° acting: *let him follow Me.*"

In the ardent Commentary which follows, Montfort sounds the rallying cry of brave souls. He is on his terrain; he himself lived the lessons which he gives to others, because it is rare to find, even among the saints, a man so scoffed at, so humiliated, so calumniated, and at the same time so heroic in his patience.

*
* *

The Secret of Mary is also a letter which Father de Montfort wrote, not to a group, like the previous one, but to a fervent soul, so that she herself might read and share it *"with persons who merit by their prayers, alms, mortifications, persecutions, zeal for the salvation of souls and detachment."*

This letter briefly explains the Holy Slavery, such as it can be practiced by souls advanced in perfection. This Marian synthesis is at the same time more lively and more accessible to the simple faithful than the *Treatise* itself. Special aspects are also found in it. "The dominant idea of the *Great Secret*, which he confides to us so that we might become saints, is not found in the same way in the *True Devotion*, and the necessity of sanctifying ourselves through Mary seems to us here more demonstrative than in the *Treatise*. Finally, in the *Secret* Montfort directly addresses the soul: he also gives her extremely important insights and advice (useful even for readers of the *True Devotion*)."

After a short *Introduction* (n°s 1 and 2) where the saint says on which conditions the Secret of Mary will be engaged in and profitable, a *first part*, which goes from n° 3 to n° 27 teaches us the *necessity of a true devotion in general*.

It is necessary to become a saint (n° 3):
grace is necessary for this (n°s 4-6);
which we find only through Mary (n°s 7-23);
on the condition of having a true devotion to her (n°s 23-27).

A *second part* explains the special true Devotion of Montfort, but by following a less rigorous plan than in the first part. This true Devotion is the *Holy Slavery*.

He goes on to discuss its:

> 1°) nature and extent (28-34);
> 2°) excellence (35-42);
> 3°) interior practices (43-52);
> 4°) wonderful fruits (52-57);
> 5°) efficacy at the end of time (58-59);
> 6°) exterior practices (60-65).

The short work ends with a prayer to Jesus and a prayer to Mary (66-69), and with some advice on the cultivation and the increase of the tree of life, or on the manner of making Mary live and reign in our souls (70-78). This is the natural *conclusion* of this letter.

*
* *

The admirable Secret of the Most Holy Rosary.

This book, which remained in manuscript form for a long time, is an original adaptation of the great work of *Antonin Thomas*, entitled *Le Rosier mystique de la Vierge* (The mystical Rosebush of the Virgin), of which the Rennes edition, in 1698, enjoyed great celebrity.

The book appears differently depending on whether we consider the original manuscript or the printed editions.

The manuscript contains, first of all, 49 chapters, entitled: 1st rose, 2nd rose, 3rd rose, etc. Next comes a first method to recite the Rosary well. Then the main rules of the Holy Rosary. Then two roses, one white and one red, a mystical rosebush and a rosebud. These last passages are not chapters like the previous roses, but dedications: 1° to priests (white rose); 2° to sinners (red rose); 3° to devout souls (mystical rosebush) and 4° to little children (rosebud). Then a more abbreviated method. Finally, two Latin notes end the book.

The printed edition modified this order, and for good reasons. They placed at the head of the book the four dedications which Montfort had put at the end; which is very natural. And, to finish a number which seems incomplete (49), they entitled the 50th rose the presentation of the methods, which corresponds well enough to the logical order.

*
* *

The Hymns.

Montfort was above all a missionary. All his other works are at the service of this essential work. So, throughout his priestly career, and even already during his time in seminary, but with a view to the future, he was led to compose a considerable number of hymns.

Because he was sufficiently prolific, however, much was attributed to him. Numerous hymns, reproduced in collections without the name of the author, or with the initials D.S., were wrongly considered as being by him. A serious work of discrimination was imperative.

This work was undertaken and successfully completed by *Rev. Fr. Fernand Fradet, S.M.M.* From this extensively documented study, it turns out that Fr. de Montfort is the indisputable author of 166 hymns; that he reworked 9, and that 30 are attributed to him by tradition, without there being any proof of the contrary. This makes the surprising total of 23,418 verses.

Other very beautiful hymns still pass under his name. But we possess proofs that they come from other sources.

The verses which he wrote are not polished for the pleasure of balance and rhyme. They are for him only a means of preaching. His poetry exists only with the aim of teaching.

What also characterizes it is that it is strongly Marian. To be convinced of this, it is enough to glance at hymns like *What my soul sings and proclaims, – I love Mary ardently, – Let everything sing and proclaim,* etc.... Even if the *Treatise on the True Devotion* did not exist, Montfort would appear here as a slave of Mary. There is no poetry in which a more filial or more tender love is expressed, nor more passionate admiration.

But there is more in his work. If Mary holds in the divine plan the place that the Saint, along with Tradition, assigns to her, it is logical that we should find it in all subjects, even when we least expect it. One or several stanzas, in the form of allusion or prayer, are the usual conclusion of the hymns, whatever subject is treated.

We shall particularly make use of his hymns on contempt of the world and its snares, to explain some of the exterior practices of the Holy Slavery.

§ III. – THE TREATISE ON THE TRUE DEVOTION

Whatever may be the merit of his other works, it is to the *Treatise on the True Devotion* that Fr. de Montfort presently owes his greatest renown. His Holiness Benedict XV, writing to the Very Rev. Fr. Lhoumeau, Superior General of both Montfortian Congregations, on the occasion of the second centenary of the death of their holy founder, on April 28, 1916, said to him:

"Blessed de Montfort wanted this to be your particular and proper spirit to promote among men the reign of Jesus by propagating the veneration of His holy Mother. Now, as a very efficacious means of this apostolate, he bequeathed to you, so that you may explain it carefully to the faithful, this book written by his hand: *On the True Devotion to the Blessed Virgin*, a book small in size, but one of such great authority and unction."

It is, then, to respond to this Montfortian vocation and to this desire of the Supreme Pontiff that we shall try to explain this *Treatise* carefully, hoping thus to work effectively for the establishment of the reign of Jesus through Mary.

Let us briefly state, first of all, the *history*, the *current state*, the *divisions* and the *title* of this *Treatise*. These general questions, once resolved, will be of great help to help us later in situating each detail again into the whole of this incomparable monument, raised to the glory of Mary.

A) HISTORY OF THE TREATISE.

Montfort, we have already said, was above all a missionary. But, in every place where he gave the exercises of the mission, he applied himself to establishing the devotion of the Holy Slavery. "I know," said Fr. de Bastières, "a very large number of scandalous sinners, in whom he inspired this devotion…, who are perfectly converted, and whose conduct is very exemplary." It is obvious, however, that good Christians especially appreciated his doctrine and profited from this devotion.

The holy missionary had given this teaching verbally at first, in the pulpit and in the confessional. He resolved to put it down in writing at the end of his life, that is, towards the age of 40 years: perhaps even in the time which preceded his death, having been warned, during the mission of Villiers-en-Plaine, that this was imminent. To have the tranquility necessary for this great work, Montfort withdrew either into the cave of Mervent, in the diocese of Luçon, or in that of Saint-Eloi, near La Rochelle. Anyway, he worked quickly, enthusiastically, and as though urged by divine inspiration. His biographer Grandet even goes so far as to say: "He composed *in three days* a book of the advantages of this slavery, which was found admirable." We are, however, allowed to wonder if these words apply to the *Treatise on the True Devotion* or to the *Secret of Mary*.

At his death, Montfort bequeathed his intact manuscript to Rev. Fr. Mulot, whom he had chosen as successor and executor of his estate. The latter knew what a treasure he held in his hands. Sheltered at first at Saint-Pompain in the hospitable rectory of the Prior, the brother of Rev. Fr. Mulot, this treasure was returned, from the year 1722, to Saint-Laurent-sur-Sèvre, where Father de Montfort had died in 1716, and where the Fathers of the Company of Mary had just established their Motherhouse near the grave of their Founder.

Until the Revolution, the Company of Mary would grow slowly, hampered in its expansion by the royal decrees limiting the number of its members to twelve. These nevertheless worked courageously, preaching missions and retreats in the whole West of France. Their preaching would always be inspired by the doctrine of the *Treatise*. All their missions were consecrated to Mary, Queen of Hearts, and, wherever possible, they set up Confraternities of the Holy Slavery. This was even one of the grievances which was asserted against them to try to obtain their suppression from the King.

Consequently, the Montfortian religious did not dare to ask for the "Privilege of the King," necessary for the publication of any book, and the work of their Father remained in manuscript form.

Then came troubles in 1789 and 1791. The revolutionaries of all stripes did not hesitate to indicate Saint-Laurent-sur-Sèvre as the home from which this flame of fanaticism rises which would soon set the Vendée on fire. To overcome this resistance to the laws, the national Guards of Cholet multiplied their searches in the house of the missionaries. They seized all that they found: private letters, papers, brochures, manuscripts. This was the moment of the fulfillment of the prophecy that Montfort had written in his *Treatise* seventy years previously: "I clearly foresee that raging beasts shall come in fury to tear with their diabolical teeth this little writing and him whom the Holy Ghost has made use of to write it" (n° 114). In these raging beasts, which tear the book of Fr. de Montfort as well as his reputation, demons were seen at first, using all kinds of instruments, even well-intentioned ones, to tear physically the book of the Saint, and to tear morally his reputation. These same attacks were directed, besides, at "those who shall read it (this writing) and carry it out in practice."

This can of course be true of all times, but it came true more particularly during the Revolution. Perhaps, indeed, the manuscript fell under the eyes of the national guards? Perhaps it was examined, manhandled, thrown on the ground, torn up, deprived of some of its pages. In any case, the second part of the prophecy came true literally. If these enraged men did not manage to destroy the *Treatise on the True Devotion* with their diabolical teeth, "at least" they obliged the missionaries "to wrap it in the darkness and silence of a chest."

It is likely then, indeed, that the Fathers of Saint-Laurent-sur-Sèvre, having learned from the experience, and being able to expect new searches, had someone contrive a sort of cellar in a field. All the precious things which they wanted to save, in particular the *Treatise on the True Devotion*, were deposited there, "in the darkness and silence of a chest."

Toward the end of the 18th century, the storm seemed to calm down. Is it from this moment or a little later that they brought back to the Motherhouse that which had been hidden a decade previously? Thus far, scholars have not been able to determine the date of this return. The fact remains that in the following years all the writings of Montfort were collected with a view to the process of beatification. The list of these writings is long, because they number 291 items. But the principal one is missing from them: the *Treatise on the True Devotion*. The disappearance was almost as inexplicable as the total absence of searches or at least worries about the precious manuscript. The devil could indeed triumph. He kept the *Treatise* deeply buried in the darkness and silence of a chest, *"that it may not appear"* (*True Devotion*, n° 114). Satan dreaded nothing as much as its publication.

Finally, on April 22, 1842, a Montfortian religious, needing documents to compose a sermon on the Most Blessed Virgin, went to search, in the common library, in a box or a cupboard containing a large number of old notebooks and truncated books. He happened to find a manuscript whose yellowed pages betrayed its antiquity. After having read some pages of it, he took it, hoping to derive some benefit from it for the composition of his sermon. He read by chance the passage where the author speaks about missionaries of the Company of Mary, and he recognized the style and the thoughts of the Allocution of Father de Montfort to his missionaries. From then on, he no longer doubted that this exercise book was from him. He carried it to the Superior at that time, who recognized perfectly the writing of the Saint. Had he not just followed, indeed, this writing throughout the 291 items gathered in the process?...

The few missionaries who had escaped death had too much to do to reorganize the library. Upheavals and changes of personnel led to the forgetting of several traditions, and nobody knew any longer what had become of the manuscript.

In announcing these persecutions against his little writing, Montfort had added: "But what matter? On the contrary, so much the better! This very foresight encourages me, and makes me hope for a great success" (n° 114).

This prophecy also came true, because, coming out of the darkness and silence of a chest, the manuscript was published in early 1843. The next year, a new edition. In 1900, at least sixteen French editions, four English, four Italian, three Polish, two Canadian, two Dutch, one German, one Spanish and one American can be counted. And nowadays this circulation is at least tripled.

Finally, so that all the readers of the *True Devotion* might be able to consult the original text of the holy Missionary themselves, this text was photographed page by page and reproduced on copper plates. And the centenary 1942 saw the first publication of this manuscript edition.

B) THE PRESENT STATE OF THE TREATISE

In what state was the *Treatise* found? In his foreword, the first editor wrote: "We notice that, by a kind of providence, although all the sheets of the manuscript were separated from one another, all, however, were in their place and well-preserved."

Certain passages of the book, however, may lead us to doubt that we possess the whole work.

In n° 227, Montfort writes: "After having, as I said *in the first part* of this preparation for the reign of Jesus Christ, employed twelve days at least in emptying themselves of the spirit of the world, which is contrary to the spirit of Jesus Christ." Now, in the book such as we possess it, there is no mention of these twelve necessary days to empty oneself of the spirit of the world. The first part in which this practice was discussed and recommended has then disappeared.

The same is true of n° 256, where Montfort writes: "Those faithful servants of Mary who adopt this devotion ought always greatly to despise, to hate, and to eschew the corrupted world, and to make use of those practices of the contempt of the world which we have given *in the first part*." There is no trace of these practices in the current *Treatise*. The "first part," in which they were recommended, thus no longer exist.

In n° 228, the author indicates, as a prayer to be recited every day of the first week, the litanies of the Holy Ghost and the prayer which follows, as it is marked "*in the first part of this work.*" Now, these prayers cannot be found in the work such as we possess it at present.

Finally, in n° 231, we read: "They should recite the formula of their consecration, which they will find *afterwards.*" And n° 236 also mentions the blessing of little chains, "which is *afterwards.*" Now, the manuscript does not contain either the formula or the blessing indicated.

All this obliges us to conclude that there existed, in the work of Montfort, a first part, which did not come down to us, and which was detached from the second: the Marian part, which we possess. On the other hand, there are also some pages missing at the end of this Marian part, which contain the formula of consecration and the blessing of little chains.

A serious study, however, of the *Treatise* such as we possess it shows that we have in this a complete whole. We have the introduction of it, which, to all appearances, is intact, with the proposition, demonstration and conclusion. The *Treatise* itself deals with all the questions raised by the evolution of the subject. What, then, could the first part contain?

It had to be a kind of *Treatise* on the spirit of the world against the spirit of Jesus Christ. We know, indeed, with certainty (n°s 227 and 256) that in it were indicated certain practices of contempt of the world, and that directives were given in it to empty oneself of the spirit of the world.

The two parts together formed a complete preparation for the reign of Jesus Christ (n° 227), a negative preparation, first of all, by emptying oneself of the spirit of the world, which is against that of Jesus Christ; a positive preparation, secondly, by the use of the great means of establishing this reign: the Most Blessed Virgin Mary and the perfect devotion to her.

What remains is the Marian part in its entirety. And this is straightaway the most important part of Father de Montfort's work.

*
* *

C) DIVISIONS OF THE TREATISE

The Saint wrote this book in one stroke without marking himself the divisions outside the text, with the exception of some chapters, indicated now by means of an asterisk. In the text, however, he gave some precious indications, pointed out by successive editors, the last ones principally. They correspond faithfully to the thought of Father de Montfort, and we can rely on them, to look for and find the major developments of this luminous thought. As Fr. J.-B. Arnaud, a Montfortian Missionary, says: "The author indicates all his divisions, not in the style of someone who is going to send his manuscript to the printer, but rather in the style of a preacher, with transitions which recall what was said and prepare what follows."

Furthermore, by undertaking his work, Montfort intends only to form a true devotee to the Blessed Virgin (n° 110), and consequently to teach him the Holy Slavery. From the first line to the last, this form of devotion is what he tries to explain. Numerous are the formulas which prove it. Before being able to devote ourselves to this in-depth study of the Holy Slavery itself, however, we are obliged to speak about more general questions, relating to every devotion to the Most Blessed Virgin, although they are verified very specially and very perfectly in the slavery of love. As a result, putting on one hand what concerns every devotion to Mary and, on the other hand, what has for its unique object the perfect devotion to Mary, we ourselves can distinguish two major parts in the *Treatise*:

1° Of the true devotion to the Most Blessed Virgin in general.

2° Of the perfect devotion in particular.

Let us now go into more detail.

It is debated whether n°s 1 to 13 constitute an **Introduction**. Modern editors solved this question in the affirmative, by giving this title to the first thirteen numbers, and by making the first chapter of the first part begin only at n° 14.

The dominant idea is this one: The knowledge and reign of Jesus will be the necessary continuation of the knowledge and reign of Mary. Now, Mary is not known enough: first of all, because she herself wanted to remain hidden out of humility, then because God made her too beautiful and too far above us. Then how do you want the reign of Jesus to come? That is why Montfort devotes himself in every way to preach about Mary during his whole life, and, so that his preaching might not die with him, he commits it to writing in his *Treatise*.

Is that not a true introduction?...

The **first part**, which goes from n° 14 to n° 119 inclusively, speaks about the True Devotion to the Most Blessed Virgin in general. What is said about it is then applied to all true devotion, while being preeminently true of the perfect devotion.

This first part is divided into two chapters:

CH. I: The *necessity* of the True Devotion (14-59).

CH. II. The *nature* of the True Devotion (60-119).

In **chapter I**, having stated briefly the *nature of this necessity* (14-15), Montfort explains the *principles on which it is based*:

1st PRINCIPLE: God willed to make use of Mary *before* the Incarnation (n° 16);

2nd PRINCIPLE: God willed to make use of Mary *in* the Incarnation (n°s 17-21);

3rd PRINCIPLE: God wills to make use of Mary *after* the Incarnation, in the sanctification of souls (n°s 22-36).

In each of these principles Fr. de Montfort examines separately the conduct of each of the three divine Persons, and draws from them the appropriate conclusions.

From all this it results that the true title of Mary is that of "*Queen of Hearts*" (n°s 37-38).

From n° 39 to n° 59, Montfort explains *the extent of this necessity*, namely:

Mary is necessary: 1°) to all men in order to work out their salvation (n°s 39-42); – 2°) specially for those who are called to a high perfection (n°s 43-46); – 3°) more specially still to those who will live in the last times (n°s 47-59).

In **chapter II**, Montfort explains the *nature of the True Devotion*. He does so with the rigor of classification of a philosopher, by distinguishing, so to speak, the genus and kind.

He establishes a certain number of *fundamental truths*, which must be found in any devotion, and in particular in any devotion to Mary (n°s 61-89).

But some so-called devotees exaggerate these fundamental principles, or understand them badly, and apply them incorrectly. Whence comes the necessity of distinguishing the marks of each of the two opposite devotions, false or true, so that we can choose in complete safety (n°s 90-114).

To complete the chapter on the nature of the *True Devotion*, the Saint briefly enumerates the different forms that it can assume, and the different practices which it involves (n°s 115-119).

The last numbers (118-119), however, are transitional. Already they speak about the perfect practice, to which Montfort is going to dedicate himself later. And it is understandable that certain authors, like *Father Faber*, in his English edition of the *Treatise*, made the second part begin at n° 118.

This **second part** speaks, then, exclusively about the Perfect Devotion, or the Holy Slavery.

In **chapter I**, Montfort gives the nature of it: it is a consecration of oneself to Jesus Christ through the hands of Mary, and this in the capacity as a slave of love. This donation has, then, in the supernatural order, the same extension as the donation of a slave in the natural order (n°s 120-133 to compare with n°s 68 to 77).

In **chapter II**, he explains the reasons which justify this devotion and recommend it to souls. This chapter is divided into two sections:

1st *Section*: An enumeration of the "*motives* which must make this devotion advisable to us." There are eight of these motives (135-182). The most developed is the fifth: this devotion leads to union with Our Lord. Montfort traces the history of this devotion in it.

2nd *Section*: The same truths, but especially those which were enumerated in article III of the previous section (see the end of n° 150), are explained under the biblical figure of the good offices of Rebecca to Jacob, and Jacob's devotion to Rebecca to bring upon himself these good offices (183-212).

In **chapter III**, the Saint studies "the wonderful effects that it (this devotion) produces in faithful souls," another aspect of the advantages which it obtains. There are seven of these effects, and they are linked to one another with a logic that we shall have the opportunity to admire later (213-225).

Finally, in **chapter IV**, he draws attention to the *practices of the perfect devotion*, *exterior* and *interior* practices which are necessary so that the initial consecration always keeps its full efficacy, and maintains the soul in dependence on Mary (226-265).

A supplement of this chapter IV shows this devotion perfectly realized in the principal act of the Christian life: *communion with Mary* (226-273).

We have given the divisions and subdivisions to which we shall devote our attention in the rest of the *Commentary*. Certain questions of detail could be differently envisaged. It will be very difficult, perhaps, to satisfy all tastes on this point. We were inspired as much as possible, and even solely by Fr. de Montfort himself and by the most obvious meaning of the texts. This will be at least our excuse with those who think otherwise.

*
* *

D) THE TITLE OF THE TREATISE

There is a question to solve before approaching the commentary.

Montfort did not put a title on his manuscript. Is this an omission on his part? Did the first page, on which the title was written, get lost?...

This second hypothesis is the most natural. The manuscript does begin with a blank page, which seems however to have been added afterward, because the first page, we see, was attached to it. This first page does not imply there is a title to come. It is like all the others: a small cross at the top, a very regular margin on both sides, and twenty four lines of text. Only the number of lines sometimes varies from one page to another, 25, 26, and even 27.

But although we have no authentic title of the manuscript, all admit the title given by the first editors: *Treatise on the True Devotion to the Blessed Virgin*. Only, Canon Didiot, in the edition that he published in 1891, in Rennes, at the printing house Caillière, finds it too pretentious and substitutes for it by his own reckoning the more modest title: *Treatise on the Devotion to the Blessed Virgin*.

And nevertheless, all the efforts of the Saint tend to reveal the *true devotion to Mary* (Cf. n°s 82, 90, 91, 110, 111, etc...) and to form "*a true devotee of Mary*" (n° 111). Since devotion to the Most Blessed Virgin can be *true* or *false*, as Montfort teaches from n° 90 to n° 119, it is not enough to say: *Treatise on the devotion to the Blessed Virgin*, to express the proper nature of his book. Devotion is a term which can be applied to two different things. As long as we do not specify about which we want to speak, we shall not have given the necessary determinations.

And this justifies the title: *Treatise on the **true** Devotion to the Blessed Virgin*.

We could also say: *Treatise on the Holy Slavery*, because such is the special form of true devotion to which Montfort wants to lead his followers.

The first name is the one that has prevailed, and quite rightly, because it encompasses the two great divisions of the *Treatise*, the Holy Slavery being the most perfect of all true devotions to Mary, or, if we prefer, the true devotion *par excellence*, the true devotion without any qualification.

Logic imposes it, then, and it is probable that if Montfort himself had wanted to take a title for his manuscript, he would not have chosen another.

COMMENTARY
ON THE TREATISE ON THE TRUE DEVOTION

INTRODUCTION

Montfort develops a thought, the main lines of which are as follows:

Mary is the means by which Jesus came to us and is to reign over us (n° 1).

Now, how could this be, if Mary continues to be either unknown, or insufficiently known? (numbers 2 to 12).

If then, as is certain, the reign of Jesus is to be established in the world, it is because the reign of Mary will be recognized there beforehand (n° 13).

§ I. – THE REIGN OF JESUS THROUGH MARY.
(1)

N° 1

*It is through the most holy Virgin Mary that Jesus has **come** into the world, and it is also through her that He has to **reign** in the world.*

This first sentence gives us the summary of the whole *Treatise*. Several times, the Saint will return to the same idea (n°s 13, 22, 49, 158), and each time he will add very suggestive variations to this primary theme.

That Jesus was born from Mary is a fact which belongs to history and which nobody has the right to call into question, even if he does not believe in the divinity of the Savior. But Jesus was not only born from Mary. He took her as an associate in the whole work of Redemption. He established her as universal Mediatrix in the acquisition and distribution of grace. Already the Proto-evangelium announced the part that she would take in the victory of her Son over the serpent and its offspring (Gen. 3:15). And the Apocalypse (12:1) shows her to us actively involved in the final battle which will pit Christ against Satan. A conclusion was imperative, and Montfort is eager to draw it: Jesus has to reign in the world through Mary, because it is through her that He came into the world. Thus is explained and justified the intention to confine himself to the presentation of Marian devotion. The reign of Mary will precede and prepare for the reign of Jesus in souls.

*
* *

§ II. – MARY IS NOT KNOWN ENOUGH
(2-12)

N° 2

There, we said, is the whole idea which rules n°s 2 to 12. A cry of very understandable anguish, when we know that the reign of Jesus must be the consequence of the reign of Mary. (See n° 13.)

Let us see how Montfort proves this truth.

1° MARY HIDDEN DURING HER MORTAL LIFE

The Saint writes in n° 2:

Mary has been singularly hidden **during her life**. *It is on this account that the* Holy Ghost *and the* Church *call her* alma Mater – *Mother secret and hidden*.

The meaning which he gives to this word "*alma*," hidden and secret, the fact that he attributes this name to the Holy Ghost and to the Church (to the Holy Ghost in Scripture and to the Church in the Liturgy), proves that he chooses as the origin of this word, not the Latin *alere*, to nourish, but the Hebrew word *alam*, to hide oneself, to be hidden. From this word, in Hebrew, is derived the substantive *almah*, virgin, a young girl living in solitude, hidden from the eyes of men because she is a virgin. Such was, indeed, the oriental custom. In St. Jerome's testimony, the Aquila version, in chapter 24 of Genesis, he translates the word *almah*, said about Rébecca, by the adjective *hidden* alone. From which the Latins took this name to signify *holy* things or persons, because the more sacred a thing is, the less it is put on display, and the more it is hidden.

Grammatically, both etymologies are possible, and "alma Mater" can mean either nourishing mother, as a student will say about his college, or hidden and secret mother, as Father de Montfort says about Mary. This last explanation is very much in keeping with the meaning given by the Holy Ghost to the word "almah" (Is. 7:14) and it puts in striking relief the intonation of the antiphon, where the word "alma" is so clearly distinguished from others. Mary is, then, well-named "*by the Holy Ghost and the Church*" a hidden and secret Mother.

2° TWO REASONS FOR THIS EFFACEMENT

Montfort gives two reasons for this effacement: the humility and the transcendence of the Virgin. Mary asked the Lord to hide her as much as possible, and for His part God wanted her to be so beautiful that He alone is capable of knowing her.

a) The humility of Mary.

Her humility was so profound that she had no propensity on earth more powerful or more unremitting than that of **hiding herself**, *even from herself, as well as from every other creature, so as to be known to God only* (N° 2).

Mary is, indeed, the ideal woman, and, as such, she had to have a marked preference for *modesty*, the most beautiful ornament of woman. She is, moreover the *holy woman par excellence*, and so humility is absolutely imperative. The higher the building of holiness is to rise, the deeper the foundations of humility must be.

N° 3

Not only does Mary hide herself, *but she begs God to hide her:*

He heard her prayers to Him, when she begged to be hidden, to be humbled, and to be treated as in all respects poor and of no account.

Such prayers were so pleasing to Him! It is not surprising, then, that He

…took pleasure in hiding her from all human creatures in her conception, in her birth, in her life, and in her resurrection and assumption (N° 3).

All these mysteries, indeed, remained nearly unknown, even with those with whom she lived.

First of all, *her parents:*

Her parents even did not know her…

…whatever the apocryphal books said about it, especially the *Proto-evangelium of James*. They had to suspect something of her holiness, either because they had been informed of it by an angel, as the same Proto-evangelium says, or else because of the miracle of fruitful sterility. But they "*did not know her*," because they could have no idea of her real greatness: her being destined for the divine Maternity. Besides, she did not know it herself at that time.

Then *the Angels:*

And the angels often asked of each other: Quae est ista... *Who is that? Because the Most High either hid her from them, or if He revealed anything of her to them, it was nothing compared to what He kept undisclosed.*

Indeed, from *natural knowledge*, the Angels could know the exterior side of Mary's life. But her inner life, her interior acts, which followed one another uninterruptedly day and night, since her Immaculate Conception, and which made her grow in grace at every moment in incredible proportions, nobody could know them, if he is not God, and those to whom God *revealed* them. Through the *beatific vision*, the Angels saw, but did not understand the grandeurs of Mary, these coming to her from the divine Maternity and, in last analysis, from God. That is why *"if He revealed anything of her to them, it was nothing compared to what He kept undisclosed."*

N° 4

Finally, *from the men who saw her:*

God the Father *consented that she should do no miracle, at least no public one, during her life, although He had given her the power.* God the Son *consented that she should hardly ever speak, though He had communicated His wisdom to her.* God the Holy Ghost, *though she was His faithful Spouse, consented that His Apostles and Evangelists should speak but very little of her, and no more than was necessary to make Jesus Christ known.*

This conspiracy of silence, desired by Mary, requested by Mary, gives us partially the reason why Mary remained unknown *in her lifetime*. How would men have known Mary, since any light for this was providentially withheld from them?

N° 5

b) **The transcendence of Mary** explains to us why the Virgin remained hidden **even after her death**.

God wanted Mary so beautiful that He alone is capable of knowing her.

She belongs to a special, unique order in the supernatural world, the order of the divine Maternity, intermediate between the order of the hypostatic union and the order of grace and glory. It is thus impossible to apply to her the ordinary methods of human reasoning by rigorous deductions. She is the exclusive domain of the sovereign liberality and of the all-powerful freedom of God. Our duty is only to admire and to show the suitability of what it pleased God to do.

Montfort sides with those who *admire*. More than that, he asserts in n° 5 and proves in the following numbers (6-12) that nobody *can* understand Mary as much as she can be understood, except God alone.

Affirmation:

Mary is **the excellent masterpiece of the Most High** *(God the Father), of which He has reserved to Himself both the knowledge and the possession. Mary is* **the admirable Mother of the Son**, *Who took pleasure in humbling and concealing her during her life, in order to favour her humility, calling her by the name of woman (mulier), as if she was a stranger, although in His heart He esteemed and loved her above all angels and all men. Mary is* **the sealed fountain and the faithful Spouse of the Holy Ghost**, *to whom He alone has entrance. Mary is* **the sanctuary and the repose of the Holy Trinity**, *where God dwells more magnificently and more divinely than in any other place in the universe, without excepting His dwelling between the Cherubim and Seraphim. Neither is it allowed to any creature, no matter how pure, to enter into that sanctuary without a great and special privilege.*

In this passage Montfort heaps up biblical expressions to show up to what point God reserves to Himself the possession of Mary, as He formerly reserved to Himself the possession of the Temple and the Ark (surmounted by Cherubim), as the spouse of the Canticle of Canticles reserved to himself the possession of the bride, by calling her the closed garden, the sealed fountain, etc.... To guard his treasure even more surely, he affects exteriorly not to attach to it so great a price. The expression *"Woman, Mulier,"* however, that is at issue here does not necessarily take on this idea of indifference. Our Lord uses it only in great circumstances (Cana, Calvary), where the Redeemer calls on the Co-redemptrix, the New Adam on the New Eve. Inasmuch as Eve contributes to the fall, she is named "Mulier". When Mary collaborates in the reparation, she is named "Mulier".

N° 6

Proofs. In spite of the lyrical enthusiasm with which this passage overflows, the argumentation is very well drawn out. Father de Montfort's discourse is loaded with biblical, liturgical and patristic allusions, which would take us too far afield if it was necessary to reconstitute everything. Let us be content to indicate the main themes of his thought.

The first proof is sought in the incomprehensible marvels which God worked in Mary.

I say with the Saints, the divine Mary is the terrestrial Paradise of the New Adam, *where He is incarnate by the operation of the Holy Ghost, in order to work there incomprehensible marvels. She is the grand and divine* World of God, *where there are beauties and treasures unspeakable. She is the* magnificence of the Most High, *where He has hidden, as in her bosom, His only Son, and in Him all that is most excellent and most precious. O, what grand and hidden things that mighty God has wrought in this admirable creature! How has she herself been compelled to say it, in spite of her profound humility:* Fecit mihi magna, qui potens est! *The world knows them not, because it is at once* incapable and unworthy *of such knowledge.*

Thus, it is not surprising that Mary is not known, because nobody can know her. This is what stands out from this first proof, the elements of which will be developed at length later. It is useless to linger there for the moment.

N° 7

The second proof invokes the *testimony*, first, of the saints, then of the world in general, finally of Heaven, earth and hell in particular.

Here is the testimony of the *Saints:*

The Saints have said admirable things of this Holy City of God; and, as they themselves avow, they have never been more eloquent and more content than when they have spoken of her. Yet, after all they have said, they cry out that the height of her merits which she has raised up to the throne of the Divinity, cannot be fully seen; that the breadth of her charity, which is broader than the earth, is in truth immeasurable; that the grandeur of her power, which she exercises even over God Himself, is incomprehensible; and finally, that the depth of her humility, and of all her virtues and graces, is an abyss which never can be sounded. O height incomprehensible! O breadth unspeakable! O grandeur immeasurable! O abyss impenetrable!

If the souls most elevated in sanctity and the most accustomed to scrutinizing the supernatural world thus proclaim in this way their powerlessness to scrutinize the mystery of Mary, what will it be like for ordinary souls?...

N° 8

Here is now the testimony of *the whole universe:*

Every day, from one end of the earth to the other, in the highest heights of the heavens and in the profoundest depths of the abysses, everything preaches, everything publishes, the admirable Mary! The nine choirs of Angels (in Heaven), *men of all ages, sexes, conditions, and religions, good or bad* (on earth), *nay, even the devils themselves* (in hell), *willingly or unwittingly, are compelled by the force of truth to call her Blessed.*

After this overview, let us enter **into detail**, and see what takes place *in Heaven:*

St. Bonaventure tells us that all the Angels in Heaven cry out incessantly to her: Sancta, sancta, sancta Maria Dei Genetrix et Virgo – "Holy, holy, holy Mary, Mother of God and Virgin," *and that they offer to her millions and millions of times a day the Angelical Salutation:* Ave Maria; *prostrating themselves before her, and begging of her in her graciousness to honour them with some of her commands. St. Michael, as St. Augustine says, although the prince of all the heavenly court, is the most zealous in honouring her and causing her to be honoured, while he waits always in expectation that he may have the honour to go at her bidding to render service to some one of her servants.*

What a queen, to whom such great princes glory to be subjected!...

N° 9

Then the special testimony *of the earth:*

The whole earth is full of her glory, especially among Christians, amongst whom she is taken as the protectress of many kingdoms, provinces, dioceses, and cities. Numbers of cathedrals are consecrated to God under her name. There is not a church without an altar in her honour, not a country or a canton where there are not some miraculous images, where all sorts of evil are cured, and all sorts of good gifts obtained. Who can count the confraternities and congregations in her honour? How many religious orders have been founded in her name and under her protection? What numbers there are of Brothers and Sisters of all these confraternities, and of religious men and woman of all these orders, who publish her praises and confess her mercies! There is not a little child who, as it lisps the Ave Maria, *does not praise her. There is scarcely a sinner who, even in his obduracy, has not some spark of confidence in her.*

And to end, the testimony of *hell:*

Nay, the very devils in hell respect her while they fear her.

*
* *

Carried away by his fervor, **might not Montfort have exceeded his purpose?** He wanted to prove that Mary is not known enough, and he has just said that she is everywhere exalted, honored, or at least feared.

It is nothing of the sort, however. A series of three short remarks gives the real conclusion, the one which constitutes the proof of the assertions previously expressed:

N° 10

First remark. – Mary is already praised much, but *we shall never praise her enough:*

After that we must surely say with the Saints:

De Maria numquam satis…
"Of Mary there is never enough"

We have not yet praised, exalted, honoured, loved, and served Mary as we ought to do. She has deserved still more praise, still more respect, still more love, and far more service.

The words *De Maria numquam satis* are written in the manuscript in very big characters. And we guess by considering them the joy which the Saint felt in drawing them.

N° 11

Second remark. – The exterior glory that is known is nothing *compared to the interior glory that is not known:*

After that we must say with the Holy Ghost: Omnis gloria eius filiae Regis ab intus – *"All the glory of the King's daughter is within." It is as if all the outward glory, which heaven and earth rival each other in laying at her feet, is nothing in comparison with that which she receives within from the Creator, and which is not known by creatures, who in their littleness are unable to penetrate the secret of the secrets of the King.*

N° 12

Third remark. – In order to know the Mother, *it would be necessary to know the Son*, because she is the worthy Mother of God:

After that we must cry out with the Apostle: Nec oculus vidit, nec auris audivit, nec in cor hominis ascendit – *"Eye has not seen, nor ear heard, nor man's heart comprehended," the beauties, the grandeurs, the excellences of Mary – the miracle of the miracles of grace, of nature, and of glory. If you wish to comprehend the Mother, says a saint, comprehend the Son; for she is the worthy Mother of God.* Hic taceat omnis lingua – *"Here let every tongue be mute."*

Indeed, the divine Maternity is what explains the incomparable grandeur of Mary. And it is itself so new, so unique: *Habet dignitatem quamdam infinitam*, says St. Thomas (I, q. XXV, art. VI, ad 4). It confers a dignity in some way infinite. How can we not remain speechless in admiration before such a miracle? But also, how can we dare to assert that Mary is honored enough?...

*
* *

§ III. – MARY MUST BE MORE KNOWN
(13)

N° 13

This conclusion is expressed at the end of n° 13. But it is prepared by the beginning of the same number, where Father de Montfort briefly recalls what he previously said:

It is with a particular joy that my heart *has dictated what I have just written, in order to show that the divine Mary has been up to this time unknown, and that this is one of the reasons that Jesus Christ is not known as He ought to be.*

We are capable from now on of understanding this sentence, in the light of the previous context. It is not in an absolute sense that Mary is unknown. It is in a relative sense only. She is not known as much as she ought to be.

Surely, the Scriptures give few details about her life. But all the same, they say the main thi*ng: "Mary, of whom was born Jesus, Who is called Christ"* (Mt. 1:16). "What more do you want," writes St. Thomas of Villanova, "what more do you seek in the Virgin? Is it not enough for you that she is the Mother of God? I ask you: what beauty, what virtue, what perfection, what grace, what glory could be lacking to the Mother of God? Give free rein to your thoughts. Unleash your boldest imaginations. Imagine a very pure Virgin, very prudent, very beautiful, very devout, very humble, very sweet, full of every grace, overflowing with all holiness, adorned with every virtue, enriched with all charisms, very pleasing to God. Elevate as much as you can the impressive figure of such a

Virgin: Mary is even greater, more excellent, superior to the most splendid thing that you can imagine."

Let us also gather from the passage the proof of *the enthusiasm* with which Montfort dedicated himself to the composition of his work. *"My heart has just dictated to me with a particular joy."* And let us try to imitate this enthusiasm in the study which we ourselves are undertaking.

And let us return to our conclusion:

If, then, as is certain, the kingdom of Jesus Christ is to come into the world, it will be but **a necessary consequence of the knowledge of the kingdom of the most holy Virgin Mary**, *who brought Him into the world for the first time, and will make His second advent full of splendor.*

A conclusion would not deserve this name if it needed to be explained. This one results clearly from all which precedes, especially when we recall the first sentence: *"It is through Mary that Jesus has to reign in the world."*

This introduction fulfills well its role. It admirably disposes minds to undertake the study of the book which it announces. It already prepares us for the marvels which we shall have to examine, as a majestic portico of a cathedral throws visitors into admiration, and invites them to come inside to contemplate in detail the splendors of the house of God. Before this *"miracle of the miracles of grace, of nature, and of glory"* (n° 12) admiration will be changed into a zeal for the work. We shall be led to study, because we shall want to know a little better the great things worked by God in favor of this humble little Virgin.

PART I

OF THE TRUE DEVOTION IN GENERAL

CHAPTER I

THE NECESSITY OF THE TRUE DEVOTION

We have already indicated above the divisions and subdivisions of this first chapter. Consequently, we shall study it according to the following plan:

Article I: **The nature of the necessity of the True Devotion** (14-15).

Article II: **The foundation of this necessity: the divine Will.**
> SECTION I: *Before* the Incarnation (16).
> SECTION II: *In* the Incarnation (17-21).
> SECTION III: *After* the Incarnation (22-36).
> CONCLUSION: Mary Queen of Hearts (37-38).

Article III: **The extent of this necessity** (39-59).
Mary is *necessary to men:*
> 1° to *save* themselves (39-42).
> 2° to *reach* perfection (43-48).
> 3° *in the last times* (49-59).

ARTICLE I

The Nature of the Necessity of the true devotion
(14-15)

N° 14

I avow, with all the Church, that Mary, being but a mere creature that has come from the hands of the Most High, is, in comparison with His infinite Majesty, less than an atom; or rather she is nothing at all, because He only is "He Who is,"

(Ex. 3:14), and thus by consequence that grand Lord, always independent and sufficient to Himself, never had, and has not now, any absolute need of the Holy Virgin for the accomplishment of His will and for the manifestation of His glory. He has but to will, in order to do everything.

N° 15

Nevertheless I say that, things being supposed as they are now, God having willed to commence and to complete His greatest works through the most holy Virgin, since He created her, we may well think He will not change His conduct in the eternal ages; for He is God, and He changes not either in His sentiments or in His conduct.

Mary is necessary, as well to God as to men. But, let us be clear!

1° It is not about an absolute necessity, resulting from the *nature* of things or imposed on God by violence or for lack of other means. God is *"He Who is,"* that is to say, whose existence is identified with His essence. He is, then, alone the absolutely necessary being, Who cannot not exist, and Who needs nothing and no one. Everything which exists outside of Him is a supremely free work of His creative omnipotence. Compared to God, Mary is *"less than an atom; or rather she is nothing at all."* She might very well not have existed. She is not, then, necessary. And furthermore, nobody can impose her on *"that grand Lord, always independent and sufficient to Himself,"* Who *"has but to will, in order to do everything."*

2° It is about a hypothetical necessity. A thing which is not necessary, absolutely speaking, can become so following an irrevocable intention, which chose it freely and was also freely imposed. Thus it was for Mary. God wanted to begin and finish His greatest works through her. Without being indispensable, this means seemed to Him more appropriate to attain the end which He was pursuing. It fulfilled the plan of revenge corresponding to the first fall and was the most suitable for proclaiming Himself and of establishing in the world the greatest glory of God alone.

Now God described Himself in Malachi (3:6): *"Ego enim Dominus et non mutor.* For I am the Lord and I change not." What reason besides would He have to change? Because He made a mistake the first time? This is repugnant to His infinite Wisdom and is no less contradicted by the impartial study of the facts such as they have come about, because could the beauty which He gave to Mary overshadow Him? He alone is *"He Who is"* and *in comparison with His infinite Majesty,"* Mary, with all the natural and supernatural riches with which she was filled, *"is less than an atom; or rather she is nothing at all"*; she recognizes this herself in her *Magnificat*: *"Because He hath regarded the humility of His handmaid"* (Lk. 1:48). Still all this was given to her only with a view to her co-redeeming maternity: *"In order to begin… His great works"* through her.

The conclusion is, then, imperative: "he is to believe that He (God) will not change His conduct throughout the centuries," and so Mary is necessary due to the divine will, that is to say, to a hypothetical necessity (n° 39).

ARTICLE II

The foundation of the necessity of the true devotion: - the divine will -
(16-38)

After having asserted in n°s 14 and 15 that the necessity of devotion to Mary results from the free divine will, Montfort rigorously proves this truth from n° 16 to n° 36. It cannot be denied, indeed: if we study the conduct of each of the divine Persons: 1° *before* the Incarnation, 2° *in the* Incarnation, and, 3° *after* the Incarnation, Mary appears invariably as the means which God wanted to use.

The Saint proceeds very briefly. Knowing that he does not have to deal with *"strong minds,"* he is content with expressing the facts without proving them. (See n° 26.) There is nothing easier, however, than to support his assertions by a simple reminder of the theological truths explained elsewhere and to show that his assertions are quite in conformity with the purest doctrine of the Church.

SECTION I

Before the Incarnation
(16)

Following the rule of *appropriations*, Montfort always speaks separately of each of the Persons of the Most Holy Trinity. He thus manages to make us admire more and under all its aspects this fundamental truth: **God wanted to make use of the Most Blessed Virgin.**

N° 16

§ I. THE CONDUCT OF GOD THE FATHER BEFORE THE INCARNATION.

God the Father has not given His Only-begotten to the world except through Mary. Whatever sighs the patriarchs may have sent forth – whatever prayers the prophets and the saints of the ancient law may have offered up to obtain the treasure for full four thousand years – it was but Mary that **merited it***; it was but Mary who found grace before God by the force of her prayers and the eminence of her virtues. The world was unworthy, says St. Augustine, to receive the Son of God immediately from the Father's hands. He has given Him to Mary in order that the world might receive Him through her.*

A work of power, the Incarnation is ordinarily *attributed* to God the Father. It is He, according to our ordinary way of understanding, Who decides on the sending of His Son to earth at the moment He will choose. Now, says the Saint, He willed to give Him only through Mary. She was the only one *to merit* it.

The merit of Mary with regard to the Incarnation is a merit of suitability. It has for its object not the Incarnation itself, but some of its circumstances. By the vehemence of her prayers and by the sublimity of her virtues, Mary merited and obtained what so many others had hoped in vain to see for four thousand years. God wanted to begin His greatest work through her. How could He now reject the one who served Him so marvelously? Or then why so many virtues and graces?

§ II. THE CONDUCT OF GOD THE SON BEFORE THE INCARNATION.

God the Son has made Himself Man; but it was in *Mary and* through *Mary.*

These two lines give us the whole plan of the Incarnation, attributed to the Wisdom of the Son.

To accomplish His work, the Son of God had many other ways at His disposal (See n° 139). If He chose that one, it is quite freely, because He considered it better, although not absolutely necessary, to make use of Mary. His conception and birth prove the reality of His human nature. The role exercised by Mary from this moment on makes more obvious the Word's intention to "recapitulate," to repeat His whole work from the beginning. He Himself will be the new Adam, and Mary will be the new Eve. It is, then, the entire predestination of the Virgin that is asserted in these words. Next to Jesus, predestined to be the incarnate Word, Mary, from all eternity, appears predestined to be His Mother, the true Mother of God. It is a predestination superior to that of any creature, a superiority not only of degree, but of order. It is not surprising that it involves an unrivalled profusion of graces, to such a point that God alone is capable of measuring the extent of it.

Let us remember, too, that it is not only *in* Mary, but *through* Mary that the Son of God became man for our salvation. By this eternal predestination, divine Wisdom willed to unite Mary to Jesus and make use of her for the accomplishment of His works. Not only in the Incarnation, but during every century, Jesus saves souls in Mary and through Mary. And the ancient Fathers were right to describe the Incarnation as: "The economy, that is to say, the plan of salvation, *through the Virgin Mary*." Equally right were the artists, who left us the graceful image of "*the Virgin at the inkwell*"; Mary carries on her left arm her divine Son, and she presents to Him with her right hand an inkwell, so that He may be pleased to write in *the book of life* the names of all those whom she recommends to Him. The faithful, indeed, have never forgotten that Mary, the great predestined woman, is the means par excellence to assure their own eternal predestination.

§ III. THE CONDUCT OF THE HOLY GHOST BEFORE THE INCARNATION.

God the Holy Ghost has formed Jesus Christ in Mary; but it was only after having asked her consent by one of the first ministers of His court.

Although it is an exterior work, and, as such, common to the three divine Persons, the formation of the humanity of the Word incarnate in the womb of Mary is usually *attributed* to the Holy Ghost. That is why the Holy Ghost is called the "active principle" of the conception of Jesus Christ.

Montfort considers, in this formation, what would lay the foundation of devotion to Mary, and he expresses this principal truth: the Holy Ghost formed Jesus Christ in Mary only after having asked her for her consent by one of the first ministers of His court.

We are here in the presence of the historic fact of the Annunciation. Obviously, the consent of the Virgin was not *absolutely* necessary. Strictly speaking even, the Word would have been able to take on human nature in her womb in spite of her. But "*things being supposed as they are*" (n° 15), since God willed to make the Incarnation depend on the free consent of Mary, as a result the Virgin was placed by the Holy Ghost at the beginning of this great work, of this miracle of miracles: the Incarnation of the Word. Is there not already there a magnificent announcement of the active and continual union of the Co-redemptrix beside the Redeemer? One does not proceed with so much respect and magnificence when one is thinking of discarding the instrument which was used!

SECTION II

In the Incarnation

1st Question

The conduct of God the Father in the Incarnation
(17)

N° 17

God the Father has communicated to Mary His fruitfulness, as far as a mere creature was capable of it, *in order that He might give her the power to produce* **His Son,** *and* **all the members of His mystical body**.

In this sentence, there are two key parts: God the Father, indeed, communicated to Mary His fruitfulness in order to give her the power to produce: 1° *His Son*; 2° *all the members of His mystical body*. There is also a restrictive parenthetical clause modifying each of the two propositions: "*as far as a mere creature was capable of it.*"

1° The power to produce the Son: in what sense is this true?...

God the Father has communicated to Mary His fruitfulness, as far as a mere creature was capable of it, *in order that He might give her the power to produce* **His Son**.

This first proposition obliges us to recall some rather lofty theological notions.

Saint Thomas distinguishes the cause and the subject of filiation. The *cause* is birth, by means of which a living person proceeds from another living person, by receiving from the latter a nature similar to the one that she herself possesses. The *subject* of filiation is the person who proceeds from the other by birth.

Now the Son of God has two births, one by which He proceeds from the Father from all eternity and according to His divine nature; the other by which He proceeds from Mary in time and according to His human nature.

The Son of God has, then, two reasons for being called Son, although He has only a single filiation: birth, which causes filiation, affects nature, which is twofold in Our Lord. *The same* Incarnate Word is, then, really the *Son of Mary* as He is really the *Son of the Eternal Father*, in spite of two really distinct births.

But how does Mary participate in *the fruitfulness of the Father?*

She had obviously no part in *the act* by which God the Father engenders His Son, neither before, nor during, nor after the Incarnation, although this act is eternal, and consequently permanent. It is simply a question of a participation in the fruitfulness of the Father Who allowed her to produce in time and according to a temporal birth the same Son Who proceeds from the Father in eternity and by an eternal birth. It is not, then, in birth, the cause of filiation, that God the Father and Mary are associated, it is *in the terminus of this twofold birth*: both have the same Son. But as God, this Son has no mother; as man, He has no father.

Such an association, however, is supremely honorable for Mary: the same Son, common to one and the other, is the inviolable knot of her alliance with God the Father and the eternal pledge of their mutual affections. The generative act of the Father is eternal and is reproduced at every instant. At the time of the Incarnation, this act coincided with Mary's generative act. And, at this moment as in that of the Nativity, both could say to the same Jesus: *Thou art my Son, this day have I begotten Thee* (Ps. 2:7). So, Mary is associated *in a certain way*, and as much as a mere creature is capable of it, with the eternal generation of the Word.

Furthermore, the temporal generation of the Word is the replica of His eternal generation. The Incarnate Word is thus the perfect image of His Father in His divinity and the perfect image of His Mother in His humanity. And so Mary receives from God the Father the power to reproduce *in His image* in human nature a Son Who preexists her in His divine nature; to reproduce Him *alone* and without the help of any other principle; to reproduce Him with such *perfection*, that, from the first instant of His conception, nothing in His human nature was lacking, and that the fruitfulness of Mary, without being exhausted by this conception, produced, however, no other fruit; to reproduce Him without harming her *virginity*, but much rather by consecrating it: "*He did not decrease, but consecrated the integrity of His Mother*"; to produce it in joy, and as cause of joy for herself and the world; *not by separating herself from it* by producing Him, as by a kind of circuminsession, first of all, during the nine months of gestation, then during the thirty years of the hidden life, finally during the whole work of Redemption, formerly, and now, for the sanctification of souls.

2° To be able to produce the members of the mystical body: in what sense also?...

The same restrictive parenthetical clause also modifies the second part:

God the Father has communicated to Mary His fruitfulness, as far as a mere creature was capable of it, in order that He might give her the power to produce **His Son**, *and* **all the members of His mystical body**.

God alone, indeed, can adopt us as children. He alone can communicate to us a nature which it is His alone to possess. In other words, God alone is the principal efficient cause of grace. But He can give to a creature the power to cause it *instrumentally*. So the sacred humanity of Christ, the Sacraments and Priests are, at the same time as God, truly causes of grace. In the same way, He was pleased to communicate His own fruitfulness to Mary, "*as far as a mere creature was capable of it*," so that she might become the **Mother of divine grace**, the Mother of all those who live the life of God, who are the adopted children of God and members of the mystical body of her Son.

And it is with just cause that Montfort attributes the communication of this power concerning the mystical body to God the Father, because just as it is in all truth the principle of natural filiation, so too we like to consider it as the principle of adoptive filiation. It is He Who ordered it from all eternity. The Holy Ghost carried it out, and the Son was its exemplary and meritorious cause.

Let us note here the moment when Mary became our Mother: from the day of the Annunciation and not only on Calvary. When God the Father made her share His fruitfulness, it was to produce simultaneously both the physical body and the mystical body of the Savior. See n° 32: "*One and the same mother does not bring forth into the world the head without the members...*," etc.

2nd Question

The conduct of God the Son in the Incarnation
(18-19)

Speaking about the relations of God the Son with His divine Mother, Montfort reduces them to two main things: *filial love* and *dependence*. The Incarnate Word is truly the Son of Mary. He loved her, then, as such a Son could love such a Mother: divinely, immensely, and infinitely. But, far from being satisfied by this love, He also associated His Mother with His work of Redemption, and in such an admirable way that He willed to depend on her.

§ I. – THE FILIAL LOVE OF JESUS FOR MARY

N° 18

God the Son has descended into her virginal womb, as the new Adam into the terrestrial paradise, to take His pleasure there, *and* to work in secret the marvels of His grace.

The comparison of the virginal womb of Mary with the earthly Paradise, with *Eden*, that is to say, the virgin earth, filled with riches and delights, is traditional in the Church. We find it in *St. John Chrysostom, St. Gregory the Thaumaturge, St. Ephrem*, etc.... Montfort was thus authorized to use this image. He was fond of it besides, and returns to it at length later (n° 261) in order to explain the interior practice of the slave of love who carries out all his actions in Mary.

Jesus *takes His delight* in Mary: the womb of the Virgin is for Him a place of delights, where He stays not by constraint, but by free choice. If He gives the name of *spouses* to all holy souls in general, and specially to the virgins consecrated by the Church; if He goes so far as to contract with some of them a real *mystical marriage*, what shall we say about her who is the saint *par excellence*, the Virgin by antonomasia and the mystical Rose! She is the Spouse *par excellence*, the unique Spouse, because no one in the world is a Spouse like her. In her alone, God can freely and always take pleasure. To her, above any other, is the song of love of the wedding of the Lamb befitting.

But the love of Jesus for His Mother is an effective love. *He works in secret marvels of grace.* These are already incomprehensible miracles for us, and moreover worked "*in secret.*" God made Mary too beautiful for us to be able to understand her. He wants to reserve to Himself the knowledge and possession of her (See n° 5). Jesus is the only son who had in his power all the means to enrich and satisfy His Mother. Not only was He allowed to use this power, but He had to do so as son and as a good son. This is the order of divine Wisdom itself, and nature demands it. So that, even there, if we want to understand the Mother, it is necessary, first of all, to understand the Son. Let every tongue remain silent here (n° 12), especially the one which, after so many proofs of the filial love of Jesus for His Mother, would again dare to treat our devotion to Mary as excessive.

*
* *

§ II. – THE ADMIRABLE DEPENDENCE OF JESUS UPON MARY

This second relation of the Incarnate Word with His Mother disconcerts our modest notions. As Montfort will say in n° 139, "*the human mind loses itself when it seriously reflects on the conduct of the Incarnate Wisdom.*" This is the great argument on which he will found the perfect devotion. "*It is through the most holy Virgin Mary that Jesus has come into the world, and it is also through her that He has to reign in the world.*" That is why He elaborates on this dependence at length, establishing at first **the fact**, then **the reasons**, and finally **the nature** of this dependence. We shall go through the passage several times, to express all the richness of it.

1° THE FACT OF THIS DEPENDENCE

This fact is incontestable. It is even of divine faith, because it is expressed very clearly in the Gospel: "*Et erat subditus illis*, and was subject to them," that is to say, to Mary and Joseph (Lk. 2:51). This obedience was exalted by St. Bernard in his first homily on *Missus est* (P.L. CLXXXIII, 60). And Montfort, the new St. Bernard, proclaims in n° 18, in the second paragraph: "*O admirable and incomprehensible dependence of a God, which the Holy Ghost could not pass in silence in the Gospel, although He has hidden from us nearly all the admirable things which that Incarnate Wisdom did in His Hidden Life.*"

He summarizes the life of Jesus in two parts: the one concerns His direct relations with *the Virgin*, the other His relations with *others*.

a) **His direct relations with the Virgin.** – The Saint speaks enthusiastically about this miracle of a God, which gives a new splendor to His own attributes, when it seems to lose them for the love of Mary.

God made Man has found His liberty *in seeing Himself imprisoned in her womb. He has made* His Omnipotence *shine forth in letting Himself be carried by that blessed Virgin. He has found* His glory *and His Father's in hiding His splendours from all creatures here below, and revealing them to Mary only.*

And he continues by enumerating the various stages of Jesus' life to which he just alluded:

He has glorified His Independence and His Majesty in depending on that sweet Virgin in His Conception, *in* His Birth, *in* His Presentation in the Temple, *in* His Hidden Life of thirty years.

Then, unable to forget that Jesus is above all Jesus, that is to say, Savior, he lifts his sights in a leap to the sacrifice and adds:

And even in His Death, where she was to be present, *in order that He might make with her but one same sacrifice, and be immolated to the Eternal Father by her consent; just as Isaac of old was offered by Abraham's consent to the Will of God.*

Finally, to give a complete idea of the office of the Virgin with regard to the Lamb of God Who bears the sins of the world, he ends by these words:

It is she who has suckled Him, nourished Him, supported Him, brought Him up, and then sacrificed Him for us.

N° 19

b) **His relations with others.** – The Saint quickly examines the rest of the life of the Savior and shows Him to us beginning His miracles through Mary:

He sanctified St. John *in the womb of St. Elizabeth his mother; but it was through Mary's word. No sooner had she spoken than John was sanctified; and this was His first and greatest miracle of grace.* At the marriage of Cana He changed the water into wine; *but it was at Mary's humble prayer; and this was His first miracle of nature.*

Father de Montfort makes us observe besides that Jesus is not content to begin, but that He has

continued *His miracles through Mary, and He* will continue *them to the end of ages through Mary* (N° 19).

These are simple assertions. But there is no need to accumulate proofs to notice the real dependence of Our Lord upon His Mother in all the circumstances mentioned by Montfort: conception, birth, presentation in the Temple, hidden life of thirty years, preparation and immolation of Jesus, and miracles of grace and nature. To be convinced of it, it suffices to recall the absolute dependence of the child upon his mother during the first years of his existence, and, as far as Jesus is concerned, to read and understand the Gospel.

It should be noted that, alone, the explanation given by Montfort shows the real purpose of Mary's presence on Calvary. She was not there to console her Son; much less to snatch Him from the hands of His executioners; nor driven by her immense sorrow. "When the supreme hour of the Son came, beside the Cross of Jesus there *stood* Mary His Mother, not merely occupied in contemplating the cruel spectacle, but *rejoicing* that her Only Son was offered for the salvation of mankind, and so entirely participating in His Passion, that if it had been possible she would have gladly borne all the torments that her Son bore" (Pope St. Pius X, Encyclical, *Ad diem illum*).

2° THE REASON FOR THIS DEPENDENCE

It does not ensue from an obligation imposed on the Incarnate Word because of His human nature, or the prejudices of His fellow countrymen; because then Jesus could have at least contented Himself with what is required from an ordinary child. And, yet, He went much farther (See n° 139). He depended on His Mother during all His earthly life and even to His death and His miracles (n°s 18 and 19). We can thus look for the reason for this dependence only in the *divine will*: the Incarnate Word willed it so. This reason asserts itself when we come to the last and more sublime categories of dependence: that of Calvary and that of the miracles. It is also the only reason that completely explains all the others. As Bishop Gay says: "The intention which the Word had of belonging above all and completely to Mary must have entered as a powerful reason into the plan which He had devised to begin His temporal life with infancy." This reason honors the sovereign liberty of God and completely satisfies our faith which seeks to understand, because, as a matter of fact, if God willed it, it was for the best: is He not infinite Wisdom?...

Now, **why did God want it so?** Montfort tells us in n° 18, paragraph 2:

O admirable and incomprehensible dependence of a God, which the Holy Ghost could not pass in silence in the Gospel, *although He has hidden from us nearly all the admirable things which that Incarnate Wisdom did in His Hidden Life,* as if He would enable us, by His revelation of that at least, to understand something of its price!

Such is indeed the ultimate reason for this dependence: **its price and His infinite glory**. That is why:

Jesus Christ gave more glory to God the Father by submission to His Mother during those thirty years than He would have given Him in converting the whole world by the working of the most stupendous miracles.

Then recalling that Jesus gave us the example, Montfort completes his idea by exclaiming:

O, how highly we glorify God, when, to please Him, we submit ourselves to Mary, after the example of Jesus Christ, our sole Exemplar!

Obviously this supposes that the heavenly Father had so settled it, because if He had willed that His Son should employ the same time in working miracles and preaching to the whole world, He would not have glorified His Father by persisting in submission to Mary. Besides, the question does not even arise: God the Son is infinite Wisdom and the means which He chooses lead inevitably and most perfectly to the purpose that He proposes. In n° 139, the same sentence will be found, with an addition, however, which clarifies the meaning of it, although it was often wrongly interpreted. We quote it according to the original text. The punctuation, often neglected elsewhere, is indicated here clearly, since the meaning depends on this punctuation.

He (Wisdom Incarnate) gave more glory to God His Father during this time of submission and dependence to the Most Blessed Virgin than He would have given Him in employing these thirty years by working miracles, preaching to the whole world, and converting all men; if He WOULD HAVE acted differently.

In this sentence, the semicolon separates the last proposition from the previous one, and makes of it a separate unit. Furthermore, the word "*if*" written in the manuscript afterward and above the line, as well as the conditional form of the verb: *would have acted*, which would not be correct if it was the only verb of the sentence, show an elliptical, concise expression, which could be translated as follows: (if it had been) otherwise, divine Wisdom would have acted another way and precisely in the one which would have been best.

The thought of Father de Montfort is, therefore, indeed this one: divine Wisdom settled on this means of glorifying God, because it was indisputably the best. If another had been better, that is the one that He would have taken.

3° THE NATURE OF THIS DEPENDENCE

There are three kinds of dependence:

a) – The dependence **of inferiority**, which the *Incarnate* Word proclaims towards His *Father* (Jn. 12:28), but that He can have towards no creature, not even towards His Mother. See N° 27: "*For Mary is infinitely below her Son, Who is God, and therefore she does not command Him, as a mother here below would command her child, who is below her.*" The fact of having received from another the nature which we possess does not imply for that reason an inferiority, especially when, for other reasons than the transmission itself, the nature transmitted, while being substantially identical to the one who transmits, is accidentally much more perfect. Such was the case of the human nature of Jesus with regard to that of Mary. Is not Jesus the head of the mystical body, including His Mother, by the capital grace with which He is filled in His human nature?...

    b) – The dependence **of servitude** or **slavery**, by which, willy-nilly, the creature is subjected to his Creator and consequently:

    c) – The dependence **of obedience**, by which the creature recognizes, accepts and proclaims the relation of servitude which binds him to his Creator.

    By right, the Incarnate Word was not bound to submit Himself to Mary in either of these last two manners: it would be against His dignity as supreme Head of humanity. Therefore it is not a matter of obedience but rather of respect and filial love. Jesus owed to His Mother respect and filial love, based on the very essence of things; He did not owe her obedience. **In fact**, however, Jesus willed to obey His Mother, "*not only during the first eight, ten, or fifteen years of His life, like other children, but for thirty years*" (n° 139) and even "*even in His death, where she was to be present, in order that He might make with her but one same sacrifice, and be immolated to the Eternal Father by her consent; just as Isaac of old was offered by Abraham's consent to the Will of God*" (n° 18). The spontaneity of His submission gives greater importance to this *de facto* obedience, for the point of view of devotion to Mary. The Incarnate Word thus could not affirm to us more clearly that He willed to make use of Mary.

    Even if we consider the life of Jesus IN THE WOMB OF HIS MOTHER, we shall find a certain dependence of servitude there which will make Montfort say, n° 139: "*This good Master has not disdained to shut Himself up in the womb of the Blessed Virgin,* **as a captive and as a loving slave**," and in n° 243: in the mystery of the Incarnation "*Jesus is a* **captive and a slave** *in the bosom of the divine Mary, and depends upon her for all* *things.*" Likewise, as long as HIS VERY EARLY INFANCY will last. In these two cases, however, the dependence of servitude concerned only the preservation of His temporal life; but, mindful of this reservation, it was a dependence not only in fact, but *by right*, as a result of the intention of the Word to take human nature, and to take it in the *true* form of infancy. Otherwise, it would be necessary to see in the infancy of the Savior a continual miracle. The only difference distinguishing it from ordinary infancy is that it was a chosen state; this allows Montfort to call it in all truth a "**slavery of love**."

On Golgotha and during "*the rest of His life*" (the Visitation and the Wedding at Cana), the dependence which Jesus showed towards Mary (dependence in fact, but not by right) was that of the Redeemer towards the Co-redemptrix, of the new Adam towards the new Eve. The execution of the plan of vengeance, decided freely by Him, entails the active participation of Mary in the acquisition and distribution of the fruits of the Redemption.

On **Calvary**, it is the **acquisition**, the Redemption properly so-called, caused by Jesus' death. Now, just as Jesus' death was necessary to redeem the world since God willed it so, so too Mary's presence attending this death, accepting and offering Him to God for the salvation of the world, was necessary so that Mary might effectively be Co-redemptrix and engender us into the life of grace. It is this universal human maternity that Jesus, on the point of dying, solemnly proclaimed by saying to this Woman (a replica of the one of the earthly Paradise): "Woman, behold thy son"; and to the beloved disciple: "Behold thy Mother." By her "Fiat" at the Annunciation, Mary had already accepted the future death of the Redeemer; since that time, she "*had nursed, fed, supported and raised*" the victim for the sacrifice. On Calvary, she truly "*sacrificed Him for us*," by the resigned and even eager acceptance that she made of His death for us. St. Antoninus is not afraid of asserting that, if no one had reported for duty to crucify her Son, she herself would have affixed Him to the Cross: would her obedience to God have been less perfect than that of Abraham? (See n° 18)

At the Visitation, it is already the **distribution** of the fruits of the Redemption. The Word became incarnate to save the world, and He will begin His redemptive work by His Precursor. He first frees him from the bonds of slavery: "*This is His* **first** *miracle in the order of* **grace**." And He carries it out with such generosity that John is also His "**greatest**" miracle in the same order. But this miracle was carried out through Mary. Jesus did not need to be transported to Ain-Karim to perform it. Also, he could have left the action of Mary in the shadows. This is just the opposite which is manifested in the Gospel narrative. Mary appears to us as the great means, the great sacrament which Jesus wanted to use to sanctify the soul of His Precursor.

"**At the marriage of Cana**, *He changed the water into wine; but it was at Mary's humble prayer; and this was His* **first miracle** *(in the order) of* **nature**. Let us note, first of all, that the presence of Jesus is due to the presence of Mary. "And the third day, there was a marriage in Cana of Galilee: and the mother of Jesus was there. And Jesus was also invited, and His disciples, to the marriage" (Jn. 2:1-2). Why this *He also*, if not because Mary was there, and that they wanted to please her also by inviting her Son? What stands out then is the fact of "*Mary's humble prayer*." "And the wine failing, the mother of Jesus saith to Him: They have no wine" (Jn. 2:3). Mary, so respectful of her Son, is content to make known to Him the embarrassment of the couple and her own desire to help them. For the rest, she leaves it to the good pleasure of Jesus. The purpose of her request, however, is very clear: to ask Jesus to compensate for the lack of wine by a miracle. And her request was fulfilled. From the whole narration, it emerges that, if Jesus works this miracle, it was to fulfill Mary's prayer. This is what Mary had very well understood when she had said to the servants: "Whatsoever He shall say to you, do ye" (Jn. 2:5). How thus explain Jesus' answer, which has all the appearances of a refusal: "Woman, what is that to Me and to thee? My hour is not yet come" (Jn. 2:4). In this answer there is neither disapproval, as St. John Chrysostom believed, nor refusal, as the continuation of the narrative proves. St. Bernard explained this obscure passage very well. Here are his words:

"What is there between you and her, Lord? Is there not what is between a son and his mother? You seek for what is common to You with her? But are You not the blessed fruit of her immaculate womb? Is it not she who conceived You without damage to her modesty and who brought You into the world while remaining a virgin? Did You not remain nine months in her womb; were You not fed by her virginal milk? Well then, why do You sadden her by saying to her: What is that to Me and to thee? – But I see that it is not to grow indignant, nor to upset the tender shyness of the Virgin Mother that You speak thus to her, because upon seeing the servants approaching whom your Mother sends You, You do without delay what she suggested to You."

In other words, Jesus admires here the sweet violence exercised on Him by the bond which connects Him to His Mother and which is going to lead Him to anticipate the hour of His manifestation, because He truly anticipated it, given the very clear sense of the words: "My hour is not yet come," and the succession of events which took place immediately after. "The Lord," says St. Ambrose (Sermo XVI, 38), "wants to be importuned by us... Hardly had He finished saying that His hour had not come yet than He worked, nevertheless, the requested miracle."

It is therefore indeed "*at Mary's humble prayer*," that Jesus changed the water into wine and worked "*His first miracle of nature.*"

Thus Jesus "*has* **begun and continued** *His miracles through Mary, and He will* **continue** *them to the end of the ages through Mary also.*" In these two miracles, indeed, the one in Hebron and the one in Cana, it is about *initial* works, about the *first miracle* in each of the two orders, that of nature and that of grace. Now, the initial works have this unusual feature that they indicate the nature of those which will follow. And when these initial works have God Himself as the author, that is to say, the One Who does not need to be familiarized with the work, to acquire the skill, all the perfection that He desires is found in the first work. There is thus nothing to change afterward. (See n° 15)

3rd Question

The conduct of God the Holy Ghost in the Incarnation
(20-21)

N° 20

God the Holy Ghost being barren in God – that is to say, not producing another Divine Person – is become fruitful through Mary, whom He has espoused.

Mary can be called the *Spouse of the Holy Ghost*. First of all, because of the love God has for her and that she has for God. But it is not for this reason that Montfort gives her this title; it is because of *her fruitfulness:*

It is with her, in her, and of her, that He has produced His Masterpiece, which is a God made Man, *and Whom He goes on producing in the persons of His members daily to the end of the world.* The predestinate *are the members of that Adorable Head.*

What name would indicate better this fertility than that of Spouse? It entails by no means, besides, the appellation of "Father" given to the Holy Ghost with regard to the Incarnate Word; because, although the active principle of His conception, He did not form the humanity of Christ from His substance and in His likeness. But how did the Holy Ghost become fruitful through Mary? In analyzing the text of our Saint, we shall discover: 1° the object of this fruitfulness; 2°

the part which Mary took in it and the consequence which results from it; 3° an error of which we must beware.

§ I. – THE OBJECT OF THE FRUITFULNESS OF THE HOLY GHOST

This object is twofold: "*Jesus Christ and His members*," according to the concise formula found at the end of n° 21.

The role of the Holy Ghost in the conception of Jesus Himself is known.

For the members of the mystical body of Jesus, according to St. Paul, they all have to bear the likeness of this adorable Head, by receiving sanctifying grace from Him. This work of assimilation is also attributed to the Holy Ghost, as its efficient cause. He is the one Who "*produces Jesus Christ in the soul and the soul in Jesus Christ*," by imprinting on it the seal of Christ. "Charity (the inseparable effect of sanctifying grace itself) was poured forth in our hearts by the Holy Ghost Who was given to us."

Note: a) that the Holy Ghost forms *at the same time* Jesus Christ and all the members of His mystical body. With Jesus, in the womb of Mary, all His members were already conceived in grace. From His fullness, until the end of time, all just men will receive grace, as all the elect will receive glory, and this by the divine Paraclete.

b) that Montfort does not distinguish without reason "*the* **predestined** *and the* **members** *of the body of this adorable Head.*" Those are not, indeed, two synonymous terms. According to St. Thomas, by members of Christ, we understand not only men who are in a state of grace, but also those who simply have faith, or even who can have it. They will completely cease being members of Christ only at their impenitent death. By predestined, on the contrary, we understand those who are already in glory or will enter it one day. All the predestined are members of Christ, but all the members of Christ are not predestined.

*
* *

§ II. – MARY'S PART IN THE FRUITFULNESS OF THE HOLY GHOST AND THE CONSEQUENCE WHICH RESULTS FROM IT

1° **Mary's part:**

The Holy Ghost has become fruitful *"through Mary, whom He has espoused"*; *"the Holy Ghost chose to make use of our Blessed Lady, though He has no absolute need of her, to bring His fruitfulness to action* (n° 21)."

It is **with** *her,* **in** *her, and* **of** *her, that He has produced His Masterpiece, which is a God made Man, and Whom He goes on producing in the persons of His members daily to the end of the world. The predestinate are the members of that adorable Head (N° 20).*

a) *In regard to Jesus.* – *With Mary:* this expression marks the *moral* collaboration of Mary; Mary gave her consent to the work of the Holy Ghost concerning the formation of the body of Christ, as the Holy Ghost had asked her for it (n° 16).

In Mary and of Mary. These two expressions complement one another. They simultaneously prove the physical reality of the flesh of the Savior, against the Docetists, Valentinians and other heretics of the first centuries; the perpetual virginity of Mary, by the exclusion of any other human principle, against all those ancient or modern thinkers who deny this privilege of our Mother; finally the *physical* cooperation in what concerns the formation of the real body of Jesus.

b) *In regard to the mystical body of Jesus.* – It is also very clear that He was formed *with* Mary, because of the import of her "Fiat"; *in Mary*, because the members are engendered with the head and in the same place; and *of* Mary, because she is at the origin of the acquisition of grace and because, having given us Jesus, she gave us by that very fact the source from whose fullness we are going to draw. Because she is the Mother of divine grace, grace is truly something which belongs to her and which comes from her.

2º **Practical consequence:**

This is the reason why He, the Holy Ghost, the more He finds Mary, His dear and inseparable Spouse, in any soul, becomes the more active and mighty in producing Jesus Christ in that soul, and that soul in Jesus Christ (Nº 20).

This passage speaks ABOUT THE PRESENCE OF JESUS AND MARY IN SOULS, about that of *Mary* as a required **condition** so that the action of the Holy Ghost may be more fruitful; about that of **Jesus** as being the **result** of the combined action of the Holy Ghost and Mary. By this new infusion of grace, indeed, the Holy Ghost makes us more like Jesus and incorporates us into Him more and more, as a member to the head of the same mystical body. It is what Montfort calls "*producing Jesus Christ in that soul, and that soul in Jesus Christ* (nº 20)."

All this is the normal consequence of the conditions which the Holy Ghost has set out. If, indeed, He becomes fruitful through Mary whom He espoused; if with her, in her and of her, He produces Jesus and produces Him every day, it is clear that the more He finds Mary in a soul, the more He will be able to exercise his own fruitfulness. And even, because the Virgin is "*the means of which He wills indeed to make use, although He had no absolute need of her*," she has to be in a soul so that the Holy Ghost can operate in it, given that He does not want to act without her.

IT IS ASKED: What sort of presence is meant here?

Obviously, it is necessary to reject any *substantial* presence similar to the Eucharistic presence. The body and soul of Mary cannot be in us physically.

It is necessary to distinguish then two other types of Mary's presence in us: the one which **attracts** the operation of the Holy Ghost, and the one which **accompanies** this divine action. The first one is doubtless, a presence of a *moral* order; it is Mary's presence as the object of our knowledge and love. The second is a presence of *action*, which will be called *physical* or *moral* according to the nature of the action itself, or according to the previously adopted theological opinion.

1° The Marian presence attracting the action of the Holy Ghost.

In his practical conclusion and in his whole *Treatise*, Montfort insists especially on the *moral presence*, the one which *attracts* the action of the Holy Ghost. Because if this divine Spirit even here, if three Persons of the Holy Trinity elsewhere, wanted to make use of the Virgin as a *means*, it follows that, the more we make use of this means, the more we shall enter the views of God and shall facilitate His activity in our soul.

This moral presence of Mary, all the more perfect the more frequently we think of her and the more we love her, will be the very measure of the action of the Holy Ghost in us: "*The more the Holy Ghost finds Mary in a soul, the more active and mighty He becomes.*" (See n° 36: *When the Holy Ghost, her Spouse, has found Mary in a soul*, etc. This correlation between Mary's presence and the action of the Holy Ghost, Montfort calls a "*mystery of grace unknown to even the wisest and most spiritual among Christians* (n° 21)." This idea of mystery, of secret, is dear to Father de Montfort to indicate his spirituality. He returns to it frequently, particularly in n° 82 and at the beginning of the "*Secret of Mary.*" We shall also have the opportunity to speak again of it. Let us note only the general sense of this formula: the great majority of the faithful, and even of theologians and pious persons do not understand *up to which point* Mary is, due to the divine will, an habitual and universal means of sanctification. Doubtless, there is no Christian who does not have some devotion to Mary, and therefore, who does not know her and love her, and does not enjoy her moral presence in his soul. But few nourish the *true devotion* towards her, based on the role entrusted by God to Mary in the supernatural economy.

How can this moral presence of Mary be explained?

There are, Montfort will say in n° 119, degrees in the practice of the Holy Slavery itself, which is nevertheless the most perfect form of true devotion. There is therefore also a mysterious gradation of souls in the knowledge and love of Mary and consequently in the presence of Mary in them. For the most faithful, the presence of Mary, always of a moral order, can be so extraordinary and so perceptible, that in reality it will touch upon the mystical life:

> *This is what cannot be believed,*
> *I carry her in the midst of myself,*
> *Engraved with traits of glory,*
> *Although in the darkness of faith.*

The Saint explains the means to acquire this presence in the following way: "*It is necessary to do all things IN MARY, that is to say, that it is necessary to become accustomed little by little to recollecting oneself interiorly, in order to form a small idea or spiritual image of the Blessed Virgin.*" (*Secret of Mary* N° 47).

Indeed, the known object must penetrate into the knowing subject under the form of an immaterial image. This image represents it to perfection, if the object is directly known. It represents it in a more or less perfect way, if the object is indirectly known. The more lively our faith is and the more profound our knowledge, the more the image of Mary representing her to our intellect will approach the reality.

Likewise, the being who loves is in the being loved and mutually by the inclination which carries them toward one another; and in this way also we shall have with Mary a union of a truly inexpressible presence. Our daily faults and imperfections prevent us too often from understanding and experiencing it, because such a union is unveiled magnificently only to simple and faithful souls that thirst for purity and love. (See *Secret of Mary*, Note on N° 15).

This presence is, one might say, acquired and corresponds to our effort, although under the prompting of divine grace and making use of the infused virtues of faith and charity.

But there exists besides a more perfect presence, of a superior order even, resulting from the lights that God pours directly into the soul, and from the fire of love that He ignites in it. It is about this presence especially that the above-quoted quatrain speaks. Here there is no longer a need for images and representations. They are even radically impossible. Mary lives mysteriously in the soul which she subjects totally to her action. Without causing either efforts, or fatigue, the thought of the Virgin constantly occupies the mind, and her love vibrates in the heart. The soul overwhelmed by this divine favor is, so to speak, possessed by Mary and it enthusiastically devotes itself to the one who shows him so much love.

This grace, however, is not granted to all indiscriminately. And it requires great fidelity and great purity. So Montfort is right to add:

"Take care not to torment yourself if you do not immediately enjoy the sweet presence of the Blessed Virgin in your interior; this grace is not given to all; and when God favors a soul by great mercy, it is very easy for it to lose it, if it is not faithful to recollect itself often, and, if this misfortune happened to you, return meekly and make amends to your Sovereign" (*Secret of Mary*, n° 52).

So, we have said, Mary *will attract* the operation of the Holy Ghost.

2° The Marian presence accompanying the action of the Holy Ghost.

There is, moreover, a presence of Mary which *accompanies* this operation. Because it is impossible to have any influence whatsoever on a totally distant object, Mary is thus necessarily in the soul in which she acts.

Of what nature will this new presence be?

Being a presence of action, it will be accidental and not substantial. But will it be *physical* or *moral*? The answer to this question would be easy if we knew clearly the nature of Mary's action in us. But precisely, that is a theological question that has been very little studied up to now. Rev. Fr. Hugon saw in this passage of Father de Montfort the proof of the instrumental physical causality of Mary in the production of grace:

"The exterior fruitfulness of the divine Paraclete is the production of grace, not in the order of moral causality, because the Holy Ghost is not a meritorious or impetratory cause, but in the order of physical causality. To bring this fruitfulness to action thus amounts to producing physically the grace and works of holiness which are appropriated to the third Person. If it is true that the Holy Ghost brings into action His own fruitfulness by the intervention of Mary, if He becomes powerful and effective thanks to her, it is through her that He physically produces grace in souls. Mary is, therefore, the secondary physical instrument of the Holy Ghost."

*
* *

§ III. – AN ERROR OF WHICH IT IS NECESSARY TO BEWARE

N° 21

In n° 21, the Saint warns us against an error of interpretation, and shows us in what sense it is necessary to take his words.

Here is, first of all, what he does not want to say:

It is not that we may say that our Blessed Lady gives the Holy Ghost His fruitfulness, as if He had it not Himself.

Why does he not want to say this? Because it would be a very grave error,

for inasmuch as He is God He has the same fruitfulness or capacity of producing as the Father and the Son, only that He does not bring it into action, as He does not produce another Divine Person.

This explanation constitutes a digression in the thought of Father de Montfort, as the dash placed in the manuscript after the words "*as if He had it not Himself* proves." If we skip the digression, the opposition of the parts of the sentence is even more marked: "*It is not that we may say…*"

But what we want to say is that the Holy Ghost chose to make use of our Blessed Lady, though He had no absolute need of her, to bring His fruitfulness into action, by producing in her and through her Jesus Christ in His members…

And he concluded as we have seen: "*A mystery of grace unknown to even the wisest and most spiritual among Christians.*

In this passage, besides the exterior fruitfulness about which he spoke and which causes no difficulty, it says: *a)* that the Holy Ghost has interior fruitfulness like the Father and the Son; *b)* that He has it because he is God.

Is this exact from the theological point of view?

It is necessary to answer this question affirmatively for each of the two propositions.

a) **The Holy Ghost has fruitfulness**, that is to say, the capacity to produce, no more and no less than the Father and the Son, because the capacity to produce is directly proportionate to the perfection of nature. The three Divine Persons have numerically the same nature. Hence, they also have the same capacity to produce. But each with a different relation. In the Father, this relation is that He engenders the Son and, with the Son, produces the Holy Ghost; in the Son, that He is engendered by the Father, and with Him produces the Holy Ghost; in the Holy Ghost, that He proceeds from the Father and the Son. The Holy Ghost does have therefore the same power, the same fruitfulness as the Father and the Son, but with this special relation that He does not have it to produce another person, but only to proceed Himself from the Father and the Son. That is why "*He is barren in God*" while having fruitfulness.

b) The Holy Ghost has fruitfulness **because He is God**.

According to St. Thomas, indeed, the capacity to produce regards *principally and directly the divine nature*, and only in an indirect and secondary way the Persons. Montfort is thus right to assert that the Holy Ghost possesses fruitfulness *as God* and that He does not possess it as the third Person of the Most Holy Trinity.

Then, because of this second point of view, he shows us the Holy Ghost "*is become fruitful through Mary, whom He has espoused,*" that is to say, exercising outside the Trinity, as the third Person, a fruitfulness that He possesses in the Trinity, as God, without having the possibility of exercising it. But it is not Mary who communicates this fruitfulness to Him. Furthermore, He could exercise it alone. *"He has no need of anything or anyone."* (See n° 14.)

We shall admire here the simultaneously very simple and profoundly theological language of Father de Montfort. We shall also see that it is mainly because of her relations with the Holy Ghost that the Most Blessed Virgin was called the **extension of the Most Holy Trinity**.

SECTION III

After the Incarnation
(22-38)

In n°s 22 to 38, Fr. de Montfort considers the conduct of the three Divine Persons after the Incarnation. He shows us, first of all, in n°s 23-25, *the investiture* that the Virgin received from each of the Persons of the Most Holy Trinity, then the *consequence* which immediately flows from it: the *power* of Mary over God Himself (n° 27), over *heaven and earth* (n° 28) and over the *predestined* (n°s 29-38).

N° 22

This is briefly announced in n° 22:

The conduct which the three Persons of the Most Holy Trinity have deigned to pursue in the Incarnation and first coming of Jesus Christ, They still pursue daily in an invisible manner throughout the whole Church, and They will still pursue it even to the consummation of the ages in the last coming of Jesus Christ.

A new and rich variation on the theme expressed in n° 1.

Let us notice, first of all, that, if the Saint does not prove in great detail and in the manner of theologians everything that he sets forth, he is, nevertheless, anxious to notify his readers that he has in his hands all the necessary documents for this. They are contained in the powerful work of **Rev. Fr. Poiré, S.J.** (1584-1637): *La Triple Couronne de la Bienheureuse Vierge Mère de Dieu* (The Triple Crown of the Blessed Virgin Mother of God). A notebook of handwritten notes attests to the serious study which Montfort made of this book. On one side, to the right, we find the summary of the noteworthy things gleaned from the author: to the left, the notes of the Saint, and in particular the Latin texts to which he alludes in n° 26.

Let us also notice the particular sense which Montfort seems to give to the words *"the last coming of Jesus Christ."* This coming is set in opposition to the first one, which was accomplished in the Incarnation. It is asserted that it will last every day until the consummation of the ages. This cannot be the Last Judgment. This is what Montfort names elsewhere (n°s 49 and 50), and in the same sense, the *second* coming, that is to say, Jesus' coming among men by means of His grace. In this coming, Mary is and will be the Mediatrix more and more visibly, as she was for the first one. The Last Judgment will be, on the contrary, the Jesus' *third* coming, as St. Thomas said, following St. Bernard and as we commonly say.

Better yet. In the text of n° 22, we can find a very clear allusion to each of three advents: 1° "The conduct which the three Persons of the Most Holy Trinity have deigned to pursue in the Incarnation and first coming of Jesus Christ"; 2° "They still pursue daily in an invisible manner throughout the whole Church"; 3° "and (They) will still pursue it even to the consummation of ages in the last coming of Jesus Christ."

1st Question

The solemn investiture of Mary
(23-25)

God the Father, on His own authority, enriched Mary for herself and for all men; God the Son communicated to His Mother everything that He received from His Father for the sake of His Passion; God the Holy Ghost makes use of her to carry out His sanctifying mission.

*
* *

§ I. GOD THE FATHER CREATED MARY AS HIS TREASURY
(23)

N° 23

God the Father made an assemblage of all the waters, and He named it **the sea** *(mare). He has made an assemblage of all His graces, and He has called it* **Mary** *(Maria). This great God has a most rich* treasury or storehouse *in which He has laid up all that He has of beauty, and splendor, of rarity, and of preciousness, even to His own Son; and this immense treasury is none other than Mary, whom the Saints have named the Treasure of the Lord,* out of whose plenitude all men are made rich (N° 23).

Montfort uses here several words in order to signify the spiritual riches with which Mary has been filled. But the word which returns most often is that of *treasury*, which he even calls synonymous with *storehouse*. Between the two, indeed, there are great resemblances, but also great differences, which justifies the use of both words in the same sentence.

A *treasury* is a place where precious and rich things which are not of daily use are contained: *"Everything which there is of beauty, of splendor, of rarity, and of preciousness"…*

A *storehouse* is a place where the most varied things in relation with the ordinary needs of life are put.

Mary is at the same time a treasury for the Lord, and a storehouse for men, because all the riches contained in Mary are not only for her; they are also for all the members of the immense human family, from the greatest saint to the most miserable sinner. Each can come there to seek what he needs to grow rich, without being afraid of ever exhausting it.

Montfort describes, first of all, the richness of the treasury in itself, then the richness which poured forth from the treasury on all men.

1° THE RICHNESS OF THE TREASURY ITSELF

God the Father made an assemblage of all the waters, and He named it the sea. He has made an assemblage of all His graces, and He has called it Mary.

We see here an unambiguous allusion to this theological opinion according to which the first grace granted to Mary in her conception exceeds in intensity and in extension the consummate grace of all the Angels and Saints together.

The reason for this divine generosity is because, from her Conception, Mary is considered as Mother of God. Her predestination already puts her in an order apart, the unique order of the divine Maternity, bordering on the hypostatic union. That is why even the crowned holiness of the elect is not a sufficient ideal for us when we think of the incomprehensible dignity of Mother of God. So we can assert with *St. Antoninus*: "Mary had, and in the highest degree, all the general and particular graces granted to all creatures." But let us hasten to add with the same saint: "She was also showered with graces which were conferred on no other creature." Thus, "the grace of Mary was so great, that a simple creature cannot have a greater." Why? Because "Mary contained in herself uncreated grace itself, that is to say, God."

Do we not find here an echo of this passage of our Saint: "(God) *has laid up* (in Mary) *all that He has of beauty, and splendor, of rarity, and of preciousness,* **even to His own Son?**"

And an echo of the words of St. Bernard: "How would God the Father not have granted all His other gifts to the one to whom alone He gave His own Son, as to His true Mother?"

Montfort too, looking for a comparison to express this *immense greatness*, has recourse to this image of an object, by definition, very vast and unlimited: **the sea**. "*God the Father has made an assemblage of all His graces* (granted to other saints), *and He has called it Mary.*"

Also to express the *variety* of the riches contained in this unlimited expanse, he recalls, first of all, that it contains everything which was granted to the other saints: "*Everything which there is of beauty, of splendor, of rarity, and of preciousness*"; and what is special to Mary, "*even to His own Son.*"

Under all aspects this is *plenitude*. Mary lacks nothing of what she can and must have to be a worthy Mother of God: "**Gratia plena.**"

2° THE INEXHAUSTIBLE RICHES OF THE TREASURY FOR MEN

The Saints call Mary *the treasure of the Lord,* out of whose plenitude all men are made rich.

And they are made rich from the treasure of Mary, because the Virgin is, with her Son, the exemplary cause, the efficient cause, and the final cause of their sanctification.

a) Mary, indeed, is inseparable from Jesus Christ. United with Him in the same decree of predestination, she has become with Jesus Christ the *exemplary cause* of our spiritual riches. With Jesus and because of Jesus, she is the divine ideal of all things. The material and spiritual world is made in the image of the Incarnate Word and of His holy Mother. And every created being will be beautiful only in the measure in which it will reproduce some of the beauties contained in the Incarnate Word and His Mother; and it will be that much richer, the more it reproduces their riches in himself.

b) With Jesus and because of Jesus, Mary is also the *efficient cause* of our spiritual riches. The Incarnate Word is the source of all graces. And the mystery of the Incarnation depended on Mary's consent. It is obvious that, by this consent, the Virgin truly gave salvation to the world: "For herself and the whole human race she has become the cause of salvation."

c) Finally Mary is also, with Jesus and because of Jesus, the *final cause* of our spiritual riches. For God arranged everything for His glory by bringing everything back to Christ. And Mary is inseparable from Christ in the divine decrees. "To end briefly, through her, because of her and for her all of Holy Scripture was made; the whole world was created for her. She is full of graces and it is for her that man was redeemed, that the Word became flesh, that God humbled Himself, and that man was raised."

So all our riches of nature, grace and glory are modeled on those of Mary, have come to us through her intervention, and are so many rays of her heavenly crown. Mary is truly *"the treasure of the Lord, out of whose plenitude all men are made rich."*

§ II. – GOD THE SON HAS COMMUNICATED TO HIS MOTHER ALL THAT HE HAS ACQUIRED BY HIS LIFE AND DEATH
(24)

N° 24

*God the Son has communicated to **His Mother** all that He has acquired by His Life and His Death, His infinite merits and His admirable virtues; and He has made her the **treasuress** of all that His Father has given Him for His inheritance. It is **through her** that He applies His merits to His members, and that He communicates His virtues, and distributes His graces. She is His mysterious **canal**; she is His **aqueduct**, through which He made His mercies flow* gently and abundantly.

"All that He has acquired by His life and His death…" Jesus saved the world (Acts 2:21) by dying on the Cross for us. Only then did His merits produce their effect. Because of His voluntarily accepted death, however, and from the first moment of His conception (Hebr. 10:5), the whole life of the Savior was meritorious. The Saint can therefore say: *"All that He has acquired by His **life** and His **death**."*

But what exactly did he intend to understand by this general assertion? He enumerates: 1° *"His infinite merits"*; 2° *"His admirable virtues"*; 3° *"all that His Father has given Him for His inheritance."*

How does He give all this to His Mother? 1° For herself: *"God the Son **has communicated to His Mother…**"* 2° For all of us *"It is **through her that He applies** His merits to His members,"* etc…

1° **For Mary herself:**

1°) *Jesus communicates His infinite merits to her.* This formula appears susceptible to a twofold interpretation.

On one hand, indeed, Jesus, the new Adam, associated Mary, the new Eve, in His whole work of Redemption. What He Himself merited in strict justice and for us, Mary merited by fittingness and according to the same modalities. Thus did she participate in the whole causality which is found in the Passion of the Savior for our salvation. Jesus truly communicates to her *"His infinite merits."*

On the other hand, already entering into the way of fulfillment, Jesus communicates to His Mother the whole plenitude of graces that He will spread through her over the rest of the world. Sublime endowment, which will allow the Virgin to give without becoming impoverished, and which will make all souls a living copy of hers, reproducing some detail of her perfection in itself.

2°) *Jesus communicates His admirable virtues to her.* In n° 214 where the question will be posed more pointedly, we shall prove that virtues themselves cannot pass from one subject to another. On the other hand, the moral dispositions with which Jesus practiced these virtues can be reproduced in a soul under the action of grace. Jesus reproduced them, first of all, and as perfectly as possible, in His beloved Mother. Thus Mary gave the example of these astonishing virtues that Montfort enumerates in n° 108. These virtues developed in her all the more freely as no obstacle ever hindered the divine action of grace there.

3°) *Jesus made her the treasuress of all that His Father has given Him for His inheritance.* As a personal reward of His sacrifice, Jesus received "a name which is above all names, that in the name of Jesus every knee should bow, of those that are in heaven, on earth, and under the earth" (Ph. 2:9-10). At His request, his Father gave Him as His inheritance all the nations of the earth. Associated with the sorrows of her Son, Mary also shares His triumphs. She is exalted above all the angels and saints, and she participates in Jesus' Kingship over heaven and earth. She is Queen, as

Jesus is King (see n° 38). Not only is she Queen, but His *treasuress*, officially charged with administering the incomparable riches of the kingdom of Christ.

2° For all of us:

1°) *Mary applies the merits of Jesus to us. She communicates His virtues and distributes His graces to us.* All this corresponds entirely to what we have just admired in Mary, and shows us that, if she was showered with so many favors, it is with a view to the mission which was to be entrusted to her. Indeed, if she collaborated in the acquisition of the merits of the Redeemer, it is right that she should collaborate in the application of these same merits. If she reproduced perfectly in her soul the admirable virtues of the Savior, she must help arouse in souls these very perfect dispositions which will allow the infused virtues to blossom there freely. If she participated in the acquisition of all graces, it is fitting that she should participate in their distribution. Thus will she exercise her functions of Co-redemptrix, model, and treasuress. The royal power which will be hers will be an altogether *supernatural* power.

2°) Mary is the *mysterious canal, the aqueduct* through which Jesus makes His mercies flow *gently* and *abundantly*. The sovereignty of Mary is not only supernatural. It is also *merciful*.

Let us note, first of all, the comparisons of canal and aqueduct, already used by *Richard of St. Victor* and *St. Bernard*. They are justified by the very fact that Mary communicates to us torrents of graces drawn from the treasury of her Son. She herself is not the source. She is only the canal.

Another very important remark: only *the mercies* of Jesus pass through this canal, the divine Master reserving to Himself the exercise of justice (see n° 31). This idea of the division between the kingdom of justice and that of mercy was inspired by the words of Assuerus to Esther: "If thou shouldst even ask one half of the kingdom, it shall be given to thee" (Est. 5:3). *St. Thomas* applies these words to Mary, and says that "she obtained half of the kingdom of God by becoming the Queen of mercy, while her Son remained the King of justice." This division is commonly admitted in the Church. Jansenists have, then, attacked her very wrongly in the "*Monita*": "Do not say that Jesus is a severe judge and I am a Mother of mercy; that He reserved justice to Himself and that He gave me the dispensation of mercy." Why must we not say this? – Because "God is a very simple and indivisible being: I have no mercy if it does not come to me from Him, and as much as it pleases Him to give me: it is He Who is the source of all graces and mercies, and it would not be possible to exhaust them." In truth, who says otherwise?... In any case, not Father de Montfort, because, according to him, it is *Jesus* Himself who makes *His* mercies pass through Mary. Everybody understands that mercy is a divine attribute and that God the Son cannot divest Himself of it. But He is quite free to make use of His Mother to manifest it.

And it is not without reason that he has recourse to this intermediary. Every instrument exercises its own causality, and it is because of this that it is employed. Mary is a woman, a mother and a queen. As **Woman**, she is distinguished by her lovable sweetness which is all the more attractive as it is more supernatural. And it is understood that Jesus makes His mercies pass "*sweetly*" through her. As **Mother**, she represents goodness, always ready to forgive the guilty child, and even to intercede for him with the angered Father. As **Queen**, she personifies clemency, which causes the rightly deserved punishment to be diminished, interposing if necessary her own authority between justice and the culprit. In this twofold point of view, Jesus will make His mercies pass "*abundantly*" through her.

§ III. – GOD THE HOLY GHOST HAS CHOSEN MARY AS THE DISPENSATRIX OF HIS GIFTS
(25)

N° 25

To Mary, His faithful Spouse, God the Holy Ghost has communicated **His unspeakable gifts**; *and He has chosen her to be* **the dispensatrix** *of all He possesses, in such sort that she distributes to whom she wills, as much as she wills, as she wills, and when she wills, all His gifts and graces. The Holy Ghost gives no heavenly gift to men which He does not pass through her virginal hands. Such has been the will of God, Who has willed that we should have everything in Mary; so that she who impoverished, humbled, and hid herself even to the abyss of nothingness by her profound humility her whole life long, should now be enriched and exalted by the Most High. Such are the sentiments of the Church and the Holy Fathers.*

This passage contains two assertions: 1° "*God the Holy Ghost has communicated to Mary, His faithful Spouse, His unspeakable gifts…*" 2° "*And He has chosen her to be the dispensatrix of all He possesses.*" The Saint develops the second idea especially, because it leads more directly to his subject: to establish the necessity of the True Devotion to Mary.

1° THE COMMUNICATION OF THE UNSPEAKABLE GIFTS OF THE HOLY GHOST

Mary has possessed the Holy Ghost fully since her Immaculate Conception. Nevertheless, He descended upon her several times in a special way in the Incarnation of the Word and at Pentecost. And each time He poured out into her soul a new effusion of His unspeakable gifts.

2° MARY IS ESTABLISHED AS THE DISPENSATRIX OF THE GIFTS OF THE HOLY GHOST

She is the dispensatrix "*of all the Holy Ghost possesses,*" that is to say, "*of all His gifts and graces,*" in such a way that *"no heavenly gift is granted to men without passing through her virginal hands."* She is such, moreover, so completely that she distributes *"**to whom** she wills, **as much as** she wills, **as** she wills, and **when** she wills, His gifts and graces."*

These words manifest *the universality* and *extension* of Mary's mediation.

a) **Universality.** Everything which comes to us from God, in the natural order as in the supernatural order, comes to us through Mary: *"**No heavenly gift** (in the most general sense) is given to men which does not pass through her virginal hands"*. Montfort drew this doctrine from *"the sentiments of the Church and the Holy Fathers."*

b) **Extension**. The mediation of Mary extends to every man in particular. It is **free** on the part of the Virgin and **unequal** in the application to souls. Free, first of all: *the subject* (to whom she wills); *quantity* (as much as she wills); *mode* (as she wills) and the *opportune time* (when she wills), everything is left to Mary's free choice. This freedom will not harm either the interest of God, or the interests of souls, because, Montfort says in n° 27: *"Mary, being altogether transformed into God by grace, and by the glory which transforms all the Saints into Him, asks nothing, wishes nothing, does nothing which is contrary to the Eternal and Immutable Will of God."* As for the inequality of her maternal Providence, this depends essentially on the very will of God and secondarily on the dispositions of those who are the object of it. (See the symbolic history of Rebecca and Jacob.)

We find in their entirety in this passage:

1) A passage from St. Bernardine of Siena: "Mary is that Mother of the Son of God Who produces the Holy Ghost. That is why the virtues and graces of the same Holy Ghost are all distributed through the hands of Mary, to whom she wills, when she wills, as she wills and as much as she wills."

The same sentence is found also in the first sermon on the *Salve Regina*, falsely attributed to St. Bernard, and in the *Biblia Mariana*, of St. Albert the Great, on the book of Esther N° 1.

2) Two passages from St. Bernard: "Nihil nos Deus habere voluit, quod per Mariae manus non transiret." Which Montfort translates: *"No heavenly gift is given to men without passing through the hands of Mary."*

And *"such has been the will of the One Who has arranged that anything would come to us through the hands of Mary."*

The theological reason itself: *"So that she who impoverished, humbled, and hid herself even to the abyss of nothingness by her profound humility her whole life long, should now be enriched and exalted by the Most High,"* is the concise translation of a passage of St. Bernard on the crown of twelve stars (n° 11). This reason, moreover, is undeniable. Where humility is lacking, the grace of God is impossible. It is, then, necessary for Mary, first of all, in a private capacity, for her own holiness, then as Mediatrix: she has to recognize that the graces which she distributes come from God alone (spirit of *poverty*); that the glory of them must return to Him alone (spirit of *humility*); and that, if He deigns to make use of her to carry out His plans, she must hide herself in the depth of nothingness (to seek the *hidden* life). By becoming impoverished, by humbling herself, and by hiding herself, Mary allowed God to make use of her in all His works of grace, and thus exalt her in the measure of her humility.

OBJECTION. We read in the *Secret of Mary*, n° 23:

"God, being absolute Master, can communicate by Himself what He communicates ordinarily only through Mary; we cannot even without temerity deny that He sometimes does this; however, according to the order which divine

Wisdom has established, He ordinarily communicates Himself to men only through Mary in the order of the grace, as Saint Thomas says."

How to reconcile this passage with what was just said about the universal Mediation of Mary?

RESPONSE. There can be no question of doubting the doctrine of Montfort on the universal Mediation. It is clearly expressed in the *Treatise*, which is his principal work. Furthermore, n° 10 of the *Secret of Mary* gives verbatim the words of St. Bernardine of Siena: "To whom she wills..." and those of St. Bernard. Also, n° 207 of *The Love of Eternal Wisdom.* It is even interesting to compare these different passages, belonging to writings composed at different times in the life of the Saint, to realize the unity and surety of his Marian doctrine.

The sentence that was challenged thus constitutes a difficulty, which is necessary to explain, according to the general rules of interpretation, by parallel and clearer passages.

If, however, a more direct answer is desired, we can propose several of them.

1°) It would be a question here, not of Mary's Mediation, but of recourse to her intercession. This recourse is essential ordinarily. Sometimes, however, Mary grants us graces which we did not request.

This answer is not very satisfactory, because Father de Montfort supposes very rare exceptions, whereas the answer supposes many of them. It is not simply at one time or another that Mary grants us graces without our having requested them; it is every day.

2°) In the time of the Saint, the doctrine of Mary's universal Mediation was much less common than now. This is perhaps because of the opposite opinion that he made use of a prudent restriction.

Yes, but then why so many explicit texts elsewhere against this unique restriction?

3°) Montfort quotes St. Thomas, and yet there is no text of the Angelic Doctor coming close to his. Would he not rely on the doctrine of St. Thomas distinguishing between the *absolute* divine power and the *ordered* divine power? God can accomplish, with absolute power, all that does not imply a contradiction. But with ordered power, He can do only what fits into the plan freely determined by Him.

Let us read again now the text of the *Secret* while deleting the parenthetical phrase; the echo of this doctrine will appear at once.

"God, being absolute Master, can communicate by Himself what He communicates ordinarily only through Mary; however, according to the order which divine Wisdom has established, He ordinarily communicates Himself to men only through Mary."

The sense of the parenthetical phrase would thus be this one: we know well the usual economy of salvation, and we can easily believe that God does not usually derogate from it. But, if there are many miracles in the natural order, could we without rashness deny that He can make or even that He does make exceptions in the supernatural order?... The saint does not, therefore, assert that there are any exceptions; he says simply that it would be rash to want to deny it. Who could hold it against him?... In any case, if they occur, which nobody can assert unless by revelation, they will no more destroy the general rule than the miraculous cure of a fatal disease prevents the same disease from causing death in all other cases.

N.B. – N° 26 constitutes a digression, a pause in the argumentation. Father de Montfort asserts in it only that, since he is dealing with simple people, he will not prove what he advances in the usual manner of theologians, that is to say, by Scripture, Tradition and reason. He is content with citing the clearest texts in the passage. For more details on this point, he refers the reader to *Rev. Fr. Poiré*.

2nd Question

The power of Mary over God
(27)

N° 27

Here begins the presentation of the immediate consequences of this solemn investiture that Mary received from the three divine Persons.

Fr. de Montfort cites, first of all, an axiom well known to theologians: "*Grace perfects nature, and glory perfects grace.*" Indeed, God is at the same time the author of nature, grace and glory. He arranged everything with admirable wisdom. It is not possible, therefore, that the three orders should contradict themselves. They can overlap, perfect, but not destroy each other. Otherwise, God would have made a mistake by giving to such a thing such a nature.

Applied to Our Lord, the axiom supplies the following argument:

Inasmuch as grace perfects nature, and glory perfects grace, it is certain that Our Lord is still, in heaven, **as much** *the Son of Mary as He was on earth; and that,* consequently, *He has preserved the most perfect obedience and submission of all children towards the best of all mothers.*

That is to say, we must find in Jesus, Son of Mary, what is essential and desired by nature in the relationships of a son with his own mother. We shall find it, even necessarily, in an absolutely superior degree, because Jesus "*is the most perfect of all sons*," and Mary "*the best of all mothers*."

Jesus, from His first moment, possessed all His grace and even all His glory. There would be no question for Him of progress towards a greater perfection, even when He entered heaven. At the least *an equality* could be spoken of, "*He is* **as much** *the Son of Mary as He was on earth*," "*He has preserved the submission and obedience*" that He had here on earth.

But we must take great pains not to conceive of this dependence as any abasement or imperfection in Jesus Christ. For Mary is infinitely below her Son, Who is God, and therefore she does not command Him as a mother here below would command her child, who is below her.

We have already said it is a *de facto* obedience, but not one of right. Jesus was free from His conception. Mary does not, then, command her Son "*as a mother here below would command her child*," *requiring* obedience from him, as long as he is at least a minor. The expression which the Saint uses, far from excluding the command, presupposes it. She does not command "*like other mothers*," that is to say, in the same way. But nevertheless she commands! The reality of her maternal rights over the heart of her Son caused the faithful to give her the beautiful title of **Our Lady of the Sacred Heart**.

IT IS ASKED: How does Mary reign over the heart of her Son?

There are many ways to reign over the heart of someone.

There is, first of all, an **authority** which asserts itself. But if the sovereignty that it creates is the strongest, it is also the least pleasant of all. We excluded this type for Mary.

There is **friendship** which is sweeter and more penetrating, because it makes everything common between the friends: *To want the same things, and not to want the same things, such is the law of firm friendship.* These rights can be claimed for Mary in the supreme degree of intensity, now especially that the beatific vision allows her to know the divine will perfectly.

Mary, being altogether transformed into God by grace (on earth), *and by the glory* (in heaven) *which transforms all the Saints into Him, asks nothing, wishes nothing, does nothing which is contrary to the Eternal and Immutable Will of God.*

There is especially the **maternity**, which surpasses all others in sweetness and is uncontrollable in its penetration. By this sovereignty, it can truly be said that the heart of the son is the full possession and the perfect property of the mother. Mary possesses, in this respect, a unique right to the respect and love of her Son: she is *"the best of all mothers."* And Jesus gladly preserves towards her the submission which He willed to show her here on earth. No gift descends from His divine heart to men, except through the intervention of His Mother.

Does this mean that Mary has the same power as God? By no means. Her authority over the heart of her Son does not come to her from herself: it is the authority *"which God wanted to give to her."* And she makes use of it only with the humble dependence which is becoming for a creature: she *prays*, and God listens to her.

When we read, says Montfort, *in the writings of SS. Bernard, Bernardine, Bonaventure, and others, that in heaven and on earth everything, even to God Himself, is subject to the*

Blessed Virgin, they mean to say that the authority which God has been well pleased to give her is so great that it seems as if she has the same power as God, and that her prayers and petitions are so powerful with God, that they always pass for commandments with His Majesty, Who never resists the prayer of His dear Mother, because she is always **humble** *and* **conformed** *to His Will.*

It is what is called the "pleading Omnipotence" of Mary, **Omnipotentia supplex**. If Jesus promised to grant all the prayers made in His name by whoever it may be, all the more reason will He grant the prayers of His Mother: they *always have the two qualities required to be granted.*

First of all, they are **humble**: sovereignty is exercised by means of prayer, revolves completely around the glory of God, because it recognizes, by the same prayer, that God alone is the source of all good. Pleading omnipotence is nothing and has nothing by itself. But it obeys the divine order: "*Ask, and it shall be given you*" (Mt. 7:7). She asks and she receives. She asks continually, and God grants to her continually also.

Thus, the prayers of Mary are **conformed to the divine will**. They are made in the name of Christ, and rely on His merit. The Virgin's dispositions of soul are the ones that Jesus desires: "*She neither* **asks**, *nor* **wills** *nor* **does** *anything which is contrary to the eternal and immutable will of God.*" And by that very fact are excluded all the causes which so often make our prayers fruitless: they lack of orientation towards the only thing necessary; they lack of submission to the divine good pleasure; they especially lack of practical conformity to the will of God by the practice of the Christian virtues, which make us worthy to be heard. Besides, is it not the divine will that Mary should intervene thus in all graces? And is it not the will of Jesus always to grant the prayers of His beloved Mother?

The fact that this will is *"eternal and immutable"* raises no difficulty against the prayer of Mary; because, from all eternity, God had decreed to grant such a grace to such a soul because of Mary's intervention for it at this precise moment. This intercession is one of the laws of the supernatural world. Sometimes even she is the only one to appear, and we attribute to her the totality of the effect. So, in the physical order, does not God seem to hide behind the secondary causes and does not nature seem to provide the reason for everything? But it is the eternal and immutable will of God which is being carried out. It maneuvers the secondary causes as it pleases, without impairing their freedom, when these causes are themselves endowed with freedom.

The end of n° 27 exalts the power of Mary's prayer. Did not that of Moses already prevent God from chastising His people, in spite of His sovereign independence and spontaneous mercy?

If Moses, by the force of his prayer, arrested the anger of God against the Israelites, in a manner so powerful that the Most High and infinitely merciful Lord, being unable to resist him, told him to let Him alone, that He might be angry with and punish that rebellious people, what must we not with much greater reason think of the prayer of the humble Mary, that worthy Mother of God, which is more powerful with His Majesty than the prayers and intercessions of all the Angels and Saints both in heaven and on earth?

3rd Question

Mary, Queen of heaven and earth
(28)

N° 28

In n° 28, Fr. de Montfort studies: 1° the foundations of the queenship of Mary; 2° its nature; 3° its practice.

1° THE FOUNDATIONS OF THE QUEENSHIP OF MARY

This queenship is affirmed in these words:

Mary commands in the heavens the **Angels** *and the* **Blessed**... **Heaven, earth,** *and* **hell** *bend with good will or bad will to the commandments of the humble Mary, whom He has made sovereign of heaven and earth.*

This queenship, proclaimed a large number of times by the Liturgy and the Holy Fathers, relies, like that of Our Lord Himself, on a threefold foundation (28):

a) The **personal dignity** of Mary, which comes to her from her divine Maternity or is required thereby, and confers on her the right "*to command in the heavens the Angels and the Blessed.*" But, as the divine Maternity entails with it *de facto* the Immaculate Conception with the fullness of grace, and as the smallest degree of sanctifying grace surpasses in value all the treasures of earth, we shall not wonder that Mary received the power to command the devils and all material beings. "The Blessed Virgin Mary is the noblest person who ever existed or who ever has to exist in the universe. Her perfection is such that, even if she had not had to be the Mother of God, she would have had to be Queen of the world."

b) **The mandate which she received from God:**

God has given her the power and permission to fill with Saints the empty thrones from which the apostate angels fell by pride.

If, as St. Paul testifies, each one of the elect is a king and master of everything which surrounds him, when it concerns the conquest of his heavenly throne, how would Mary not be universal sovereign, since she received the responsibility to fill all these empty thrones. She sends the Angels to the aid of those who are called to the heavenly inheritance. Things and people will be everywhere and always at her command for the same purpose. "To them that love God, all things work together unto good," and demons will run away frightened when she takes the elect under her protection.

c) **The incomparable merit of her profound humility.** Mary was not only very humble personally, but she was also, at the same time as Christ, exposed to humiliations and opprobrium of every sort at the foot of the Cross of the Savior. That is why God exalted her and gave her a name which, after Jesus' name, is raised above all names. God granted her such power *"that Heaven, earth, and hell bend with good will or bad will to the commandments of the humble Mary."*

2° THE NATURE OF THE QUEENSHIP OF MARY

This is a queenship of *mercy*. Its sole purpose is to lead the elect to eternal bliss. She is not interested in judging or chastising the culpable. She has power over the demons only to prevent them from harming her children. And so, she will fill the thrones with saints, very numerous certainly, left empty by the fall of the evil angels. This reign of mercy, explains St. Albert the Great, extends well beyond the reign of justice, grace and glory; because the latter supposes only the conferring of good, whereas the former not only confers good, but removes evil. That is why, under one aspect or another, it can be practiced everywhere: in Heaven, on earth and in purgatory.

3° THE PRACTICE OF THE QUEENSHIP OF MARY

It is quickly described here, because the following pages speak about it at length (n°s 29 and 30).

First of all, the reign of Mary is an **infallible** reign. It always reaches the desired end, namely the predestination of the saints, in keeping with the eternal and immutable will of God.

It is nevertheless **fought against**, like that of her Son, and for the same motives. The good accept it eagerly, and the miserable, especially the demons, suffer it enraged.

This double consideration is suggested by the sentence: "*Such has been the will of the Most High, Who exalts the humble, that heaven, earth, and hell bend with* **good will or bad will** *to the commandments of the humble Mary…*"

And the Saint continues by listing the titles of Mary: …"*Whom He has made sovereign of heaven and earth* (a title encompassing all the others), *general of His armies* (in keeping with the original plan of revenge (Gen. 3:15)), *treasurer of His treasures* (endowed so that she might truly be, alongside the great conqueror, a help similar to Him), *dispenser of His graces* (in order to spread over others the fullness of His treasure), *worker of His greatest marvels* (since the Incarnation), *restorer of the human race* (because of the part which she took in the sacrifice of the Cross), *Mediatrix of men* (who were entrusted to her by the dying Jesus), *the exterminator of the enemies of God* (who still continually put the salvation of souls in danger), *and the faithful companion of His grandeurs and His triumphs*" (at the Last Judgment and in eternity). This long series of titles is a chronological overview of Mary's role in the history of the world.

4th Question

The power of Mary over the predestined
(29-38)

N° 29

From n° 29 to n° 38, the Saint considers the functions allocated to the Virgin by each of the divine Persons in the conduct of this most intimate portion of the kingdom of God on earth, the true dwelling of this great Queen: the heart of the elect. Commenting and applying to the elect the words of Ecclesiasticus, chapter 24:8 (13 according to the Vulgate): "*Let thy dwelling be in Jacob, and thy inheritance in Israel, and take root in my elect*," he shows God the Father forming through Mary a multitude of **adoptive children** (n°s 29-30); God the Son attaining through Mary the fullness of His **Mystical Body** (n°s 31-33); and God the Holy Ghost exercising through Mary His **sanctifying mission** in the elect (n°s 34-36). From this whole passage, it becomes clear that Mary's real title is that of **Queen of Hearts** (n°s 37-38).

*
* *

§ I. – MARY, MOTHER OF ALL THE CHILDREN OF GOD
(29-30)

In n° 29, Montfort speaks briefly about the existence of divine adoption, as well as its nature and extension. Then he highlights the part which belongs to Mary by a definite intention of God. Finally, he proves this divine intention by a text drawn from Scripture.

In n° 30, he draws a twofold conclusion from what precedes, one is *positive*: Mary Mother of all the children of God, the other *negative*: he who does not have Mary as his Mother does not have God for his Father; he is a reprobate.

1° THE ADOPTION OF LOVE

"*God the Father wishes to have children...*" It is, then, a filiation quite different from the eternal and necessary filiation of the Word. It is completely free. Because He loved us, for the unique purpose of pouring upon us something of His infinite abundance, God established that to all His creatures capable of understanding and love, He would give Himself, by means of grace here on earth and of glory in heaven. By communicating to us His nature, He adopted us as children. This adoption is quite special: it puts in us something other than a purely fictitious title. And this divine plan embraces every century and all generations. *"God the Father* (through appropriation) *wishes to have children...***till the consummation of the world.**"

2° THE PART WHICH BELONGS TO MARY IN THIS ADOPTION

"God the Father wishes to have children **by Mary**." Having associated Mary, as much as a pure creature was capable of it, with His natural fruitfulness (n° 17), He also wants to associate her with His fruitfulness of love. Thus, Mary is at the origin of our adoption, that is to say, at the Incarnation; she is also in its accomplishment on Calvary; she is, finally, in its application, when God spreads in souls this intrinsic quality, which is called sanctifying grace and truly makes us His children.

3° PROOF DRAWN FROM SCRIPTURE

The Saint applies to the elect, according to the spiritual sense, the word which is said, according to the literal sense, about Jacob and his descendants, the only one in possession of the knowledge of the true God. This application to the elect becomes clear, if we examine the context:

And He (God the Father) *said to her these words:* **In Iacob inhabita,** – *"Dwell in Jacob"* – *that is to say, make your dwelling and residence in My predestinated children, figured by Jacob, and not in the reprobate children of the devil, figured by Esau.*

We can admit without any trouble the interpretation according to which Jacob is the figure of the predestined, and Esau that of the reprobates. It is commonly found in commentators on Holy Scripture, either about Malachy (1:2), or the Epistle to the Romans (9:13): "Jacob I have loved, but Esau I have hated." Also, it is possible to show as being said to Mary the words which apply to the first head of eternal

Wisdom. The Church herself gives us multiple examples of this application in the liturgy.

The association of the words: "**Children** *of God and* **predestined**," opposed to "**children** of the devil and **reprobates**" is explained in the same way that the words "*predestined and members of the body of Christ*" encountered in n° 20. He who is just today can lose grace tomorrow and die damned. On the other hand, the sinner can return to God and be changed into a vessel of election. Jacob is the figure of those who will enjoy the divine adoption not in a passing way, but in a long-lasting and eternal way. The same are called farther on "*the* **true** *children of God, the predestinate* (n° 30)."

Also "*make your* **dwelling and residence**..." Both terms are more or less synonymous. If "dwelling," however, indicates the place where we actually live, "residence" takes on a rather legal and official sense. A person is said to reside in such a place. He does not perhaps live there always. But this place is intended for him before the law and public opinion. Now Mary establishes at the same time her dwelling and residence in the elect. She actually lives among them, and they are legally intended for her. These words, however, must be understood in the metaphoric sense, because it is not about a substantial presence. (See n° 20 and its commentary.)

4° SUPERNATURAL AND SPIRITUAL GENERATION

N° 30

In the first place, the Saint considers "*the physical and natural generation*," the one which communicates to children a nature specifically similar to that of their parents, and which arrives at this purpose by forming a *body* capable of receiving a soul created directly by God. And he points out that parenthood is not single: "*there is a father and a mother*."

He then looks at "*the supernatural and spiritual generation,*" the one which communicates to children a being *surpassing* all the requirements of their *nature*, because it is a participation in the very nature of God: in the production of this being nothing is visible to the senses, because it takes place in the soul *spiritually*. And he points out here again that parenthood is not single: "*There is a Father, Who is God, and a Mother, who is Mary.*" It is, besides, the rigorous consequence of what was said in n° 29: God the Father decrees to make use of Mary to achieve His adoption of love. Why? Is not His love infinite and can it not compensate for maternal love? Precisely by choosing Mary as intermediary between Him and us, He shows the delicacy of His love. He takes into account the noblest aspirations of our human heart, the first impulses which were caused by maternal love.

And so the **positive conclusion**: "*All the true children of God, the predestinate, have God for their Father, and Mary for their Mother.*" Mary participates in the fruitfulness of the Father, as much as a simple creature is capable of it, to produce at the same time as He and, as much as it is possible, like Him, "*Jesus Christ and all the members of His Mystical Body.*" (See n° 17.)

5° THE ESAUS AND THEIR DISTINCTIVE MARK

From the argument explained above, Montfort also draws a **negative conclusion**, to which he gives more considerable development: "*He who has not Mary for his Mother, has not God for his Father.*"

Based on this principle, he asserts, first of all, in a general way:

This is the reason why the reprobate, such as heretics, schismatics, and others, who hate our Blessed Lady, or regard her with contempt and indifference, have not God for their Father, however much they boast of it, simply because they have not Mary for their Mother…

Descending then to a more concrete deduction, he maintains that lack of devotion to Mary is

the most infallible and indubitable sign by which we may distinguish a heretic, a man of bad doctrine, a reprobate, from one of the predestinate.

This is, then, the **true distinctive mark of the Esaus.**

a) *By what sign, does Montfort recognize a reprobate?* He speaks to us about heretics and schismatics, because they are outside the *unity* of the Church. But it is not on this mark that he bases his argument. It is on the fact that they do not have Mary for their Mother. Do they not show it by their conduct?

For if they had her for their Mother, they would love and honour her as a true and good child naturally loves and honours the mother who has given him life.

Universal, indeed, among Catholics, is the sentiment which leads us to honor Mary as our Mother. Such a sentiment, approved, moreover, and encouraged by the Church, cannot be erroneous. It must have a secret but necessary connection with some religious truth. By their contempt towards Mary, heretics and schismatics are opposed to this universal Catholic sentiment, they deny this truth, and consequently proclaim in spite of themselves that they do not have God for their Father, and they side with the reprobates.

b) *Opposition to Mary is the distinctive mark of the reprobates.* It is not always easy to distinguish, certainly, "*a heretic, a man of bad doctrine, a reprobate, from one of the predestinate.*" Now, among all the signs which can enlighten us on this subject, here is the one which is "*the most infallible and indubitable.*" He bases himself on a fact easy to verify:

The heretic and reprobate have nothing but contempt and indifference for our Blessed Lady, endeavouring by their words and examples to diminish the worship and love of her openly or hiddenly, and sometimes under specious pretexts.

Montfort will later (n°s 63-65) give striking examples of this. For the moment, he contents himself with a painful sigh:

Alas! God the Father has not told Mary to dwell in them, for they are Esaus.

Indeed, *Billot* admits that devotion to Mary is a negative mark of the true Church. That is to say, the Church necessarily possesses the true devotion to Mary. This devotion, however, is not easy to determine. Furthermore, many non-Catholic sects have preserved Marian veneration. The presence of this devotion cannot, then, be enough to show the true Church of Christ. But does a sect possess no devotion to Mary at all? More than that, does it not boast of having it? Then we are sure: it is certainly not the true Church of Christ.

Such are the practical conclusions of the spiritual Maternity of Mary, considered in its relationship with God the Father. When the author will have considered the same Maternity in connection with God the Son and God the Holy Ghost, his deductions will be even more extended. They will apply, then, not only to men of bad doctrine, but to Catholics themselves. And the true devotion to Mary will show itself, with ever-increasing evidence, as the touchstone serving to recognize predestined and perfect souls.

§ II. – MARY, MOTHER OF THE WHOLE MYSTICAL BODY OF CHRIST
(31-33)

From n° 31 to n° 33, there is discussion of the spiritual Maternity of Mary in her relations with God the Son. Now, just as the divine adoption of which we are the object is the image of the eternal generation of the Word by the Father, so too the adoptive filiation which results from it for us is the image of the natural filiation of the second Person of the Most Holy Trinity.

N° 31

God the Son wishes to form Himself, and, so to speak, **to incarnate Himself**, *every day by His dear Mother in His members.*

Is not the Christian life the reproduction of the life of Jesus in us? It is not an incarnation strictly speaking, as when the Word became flesh. That is why it is specified: "*God the Son wishes…***so to speak**, *to incarnate Himself.*" There are resemblances, however, which should now be brought to light.

Montfort establishes successively what is: 1° *the inheritance of Mary*; 2° *her double maternity*; 3° *her blessed fruit*; 4° *our true day of birth*.

1° THE INHERITANCE OF MARY

Taking up again the text of Ecclesiasticus, he puts the second part on the lips of the Son, addressing Mary:

And He has said to her: **In Israel haereditare**-"*Take Israel for you inheritance." It is as if He had said, God the Father has given Me for an inheritance all the nations of the earth, all the men good and bad, predestinate and reprobate. The one I will lead with a rod of gold, and the others with a rod of iron. Of one I will be the Father and the advocate, the Just Punisher of others, and the Judge of all. But as for you, My dear Mother – you shall have for your heritage and possession only* **the predestinate**, *figured by Israel; and,* as their good Mother, *you shall bring them forth and maintain them; and* as their sovereign, *you shall conduct them, govern and defend them.*

This passage, as regards the judiciary power of Christ, is quite steeped in biblical recollections drawn from Psalm 2. For the good, Jesus will be all love; for the wicked, He will have only rigor; to the ones and the others, He will give what they will have deserved. And His judgment will have an absolute validity, because it will have been pronounced with full knowledge of the facts and irrespective of persons.

Of this kingdom, Jesus communicates to His Mother the best part, the one which concerns the predestined. We have already explained, in commenting on n° 24, the foundation of this division. Let us observe now who are the predestined. Not only those who are in a state of grace at one moment or another of their earthly existence, but those who will die in a state of grace and be admitted into Heaven. Consequently, "*true children of God*" is equal to "*predestinate*" (see n° 30) and "*predestinate*" is equivalent to "*heirs of the heavenly kingdom.*" And as this heavenly inheritance consists in the vision of God face to face, we shall understand why "*the predestinate are figured by Israel.*" Indeed, St. Augustine writes: "Israel means *the one who sees God*," and he adds: "This will one day be the reward for all the saints." St. Jerome gives another meaning to the Hebrew word. According to him, this word would signify "strong against God." But the context seems to agree with St. Augustine, because Jacob exclaimed immediately after having received his new name: "I have seen God face to face, and my soul has been saved" (Gen. 32:30).

To these predestined, heirs of the celestial kingdom, Mary *gives* life, *nourishes* it so that it does not decrease and *develops* it according to all the effects of grace, as a **Mother** towards her children. Then, as **sovereign**, she rules the activity of her subjects, by *leading* them: she makes every effort to insure their predestination, by *governing* them, and finally, she *protects* them victoriously against the rage of the demons and their emissaries.

2° THE TWOFOLD MATERNITY OF MARY

N° 32

God the Son, the great victor about whom Montfort just spoke, is not simply Son of God; He is also Son of Mary. And in being born from her, He caused a twofold maternity in her. He is Himself her only Son by physical birth. But all the members of His Mystical Body are born from her spiritually at the same time as their divine Head.

a) **Proof from Sacred Scripture.**

"This man and that man is born in her," says the Holy Ghost: **Homo et homo natus est in ea** *(Ps. 86:5). According to the explanation of some of the Fathers, the first man that is born in Mary is the Man-God, Jesus Christ; the second is a mere man, the child of God and Mary by adoption.*

The passage of Origen to which the Saint alludes seems to be drawn from the prologue to the Commentary on the Gospel according to St. John. "Nobody can understand the sense (of this Gospel) if he has not, first of all, rested on the heart of Jesus and if he has not received from Jesus, Mary for his Mother..." It is necessary that Jesus be able to say about him in addressing Mary: "This one is Jesus to whom you gave birth."

And in a brief commentary on Psalm 86, verse 5, he says: "The child Jesus was born in Bethlehem: man was born in Zion."

As for the passage by St. Bonaventure, we find it in the *Speculum Beatae Mariae Virginis*, lect. III; "The two sons of Mary are a Man-God and a pure man, because she is the mother of the One physically and of the other spiritually."

All commentators recognize that Psalm 86 is messianic, and it has very often been applied to Mary. It is admitted that she herself is this grand city which the Lord built with His own hands. The Hebrew text favors the spiritual maternity of Mary in another way, because the expression "homo et homo" means literally "*every man.*" Canon Pannier translates: "All men became her sons," and Vigouroux: "A multitude of men are born from her."

b) **Theological reason.**

If Jesus Christ the Head of men is born in her, the predestinate, who are the members of that Head, ought also to be born in her by a necessary consequence. One and the same mother does not bring forth into the world the head without the members, nor the members without the head; for this would be a monster of nature. So in like manner, in the order of grace, the Head and the members are born of one and the same Mother; and if a member of the Mystical Body of Jesus Christ – that is to say, one of the predestinate – was born of any other mother than Mary, who has produced the Head, he would not be one of the predestinate, nor a member of Jesus Christ, but simply a monster in the order of grace.

This is the doctrine of the Mystical Body, as it is already explained by St. Paul. It is also the traditional doctrine of the Church. Let us quote only St. Antoninus: "Mary will not give birth to a Son only, but to a multitude of sons, that is to say, to all those who are redeemed by the Lord. She gave birth to them all at the same time, inasmuch as by a single act and in a single instant, she gave birth to what was for everyone the cause of life. And, yet, she did not engender them all at the same time, if it concerns the application of the fruits of the Passion in souls. This application, which produces, in fact, life in every soul, comes about in each only in the course of time."

Furthermore, our Saint continues his *progressive* exposition. In n° 28, he described the *universal* domain of Mary. He speaks now about her **favorite** domain: the heart of the elect. Among all the categories of the members of Christ, he deals especially with the one which is definitive: the predestined. He does not exclude the others. He does not denote his attention to them. Getting straight to the final point, he shows who the *true children* of God and Mary are.

Now, these predestined, redeemed by Christ, form a single body with Him. We cannot, without destroying Christ, either separate His human nature from His divine nature which are united hypostatically, nor separate the redeemed from the Redeemer. This consequence results from it, which Montfort proclaims necessary, and which Pius X set down in his encyclical "**Ad diem illum**": Mary being Mother of the Christ must also be our mother. To such a point that, if one of the predestined was born from another mother than Mary, he would not be one of the predestined, nor a member of Christ, but a *monster* in the order of grace, because it would mean to say that Mary did not give birth to the *whole* Christ.

3° THE FRUIT OF MARY

N° 33

Mary is, then, Mother both of the Head and of the members of the Mystical Body of Jesus. But, as St. Antoninus remarks, her maternity comes about for each in particular only at the moment in which grace occurs or increases in him. So:

Jesus being at present as much as ever the fruit of Mary – as heaven and earth repeat thousands and thousands of times a day, "**and Blessed be the Fruit of thy womb, Jesus**" *– it is certain that Jesus Christ is, for each man in particular who possesses Him, as truly the fruit of the womb of Mary, as He is for the whole world in general.*

That Jesus is the fruit of Mary's womb and became man only following the "*Fiat*" of the Virgin, no longer needs to be proved. That Jesus is also born in souls by the intervention of Mary follows clearly from the universal Mediation.

The result:

If any one of the faithful has Jesus Christ formed in his heart, he can say boldly: **All thanks be to Mary!** *What I possess is her effect and her fruit, and without her I should never have had it.*

The Virgin can repeat words of the Apostle to the inhabitants of Galatia: "My little children, of whom I am in labour again, until Christ be formed in you" (4:19) with more reason. Her action is limited neither by time nor space. It extends to the whole world, for the good of all men, and till the end of the ages:

We can apply to her more than St. Paul applied to himself those words: "**Quos iterum parturio donec formetur Christus in vobis:** *I am in labour again with all the children of God, until Jesus Christ my Son be formed in them in the fullness of His age.*"

4° OUR TRUE DAY OF BIRTH

Taking his considerations still farther, and drawing the last conclusion of his argumentation, Montfort writes:

St. Augustine, surpassing himself, and going beyond all I have yet said, affirms that all the predestinate, in order to be conformed to the image of the Son of God, are in this world hidden in the womb of the most holy Virgin; where they are guarded, nourished, brought up, and made to grow by that good Mother until she has brought them forth to glory after **death, which is probably the day of their birth**, *as the Church calls the death of the just.*

In his notebook on the book by Father Poiré, "*La Triple Couronne*" (The Triple Crown), on page 75, the Saint transcribes literally this passage: "I base myself on a rich conception of the great St. Augustine in the book *On Holy Virginity* (Chap. VI), where, after saying that the Virgin is our Mother by spirit and by grace, just as she is the Mother of the Savior by nature, he takes his thought further and he remarks that she delivers her spiritual children when she gives birth to them for heaven, consequently that she carries them in her womb when they are here on earth, while waiting for a better condition."

St. Augustine speaks, however, in the place indicated, only about the spiritual maternity of Mary with respect to the Mystical Body of Jesus, comparing it to that of the Church with respect to the predestined: "In sanctis regnum Dei possessuris" ("In the holy ones who are to possess the kingdom of God"). It is by no means a question about the day of birth. It seems that the place where the Holy Doctor "*surpasses himself*," must be sought in the *Treatise on the Creed*, addressed to catechumens, which unfortunately is at present of dubious authenticity. He speaks about catechumens, welcomed into the bosom of the Church, supported by the appropriate food, and brought into the world on the day of their baptism: no longer in sorrow, but in joy, because Mary has broken, by her obedience, the chains which Eve had bequeathed us by her disobedience. Did not Montfort merge these two passages? Applying to Mary what is said about the Church, he borrows from the *Treatise on the Creed* the comparison of the sons nourished at the breast of their mother until the day of their spiritual birth. But instead of stopping at the catechumens and Baptism, he continues to the more general idea developed in the book *On Holy Virginity*, and he speaks to us about the predestined and about their definitive birth to the divine life. It is enough, indeed, to read again the end of the number 33 in order to find the faithful echo of the thought of St. Augustine there, made still more beautiful by the learned meditations of the great Servant of Mary.

And this is a perfectly correct idea. In order for the predestined to resemble their divine model and receive the adoption of the children of God, it is necessary for them to be *formed by the woman* too. Jesus is now as always the fruit of Mary. The latter is the universal mediatrix of grace. She has to form in us Jesus Christ, her Son, until the fullness of His age. The predestined, then, have to remain hidden in her womb, to be "*protected*" against everything which compromises their divine life; "*nourished*" by grace under all its forms; "*supported*" so that the natural decrease of their spiritual strength is constantly repaired; and "*enlarged*" by the increase of this supernatural life, which will make them come to the fullness of the age of Christ. And the day of their *death* will truly be the day of their birth, as the Church, in the Martyrology, calls the death of the saints.

This is the mystery of the Incarnation lived by the elect. The womb of Mary will become the divine mold "where the saints are formed and molded" (n°s 218,219).

O mystery of grace, unknown to the reprobate, and but little known even to the predestinate!

Some people do not want to admit this role of Mary: others do not understand the full reach of it. Let us ask the Virgin to be our mother, to be kept hidden in her womb, so that the day of our death may truly be the day of our birth.

§ III. – MARY AND THE SANCTIFICATION OF THE ELECT
(34-36)

Numbers 34-36 describe: 1° the mandate of the Holy Ghost; 2° the two claims of Mary to receive this mandate: she is the well-beloved and she is the spouse; 3° the virtues of the well-beloved; 4° the fruitfulness of the spouse; 5° the practical consequences of this doctrine.

1° THE MANDATE OF THE HOLY GHOST

N° 34

God the Holy Ghost wishes to form Himself **in** *her, and to form elect for Himself* **through** *her, and He has said to her:* **"In electis meis mitte radices**: *Strike the roots, My Well-beloved and My Spouse, of all your virtues in My elect."*

Charged with executing the designs of love of the Father and the Son, He does not want to acquit Himself of them without turning to Mary. On the contrary, He wants to form His elect, that is to say, the predestined, *in Mary*, because the Head of the Mystical Body was formed in her, and *through Mary*, because through her He distributes all His graces. The explanations, given previously about n° 20, again have their reasons for being here.

According to this mandate, Mary must strike the root of *all* her virtues in the elect. Hence, if they did not resemble Mary, they would not be of the elect. But obviously, once planted, these roots will have to develop and produce flowers and fruits. Montfort suggests it in alluding, first of all, to Psalm 83:8, "*they shall go from virtue to virtue,*" then to the Gospel (Jn. 1:16) "*and grace for grace.*" The elect will thus come to reproduce little by little the ideal of all holiness, Jesus.

Therefore, it is not Mary who will produce grace by her own authority; God alone can give it. But He will give it by the intervention of Mary, and He will make use of her in such a way that, to imprint perfectly on His elect the image of His Son, He will have only to form them on her image.

2° THE WELL-BELOVED AND SPOUSE

"*Strike, My* **Well-beloved** *and My* **Spouse…**" These two titles explain the reason for the mandate entrusted to Mary.

The work of sanctification is a work of love. That is why it is attributed to the Holy Ghost, the substantial Love of the Father and the Son. That is also why the Holy Ghost wants to accomplish it through Mary.

a) The **Well-Beloved** serves Him as a *model:*

I took so much complacence in you when you lived on earth in the practice of the most sublime virtues, that I desire still to find you on earth, without your ceasing to be in heaven. For this end, reproduce yourself in My elect, that I may behold in them with complacence the roots of your invincible faith, of your profound humility, of your universal mortification, of your sublime prayer, of your ardent charity, of your firm hope, and all your virtues.

This does not prevent the elect from being formed in the image of Jesus, as St. Paul says. On the contrary: because Mary is herself completely transformed into Jesus (see n° 63), to form souls on the model of Mary is to form them on the model of Jesus. But Mary is a mere creature. She is more within the reach of our small imitation.

We find in these words of the Saint the echo of the words of God the Father at the baptism of Our Lord: "This is My beloved Son, in Whom I am well pleased," and the practical consequence: "Hear ye Him" (Mt. 17:5). The Holy Ghost was well-pleased in Mary; that is why He wants all the elect to reproduce her virtues: some more perfectly, others less perfectly, according to the richness of the soil in which these roots are struck. The flowers, however, which will bloom in this soil will be of the same kind as those admired formerly by the Holy Ghost, and they themselves will be regarded with good pleasure.

Thus it is explained how the Virgin, who no longer has faith for herself, preserved it for others by this wonderful reproduction of herself in the elect. And the Holy Ghost finds her on earth today, where all her virtues live again morally, without her ceasing for that reason to be bodily in heaven.

b) But it is the Virgin herself who *reproduces herself* in the elect. This follows still more from the title of **Spouse** which is given to her:

You are always My Spouse, as faithful, as pure, and as fruitful as ever. Let your faith give Me My faithful, your purity My virgins, and your fertility My temples and My elect.

Like every mother, Mary will nurse the children to whom she will transmit supernatural life. She will be only the instrumental cause. And yet what sweetness she will confer on the grace passing through her! The *fidelity* of Mary since the Incarnation of the Word calls for that of the Holy Ghost till the end of time, because God never withdraws first (Rom. 11:29). Her *purity* is a guarantee for God that souls will never find in her an obstacle to divine union. Her *fruitfulness* is proof that she can always make use of the effects of grace produced by the Holy Ghost in souls. And since, according to the proverb: "Every agent acts like itself," to keep the *faithful*, the Holy Ghost will reproduce the *faith* of Mary by utilizing the services of Mary herself. And so on for the other virtues.

3° THE VIRTUES OF THE WELL-BELOVED

Montfort speaks several times about the virtues of Mary (n°s 34, 108, 144, 260). He does not always list them in the same order, but the principle is still the same: Mary is the model of all the Christian virtues. Number 108, the most complete, lists: "*her* **profound humility** (the fundamental virtue, the foundation of all holiness), *her* **lively faith** (by which Mary sets aside her way of seeing things to adopt that of God), *her* **blind obedience** (which summarizes her whole life and immolates her own will), *her* **continual prayer** (a natural movement in a soul completely molded by faith), *her* **universal mortification** (not so much that she must distrust creatures, but to fill up what is lacking in the Passion of the Savior), *her* **divine purity** (which extends as far as the Immaculate Conception), *her* **ardent charity** (which nothing delays), *her* **heroic patience** (at the foot of the Cross), *her* **angelical sweetness** (the smile on the lips even in trials) and *her* **divine wisdom** (the crowning of everything). These are the virtues that the true devotee of Mary must especially imitate and reproduce.

4° THE FRUITFULNESS OF THE SPOUSE

N° 35

a) In general:

When Mary has struck her roots in a soul, she produces there marvels of grace, which she alone can produce, because she alone is the fruitful Virgin, who never has had, and never will have, her equal in purity and in fruitfulness.

These words show, first of all, the **condition** indispensable to this mysterious work of grace, namely: the taking possession of the soul by Mary: "*When Mary has struck her roots in a soul,*" by a real and interior devotion, aiming at the imitation of her virtues. – They show then the prodigious **fruitfulness** of Mary's action: "*She produces there marvels of grace, which she alone can produce,*" that is to say, the ever more perfect image of Jesus, by means of the reproduction of her own virtues. – They show finally **why** God gave such a power to Mary. "*Because she alone is the fruitful Virgin…,*" etc. The fruitful virginity puts her in a unique rank, and it was required as much for her divine maternity as for her spiritual maternity, as well as all her negative and positive holiness. By this incomparable purity and this unequaled fruitfulness, Mary's sanctifying action is universal and extends to all the effects of grace in souls.

b) In particular:

Mary has produced, together with the Holy Ghost, the greatest thing which has been, or ever will be – a God-Man; and she will consequently produce the greatest saints that there will be in the end of time.

Because evil must have then its maximum development and efficiency, it is quite natural that the counterpart of evil, devotion to Mary, should also reach its peak.

Then she will contribute especially:

to the formation and the education of the great Saints who shall come at the end of the world.

She will raise them up and prepare them for their mission. This supremely difficult work can only have Mary as its author.

For it is only that singular and miraculous Virgin who can produce, in union with the Holy Ghost, singular and extraordinary things.

The Virgin, *singular* and *miraculous* by her fruitfulness, is alone equal to the events *singular* (not yet seen) and *extraordinary* (because good like evil will be taken to the extreme) which will confront each other in this supreme fight. And if Mary is capable of accomplishing such prodigies, it is not by herself alone: it is because she will work "in union (with the) Holy Ghost."

The Saint will give farther on (n°s 47-59) a wide development to these few ideas.

5° PRACTICAL CONSEQUENCES

N° 36

They are explained, first of all, under a **positive** form:

When the Holy Ghost, her Spouse, has found Mary in a soul, He flies there. He enters there in His fullness; He communicates Himself to that soul abundantly, and to the full extent to which she makes room for her Spouse.

Then under a **negative** form:

Nay, one of the great reasons why the Holy Ghost does not now do startling wonders in our souls is because He does not find there a sufficiently great union with His faithful and inseparable Spouse.

These two consequences follow from the fact that Mary is the **Spouse of the Holy Ghost**, the faithful Spouse, the fruitful Spouse, the inseparable Spouse.

Father Terrien asserts having found this title only twice in Tradition, once in St. Peter Damian and another time in a Greek Father whom he does not name. At the extreme opposite, Father Poiré, quoted by Montfort, asserts: "Why go to any trouble to prove this truth, because all the holy Fathers unanimously preach it and because this is the ordinary opinion of the Catholic Church? St. Ildephonsus, St. Bernard, and St. Bonaventure, speak of it so often as to amaze us. St. Gemanus, Patriarch of Constantinople, calls her on this occasion, the spotless and irreproachable Spouse (Oratio de Praesentatione B.M.V.). Others, along the same lines, name her: the royal couch and the nuptial bed of the Holy Ghost. The Blessed Holy Ghost, says St. Anselm (Lib. De Excel. Virg., cap. 4), the Love and the Bond of the Father and the Son, the One in Whom and by Whom must be loved everything that we want to love, personally descended and in His own substance into the glorious Virgin, and, by an incomprehensible privilege, choosing her to the exclusion of every other creature, made her His Spouse, and, in the same way, the Queen and the Empress of the universe."

And the author then quotes St. Gregory of Nyssa, St. Lawrence Justinian, Tertullian, Eusebius of Caesarea, St. Epiphanius, St. Gregory of Nazianzen, etc.

Textual criticism has made progress since Father Poiré, and if it was a question of choosing at present between these two authorities, that of Fr. Terrien and that of Fr. Poiré, the question could not be settled for a long time, because the documentation of the first is extremely serious and that of the second is almost impossible to verify.

Let us recognize that the ancient Fathers seem to have been distrustful of the title "Spouse of the Holy Ghost" given to Mary. Leo XIII, however, admits it in his Encyclical *Divinum illud munus*, and for Montfort the legitimacy of this appellation arouses no hesitation.

Besides, we already know that the title of Spouse given to the Holy Ghost with regard to the Virgin does not entail the title of Father with respect to Our Lord.

Furthermore, it is the only term which can express the twofold relation which exists between Mary and the third Person of the Most Holy Trinity, because it is from the Holy Ghost that Mary received the divine fruitfulness to be the true Mother, according to nature, of the only Son of God, and, according to grace, of all the adoptive children of God. In the supernatural order as in the natural order, the husband communicates life by means of the wife. So "*since that Substantial Love of the Father and the Son has espoused Mary, in order to produce Jesus Christ, the Head of the elect and Jesus Christ in the elect, He has never repudiated her, inasmuch as she has always been fruitful and faithful.*" That is why she is the *inseparable* Spouse of the Holy Ghost.

The **positive consequence** relies on the three fundamental laws of marriage: a) *preferential love* by which the husband chooses his wife among a thousand and leaves everything to go to her: "*He* **flies** *there*"; b) a strong and indissoluble *union*, brought about by the conjugal bond and by virtue of which the husband is at home in the house of the wife: "*He* **enters** *there in His fullness*"; c) *the mutual rights* of the couple; in virtue of these rights, the husband can do with his wife what he wills and vice versa. "Mary," says St. Bernardine of Siena, "has acquired a sort of jurisdiction over the temporal mission of the Holy Ghost." She can bring Him to unite Himself with the soul with whom she herself is united: "*He* **communicates Himself** *to that soul abundantly, and to the full extent to which she makes room for her Spouse.*"

The **negative consequence** relies, on one hand, on the will of the Holy Ghost to work His marvels of grace through Mary, and, on the other hand, on the fact that Mary is not known and loved enough. This last reason will be progressively taken away, until *"the happy time, the age of Mary"* comes, in which the Holy Ghost finding Mary everywhere, will accomplish, through her, "*startling wonders in souls.*"

CONCLUSION

Mary, Queen of Hearts
(37-38)

To describe this reign of Mary over hearts, the obvious *conclusion* of everything which precedes, Montfort recalls, first of all, the *foundation* of her sovereignty; then he shows the *extension* and *principal object* of it. Finally, he adorns the head of Mary with this title so sweet, which summarizes all his doctrine: *Queen of Hearts*.

1° THE OBVIOUS CONCLUSION

N° 37

We may evidently conclude, then, from what I have said that Mary has received from God a great domination over the souls of the elect.

The one who has especially understood n°s 29-36 and what we said to explain them will admit, like Montfort, that the conclusion is obvious.

For Mary cannot make her residence in them (the elect), *as God the Father ordered her to do, and form them in*

Jesus Christ, or Jesus Christ in them, and strike the roots of her virtues in their hearts and be the inseparable companion of the Holy Ghost in all His works of grace – she cannot, I say, do all these things unless she has a right and domination over their souls by a singular grace of the Most High.

It is useless to insist. The obvious is not proven. As a queen commands in her palace, Mary commands in the soul of the elect. As a mother engenders, nourishes, and develops her children in her womb, Mary forms and educates her elect enclosed in her womb until their birth in heaven. As a gardener cultivates and sows as he pleases the land which he owns, Mary will strike, without any resistance on their part, the roots of her virtues in the souls of the elect.

All this power, Mary "*has received from God*" and "*by a singular grace of the Most High.*" God is free to carry out all that He wants. But He gave to none other than Mary a mission so universal in the whole world.

2° THE FOUNDATION OF THIS DOMAIN OF MARY

The Most High "*having given her power over His only and natural Son, has given it also to her over His adopted children.*" The grace of the divine Maternity in Mary, like that of the hypostatic union in Our Lord, like that of the predestination of the saints, depends uniquely on the pure liberality of God. But since God liberally placed this foundation, all the rest will follow of itself. Recall the text of St. John Damascene: "Mary truly became sovereign over every creature when she became Mother of the Creator."

Mary's power over the Son of God was already proved (n°s 18-19). It only remains to speak briefly about the power over the adoptive children of God.

These adoptive children are only the copy, the image of the Son of God by substance. The latter remains consequently *unique* and *natural*. But, precisely because they are the copy, they have to imitate Him in His life and mysteries, therefore in His dependence on Mary. "For whom He foreknew, He also predestinated to be made conformable to the image of His Son" (Rom. 8:29).

3° THE EXTENT OF THIS DOMINION

N° 38

"*Not only as to their bodies, which would be but little matter, but also as to their souls.*" Indeed, he who can do the greater can do the lesser. Now, we have already seen that Mary received from each of the three divine Persons the spiritual dominion over the elect. All the more so does she also possess power over their body and over the whole temporal order, provided that she makes it contribute to the good of the elect. "*Mary is the Queen of heaven and earth by grace, as Jesus is the King of them by nature and by conquest.*"

But does this sovereignty involve a **true dominion**, or is it only one of honor?

Certainly Mary surpasses all creatures by her excellence. It is also obvious that the elect, in heaven and on earth, submit themselves unconditionally to their Queen and Mistress. But to what point ought their dependence go? Besides the power to command, or the power of jurisdiction, does Mary possess true power, a title of propriety, a dominion in the true sense of the word?

It is necessary to answer this question affirmatively. But this should not frighten us. Mary's dominion is not *arbitrary*. Mary is Queen of heaven and earth; but she is also the humble slave of the Lord, subjected more than any other to the laws which He Himself established to govern the law of property. Furthermore, her power is not *tyrannical*. It does no violence to the predestined for the benefit of their sovereign: indeed they are the ones who especially profit from her dominion. It *does not destroy the freedom* of the predestined, because freedom is essential to human nature. Finally, it is not a dominion *of nature*, but *of grace*. Our Saint is anxious to underline this last point, which is of capital importance. But, except for this difference declaring the origin of the law, the extent of the domain is exactly the same for Jesus and for Mary: "*Mary is the Queen of heaven and earth* **as** *Jesus is King of them...*" The reign of Mary, then, can neither be limited, nor attributed to her because of her, without separating her from Jesus. Now one must not separate what God has so intimately united.

And just as Jesus is King, first of all, *by nature*, as Son of God and incarnate Word, then *by conquest*, because of the merits of His death on the Cross; so too Mary is Queen **by grace** and her purely *gratuitous divine Maternity* and her very *meritorious sorrowful compassion*. But, for having come from the liberality of Christ, this domain is neither any less beautiful nor less real.

4° PRINCIPAL OBJECT OF THIS DOMAIN

It is expressed in these terms:

Now, as the kingdom of Jesus Christ consists principally in the heart and interior of a man – according to that word, "**The kingdom of God is within you**" *– in like manner the kingdom of our Blessed Lady is principally in the interior of a man – that is to say, his soul; and it is principally in souls that she is more glorified with her Son than in all visible creatures...*

The Gospel passage cited by Montfort is interpreted in the same sense as *Knabenbauer* gives it, and, says the latter, by a rather considerable number (sat multi) of authors. We can thus follow this interpretation, although modern exegetes see here instead the meaning in it: *in your midst*. "Do you seek the kingdom of God? But there hath stood one in the midst of you, whom you know not" (cf. Jn. 1:26). The two explanations, moreover, overlap, because the reason why the Jews do not recognize the kingdom of God is that it is wholly interior and spiritual, and, consequently, deprived of this exterior and political splendor that the Jews expected.

Now, the reign of Mary is, by grace, exactly the same as that of Jesus by nature and by conquest. It is, therefore, above all interior, too. What the Virgin desires above everything, like her divine Son Himself, is the transformation of our soul through holiness. When they have obtained this result, they will be more honored than by the whole splendor of the universe. This mute praise of material creation, which groans, says St. Paul, in being sometimes diverted from its providential purpose by the vanity of man, will completely recover its voice, when man, the pontiff of creation, will seize it to turn it toward God.

5° MARY, QUEEN OF HEARTS

"*And we can call her as the Saints do, the* **Queen of Hearts**." This title, chosen later to indicate the confraternity of the Holy Slavery, summarizes marvelously the consecration which we make of ourselves to Mary, in order to belong totally to Jesus.

1° **The origin of this title.** – There is no new title there. "*We can call her* **as the Saints do**…" Which ones exactly? It is difficult to say. A passage attributed to St. Anselm of Lucques, but which could equally well be from St. Bonaventure or St. Bernard, contains the following expressions: "O Snatcher of hearts! O Absorber of minds…What does it profit you, lover of souls, that we love you and your Son with our love? Are not the heavens sufficient for you, that you require our hearts, when they are so smelly and earthly? Receive them, huntress of souls, and refresh them in the bosom of your grace." And farther on: "Therefore, *ave*, my Lady, my Mother, *nay, my heart and my soul*, Virgin Mary." By comparing these last words with the final prayer of the Little Crown, we shall notice that Montfort knew this text: "O Lady, who snatches hearts with your sweetness." "O Snatcher of hearts, when will you restore my heart to me?"

St. Peter Damian also exalts the dominion of Mary over our hearts in a sermon on the Annunciation: "What singular rule do you claim in our hearts for yourself."

St. John Eudes: "Consider that, after the adorable Heart of Jesus, the Supreme Monarch of Heaven and earth, the august Heart of the Queen of Angels and the Mother of the King of Kings is King of all hearts which were created to love God."

St. Bridget puts these words on Mary's lips: "As the magnet attracts iron, so I attract hardened hearts to God."

Everywhere, there is the equivalent of the title "*Queen of Hearts.*" Montfort is not, then, the only one to give it to Mary.

2° **Meanings of this title**. – This is not simply a sentimental appellation. It allows us, certainly, to express our love for Mary. *But who could blame us for it?* The Virgin is **Queen of hearts**, because she is Queen of love and the instrument of the divine mercies. All that we can imagine by way of goodness and sweetness, we can attribute to her without fear of exaggeration.

But we do not have to content ourselves with that. Sincere love is the one which observes the commandments of the beloved being. That being the case, the number of those who escape the plenitude of Marian influence is absolutely incalculable, because they removed themselves first from the law of the divine Master. And since Mary is not occupied with exercising the divine justice, she does not reign over these unrepentant sinners, who will end in the disaster of hell. They are slaves of constraint, among whom she did not receive the order to establish her residence.

On the other hand, in all the souls where God reigns undisputedly and where He will reign for all eternity, Mary is, in all truth, *Queen of hearts*. These souls submit themselves spontaneously to her royal and maternal authority and they are attached to her by the bonds of *the slavery of love* (n°s 69-70). It is in these pliant and docile hearts that Mary is truly at home, free to act as she pleases. And it is from there that she exercises most gladly her empire over heaven and earth, ordering all the rest of creation to the salvation of her children and slaves.

Sentiment? Yes. But manly sentiment, since the heart signifies here, as often in Holy Scripture, what is most intimate in us, and since the reign of God in our hearts is the equivalent of perfect holiness.

So ends, on a title at the same time so sweet and so austere, the most theological part of the *Treatise on the True Devotion*. And now, flying this name as a banner, the Archconfraternity of Mary Queen of Hearts works all over the world to subject hearts to Jesus, Who, if He must reign over souls, must also reign there through Mary.

ARTICLE III

The extent of the necessity of the True Devotion to Mary
(39-59)

N° 39

From all that we have said until now:

We must conclude that the most holy Virgin being necessary to God by a necessity which we call hypothetical, in consequence of His Will, she is far more necessary to men, in order for them to arrive at their Last End.

This is what Montfort is going to prove now, by asserting, first of all, *in a general way* the necessity of devotion to Mary. Then, descending to the practical applications, he will say that this devotion is necessary *for all men to save themselves* (n°s 40-42), and more especially *for those who want to attain high sanctity* (n°s 43-46). And, if all this is true of all times, it will be so especially *at the end of the world* (n°s 47-59).

1st Question

The Necessity of Devotion to Mary in general
(39)

"*Mary is necessary to men, in order for them to arrive at their Last End.*" God was supremely free to take another means to lead men to eternal bliss. He, however, chose this way. And now, as a result of His actual choice and of His divine immutability, He can no longer change the order which He established (at least of *prescribed* power). All the more reason man cannot change anything there himself. It is therefore very true that Mary is "*far more necessary*" to men than to God. Even there however, this is not an absolute necessity, deriving from the very nature of things. It is a necessity based, as previously, on the divine will.

Another consequence:

We must not confound devotions to our Blessed Lady with devotions to the other Saints, as if devotion to her was not far more necessary than devotion to them, or as if devotion to her were a matter of supererogation.

To Mary is due the veneration of *hyperdulia*, and to other saints the veneration of *dulia* only, whereas the worship of *latria* is reserved, whatever the Protestants say about it, to God alone. Let us recall nevertheless that between hyperdulia and dulia, there is not only a difference of degree. The two form two different species in the classification of veneration.

Several reasons can be given for this superior veneration, reserved for Mary: the fullness of grace and glory, including the Immaculate Conception; the ineffable grandeur of the divine Maternity and the bonds of consanguinity or affinity which it establishes between Mary and each of the divine Persons. But especially, for what concerns us, the altogether special role which she played and which she still plays in the economy of our salvation. She has the mission of leading the elect to heaven, and, because of this, she received a universal dominion over heaven and earth. Now the devotion which we owe to Mary is correlative to the domain which she exercises over us. This devotion must, then, be unlimited, where the domain is universal. Depending constantly on Mary in the order of grace, we are obliged to recognize this dependence by our devotion.

2nd Question

Devotion to Mary is necessary for salvation
(40-42)

After having said in what sense devotion to Mary is necessary for men to be saved, we shall see with Montfort the proofs of this truth: proofs drawn from Tradition and the Saints, from the figures and words of the Old and the New Testament, from theological reasons and experience, and, finally, from the confessions of the demons and their minions. In closing, we shall examine whether devotion to Mary is indeed a sign of predestination.

1° THE MEANING OF THIS ASSERTION

Obviously, it is not about an absolute necessity; we have already said this is a moral necessity only, as St. Alphonsus remarks. Furthermore, it is not applied to all in the same way. Children, for example, who die after baptism and before the age of reason, are incapable of displaying devotion to Mary. Likewise, adults who have never had the use of reason. Many either do not know the Blessed Virgin, or never think of invoking her. They, however, receive graces from Mary. Every difficulty will disappear once we have made the distinction between *explicit* devotion and *implicit* devotion. All those who know Mary and realize the importance of her role must have an explicit devotion towards her. For others, an implicit devotion will suffice, contained in the sincere desire to use all the means established by God to save us.

2º PROOFS DRAWN FROM TRADITION AND THE SAINTS

Nº 40

Montfort cites a great number of witnesses:

The learned and pious Suarez *the Jesuit, the erudite and devout* Justus Lipsius, *doctor of Louvain, and many others have proved invincibly, in consequence of the sentiments of the Fathers (and among others, of* St. Augustine, St. Ephrem, *deacon of Edessa,* St. Cyril *of Jerusalem,* St. Germanus *of Constantinople,* St. John Damascene, St. Anselm, St. Bernard, St. Bernardine, St. Thomas, *and* St. Bonaventure), *that devotion to our Blessed Lady is necessary to salvation.*

Almost a volume would be necessary to gather all the texts of each of the authors quoted by Montfort proving this truth. And it is certain that he did not exhaust the list of them. *Father Crasset*, known by him, and St. Alphonsus Liguori invoke still other authorities, especially among the theologians. The latter asserts that, in his time, it was the *common opinion*.

Some of the words of the Saints to which he alludes here were already reported. We know, for example, that *St. Augustine* gladly compares the role of Mary to that of the Church, and judges the one as necessary as the other. We know that *St. Ephrem* draws the necessity of devotion to Mary for our salvation from her opposition to Eve and from the plan of *recircumlatio*. In the same way *St. Cyril of Jerusalem*. We can wonder, however, whether Father de Montfort did not confuse the name of St. Cyril of Jerusalem with that of the great doctor of the divine Maternity, St. Cyril of Alexandria. It is, indeed, the latter that we read in the list of Father Crasset. As for *St. Germanus of Constantinople*, it would be necessary to recall his two homilies on the Presentation, his three discourses on the Dormition, the first in particular, where he compares devotion to Mary to the breath of the body: both are signs of life; finally his great sermon on the Cincture of the Most Blessed Virgin.

St. John Damascene is quoted verbatim in n° 41.

Among all the passages of the holy Fathers and Doctors, of which I have made an ample collection, in order to prove this truth, I shall, for brevity's sake, quote but one: Tibi devotum esse, est arma quaedam salutis, quae Deus his dat quos vult salvos fieri –"*To be devout to you, O holy Virgin, is an arm of salvation which God gives to those whom He wishes to save*" (St. John Damascene).

St. Anselm says about Mary: "If you keep silent, no saint will pray, no one will come to our aid; if you pray, everyone will also pray and come to our aid." *St. Bernard* exalted in lyrical terms the immense impact of Mary's "Fiat" for the salvation of the world. *St. Bernardine of Siena*, although belonging to the 15th century, is quoted immediately after St. Bernard (12th c.), and before St. Thomas and St. Bonaventure (13th c). This is perhaps because of the similarity of the Marian doctrine of these two saints. This similarity is especially noticeable in the comparison which both make between the Virgin and the *neck.* Mary is the neck of the Mystical Body. Now what member of the human body can claim to receive the vital impulse of the head, if this impulse is not transmitted to it through the neck? *St. Thomas*, in the *Summa Theologiae*, proclaims that Mary, by receiving Jesus in her womb, welcomed grace for the whole world. *St. Bonaventure*, in the *Speculum Beatae Mariae Virginis*, which, formerly, was commonly attributed to him, and in his commentaries on the *Salve Regina*, asserts that it is enough to be humble and to have confidence in Mary so as not to fear anything for one's salvation. Whereas we have every reason to fear if we lack this humility and confidence.

As for the *examples* given by the Saints themselves, they are so striking that Pius XI could say: "Mary is with God when He produces saints, in the sense that she raises, forms and crowns them."

3° PROOFS DRAWN FROM THE FIGURES AND WORDS OF THE OLD AND NEW TESTAMENT

N° 41

These figures and words are not enumerated here. But they are found in other places of the *Treatise*. Here are the principal ones:

That Mary is called for example, in the Old Testament, the earthly paradise, in which the tree of life grows, the earth making all sorts of plants germinate, the sun illuminating and warming everything with its rays, the moon putting the darkness of the night to flight, the star guiding the course of sailors, the dawn preceding the sunrise, the Ark of Noah saving men from the deluge, etc., the same conclusion always emerges from it: without Mary men would not reach salvation. She is the true mother of the living, like Eve; it is she who obtains for us the divine blessing as Rebecca did; because she is our sister, God treats us with mercy, as He did for Abraham because of Sara, etc.

In the Old Testament, we have the words of Genesis 3:15: "I will put enmities between thee and the woman, and thy seed and her seed…She shall crush thy head, and thou shalt lie in wait for her heel." Psalm 44:13: "All the rich among the people shall entreat thy countenance." Proverbs, ch. 8:35: "He that shall find me, shall find life, and shall have salvation from the Lord," etc.

In the New Testament, several passages show the necessity of devotion to Mary: the *Wedding at Cana*, where Jesus carries out the first of His miracles, but only at the prayer of Mary, and aroused faith in the heart of His disciples; *the Woman clothed with the sun*, who gives birth in pain to all the members of the Mystical Body of her divine Son; the *heavenly Jerusalem*, Spouse of the divine Lamb, composed of all those who will reign eternally with Jesus in Heaven and of those only.

The words of the New Testament, establishing the same necessity, are, first of all, the *angelic salutation* "Hail, full of grace...thou hast found grace with God." See n° 44: Mary found grace with God without the help of any creature. But all other creatures who have found grace since then have found it through her. This already appears very clearly in the mystery of the *Visitation*. All generations will proclaim Mary blessed and, in return, all will participate in the divine mercy and will provide the elect in heaven. In *Bethlehem* the Magi "found the Child with Mary, His Mother." And that is always the place where everyone must seek Him. Mary, like Jesus, will be a sign of contradiction; her soul will be pierced by a two-edged sword; but only those who will be on her side will be saved. Let us also point out the word of the dying Jesus to Mary: "Woman, behold thy son," and to John: "Behold thy Mother," as well as that of St. Paul: "For whom He foreknew, He also predestinated to be made conformable to the image of His Son." That is to say, to be, like Him, children of Mary.

4° PROOFS DRAWN FROM THEOLOGICAL REASONS AND THE FACTS OF EXPERIENCE

There again, the **theological reasons** are not given by the Saint. But they can be deduced from all of his doctrine. They can be reduced to five.

a) *The plenitude of grace in Mary*, which of itself, raises her to the first rank among all the saints and commands for her the respect and veneration of everyone, even of the angels and the Blessed.

b) *The divine Maternity*, which places Mary in an order apart and legitimizes an absolutely special veneration. Moreover, her perpetual virginity and Immaculate Conception have no other reasons for being and are truths of faith. Even in this regard belief in Mary *ever Virgin* and *Immaculate* proves to be necessary.

c) *The Co-redemption*, which commands our deep gratitude to the one who suffered so much for us.

d) *The spiritual Maternity*, which obliges the children to honor their mother.

e) *The universal Mediation*, in virtue of which we depend on Mary at every moment, and, normally, have to ask her for the necessary help.

For all these reasons, it is required to honor Mary in order to be saved. When it is a question of mere salvation, the degree of devotion is not indicated by the Saint. It will be later for what concerns souls aspiring to perfection.

If this veneration is so necessary why is it not imposed by a **special precept**? Because it is sufficiently contained in the obligation whereby we are *to make our salvation sure*. We are not commanded specially and formally to breathe, but breathing becomes obligatory by the law which forbids suicide. So too, in the supernatural order, everything, the omission of which compromises our salvation, is in point of fact even obligatory, and obligatory to the extent of its influence on our salvation.

N° 42

Proofs from experience.

The fact is [*and argument does not prevail against fact*] that the world is full of devotion to Mary and that all Christians turn to this good Mother to obtain all sorts of graces. How many times do they not recite the *Hail Mary* or the *Salve Regina*? And do not these two prayers eloquently express the need which we have of Mary's help, either during our life, or especially at the hour of our death? "Pray for us poor sinners, now and at the hour of our death." – "After this our exile, show unto us the blessed Fruit of thy womb, Jesus."

Among the saints who experienced the sweetness and the ease of this way, Montfort cites especially *St .Francis of Assisi*.

I could bring forward here many histories which prove the same thing, and among others, one which is related in the chronicles of St. Francis, when he saw in an ecstasy a large ladder which went to heaven, at the end of which was the Blessed Virgin, and by which it was shown to him that it was necessary to rise in order to come to heaven.

Here is the fact with more ample details, as it is contained in the *Fioretti*:

"One day, this great saint, delighted in ecstasy, saw two ladders which rose from earth up to heaven. On one of them, which was red, leaned Our Lord. On the other, which was white, stood the Virgin Mary. The sons of St. Francis zealously climbed the red ladder, to join Our Lord. But their efforts were useless, and all fell again to the ground discouraged. On seeing this, St. Francis began crying bitterly, and complaining sweetly to Jesus, Who answered him: 'Order your brothers to go to My Mother and to rise by the white ladder.' Immediately the saint passed on this order to his religious. And these rose easily along the virginal ladder, and they were received in heaven by the Virgin, who led them to Jesus."

Examples of this kind could be multiplied, drawn either from the lives of the Saints or the experience of the priestly ministry. How many poor sinners were saved at the last minute thanks to the practices of devotion which they had preserved, even in the midst of their crimes? It is not a question of adding a blind faith to the narratives, in more or less legendary form, which antiquity has passed on to us; although some are attested by authors completely deserving of our confidence (Father Crasset, St. Alphonsus Liguori, and others). It concerns actual cases, in which the exhortation to the love of Mary was the only means to approach a sinner and to convert him. Every priest accustomed to the direction of souls can give multiple examples of this.

5° PROOFS DRAWN FROM THE ADMISSIONS OF THE DEMONS AND THEIR MINIONS

The Saint appeals to the experience of virtuous souls. But he also quotes confessions extracted from demons in evidence of the truth. For this purpose, he briefly recounts the story of a possessed Albigensian delivered by St. Dominic. This story, reported by all the biographers of the saint, is given with more details by Fr. de Montfort in the *Admirable Secret of the Most Holy Rosary*. He explains in particular that, if the number of demons in the body of this possessed person was fifteen thousand, it is because the heretic had attacked the fifteen mysteries of the Rosary, and that, by the Rosary of which he had made a weapon, Dominic struck terror and dismay into all hell. This is the admission of the demons. Forced then by the Blessed Virgin, at the prayers of St. Dominic, they acknowledged before a multitude estimated at more than twelve thousand people "*several great and comforting truths concerning the devotion to the Blessed Virgin.*" These among others: as the sun dissipates the darkness, so too Mary exposes the infernal machinations contrived by the demon to lead souls into temptation. All those who serve her faithfully are assured of escaping hell. Many sinners, having only the time to call upon her at the time of death, are saved. One of her sighs alone has more weight than all the prayers of the saints. "And if this miserable *little Mary* had not opposed and repressed our efforts, we would have exterminated the whole Church a long time ago." Finally, whoever perseveres in the fervent recitation of the holy Rosary will not die without true contrition for his sins. So that, as Montfort says,

it is not possible to read this authentic history, and the panegyric which the devil made, in spite of himself, of devotion to the most holy Mary, without shedding tears of joy, however lukewarm we may be in our devotion to her.

Therefore, the demon and those that he encourages to make the greatest efforts *to turn souls away from devotion to Mary* are seen on all sides. As if it were not sufficient for them to deprive them of divine grace, they have no rest until they take them away from Mary. St. Alphonsus Liguori skillfully develops the story of Agar and Ismael: "Sarah, seeing Isaac playing with Ishmael, who was teaching him evil habits, asked Abraham to send him away, and his mother Agar also: '*Cast out this bond-woman and her son.*' She was not satisfied that the son alone should leave the house without the mother, fearing lest the child would come to visit his mother, and thus continue to frequent the house. In like manner, the devil is not satisfied with seeing Jesus cast out from a soul, if he does not see the mother also cast out: '*Cast out this bond-woman and her son.*' Otherwise he fears that the mother, by her intercession, may again obtain the return of her son. And he has cause to fear, for according to the teaching of Father Pacciuchelli: "If we are faithful in honoring the Mother of God we shall soon receive God Himself by her intervention."

6° A COROLLARY PRACTICE

DEVOTION TO MARY A SIGN OF PREDESTINATION

N°s 40-42

Here is how Montfort expresses this truth (in the opinion of all the holy and learned personages whom he quoted) and even *"in the opinion of Œcolampadius and some other heretics:"*

it is an infallible mark of reprobation to have no esteem and love for the holy Virgin; while, on the other hand, it is an infallible mark of predestination to be entirely and truly devoted to her (N° 40).

Let us notice, first of all, that Montfort speaks, on one hand, about the one who, deliberately and voluntarily, rejects any devotion to Mary, and, on the other hand, about the one who shows a *true devotion* towards her. We have already said above that devotion, in certain cases, can only be implicit. This case is formally excluded here. On the other hand, Montfort will later vehemently protest (n°s 97-100 and 102) against the presumptuous and hypocritical devotees, some claiming to be saved, in spite of their sinful life, because of some vague prayers to Mary, others covering their very numerous and very grave disorders under the mask of this same devotion. Obviously, this is not what is being discussed in n° 40. So that Mary may infallibly lead her servants to eternal salvation, these must be "*completely and truly devoted*" to her. This clarification, recalled by all authors who teach this truth, is the best response to the diatribes of the *Monita salutaria:* "Do not believe you are predestined because of some marks of veneration which you show towards me, if you do not have charity." Those who do not crucify their flesh, according to the teaching of St. Paul (Gal. 5:24), cannot "identify with either Christ or me, His Mother, even though they shower me with marks of devotion."

A distinction was essential here, and, as usual, it eluded the author of the *Monita*. It is one thing to persist in one's sin, in the vain assurance that Mary will take into account the sinner's poor practices of devotion to her, to shield him from hell, and another thing to regret his state and turn to Mary to get out of it as quickly as possible, and to persevere, then, in grace regained. "If the only power at the disposal, at certain hours, of unfortunate souls, boils down to praying to the Virgin, what will they resolve to do, if we succeed in convincing them of the uselessness of this last effort."

Montfort will say later (n°s 99-100):

I confess that, in order to be truly devout to our Blessed Lady, it is not absolutely necessary to be so holy as to avoid every sin, though this were to be wished; but so much at least is necessary, and I beg you to lay it well to heart:

1. To have a sincere resolution to avoid, at least, all mortal sin, which outrages the Mother as well as the Son;

2. I would add also that to do violence to ourselves to avoid sin, whatever it is, even venial;

3. To enroll ourselves in confraternities, etc…

This is wonderfully useful to the conversion of a sinner, however hardened: *and if my reader is such a one, even if he has his foot in the abyss, I would counsel these things to him. Nevertheless, it must be on the condition that he will only practice these good works with the intention of obtaining from God, by the intercession of the Blessed Virgin, the grace of contrition and the pardon of his sins, to conquer his evil habits, and not to remain quietly in the state of sin, in spite of the remorse of his conscience, the example of Jesus Christ and the Saints, and the maxims of the holy Gospel.*

This ambiguity having been dispelled, the twofold assertion brought out by Montfort becomes obvious, and, especially after what we said previously, it hardly needs to be proved.

Devotion to Mary being necessary for salvation, those who reject it with full knowledge of the facts put themselves outside the way indicated by God, and, as long as they persevere in this stubbornness, they cannot hope to reach eternal bliss. Those who, at the cost of violent efforts against themselves to leave their bad habits, managed to practice constantly the true devotion to Mary, are *at present* on the way to heaven. There is not the slightest doubt about this. Mary, like God Himself, necessarily loves those who love her, and those who look for her are assured of finding her.

But can the latter base themselves on their *current* devotion to Mary to believe that they possess an infallible sign of **predestination**? And likewise, can others fear, according to their current feelings, of being an object of eternal **condemnation**? That is the whole question, because, after all, the will is changeable, and whoever is holy today can become a sinner tomorrow, die in this state and be damned. It is seen sometimes, although the contrary is more frequent.

Can the Christian, who knows his weakness and trembles for his future, hope to be saved, if he is really, sincerely devout to Mary?

Montfort answers: Yes! And he relies on the authority of all the Fathers whom he quoted and whose testimonies we have already summarized. Father Crasset proves it at length: 1° by Sacred Scripture; 2° by the Fathers; 3° by theological reason. Likewise St. Alphonsus Liguori. The latter, having said in what sense it is necessary to understand his words: "It is understood, then, only of those of her servants who, with the desire to amend, faithfully honor and commend themselves to the Mother of God," adds: "That these should be lost is, I say, morally impossible." Because, just as it is impossible to save oneself, if we are not at all protected by Mary, similarly the one who becomes attached to her, and who listens to her, will not be confounded.

We can reduce to two the reasons which show this special efficacy of devotion to Mary:

a) **On Mary's part**: Mary is the spiritual Mother of all the faithful. She is capable of obtaining for them all the graces necessary for their salvation, and she wishes to obtain them for them more ardently than they themselves wish to receive them. Now, what mother, being able to protect from death a son who loved her tenderly and served her lovingly, would refuse to use her power to save him? All the more reason, Mary will do it eagerly, since she is the ideal mother from all points of view.

b) **On our part**: Whoever sincerely practices devotion to Mary is settled at present in the way of salvation, makes himself safe from his own inconstancy as surely as possible, and secures a means of rising quickly, if he has the misfortune to fall again into sin, and, by uniting with Mary, places himself through her in contact with Jesus, the principle of eternal salvation. Now, it is a maxim that the more we approach a principle, the more we participate in its influence.

For all these reasons, devotion to Mary is not yet heavenly glory, granted as a gift to the living, but it is, says the Saint, an *infallible* sign, or, as St. John Damascene says, an *assured pledge*, of such a kind, says St. Alphonsus, that damnation is *morally* impossible. We could not claim mere security, as long as we are here on earth.

3rd Question

Devotion to Mary is necessary for perfect souls
(43-46)

N° 43

Continuing his ascent in the degrees of necessity: necessary for God, more necessary for men "*simply for working out their salvation,*" Montfort comes "*to those who are called to any particular perfection,*" in any state of life whatsoever, and he proclaims devotion to Mary "*much more necessary still*" for them than for all others. "*I do not think,*" he asserts, by basing himself on his great experience with souls in all the stages of the spiritual life,

I do not think any one can acquire an intimate union with our Lord (the supreme degree of the mystical life)*, and a perfect fidelity to the Holy Ghost* (leading her from summit to summit all the way to this supreme degree)*, without a* **very great union** *with the most holy Virgin, and a great dependence on her succor.*

This assertion of the Saint follows from all that he said previously (see n° 37: "*We may conclude, then, from what I have said... secondly... that*", etc.). He could thus content himself with the proofs given above. Since it is to this category especially, however, that the perfect devotee will belong whom he intends to form (n° 110), he does not fail to offer new proofs here.

These proofs are three in number, and are clearly indicated by the expression repeated three times: "*It is Mary alone...*" It is Mary alone who possesses: 1° the key of the treasure of grace (n° 44); 2° the key of the cellars of divine love; 3° the key of the earthly Paradise (n° 45). Conclusion: "*All the rich among the people shall supplicate thy face* (n° 46)."

*
* *

§ I. – MARY ALONE POSSESSES THE KEY OF THE TREASURE OF GRACE
(44)

N° 44

Montfort rereads the sublime page of St. Luke, in which are splendidly described the dignity and role of Mary; he illuminates the major principles of Mariology, and he writes in his turn a page overflowing with enthusiasm and admiration.

The archangel Gabriel declares to Mary that she found grace before God: "Thou hast found grace with God" (Lk. 1:30). This expression is encountered several times in Holy Scripture to indicate to someone that he is the object of a great divine kindness. We understand, however, in what sense the Saint says:

It is Mary alone *who has found grace before God, without the aid of any other mere creature.*

Neither Noah, nor Moses, nor Gideon found grace with the Lord to this extent. Let us listen to St. Bernard: "You have found grace with God: what grace? The peace of God and men, the destruction of death, the reparation of life." He is quite certain that she alone merited (by suitability) such favors (see n° 16 and the commentary on it). No other creature could help her obtain what no other possessed and was incapable of obtaining for himself. *No one gives what he doesn't have.*

Mary, however, found grace, and not only for herself, but for the whole world. That is why

it is only through her that all those who have found grace before God have found it at all; and it is only through her that all those who shall come afterwards shall find it.

She was so richly endowed, indeed, only with a view to her mission: this personal endowment is recalled in broad outline:

She was full of grace when she was saluted by the Archangel Gabriel, and she was superabundantly filled with grace by the Holy Ghost when He covered her with His unspeakable shadow; and she has so augmented, from day to day and from moment to moment, this double plenitude, that she has reached a point of grace immense and inconceivable.

Rich personal endowment, we said, but with a view to her mission:

In such sort that the Most High has made her the sole treasurer of His graces, and the sole dispenser of His graces.

These words seem to be a repetition of n°s 23, 24 and 25. But whereas there they concerned all souls who want to benefit from grace, here they no longer concern anyone except perfect souls and great saints, as the continuation proves:

...to ennoble, to exalt, and to enrich whom she wishes; to give the entry to whom she wills into the narrow way of heaven; to pass whom she wills, and in spite of all obstacles, through the strait gate of life; and to give the throne, the scepter, and the crown of the King to whom she wills.

Is this not the echo of the words of the divine Master in the Sermon on the Mount, inviting souls to walk in the way of perfection and exclaiming: "Enter ye in at the narrow gate: for wide is the gate, and broad is the way that leadeth to destruction, and many there are who go in thereat. How narrow is the gate, and strait is the way that leadeth to life: and few there are that find it!" (Mt. 7:13-14)? Besides, all the words of this passage are so many biblical images, indicating those who will reach the happiness of heaven. Montfort restricts them only to the sense of eminent happiness, requiring an extraordinary merit. This is the only means to be noble, high and rich in the supernatural order.

And he ends by recalling what he already said in n° 33:

Jesus is everywhere and always the fruit and the Son of Mary, and Mary is everywhere the true tree which bears the fruit of life, the mother who produces it.

If the slightest degree of supernatural life cannot blossom without Mary's intervention, all the more reason will this also apply when it will be a matter of reproducing the life of Jesus in us, of expressing His traits in our soul.

*
* *

§ II. – MARY ALONE POSSESSES THE KEY OF THE CELLARS OF DIVINE LOVE
(45)

N° 45

This time, Montfort will no longer seek the source of his inspiration in the Gospel, but rather in the Old Testament.

And he stops now at a very beautiful image drawn from the "Canticle of Canticles". The bride is delighted at the fact that the bridegroom has made her enter into the wine cellar, *in cellam vinariam*. This wine represents the love and the fervor with which God inebriates holy souls. And the cellar symbolizes their union with God, a union which is realized in the most intimate part of the soul and in the act of the purest love.

Now

It is Mary alone *to whom God has given the keys of the cellars of divine love and the power* (not only) *to enter* (herself and at her discretion) *into the most sublime and secret ways of perfection* (but also), *to make others enter in there also.*

The bride of the "Canticles" was proud to have been introduced, by privilege, into the cellars of divine love. But it was not in her power either to enter there of herself, or to introduce others there, because she had not received the keys of this wonderful refuge. Mary can enter it when she wants, remain there as long as she wants, introduce there whom she wants, because she possesses the keys. The results have already been described many times for her and her incomparable holiness. She will produce in souls a holiness of the same kind, drawn from the same sources, which will likewise attract the glances of the divine Spouse.

*
* *

§ III. – MARY ALONE POSSESSES THE KEY OF THE EARTHLY PARADISE
(Same number)

Since the disastrous fault committed by our first parents, the earthly Paradise had been closed. It still remains so at present. Not to all, however, "*to those whom it is her pleasure,*" Mary gives access to this delightful garden, "*to make them become saints.*" How will this transformation take place? We shall learn it by following the text of the *Treatise*:

It is Mary alone *who has given to the miserable children of Eve, the faithless, the entry into the terrestrial Paradise,*

thus repairing the consequences of the first fault. This earthly Paradise will not bear any mark exteriorly distinguishing it from the earth inhabited by the other children of Eve. All its beauty will be interior and all its efficacy to produce the effects enumerated below will ensue from what the earth has become, thanks to Mary, and for her children only, the instrumental cause of the miracles of sanctification. Mary opens to her children the entrance of this regenerated world, so that they can "*walk there agreeably with God,*" like Adam before the fall, "*to hide themselves securely against their enemies,*" who have no access into this sacred refuge, "*to feed themselves there deliciously, without any more fear of death, on the fruit of the trees of life,*" which man no longer had the right to touch, "*and of the knowledge of good*" to carry it out, "*and evil*" to avoid it, "*and drink in long draughts the heavenly waters of that fair mountain, which gushes forth there with abundance."*

We recognize in these words the description of the earthly Paradise, as given in chapters II and III of Genesis. The main elements are interpreted in a spiritual sense and can be understood in *two different manners*, depending on whether the earthly Paradise is, as we said, **the regenerated world**, having become thanks to Mary an instrument of salvation, or **Mary herself**, the true earthly Paradise of the New Adam, but also containing all the members of His Mystical Body. Either way, the results will be the same. The world, transformed by faith, no longer offers to man anything except a means to go to God and to avoid the obstacles which would divert him from it.

The ambiguity disappears at the end of the paragraph, where it is said:

or rather **She is herself that terrestrial paradise**, *that virgin and blessed earth, from which Adam and Eve, the sinners, have been driven, and she gives no entry there except to those whom it is her pleasure to make Saints.*

There could be no doubt. Mary is this earthly Paradise where neither sin, nor sinners can have access, but only holy souls, or at least those who wish to be. Towards them, Mary will fulfill not only the general role which falls to her with regard to the predestined, and which was described in n° 33. She will produce the same effects with such perfection that she will incite in these souls an intense fervor, and will lead them to show themselves generous. In this earthly Paradise, the saints will not only walk, but they will also walk "*agreeably*"; they will not only hide, but they will also hide "*securely*"; they will not only feed, but they will also feed "*deliciously*" and they will drink "*in long draughts*" the heavenly waters of this beautiful fountain which gushes forth there "*with abundance.*" How could we not say with the Church: "**O felix culpa!** O happy fault!" Mary repaired the damage caused by Eve, and she restored everything to a better state than it was previously, if considered from the solely supernatural point of view.

*
* *

Conclusion: "All the rich among the people shall supplicate thy face"
(46)

N° 46

Relying on verse 13 of Psalm 44: "All the rich among the people shall entreat thy countenance," Montfort concludes that in every century, but more and more as the end of the world approaches, the greatest saints will be the work of Mary. It was already so in the past. But the Saint does not stop at this consideration. He only looks forward, into the future, and he sings in advance the triumph of these Marian souls over everything which would be opposed to their spiritual progress:

All the rich among the people, to make use of an expression of the Holy Ghost, according to the explanation of St. Bernard – all the rich among the people shall supplicate thy face from age to age, and particularly at the end of the world; that is to say, the greatest saints, the souls richest in graces and virtues, shall be the most assiduous in praying to our Blessed Lady, and in having her always present as their perfect model to imitate, and their powerful aid to give them succour.

Montfort invokes the authority of St. Bernard to interpret this verse of Psalm 44 in a Marian sense. The Church gives the example in her liturgy, by borrowing several fragments from the same Psalm to insert them into the Masses of the Most Blessed Virgin, for example, besides the verse in question: "My heart hath uttered a good word, hearken, O daughter, and see" (Ps. 44:1,11), etc.... Since this Psalm is messianic, the literal sense of verse 13 announces the future conversion of the heathen nations and their mass entrance into the bosom of the Church. But, as St. Robert Bellarmine remarks about verse 10: "The queen stood on thy right hand," whatever is said about the Church, spouse of Christ, can be applied to any perfect soul and especially to the Blessed Virgin Mary. Because although the latter is Mother of Christ according to the flesh, she is His Spouse according to the spirit, and, among all the members of the Church, she occupies the first rank. It is justifiable, then, to see in verse 13 a prediction concerning the eagerness, not of any souls whatever, but only of the richest in graces and in virtues. They will turn to Mary so as to have in this good Mother the perfect model of holiness which they aspire to, and to ask of her the powerful help which will allow them to attain it.

The Saint evidently attaches to the expression "**from age to age**" an idea of continuous progress in the intensity of this burning plea, by which the saints seek to obtain the good graces of their Sovereign, and to read on her features the answer to their prayers. Indeed, he returns to it insistently in n°s 47 and 48, which, because of this, are transitional numbers and can be connected with the present question as well as with the following one.

4th Question

Devotion to Mary is especially necessary in the end times
(47-59)

These pages of the *Treatise* attain a lyricism rarely equaled. Montfort thrills enthusiastically at the idea of Our Lord's triumph at the end of time, and he sings the merit of the Marian souls who will prepare it.

This question is divided into three great pictures. The first shows the miracles of grace, the gigantic fights and the sensational conversions which will signal the end times (n^{os}

47-48). The second describes the role reserved for Mary in the accomplishment of these miracles (n°s 49-54). The third gives a magnificent portrait of the apostles of the end times (n°s 55-59).

*
* *

§ I. – GENERAL OVERVIEW ON THE END TIMES
(47-48)

N° 47

Quoting, first of all, the revelations given to Marie des Vallées, then the preaching of St. Vincent Ferrer, and finally, a prophecy contained in Psalm 58, Montfort sings of the heroic sanctity which will be manifested at the end of the world.

1° **Marie des Vallées** (1590-1656). Spiritual daughter of St. John Eudes, she was called the Saint of Coutances. At Saint-Sulpice, Montfort had read her life handwritten by Baron de Renty (1611-1652), a close friend of St. John Eudes and Fr. Boudon. She had numerous revelations, particularly about the end of the world. Our Saint does not hide that he drew from it: "As has been revealed to a holy soul whose life has been written by Fr. de Renty."

I have said that this would come to pass particularly at the end of the world, **and indeed presently***, because the Most High with His holy Mother has to form for Himself great saints, who shall surpass most of the other saints in sanctity, as much as the cedars of Lebanon outgrow the little shrubs.*

This very biblical comparison expresses a very evangelical thought, namely, the existence of great saints at the end of the world. Our Lord opened his mind about it very clearly. Obviously, we shall not come to this end all at once. Just as evil will always keep increasing until it reaches the end of the last days, good will also always become stronger, and, in every century, very great saints will precede and prepare those who will come at the end of the world.

N° 48

2° **St. Vincent Ferrer** (1355-1419) was, as Montfort says, the "*great apostle of his age.*" He announced everywhere the imminence of the Last Judgment. God worked the most striking miracles to lend credence to the words of His messenger for souls. The very lively faith of our Saint could only surrender entirely in the presence of such manifestations.

Now, in one of his books: *Tractatus de vita spirituali* (Treatise on the Spiritual Life), St. Vincent Ferrer speaks about a new congregation which will appear in the end times. Its members will have to convert the whole world in the interval which will pass between the appearance of the Antichrist and the end of the world.

This source, also quoted by Montfort, will help us understand the whole beginning of n° 48:

These great souls, full of grace and zeal, shall be chosen to match themselves against the enemies of God, who shall rage on all sides; and they shall be singularly devout to our Blessed Lady, illuminated by her light, nourished by her milk, led by her spirit, supported by her arm, and sheltered under her protection, so that they shall fight with one hand and build with the other (N° 48), just as the Jews, having returned from captivity, were forced to do in Jerusalem.

In this description the main traits of the slave of love are already recognized, acting through Mary, with Mary, in Mary and for Mary. Not only will this good Mother lead these souls to holiness, but she will preserve them in it, by supporting them, defending them, and giving them victory over their enemies. Indeed:

With one hand, *they* (these great souls) *shall fight, overthrow, and crush the heretics with their heresies, the schismatics with their schisms, the idolaters with their idolatries, and the sinners with their impieties.*

And so, there will be nothing left of all that is opposed to the reign of God and His Christ. Evil, under all its forms and everywhere it is found, will be thrown down by the apostles of Mary, with the help of their heavenly Queen.

It will be, however, only the work of *clearing away*, the purely negative effect, obtained at the price of incredible struggles. After that will come the otherwise important work of **building**.

With the other hand *they shall build the temple of the true Solomon, and the mystical city of God, that is to say, the most holy Virgin, called by the holy Fathers the* temple of Solomon *and the* city of God.

To the one who would wish to know who gives these titles to Mary and how they are verified in her, we would recommend reading *Fr. Poiré*. This assertion of the Saint is proved there in every detail and it is very likely the latter thought of these passages of Fr. Poiré in writing these lines.

Let us note rather the idea of our Saint: in order to welcome Our Lord in the glory of His third advent, it is fitting to build Him a *temple*, and this temple is none other than Mary; to welcome this King of kings and this Lord of Lords on the very day of His triumph, it is necessary to build for Him on earth a *great city* which will be His *capital*, and this city is none other than Mary. Obviously a purely spiritual temple and city, and consequently also a building in the metaphorical sense only. This will be accomplished, when these great saints, apostles of Mary, "*by their words and their examples shall bend the whole world to true devotion to Mary.*" Mary will take possession of souls, animate them with her life and draw her divine Son into them.

But evil will not see such opposition to its destructive work **without reacting**. Before giving up definitively, it will get desperately agitated. "*This shall bring upon them* (the holy souls) *many enemies*," but will also contribute to forming and strengthening them. They will thus win for themselves "*many victories*" and obtain much glory for God alone.

3° **Psalm 58.** – These private revelations would not be enough to support a thesis on such a scale. At least they can serve to enlighten a *very obscure prophecy* contained in Psalm 58, verses 14 and 15.

It is this which the Holy Ghost seems to have prophesied in the fifty-eighth Psalm, of which these are the words: Et scient quia Deus dominabitur Iacob et finium terrae; convertentur ad vesperam et famem patientur ut canes et circuibunt civitatem: "*And they shall know that God will rule Jacob, and all the ends of the earth; they shall return at evening, and shall suffer hunger like dogs, and shall go round about the city*" (N° 48, 2nd paragraph).

The literal sense of these verses seems to concern **the Jews**. Either at the end of the world, or after the destruction of Jerusalem and their dispersion in all the nations, they were or will be obliged to recognize that Jahweh is not only the God of Jacob (that is to say, of the Jews) but rightly of the whole earth. Everywhere, indeed, idols fall and the worship of the true God is established. The Jews themselves "*will be converted in the evening*," that is to say, either *too late* to obtain mercy and then they will make a tour of the city inhabited by the elect and they will vainly try to quench their late hunger for justice; or else *they will turn to the darkness of the night* and *sensual pleasures*, like dogs roam near the walls of a city to look for the corpses of decomposing animals, to quench their hunger; or else *they will be converted at the end of the world*, they will themselves hunger for justice, like the Gentiles; they will be satisfied by the Gospel preaching, and they too will go around the city by teaching and preaching.

Montfort proposes *another explanation* based on all the preceding. The prophecy no longer concerns only the Jews, but the **whole world**, on which God will clearly manifest His power on the last day. Many men, who had let themselves be blinded by sin, *will wish to be converted* and will feel a *sincere hunger for justice*. They will look for the means to calm this supernatural hunger and **they will find Mary**, the true city of refuge which God established for their salvation. It is to this good Mother that they will go to ask to be taught the ways of justice.

This city which men shall find at the end of the world to convert themselves in, and to satisfy the hunger they have for justice, is the most holy Virgin, who is called by the Holy Ghost the City of God.

So, devotion to Mary, operating on a large scale at the end of the world, will convert idolaters, heretics, schismatics and sinners, and transform them into admirable saints, eager for justice and holiness, and working with all their strength to assure their triumph on earth.

But let us not forget that this city of God, which will save so many people on the last day, will be built by the other great saints, when they will bend the whole world, by their words and their examples, to true devotion to Mary.

*
* *

§ II. – THE SPECIAL ROLE OF MARY IN THE END TIMES
(49-54)

In n° 49, Montfort establishes the relations between the role allocated to the Virgin in the first advent and the one which will be reserved for her in the last.

In n° 50, he enumerates the reasons which prove this role.

In n°s 51-54, he shows in all this a perfect fulfillment of the prophecy contained in the Protoevangelium.

1° THE ROLE OF MARY IN THE FIRST AND LAST ADVENTS

N° 49

1° The resemblances:

It is through Mary that the salvation of the world was begun, and it is through Mary that it must be consummated.

These words echo the first phase of the Treatise. But they have a more restricted sense. The first sentence, indeed, envisaged the reign of Jesus in the world throughout the ages. The latter, on the contrary, no longer envisages anything except the last advent of Jesus Christ at the end of the world. It establishes the comparison between this advent and the first. It is in this particular sense that it will be necessary to understand each of the reasons enumerated in N° 50.

2° The differences:

Mary has hardly appeared at all in the first coming of Jesus Christ, in order that men, as yet but little instructed and enlightened on the Person of her Son, should not remove themselves from Him, in attaching themselves too strongly and too grossly to her,

and by directing to her an idolatrous worship with all the characteristics of pagan worship, when it had a feminine divinity as its object.

This statement is not made lightly. It is based on a real possibility, and on a historic fact.

a) *Real possibility:*

This would have apparently taken place if she had been known, because of the admirable charms which the Most High had bestowed even upon her exterior.

Recall that, at the beginning of the Church, Mary was not, like ancient goddesses, a vague myth, an ideology personified, a thing that we picture without knowing whether she ever existed. She lived among Christians who, twenty or twenty-five years after the Ascension of Jesus Christ, could still see her, admire her and feast their eyes and heart on her beauty, ever-young and fresh in spite of the years. Humanly speaking, and considered independently of the impression of calm that Mary's beauty produced on souls, according to St. Thomas of Villanova, there could certainly have been a too material infatuation of people towards Mary, if her role had completely been highlighted then.

b) *Historic fact:*

This is so true that St. Denys the Areopagite has informed us in his writings that when he saw our Blessed Lady, **he should have taken her for a Divinity**, *in consequence of her secret charms and incomparable beauty, had not the Faith in which he was well established taught him the contrary.*

He was well established in the faith, which is why he was able to avoid the error. Recently converted Christians, who were insufficiently educated, not yet delivered from the purely physical remnants of their pagan habits, perhaps would not have escaped the same danger.

The Saint, however, imitates most of his contemporaries. He supposes that the self-styled letter sent by St. Denys the Areopagite to the apostle Saint Paul is authentic. Undoubtedly, he had to side with the opinion expressed by Father Crasset. "Without stopping to examine if the Epistle which he sends to this great apostle is from him or not, because opinions are divided, I report what he claims to have seen with his eyes." And he quotes several authors expressing the same opinion. This is still what is done now. Our Saint is, then, in good company when he attributes this letter to St. Denys the Areopagite.

Montfort does not speak explicitly about the immense intermediate space between the first and the last advent. In the Introduction, he showed that Mary must be more and more known, to prepare for the knowledge and reign of her divine Son. One might ask, however, whether the *Second Coming*, about which he spoke at the end of n° 49 does not also belong to the second manifestation of Our Lord by His grace, but then in the time close to the Last Judgment. Thus, the Saint would not deviate from the usual distinction of the three advents of Our Lord, in His flesh to redeem us, in His grace to sanctify us, and in His glory to judge us. (See n° 22 and its commentary.)

Either way, it is about the last era. And Montfort writes:

But in the second coming of Jesus Christ, Mary has to be made known and revealed by the Holy Ghost, in order that through her Jesus Christ may be known, loved, and served. The reasons which moved the Holy Ghost to hide His Spouse during her life, and **to reveal her but a very little since the preaching of the Gospel**, *subsist no longer.*

We intentionally highlighted the penultimate interpolated clause, to show a full coinciding of doctrine between what was said in the Introduction and what is said now.

2° PROOFS OF THIS MARIAN ROLE

N° 50

God, then, wishes to reveal and discover Mary, the masterpiece of His hands, in these latter times.

This is a summary of what precedes, in which everything must be taken in the literal sense. The veil behind which Mary hid by humility, or which God cast over her to reserve for Himself the knowledge and possession of her, this veil will be torn, and Mary will appear in all the magnificence of her glory and her power. This revelation, besides, will be all for the glory of the divine Artist Who executed such a masterpiece, and it will serve to lead more to God the sincere souls who will want to be saved.

To prove this divine intention, we have the following arguments:

1° *The reward due to Mary's humility.* "He that humbleth himself shall be exalted" (Lk. 14:11).

Because Mary *hid herself in this world, and put herself lower than the dust by her profound humility, having obtained of God and of His Apostles and Evangelists that she should not be made manifest.*

2° *The glory that God desires to receive from men for His masterpiece.* "The Lord hath made all things for Himself" (Prov. 16:4). All the exterior works of God proclaim His glory, and that is why He created them. All the more reason He is anxious to be glorified, even on earth, by men, for the most beautiful work He ever accomplished in the purely created order. That is why:

Mary, being the masterpiece of the hands of God, as well here below by grace as in heaven by glory, He wishes to be glorified and praised in her by those who are living upon the earth.

3° *The different roles that Mary plays in connection with our salvation:*

a) Her appearance precedes and announces that of Jesus as *the dawn* precedes and announces the sunrise (n° 50, 3°).

b) She was physically *the way* by which *Jesus Christ came into the world* the first time. She will again be, but this time morally, the way by which He will manifest Himself to the world on the last day (n° 50, 4°).

c) She is, for men themselves, *the straight and immaculate way to go to Jesus*, and to find Him perfectly. It is, then, through her that holy souls must find Him. Let us admire here the beautiful argumentation of Father de Montfort: He who will find Mary will find Jesus: but Mary cannot be found except by searching for her; we cannot search for her unless we know her, because to search for her it is necessary to desire her, and we do not desire what we do not know: it is necessary, then, for Mary to be known and more known than ever, so that she might be desired, sought, found and so that, with her and in her, Jesus may be found, possessed and glorified. To show better the logical sequence, we neglected the first argument. It too deserves to be considered: He who will find Mary, will find *life* (Prov. 8:35). Now Jesus is the way, the truth and the *life* (Jn. 14:6). Therefore, the one who will find Mary will find Jesus (n° 50, 5°).

d) She is *the universal mediatrix* of all graces, exercising her power in favor of the predestined. She will, then, shine at the end of the world IN MERCY with regard to all those who will accept even belatedly the reign of her Son; IN STRENGTH against all those who will personally oppose it and will try to divert others from it; and IN GRACE to inspire and support the great saints who will work to win souls for her and will be the apostles of the end times. Nobody will be caught by surprise. Each will choose with full knowledge of the matter and will be treated according to his choice (n° 50, 6°).

e) Finally, her royal *power*, completely at the service of the elect, allows her to act even on demons and their henchmen, to limit their harmful power. She will be then terrible to them as an army in battle array. The demon, indeed, will know that he has little time left to ruin souls, and he will make every effort to set up pitfalls for them. He will be incensed especially against the faithful servants and the true children of Mary, over whom he triumphs with more difficulty. But we shall see Mary raising herself to defend them, and thoroughly engaged in the battle predicted from the beginning of the world (n° 50, 7°).

3° THE FULFILLMENT OF THE PROPHECY CONTAINED IN THE PROTOEVANGELIUM
(51-54)

N° 51

These cruel devilish persecutions will increase every day until the **appearance of the Antichrist**. Behold in what terms the Apostle announced to the Thessalonians the advent of this great enemy of the faith: "Let no man deceive you by any means, for unless there come a revolt first, and the man of sin be revealed, the son of perdition, who opposeth, and is lifted up above all that is called God, or that is worshipped, so that he sitteth in the temple of God, shewing himself as if he were God" (2 Th. 2:3-4). St. Augustine sees in the Antichrist not a particular person, but a *multitude* of the enemies of Christ. Other Fathers see there *a man* so villainous, that sin will be, so to speak, embodied in him. This is the sense adopted by Montfort. Jesus reigns over all men, good and bad, predestined and reprobate. He leads some with His golden scepter, others with His iron rod. Mary reigns only over the predestined, supports them with her graces and inspires them with her spirit. And she is in reality the one who can be opposed to the Antichrist, the leader of the reprobates, the mainstay and the organizer of the fight and revolt.

It is of this grand fight that we must understand "**that first and celebrated prediction**," and the "**curse of God, pronounced in the terrestrial Paradise against the serpent**": "*Inimicitias ponam inter te et mulierem, inter semen tuum et semen illius; ipsa conteret caput tuum et tu insidiaberis calcaneo eius.* I will put enmities between thee and the woman, and thy seed and her seed; she shall crush thy head, and thou shalt lie in wait for her heel."

This prophecy is like a diamond with many facets, the brightness and the glint of which are very different, according to the point of view one takes to consider it. We find the first promise of the Savior and the Redemption, the announcement of the plan of revenge, the prediction of the Virgin, her virginal Maternity, her Immaculate Conception, her Mediation in the distribution of all graces. Let us also look there for the prophetic sense explained by Montfort concerning the last times.

1° The author of the enmities: God Himself.

N° 52

God has never made or formed *but one enmity; but it is an irreconcilable one, which shall endure and develop even to the end. It is between Mary, His worthy Mother, and the devil – between the children and the servants of the Blessed Virgin and the children and instruments of Lucifer.*

And in n° 54, he adds:

God has not only set an enmity but enmities, *not simply between Mary and the devil, but* between the race of the holy Virgin and the race of the devil; *that is to say, God has set enmities, antipathies, and secret hatreds between the true children and the servants of Mary and the children and servants of the devil.*

The Latin text says "inimicitias *ponam*," I shall put, I shall found, I shall establish enmities. This "expresses the solidity of the divine work... So, then, having been placed by God, this enmity, or better these enmities, are so firm that they are unyielding and absolute." And consequently they are eternal. They will even keep increasing till the end.

Father de Montfort translates the two verbs: "God has never *made or formed* but one enmity"... "He did not simply allow it as He allows evil: He *made it Himself*. This is His work; and just as at the beginning of creation, He separated the light from the darkness, – "Divisit lumen a tenebris" – so He decreed between Mary and the serpent, as well as between their races." – "This work, like all those of God, reflects His perfections. He gave it a *form*, such as He wanted it in His Wisdom: this enmity will be essentially total, inflexible, and absolute."

2° The adversaries involved: Mary and Satan.

The most terrible of all the enemies which God has set up against the devil is His holy Mother Mary.

First of all, as for the *duration* of His enmity.

He has inspired her, even since the days of the earthly Paradise, though she existed then only in His idea, with so much hatred against that cursed enemy of God…

Before existing, Mary is the enemy of Satan, because the latter was afraid of her as soon as she was announced. And, by her privilege of the Immaculate Conception, never, not even a single moment, will she spend in the power of her adversary.

Then, as for the *vigilance* of this enmity. It will never be found lacking, neither for what concerns Mary personally, nor for what concerns her service with souls:

He has given her… so much industry in unveiling the malice of that old serpent…

Finally, as for the efficacy of this enmity:

He has given her… so much power 1° **to conquer**, 2° **to overthrow** *and* 3° **to crush** *that proud impious rebel,* that he fears her more, *not only than all Angels and men, but in some sense more* than God Himself.

The victory could not be more complete.

More terrible to the devil, *in a sense*, than God Himself!... These words demand an explanation.

It is not that the anger, the hatred, and the power of God are not infinitely greater than those of the Blessed Virgin, for the perfections of Mary are limited,

and those of God are not. Besides, as the Hebrew text explains very well, the victory of Mary herself is attributed to her divine Son. The Virgin is only the instrumental cause of it. And God resorts to this intermediary for two reasons:

a) *For a psychological reason:*

First, *because Satan, being proud, suffers infinitely more from being beaten and punished by a little and humble handmaid of God, and her humility humbles him more than the divine power.*

Goliath was more humbled to be overcome by David, and in the circumstances that are known, than if he had been able to confront, in a single combat, an opponent of his size, or of superior strength. Also, Satan would be more proud to face Our Lord, in this final struggle, even if it meant being brought down by Him. He will meet only Mary, Queen of the predestined, Mary, *"the little and humble handmaid of God,"* acting in the name of her Master, by his authority and by his strength. And, in the end, all the glory of the triumph will redound to God alone, and the whole humiliation of the defeat will be even more cutting for Satan. This height of humiliation is very well expressed by the words "*overcome and* **punished**," like a great man who sees himself treated like a little boy, is even more punished than humbled.

b) *For a reason of experience:*

Secondly, *because God has given Mary such a great power against the devils, that, as they have often been obliged to confess, in spite of themselves, by the mouths of the possessed* (see n° 42, 2°), *they fear one of her sighs for a soul more than the prayers of all the Saints, and one of her menaces against them more than all other torments.* (See above n° 42, 5°.)

N° 53

3° **The foundation of the enmities: the** *recircumlatio.*

This is shown by a double antithesis:

a) *Between Lucifer and Mary:*

What Lucifer has lost by pride, Mary has gained by humility.

Loss and gain, both personal: each was treated according to his merit.

b) *Between Eve and Mary:*

What Eve has damned and lost by disobedience, Mary has saved by obedience.

Infinite consequence and unlimited repercussion of the acts of each of the two on her respective descendants! But to these same children, whom Eve infected with death, Mary restores life. The sentence which expresses this truth could be signed by illustrious names of antiquity: St. Justin, St. Irenaeus, Tertullian, St. Ephrem, St. Cyril of Jerusalem, St. Augustine, etc...:

Eve, in obeying the serpent, has destroyed all her children together with herself, and has delivered them to him; Mary being perfectly faithful to God, has saved all her children and servants together with herself, and has consecrated them to His Majesty.

This is the slavery by right of conquest. Satan, by his victory over Eve, seized her and her children and subjects them, one way or another, to his cruel slavery. The obedience of Mary has the power to repair all the disasters caused by the disobedience of Eve. The merits, however, of her Son will be applied efficaciously only to the predestined, "*her children and servants*," and these last alone freely acknowledge their slavery of love towards their divine Conqueror.

4° The extension of the enmities: the race of Mary and the race of Satan.

Here especially it was necessary to put "enmities" and not simply only one. "An enmity can weaken or disappear, it can contain exceptions: all of which would be improbable, if it is a matter of a bundle of enmities more difficult to break, as it is a triple link: 'A threefold cord is not easily broken' (Eccles. 4:12). This bundle is composed of successive manifestations of enmity in time or multiplied by their diverse applications: antagonism in ideas, intentions and feelings; antagonism in love or hatred, in purpose as well as in means, in joys and sadness; antagonism, finally, in the life of individuals as well as in that of societies." These words of Rev. Fr. Lhoumeau seem to us the best commentary on those of Father de Montfort contained in n° 54:

N° 54

God has set enmities, antipathies, and secret hatreds between the true children and the servants of Mary and the children and servants of the devil. They do not love each other mutually. They have no inward correspondence with each other. The children of Belial, the slaves of Satan, the friends of the world (for it is the same thing), have always up to this time persecuted those who belong to our Blessed Lady, and will in future persecute them more than ever; just as of old Cain persecuted his brother Abel, and Esau his brother Jacob, who are the figures of the reprobate and the predestinate.

Let us also note, to complete the commentary, the **twin formulas**, repeated several times in these numbers: "*children and servants*" of Mary, "*children and slaves of Mary*" on one hand, and on the other "*children and servants of the devil,*" "*children and slaves of the devil,*" and even the triple formula repeating the same thing: "*children of Belial, slaves of Satan and friends of the world.*" Just as Mary is "*Mother and Mistress*" of the predestined, Mistress or Queen because she is Mother, and by virtue of her Maternity, in the same way the predestined are children of Mary and, because they are children, her faithful servants and her slaves of love. The maternity of Mary and the filiation of the elect are indeed real, although supernatural and spiritual. Mary truly transmits the life of grace to the elect. The filiation of the reprobates in regard to Satan is, on the contrary, a metaphoric filiation only. They imitate the devil. They act like him. They are inspired by his spirit. This is what puts them totally in his power. Hence the equation between "*children,*" "*slaves*" and "*friends.*" The equation between "*Belial,*" "*Satan*" and "*the world*" is not less evident. Belial is, indeed, this perverse spirit which does evil for the love of evil, without deriving any personal advantage from it. Satan is the systematic adversary of everything which is God and the work of God. And the world is the group of those who allow themselves to be led by this double spirit and profess principles absolutely opposed to those of the Gospel, for the sole pleasure of ruining souls. To have the spirit of Belial, the spirit of Satan or the spirit of the world, is, then, exactly same thing.

5° **The fight and the result of the fight.**

a) *Throughout the ages.*

The reprobate will persecute the predestined, as Cain persecuted Abel, and Esau, Jacob. The detail of these persecutions is given in n° 190. We too shall return to it later. The result is described here:

But the humble Mary will always have the victory over that proud spirit (Lucifer)*, and* (this victory will be) *so great* (so complete) *that she will go the length of crushing his head, where his pride dwells.* (By her watchful enmity) *she will always discover the malice of the serpent* (cunning and deceptive as in the earthly Paradise). *She will always counterwork his infernal mines and dissipate his diabolical counsels, and will guarantee even to the end of time her faithful servants from his cruel claw.*

Between the two races, as between the Woman and the serpent, the enmity will be unyielding. If Satan is the roaming lion seeking whom he may devour, the cruel beast which, with a strike of the claw tears his victim, the serpent with unequaled ruses which insinuates itself to slip in its poison; if he inspires his feelings in all those whom he animates, Mary is capable of standing up to all these conspired efforts, and of maintaining in her children the integrity of the faith and morals.

b) *At the end of the world:*

Satan will lay his snares against her heel, that is to say, her humble slaves and her poor children, whom she will raise up to make war against him,

against these great saints about whom we spoke.

Montfort shows the **striking contrast** between what they will be *before the world* and what they will be before God.

They shall be little and poor in the world's esteem, and abased before all, like the heel, trodden underfoot and persecuted as the heel is by the other members of the body.

Everybody will despise them and yet everybody will persecute them.

But in return for this, they shall be rich in the grace of God, which Mary shall distribute to them abundantly. They shall be great and exalted before God in sanctity, superior to all other creatures by their animated zeal.

Persecution will not only highlight more their virtue and their holiness. It will also allow them to plunge into the fray to defend their brothers. Thanks to them, "*the power of Mary over all the devils will especially break out*" then.

They will lean so strongly on the divine succor, that, with the humility of their heel, in union with Mary, they shall crush the head of the devil, and cause Jesus Christ to triumph.

In short, the demon will not appear personally. He will be content with sending henchmen and particularly the Antichrist, by means of whom he will unleash the supreme fight. Thus, Mary will act and triumph only by the Saints that she will raise up. The faith will, then, play a big role, then as now. And this explains the error of those who will enlist under the banner of the Antichrist and the hesitations of those who will not surrender at one blow to the appeal of the apostles of Mary! And nevertheless, what danger will the latter not escape?...

*
* *

§ III. – THE APOSTLES OF THE LAST TIMES

(55-59)

Number 55 describes their preparation.

Numbers 56, 57, 58, and 59 show the efficacy of their apostolate under various images.

1° THEIR PREPARATION

N° 55

The Saint again asserts what, by the very will of God, must be the foundation of all spiritual renewal, ending in the heroic holiness of the last times:

In a word, God wishes (and this reason surpasses all the others) *that His holy Mother should be* at present *more known, more loved, more honoured, than she has ever been.*

What might seem to concern only the time of the Saint: "at present," is true of every century, and with an increasing intensity. According to n[os] 58 and 59, these words apply mainly to these Marian souls who will live at the end of the world and be the apostles of the last times. But this result must begin from the time of the Saint and because of its Marian influence. The expression "at present" thus amounts to this: "From now on."

Montfort proposes the *means* which must normally lead to this result:

This, no doubt, will take place, if the predestinate enter, with the grace and light of the Holy Ghost, into the interior and perfect practice which I will disclose to them shortly.

Let us not see in the words "no doubt" a doubtful formula; it is, on the contrary, the exclusion of any possible doubt, the expression of an absolute truth: "this will happen without *any* doubt, certainly." It is the meaning which they had in the 17th century.

But for this a common devotion is not enough. A devotion in its *most perfect realization* is needed, including not only the consecration to Mary, but the Marian life, especially by the *interior practices* of the Holy Slavery. There is in it such a means of holiness, that, without a special grace of the Holy Ghost calling to this devotion, and without a special light of the Holy Ghost helping to understand it, the predestined themselves would not have recourse to this means.

And Montfort sings enthusiastically of the **effects** which this true devotion will produce in souls themselves:

First of all, as for the *infallible execution of the decree of their predestination*:

Then they (the predestined) *will see clearly, as far as faith allows, that beautiful Star of the Sea. They will arrive happily in harbour, following its guidance, in spite of the tempests and the pirates.*

Might we not think that we are listening to *St. Bernard* (Hom. II, on *Missus est*): "O you, whoever you are, who understands that, in the course of this mortal life, you navigate more on a stormy sea than you walk on dry land, never avert your eyes from this star, if you do not want to be shipwrecked. If the wind of temptations rises, if you fall against the stumbling blocks of adversities, look at the star, call upon Mary... If you follow her, you will not get lost; if you pray to her, you will not be discouraged... If she supports you, you will not fall; if she is favorable to you, you will reach the port."

Then as for the *theoretical knowledge and practice* of the grandeurs of Mary:

They will know the grandeurs of that Queen, and will consecrate themselves entirely to her service, as subjects and slaves of love.

We shall see, indeed, further on that the holy slavery is the best way of recognizing the sovereign dominion of Mary over the soul of the predestined, and, for Mary, the best way of entirely taking possession of her favorite kingdom, the heart of the predestined. It is the living title of Mary Queen of Hearts.

In the third place, as for *the experience that they will have of the goodness of Mary*:

They will experience her sweetnesses and her maternal goodnesses, and they will love her tenderly like well-beloved children.

Mary, Queen by virtue of her Maternity, lovingly exercising the responsibilities of her Maternity. The predestined slaves of Mary, because they are her children, submit themselves to their Queen with the same impetus and the same spontaneity as a child obeys his mother.

Fourthly as for the *frequent and confident recourse that they will have to her mercy*:

They will know the mercies of which she is full, and the need they have of her succour; and they will have recourse to her in all things, as to their dear advocate and mediatrix with Jesus Christ.

Mary, Queen of mercy, charged by her Son with the dispensation of mercy, will inspire in her children the most complete confidence in her merciful intervention. We cannot give any greater pleasure to somebody than to offer him the frequent occasion of exercising his office.

Finally, as for *being persuaded more and more that Mary leads to Jesus* all those who abandon themselves to her:

They will know what is the most sure, the most easy, the most short, and the most perfect means by which to go to Jesus Christ; and they will deliver themselves to Mary, body and soul, without reserve, that they may thus be all for Jesus Christ.

We have a rapid summary of everything which concerns the perfect devotion: its nature, its motives, its effects, and its practices.

2° THE EFFICACY OF THEIR APOSTOLATE
(56-59)

N° 56

Montfort asks a question, and he will give to it in rapid succession a large number of precise, ardent, biblical answers, each one beginning with "they will be":

But who shall be those servants, slaves, and children of Mary?

The description of the apostles of the last times will be provided by the enumeration of their qualities. As it concerns a prophecy, we could not expect a more precise identification.

The answer to the question which has just been posed thus describes under various figures the qualities and the zeal of these great servants of Mary, as well as the results obtained by their efforts.

1° They will be like this **burning fire** which, according to the prophet Malachy, will be ignited before the day of wrath by the messenger of Yahweh and will purify, first of all, the sons of Levi, so that their oblation may be henceforth pleasing to God. But it is obvious that they, once purified, will work to purify others, and that, to begin with them is to assure at the first try this campaign of striking conversions that will signal the end of time.

They shall be a burning fire of the ministers of the Lord, who shall kindle the fire of divine love everywhere.

The manuscript reads: *They shall be a burning fire: ministers of the Lord who shall kindle the fire of divine love everywhere.* According to this variant, the apostles of the last times would be themselves ministers of the Lord, who would ignite in souls the fire of divine love.

2° They will be like so many "**sharp arrows**" in the hands of the powerful Mary to pierce her enemies: "*Sicut sagittae in manu potentis*" (Ps. 126:3). It is by them that Mary will triumph over all the adversaries of the faith, over all the propagators of corruption, about whom it was previously spoken.

3° They will themselves be like these **sons of Levi**, who were discussed in 1°, not only purified by the fire of tribulations, but purified *well* by the fire of *great* tribulations, "such as hath not been from the beginning of the world until now, neither shall be" (Mt. 24:21) until that day. This purification constitutes only the negative element of holiness: ἅγιος detached from earth. The positive element: *sanctus*, united with God by a stable pact, will not be lacking either. They will even be, as Montfort energetically says, "*closely adhering to God.*" Thus prepared, they "*shall carry* the love of God *in their heart*, the incense of prayer *in their spirit*, and the myrrh of mortification *in their body.*" Zeal, interior life, mortification, such are indeed, indeed, the indispensable qualities of every true apostle. Thus, they "*shall be everywhere the good odour of Jesus Christ* to the poor (that is to say, to those who have the spirit of poverty) *and to the little* (that is to say, to the humble of heart), *while they shall be an odour of death to the great, and to the proud worldlings*" (this last word explaining all the others).

N° 57

4° They will be as "**clouds thundering and flying**" allowing themselves to be guided through the air, "*at the least breath of the Holy Ghost.*" Montfort is fond of this image in order to indicate the perfect docility of the apostles of the last times to the action of the Holy Ghost. He returns to it in his *Prayer for Missionaries* to ask for missionaries for his Company of Mary, and, on this occasion, he draws a rule of life for them, which of itself is capable of forming them according to the ideal described here. "What do I ask for you?... *Liberos*, clouds raised high from the earth and full of heavenly dew (see 3°), who, unhindered, fly on all sides, according to the inspiration of the Holy Ghost. They are those of whom your prophets had knowledge in part, when they asked: "Who are these that fly as clouds, and as doves to their windows (Is. 60:8)? Whither the impulse of the spirit was to go, thither they went" (Ez. 1:12). These apostles, then, will become attached to nothing which could hold them back, will be astonished at nothing in the service which will be reserved for them, will not be troubled at all to know how they will be treated, imitating in this the docility and lack of concern of the cloud. Like it, too, they "*will spread*" over souls

the rain of the Word of God and of life eternal. They shall thunder against sin; they shall storm against the world; they shall strike the devil and his crew; and they shall strike further and further, for life or for death, with their two-edged sword of the Word of God, all those to whom they shall be sent on the part of the Most High.

A *supplementary image* which fits very well here, because the great instrument of battle and victory which will be at their disposal, the one which will lead to the salvation of souls of goodwill, and will cause the fatal hardening of others, will be the *Word of God*. This Word will strike souls, like St. Paul on the road to Damascus, by the crash of its echo and the suddenness of its light, and it will force them to reflect. But regrettably, all will not believe in it!

N° 58

5° They will be **true apostles**, reproducing the model drawn for a long time by the Holy Ghost "who is explained in very obscure and secret, but completely divine words": *The Lord of power* (that is to say, of miracles) *will grant them the gift of the word and the strength to work wonders and to carry away glorious spoils from His enemies.* Having fallen in love with the apostolic ideal, *"they shall sleep without gold or silver, and, what is more, without care,"* that is to say, without any concern, in the most complete abandonment to divine Providence, and this *"in the middle of the other priests, ecclesiastics, and clerks,"* who will perhaps have not the same detachment. And yet, *"they shall have the silvered wings of the dove."* They will distribute enormous riches in order to do good. And they will go *"with the pure intention of the glory of God and the salvation of souls, wheresoever the Holy Ghost shall call them. Neither shall they leave behind them, in the places where they have preached, anything but the gold of charity, which is the accomplishment of the whole law."*

In this whole passage, Montfort comments on verses 12-14 of Psalm 67, which predict that the apostles will have, jointly, the gift of miracles and disinterestedness. And he makes the *complete* application of them to the apostles of the last times, as, in his Prayer for Missionaries, he *partially* means the Fathers of the Company of Mary. All commentators admit with Father de Montfort that the meaning of these verses is very obscure. And we must be grateful to him for having given us a plausible explanation.

N° 59

6° Finally, they will be **true disciples of Jesus Christ**. *Personally*, they will walk in the footsteps of His poverty, humility, contempt of the world and charity. In their *ministry*, they will teach, like Jesus, that the way to heaven is a narrow way, and they will be inspired by the simple truth, the one which is conformed to the holy Gospel, even if it is against the maxims of the world. They will not worry at all about the judgments which will be brought upon them. They will show no favoritism, speaking to each with complete apostolic frankness, without sparing, listening to or being afraid of any mortal, however powerful he may be. It is such a common defect not to dare to speak the truth to the great, and not to be afraid of overwhelming the young. The apostles of the last times will avoid this defect, as well as the opposite defect besides, which consists of charging the great with all the sins of the people...

To succeed in this delicate mission, they will be armed from head to foot:

They shall have in their mouths *the two-edged sword of the Word of God. They shall carry* on their shoulders *the bloody standard of the Cross, the crucifix* in their right hand *and the Rosary* in their left, *the sacred names of Jesus and Mary* in their hearts, *and the modesty and mortification of Jesus Christ* in their own behaviour.

St. Paul would say: in their whole body.

Such will be the apostles that the Saint sees advancing in the future, "*like so many new Davids, the staff of the Cross and the sling of the Rosary in their hands*, in baculo cruce et in virga virgine, *and Mary shall be there by the order of the Most High, to extend His empire over that of the impious, the idolaters, and the Mahometans.*" "Doubtless," says Rev. Fr. Lhoumeau, "he knew that these future apostles would appear like isolated and temporary meteors. They belong to a lineage, to the race of the Woman that he saw in history continuing from the beginning. Closer to him, the figure of St. Dominic was familiar to him, as well as that of St. Vincent Ferrer. And it is to assert his connection and communion of thought with them that he wanted to be affiliated with the

Dominican family through the Third Order. What he saw in these great servants of Mary, his predecessors, he shows in those who will succeed him, but with a kind of intensification and perfection, with a focus conformed to the last times, when everything will be taken to the extreme and will end."

But as for the **time** and the **manner** in which all this will come to pass, Montfort puts a big question mark. *God alone knows. It is for us to hold our tongues, to pray, to sigh, and to wait: exspectans, exspectavi.*" He sees the final result, and predicts it. He knows that these apostles will be formed by other apostles, and he draws the rules which, normally, must lead to this end (n° 55). But that is the limit of his knowledge. God reserved for Himself impenetrably the knowledge of this date, "but of that day and hour no one knoweth, no not the angels of heaven, but the Father alone" (Mt. 24:36). Now, the date of it could more or less be foreseen if the precise chain of the circumstances which will give the impetus to the great events of the end of the world was known. It is, therefore, not surprising that Montfort admits not knowing them. The opposite would be more surprising and… inadmissible.

CHAPTER II

THE NATURE OF THE TRUE DEVOTION
(60-119)

N° 60

The Saint himself manifests, in n° 60, the connection and the sequence of his ideas:

Having said something so far of the necessity which we have of the devotion to the most holy Virgin.

Here is assured the connection with what precedes and constituted our entire first chapter.

I must now show in what this devotion consists.

Here is the purpose of this second chapter. We have entitled it *nature of the true devotion*. The nature of a thing is, indeed, that in which it consists, what constitutes it.

Montfort wants to tell us the nature of the **true** *devotion*. For this purpose, he will apply himself to determining what can belong equally (although the other way around) to two very different categories: false devotion and true devotion. Then he will insist on the elements which characterize each of the two categories, by showing that *false* devotion spoils all the general principles which it claims to apply, whereas *true* devotion preserves them entirely.

He begins, then, by establishing five **fundamental truths** which must be found in any devotion to Mary (n°s 61-89).

Then, approaching the essential differences, it will be easy for him to prove that some so-called devotees of Mary exaggerate these fundamental principles or understand them incorrectly and make a bad application of them. For example:

Jesus Christ is our only Master, but this does not mean that we dishonor Him by honoring Mary, as the scrupulous devotees fear. We need a mediator with the Mediator Himself, and this mediator, or better this mediatrix is Mary, an all-powerful mediatrix who is always heard by her Son. But the aid which she assures us does not excuse the exaggerated confidence of the presumptuous devotees: that the protection of Mary would allow them to offend Jesus without having to be afraid of anything for their salvation. Those, then, have a false devotion to Mary, in spite of the principles which they invoke.

It is important to know what are the **essential marks** of each of the two contrasting devotions so that we can choose in complete safety (n°s 90-114).

To complete the chapter on the nature of the true devotion, it is enough to relate the **various forms** which it can take, and the various practices which it contains (n°s 115-119).

Let us return to the text of n° 60. We shall see whether it does not contain in germ all these divisions:

I must now show in what this devotion consists. This I will do, by God's help, after I shall have first presupposed some fundamental truths which shall throw light on that grand and solid devotion which I desire to disclose.

These last words refer to the devotion of the holy slavery, which is the most perfect among all forms of true devotion. Montfort has the sole purpose to teach it, even in writing this first part.

Here is the plan of this second chapter:

Article I: **The fundamental truths of any devotion to Mary** (61-89).

Article II: **Essential marks**:

1° Of *false* devotion to Mary (90-104).
2° Of *true* devotion to Mary (105-114).

Article III: **Various practical forms of the true devotion** (115-119).

ARTICLE I

Fundamental truths

(61-89)

Overview:

Father de Montfort, following Bérulle and the whole French School, regards devotion to the Most Blessed Virgin as something infinitely serious, something whose roots sink into the depths of dogma, and in particular into the ineffable mystery of the Incarnation. Mary is honored because of the admirable union which she contracted with her divine Son by her Maternity. And the honor which is rendered to her has no other purpose than to honor Jesus Himself better (1st *truth*).

All creatures are in a relation of servitude to the Incarnate Word. Consequently, they will be in the same relation to His Mother (2nd *truth*).

But this taking possession of us by Mary by no means tends to cover our poverty and to let it develop without any danger for us. Mary helps us to empty ourselves from the extreme corruption which we drag around in ourselves (3rd *truth*).

This original weakness is the cause nevertheless of multiple faults, at least of frailty. We are unworthy to appear before our Divine Savior, Who is purity itself. That is why we have recourse to Mary's intercession (4th *truth*).

Finally, the same weakness makes us incapable by ourselves of preserving our spiritual treasures. We entrust them to Mary so that she may guard and defend them (*5th truth*).

Montfort no longer shows himself dependent on his century anywhere in his *Treatise*. He fights the oppositions which showed themselves in his time with regard to Marian devotion. He develops the principles which are dear to the great masters of the time. Before hastening to fly with his own wings, in the second part, by teaching the form of devotion which pleases him most, he is anxious to show here that this devotion itself, being after all only the most perfect form of true devotion to Mary, rests like it, on the indisputable principles of the School.

Let us see precisely how this is so in all its details.

I. – First Truth

Jesus Christ is the last end of Devotion to the Most Blessed Virgin
(61-67)

N° 61

The Saint begins by expressing a **general principle** that he will then prove with an eloquent conviction:

Jesus Christ our Savior, true God and true Man, ought to be the last end of all our other devotions, else they are false and delusive.

By *natural* right, as Incarnate Word, by right of *conquest*, as our Savior, He concentrates on Himself all the tributes which we can and must offer to God. It is allowed to honor the Saints only to praise God for the marvels of grace which He worked in them, and to ask them to present our praises to God, to intercede for us with His divine Majesty. It is an absolutely general rule; no devotion not having Jesus Himself as the object, can make an exception to it.

§ I. – GENERAL PRINCIPLE

Jesus "ought to be the last end of all our devotions." This is proved over the course of two pages of an overflowing lyricism, written, we see, in a single breath and citing the most beautiful texts and the most beautiful comparisons found in Holy Scripture.

a) "*Jesus Christ*, the first and final cause of our salvation, *is the alpha and the omega, the beginning and the end of all things*," as it says in the Apocalypse. It is through Him, as Word, that everything was created; it is through Him, as Incarnate Word, that everything was recreated; it is through Him also that everything must return to its principle.

b) *Jesus Christ*, the exemplary cause of our salvation, *is the supreme Model*, Who not only must be reproduced by souls, but must live again in them: as the Apostle says, "*we only labor that we may present every man perfect in Jesus Christ* (cf. Col. 1:28), *for in Him dwelleth all the fullness of the Godhead corporally* (cf. Col. 2:9) *and of every other fullness of graces* (cf. Jn. 1:14), *virtues and perfections.*"

c) *Jesus Christ*, the meritorious cause of our salvation, *is the only one in Whom we have been blessed* "*with all spiritual benediction*," according to the promise which had formerly been made to Abraham.

d) *Jesus Christ*, the efficient cause of our salvation, is from every point of view *the only One Who has the authority to guide us*. This is proved in a magnificent outpouring, where the diverse titles of the Savior are enumerated with what logically and immediately follows from them to rule our relations with Him. "*He is our only* **Master**, *Who has to teach us* (submission of the intellect), *our only* **Lord**, *on Whom we* *ought to depend* (submission of the will), *our only* **Head**, *to Whom we must belong* (by sanctifying grace), *our only* **Model**, *to Whom we should conform ourselves* (by the practice of the virtues), *our only* **Physician**, *Who can heal us* (of our daily faults of mere frailty), *our only* **Shepherd**, *Who can feed us* (to repair, maintain and develop our life), *our only* **Way**, *Who can lead us* (to our last end), *our only* **Truth**, *Whom we must believe* (He not only teaches, but is Himself the truth which He teaches and towards Whom our intellect aspires; this Truth, however, is manifested to us, here on earth, only in the obscurity of Faith), *our only* **Life**, *Who can animate us* (in the whole supernatural blossoming of our personality) and (summarizing everything) *our only* **All** *in all things, Who can suffice us.*" The scriptural allusions which we indicated in the notes are clear.

§ II. – CONSEQUENCES OF THIS PRINCIPLE

These consequences are enumerated, first of all, in a negative form, then in a positive form.

a) NEGATIVE CONSEQUENCES

Three are particular and the fourth is general, embracing several points of view at the same time. But all express the same truth under various aspects.

a) **Outside of Jesus Christ no salvation is possible**, according to the answer of St. Peter to the Sanhedrin: "*No other name under heaven was given to men, than the name of Jesus whereby we must be saved*" (cf. Acts 4:12).

b) **Outside of Jesus Christ no spiritual perfection is possible**, because, according to the remark of the Apostle, comparing the work of our perfection with the construction of a building: "*God did not lay another foundation for us for our salvation, perfection, and glory* (justification, progress, crowning) *than Jesus Christ* (cf. 1 Cor. 3:11): *any building* *which is not placed on this solid ground is established on shifting sand and will fall infallibly sooner or later.*

c) **Outside of Jesus Christ not even is life possible**, because Jesus compared Himself to a vine and us with branches: "*If any one abide not in Me, he shall be cast forth as a branch, and shall wither, and they shall gather him up, and cast him into the fire, and he burneth* " (Jn. 15:6).

d) "**Outside of Jesus Christ nothing matters**. *Everything is only a distraction* (because it leads away from the goal instead of leading to it), *a lie* (presenting itself under appearances which do not correspond with reality), *injustice* (in the sense that it leads to sin), (or at least) *uselessness* (because it is of no use for the one thing necessary), *death* (spiritual and often temporal) *and damnation* (which is the definitive break between Jesus and the soul)."

b) POSITIVE CONSEQUENCES

Some are general, others concern devotion to the Blessed Virgin in particular.

1º – GENERAL CONSEQUENCES

There are two of them:

a) *With Jesus Christ, there is nothing to fear*, neither from the point of view of salvation which is assured, nor on the part of creatures which cannot prevent it:

If we are in Jesus Christ and Jesus Christ in us, we have no condemnation to fear. Neither the angels of heaven, nor the men of earth, nor the devils of hell, nor any other creatures, can injure us; because they cannot separate us from the love of God which is in Jesus Christ.

One recognizes in this passage the magnificent challenge made to all creatures by St. Paul: "Who will separate me from the love of Christ" (cf. Rom. 8:35)?

b) *With Jesus Christ, we can do all things*, that is to say, we cannot only work on our own sanctification, but also lead others to Christian perfection, and thus worthily glorify the Holy Trinity.

Through Jesus Christ, with Jesus Christ, in Jesus Christ, we can do all things; we can render all honour and glory to the Father in the unity of the Holy Ghost; we can become perfect ourselves, and be to our neighbour a good odour of eternal life.

2° – PARTICULAR CONSEQUENCES

N° 62

They concern devotion to the Blessed Virgin.

It is there that the Saint wants to come. So, after having clearly stated his principle and having briefly drawn the general conclusions, he lingers at greater length to develop this particular conclusion. He dedicates all of n°s 62-67 to it: *a)* by determining, first of all, the *true purpose* of Marian devotion; *b)* by then showing the *close and indissoluble union* which exists between her and her Son; *c)* by *defending* this devotion against the attacks of the author of the "Avis salutaires"; *d)* and finally *by ardently praying* to Our Lord to grant him a true devotion to His most holy Mother.

a) **The true purpose of devotion to Mary**: This purpose is to establish more perfectly devotion to Jesus Christ Himself. Father de Montfort had already written his book on *The Love of Eternal Wisdom*. Jesus, eternal and incarnate Wisdom, is the unique object of it, and among all the means which he enumerates to acquire and preserve this divine wisdom, the most powerful, the most perfect, the most indispensable, is "*a tender and true devotion to the Most Blessed Virgin.*" On this occasion, we have already said, the Saint quickly sketches his whole future *Treatise on the True Devotion*. Also n°s 61 and 62 can be considered as a recapitulation of *The Love of Eternal Wisdom*. We have here, then, as in several other places of the *Treatise*, for example n°s 152, 168 and 265, an insight into the complete Montfortian spirituality: "*Ad Iesum per Mariam,* Let us go to Jesus through Mary."

The existence of this purpose is asserted here in two ways, directly and indirectly.

Direct affirmation:

If, then, we establish the solid devotion to our Blessed Lady, it is only to establish more perfectly the devotion to Jesus Christ, and to put forward an easy and secure means for finding Jesus Christ.

A brief assertion which will be repeated later and amplified during the discussion of the *perfect devotion*. And it will be said that this devotion is an easy, short, perfect and secure way of arriving at union with Our Lord.

Indirect affirmation:

If devotion to our Lady removed us from Jesus Christ, we should have to reject it as an illusion of the devil.

There is not the slightest doubt in this statement. But we have nothing to fear! That is not the case:

But on the contrary, so far from this being the case, there is nothing which makes devotion to our Lady more necessary for us, as I have already shown, and will show still further hereafter, than that it is the means of finding Jesus Christ perfectly, of loving Him tenderly, and of serving Him faithfully.

N° 63

b) **The close and indissoluble union between Jesus and Mary.**

This is the reason which makes devotion to Mary necessary in order to practice perfectly devotion to Jesus Himself. Unfortunately, most Christians, and even the most learned among Christians, do not know "*the necessary union which there is between Jesus and His holy Mother.*" And Montfort complains about it to the divine Master, as if to bid Him to realize as quickly as possible His will to make Mary known (n°s 1-13):

I here turn for one moment to Thee, O my sweet Jesus, to complain lovingly to Thy Divine Majesty that the greater part of Christians, even the most learned, do not know the necessary union which there is between Thee and Thy holy Mother.

This is the beginning of a magnificent apostrophe to Our Lord. It is difficult to express its matchless accent and passionate love.

Then he continues, showing the extent to which this union is *necessary*.

Thou, Lord, art always with Mary, and Mary is always with Thee, and she cannot be without Thee, else she would cease to be what she is.

The whole reason for her beauty, her purity, her natural and supernatural endowment, and even of her existence, is because she was predestined to be and because she was in fact the Mother of Jesus, and His assiduous collaborator in the destruction of sin and the redemption of souls. Remove all this and Mary's life can no longer be explained, much less its unfathomable mystery. Far from being an obstacle to going to Jesus, she thus has for her mission to lead souls to Him.

But, furthermore, this union is so *intimate* that it reaches the highest possible degree and becomes established in it: *transforming union.*

(Mary) is so **transformed** *into Thee by grace that she lives no more, that she is as though she were not. It is Thou only, my Jesus, Who livest and reignest in her more perfectly than in all the Angels and Blessed.*

Because Mary possesses grace, the cause of this transformation, in herself alone in more fullness than all the Angels and Saints together. By grace itself, by the infused virtues and the gifts of the Holy Ghost which necessarily accompany grace, by the privileges of the state of innocence in which Mary was constituted, her soul with all its faculties and her body with all its powers were on earth, and will be eternally in heaven, under the absolute empire of Jesus. No insubordination is to be feared. And Jesus is assured of harvesting, on this blessed land, the hundredfold of everything which He sows in it:

Ah! If we knew the glory and the love which Thou receivest in this admirable creature, we should have very different thoughts both of Thee and her from what we have now.

In particular, one should not fear displeasing Jesus by honoring Mary, His Mother.

A transforming union that has been accomplished, but is also *absolutely indissoluble.*

She (Mary) is so intimately united with Thee, that it were easier to separate the light from the sun, the heat from the fire. I say more: it were easier to separate from Thee all the Angels and the Saints than the divine Mary.

The reason is because:

Mary loves Jesus more ardently, and glorifies Him more perfectly than all other creatures put together.

Grace on earth and glory in heaven are the principles of this love and glorification. Now, both exceed everything which was granted to the other saints combined and were always confirmed in Mary, grace morally, glory physically.

N° 64

c) **Response to the attacks of the "*Avis salutaires*" against Marian devotion.**

The question of the devotion of the Jansenists to the Most Blessed Virgin was recently raised again. A study, published, first of all, in *La Vie Spirituelle* (*The Spiritual Life*), in February, March and April, 1938, then in a special book entitled *Devotion to Mary at the close of the XVIIth century*, under the signature of *Rev. Fr. Hoffer*, of the Society of Mary of Father Chaminade; on the other hand a work of *Rev. Fr. Baron, S.J.*, published by the Bulletin of the French Society of Marian studies, 1938, lead, on certain points at least, to identical conclusions.

It is generally agreed – and it is enough in order to justify Montfort's critique of them in n° 64 and in n° 93 – that the Jansenists fall too much into a critical spirit. On the pretext of removing the abuses which here and there slip into the practices of popular devotion, they run the risk of attacking the devotion itself and slowing the impetus of it.

Besides, Jansenists radically distrust the affectionate part of devotion. Even in devotion, they dread and avoid everything which looks like sensible attraction. It is not always possible, they think, to discern whether this attraction comes from the Holy Ghost or from concupiscence. To give in to it would be to expose oneself to the tragic awakening of carnal enjoyment. So, they fought, on principle, any sentimental devotion to the Virgin. It was perhaps easier for a subtle Jansenist than for a simple believer to discern where rigid piety stopped and blameworthy sentimentality began. We shall find later in the text of Father de Montfort the echoes of this exaggerated ostracism.

But it is especially against the *Avis salutaires* that Montfort protests most vehemently. This venomous book, written in a spirit of frank belittlement against devotion to Mary, was sponsored by Port-Royal, and has a good share of responsibility for its anti-Marian reputation, about which the Jansenists complained. Montfort is thus right to take it to task, imitating in this Father Crasset, from whom he borrows much.

But let us come to his text itself.

After that, my sweet Master, is it not an astonishingly pitiable thing to see the ignorance and the darkness of all men here below in regard to Thy holy Mother?

Here it is no longer about this mystery willed by God, which the Introduction showed us. God spoke rather clearly. All men, absolutely all, should have understood, so much so that the fact that they did not understand *amazes* and inspires *pity*.

But here is the worst part!

I speak not so much of idolaters and pagans, who knowing Thee not, care not to know Thee.

Some are guilty, pagans *positively*, who deliberately rejected the light of the Gospel. Others are excusable, pagans *negatively*, who do not have knowledge of the doctrine of salvation. But their ignorance of Mary is nonetheless a pitiable anomaly.

I speak not even of heretics and schismatics, who care not to be devout to Thy holy Mother, being separated as they are from Thee and Thy holy Church.

In itself, devotion to Mary is a *purely negative mark* of the true Church (see N° 30). If it is lacking in a church, this church cannot be the true church, because the latter necessarily has devotion to Mary. But if it exists, it is not by itself proof that we are in the presence of the true Church, because there are sects which preserved it. In reality, however, devotion to Mary is lacking in a large number of sects, which legitimizes the remark of our Saint. We do not see why, moreover, heretics, detaching themselves from Christ Himself, or at least from His Church (which comes to the same thing), would be anxious to preserve devotion to Mary. Does not all the glory of the Virgin and all her titles for our veneration come to her from the fact that she is Mother of Christ?...

But I speak of Catholic Christians, and even of doctors amongst Catholics, who make profession of teaching truths to others, and yet know not Thee nor Thy holy Mother, except in a speculative dry, barren, and indifferent manner.

Here is indeed the disembodied, pale and narrow devotion, wanted by the puritan Jansenists. Just as they did not know the merciful and condescending side in the Savior, so too they scarcely point out the spiritual maternity of Mary towards us. This would lead too much to (exaggerated) confidence and (sensible) love.

This first criticism is thus very just.
Also, the second.

These doctors speak but rarely of Thy holy Mother, and of the devotion which we ought to have to her, because they fear, so they say, lest we should abuse it, and should do some injury to Thee in too much honouring Thy holy Mother.

Generally speaking, the abuses which they condemn are condemned by the Church every time they truly exist. But, is this a sufficient reason to suppress the thing which is abused? What would remain, both in a religious order and in all other orders, if everything which can lend itself to reprehensible abuses was suppressed?

Let us listen to the counsels of moderation that the abbot of Saint-Cyran sent to the gentle and loving Sister Marie-Claire Arnaud, whose devotion for the Virgin he found too sentimental. They singularly confirm what Montfort says in this whole passage:

"Moderation is necessary everywhere... It is only God alone Whom we can and must love immeasurably... The Virgin is raised above all the saints and all creatures and so close to God that it is easy to be mistaken in our movements and words when we have some zeal for her, and even for God, being possible to transport the same affections that we have for God, which are immeasurable, to the Virgin, who does not approve them, considering herself nothingn even in heaven in God's sight. That is why you do not praise her in praising her thus, you do not love Him in loving her, if you do not set limits to your love, since there is only the love of God, which one offers to God, that should be immeasurable."

Read Montfort now. He recalls, first of all, what their objections are:

1° *Too much importance is granted to Mary:*

If they hear or see anyone devout to our Blessed Lady, speaking often of his devotion to that good Mother in a tender, strong, and persuasive way, as of a secure means without delusion, as of a short road without danger, as of an immaculate way without imperfection, and as of a wonderful secret for finding and loving Thee perfectly, they cry out against him, and give him a thousand false reasons by way of proving to him that he ought not to talk so much of our

Blessed Lady, that there are great abuses in that devotion, and that we must direct our energies to destroy these abuses, and to speak of Thee, rather than to incline the people to devotion to our Blessed Lady, whom they already love sufficiently.

"The war on the abuses is truly declared."

Let us see what these abuses are.

We hear them sometimes speak of devotion to Thy holy Mother, not for the purpose of establishing it and persuading men to it, but to destroy the abuses which are made of it, while all the time these teachers are without piety or tender devotion towards Thyself, simply because they have none for Mary. They regard the Rosary, the Scapular, and the Chaplet as devotions proper for weak and ignorant minds, and without which men can save themselves.

The *fourth salutary opinion* said:

"The formulas and little prayers which he will have recited, the signs and instruments of piety which he will have worn, the confraternities or associations to which he will have given his name, will be of no use to the sinner."

And the *fifth*, after having denied that we are the slaves of Mary, adds:

"If, then, you are not my slaves, why continue to show it, by using these titles and signs of servitude. The world is delighted at empty marks of submission proper to people of court, I am not delighted at it."

The signs of servitude here can only be the Rosary, the Scapular and perhaps the little chains; and the vain and worldly submissions (such as we meet at court), are none other than the custom of greeting the images and statues of

Mary and bowing before them. A very grave abuse obviously which it is necessary to extirpate as quickly as possible.

That is why 2° *let us reject these ridiculous practices:*

If there falls into their hands any poor client of our Lady who says his Rosary, or has any other practice of devotion towards her, they soon change his spirit and his heart. Instead of the Rosary, they counsel him the seven Penitential Psalms. Instead of devotion to the holy Virgin, they counsel him devotion to Jesus Christ.

The warning given to indiscreet devotees is known: "Do not grant me more time and do not address more prayers to me than to God." We see rightly in these words the condemnation of the custom spread among Christians of reciting the Rosary, the litanies of the Blessed Virgin, the Little Office and other Marian prayers. And the instructor adds: "Reserve all your love and all your prayers for God." Father de Montfort is only specifying the practice more specially counseled in place of the condemned practices: the recitation of the 7 Penitential Psalms.

In a letter on justification written to Innocent XI by Choiseul, bishop of Tournai, we read these passages: "Those who are called Jansenists recommend devotees to enroll themselves in confraternities; but to silence the calumnies of the Protestants, they condemn the superstitions of *old women* (the Saint says weaklings, it is the same meaning). They declare that the wearing of a consecrated habit (scapular) honors the Virgin, but they do not attach the assurance of salvation to the habit itself, if the one who wears it does not keep God's commandments." Father de Montfort condemns the *presumptuous devotees* no less energetically in N° 97. What remains consequently of all these suspicions of abuse constantly recalled? A mistrust voluntarily or involuntarily maintained towards the true Devotion itself. Nothing more.

So, in an indignant answer, Montfort is right to ask:

O my sweet Jesus, have these people got Thy spirit? Do they please Thee in acting thus? Is it to please Thee, to spare one single effort to please Thy holy Mother for fear of thereby displeasing Thee? Does devotion to Thy holy Mother hinder devotion to Thyself? Is it that she attributes to herself the honour which we pay her? Is it that she makes a side for herself apart? Is it that she is an alien, who has no union with Thee? Does it displease Thee that we should try to please her? Is it to separate or to alienate ourselves from Thy love to give ourselves to her and to love her?

We feel in these words the emotion of the defender of the true Marian devotion against those who persist in confusing it with its counterfeits, or at least who would like to suppress the one so as more radically to prevent the others.

N° 65

All the questions asked here obviously call for a 'no' answer, right down the line.

Yet, my sweet Master, the greater part of the learned could not shrink more from devotion to Thy holy Mother, and could not show more indifference to it, if all that I have just said were true!

d) Ardent prayer to Our Lord to obtain from Him a true devotion to the Most Blessed Virgin.

First of all, in the *negative* sense:

Keep me, Lord – keep me from their sentiments and their practices.

Then in the *positive* sense:

And give me some share in the sentiments of **gratitude** (for benefits received), **esteem** (for the true dignity of Mary),

respect (due to parents whatever they are), *and* **love** (so natural for the child toward his mother) *which* **THOU** *hast* (You Yourself) *in regard to Thy holy Mother.*

In truth, can anyone do better than to address Jesus Himself to obtain from Him, not just any devotion to Mary, but a part of His own devotion towards His beloved Mother? That one at least must be above suspicion. Now (n°s 18 and 27), Jesus showed on earth and preserves now in heaven the sentiments of filial piety that a son must always show to his Mother, provided that he be a free man. It is those same which are enumerated here. Besides, the perfect devotee imitates as exactly as possible the devotion of Jesus towards His Mother (see n° 139).

Far from displeasing Jesus, this prayer aims only at obtaining from Him what will allow us to honor Him more perfectly:

In order that I may love Thee and glorify Thee all the more by imitating and following Thee more closely.

The imitation of someone is, indeed, the best way to show him how much he is esteemed.

To be himself truly devout to Mary, but also to inspire in souls this true devotion, is the purpose which Montfort pursues. So, after praying to obtain the true devotion, he prays to obtain the gift of speaking worthily about it.

N° 66

So, as if up to this point I had still said nothing in honour of Thy holy Mother, give me now the grace to praise her worthily: Fac me digne Tuam Matrem collaudare, *in spite of all her enemies, who are Thine as well.*

To these same enemies who are opposed to Marian veneration, he wishes to say loudly "*with the saints*":

Non praesumat aliquis Deum se habere propitium, qui benedictam Matrem offensam habuerit. *"Let not that man presume to look for the mercy of God who offends His holy Mother."*

N° 67

And 1° to obtain of Thy mercy a true devotion to Thy holy Mother, and 2° to inspire it to the whole earth, make me to love Thee ardently.

From the knowledge and love of Jesus, the Word incarnate, will spontaneously spring the knowledge of the grandeurs of Mary and devotion to this good Mother, as the Berullian school teaches.

And for that end receive the burning prayer which I make to Thee with St. Augustine and Thy true friends.

This term of "burning prayer" that the Saint applies here to the prayer of St. Augustine, his children apply to the prayer which he himself composed to ask God for missionaries.

The first part of this prayer is drawn from the book of *Meditations*, falsely attributed to St. Augustine. The second part seems rather to have affinities with the book of the *Confessions*.

In this prayer, all ardent with the love of Jesus, St. Augustine begins by giving to Our Lord the most beautiful titles which recommend Him to our love. Then he reproaches himself for having been insensible to His charms for so long a time. Finally, he gives free rein to his desires so that they turn solely to Jesus. By quoting him, Montfort proves definitively that it is "**the love of Jesus which we seek by the divine Mary.**"

II. – Second Truth

We belong to Jesus Christ and to Mary in the capacity of slaves
(68-77)

Jesus Christ is the first principle and last end of all things. All creatures, which are the work of His hands and which He made for His own glory, are subjected to His dominion and have contracted, due to their origin and their destination, very strict obligations towards Him.

The present article brings to light the true nature of these obligations.

By Baptism, we became *slaves of Jesus Christ* (n° 68).

Numbers 69-71 define the difference which separates the simple *servant from the slave*, as well as the various *sorts of slavery*. Numbers 72-77 prove that we have to be the *slaves of love of Our Lord and His holy Mother*: of the one by nature and by conquest, of the other by grace and as a result of the divine will associating Mary with the work of our Redemption.

*
* *

§ I. – SLAVES OF JESUS CHRIST
(68)

N° 68

We must conclude, from what Jesus Christ is with regard to us, that we do not belong to ourselves, but, as the Apostle says, are entirely His, as His **members** *and His* **slaves***, whom He has bought at an infinitely dear price – the price of all His Blood.*

Let us note, first of all, the closeness of the two terms which we underlined: *"members"* and *"slaves"*. We shall see farther on what must be the qualities of our slavery towards the good Master. These two words show us how Our Lord Himself considers and treats His slaves: as members of His Mystical Body. As ancient history testifies, all the slaves of a rich man were called a family. But we also know how the members of this family were treated. In the supernatural life, all the slaves of Jesus form one body with Him. Now nobody loathes his own flesh, but he feeds and warms it. This explains to us how, being the members and slaves of Jesus Christ, we are by that fact itself the *children* and *slaves* of Mary, the other association of words which often recurs in the writings penned by our Saint.

Montfort proves the existence of this slavery, first of all, by right of the conqueror, then by several texts of Sacred Scripture.

1º THE RIGHT OF THE CONQUEROR

Before Baptism we belonged to the devil, as his slaves; but Baptism had made us true slaves of Jesus Christ.

It is the law of war that the losers pass under the dominion of the conqueror. By that claim alone, we would already be the true slaves of Jesus Christ. But note the difference expressed in these lines: before Baptism we were *as* slaves of Satan. The latter had no right to such a dominion: it was tyranny on his part. Baptism, on the contrary, restored us to our *true* Master. To the natural right which the latter previously had over us was added the right of conquest. And this conquest was *"infinitely expensive"* to our divine Master, because, to accomplish it, He paid with His person and not only His goods; He shed all His blood, the price of which is infinite. Baptism, then, has indeed, made us the true slaves of Jesus Christ.

As a result we ought not

to live, to work, or to die, except to bring forth fruit for that God-Man, to glorify Him in our bodies, and to let Him reign in our souls, because we are His conquest, His acquired people, and His inheritance.

All nations, indeed, are often proclaimed *the inheritance* of the Servant of Yahweh, *the reward of his voluntarily accepted sacrifice.* Our whole life: the beginning, continuation and end; our whole nature: our body with its senses, our soul with its faculties; the whole multiple exercise of our natural and supernatural activity must tend to glorify Jesus Christ, to bear fruit for Him.

2° TEXTS OF HOLY SCRIPTURE

Many words drawn from Sacred Scripture, and thus inspired by the Holy Ghost, come to confirm this right of the conqueror to our humble services. They

show both that Jesus Christ is the sole principle, and ought to be the sole end, of all our good works, and also that we ought to serve Him, not as servants on wages, but as slaves of love.

Indeed, "*the Holy Ghost compares us*:

1° "*to* **trees** *planted along the waters of grace in the field of the Church, who ought to bring forth fruit in their seasons.*" This is indeed what is demanded of the just man in general in Psalm 1:3.

2° "**To the branches of a vine**, *of which Jesus Christ is the stock* (and grace the sap), *and which must yield good grapes.*" This is the famous comparison developed by St. John at the beginning of chapter 15.

3° "*To a* **flock**, *of which Jesus Christ is the shepherd* (to which He gives and sustains life through grace and the sacraments), *and which is to multiply and give milk."* Thus speaks Christ in St. John (chap. 10).

4° *"To a* **good land**, *of which God is the labourer, in which the seed multiplies itself, and brings forth thirty-fold, sixty-fold, and a hundred-fold."* This is the parable of the sower, in St. Matthew, chap. 13.

So much for direct proofs.

Here now are two indirect proofs.

Jesus Christ cursed the unfruitful fig-tree, *and gave sentence against the* useless servant, *who had not made any profit on his talent.*

Conclusion:

All this proves to us that Jesus Christ wishes to receive some fruits from our wretched selves, namely, our good works, because those good works belong to Him alone (our cooperation with grace being itself the result of a grace): Creati in bonis operibus in Christo Iesu.

But, says Montfort, in concluding, we must serve Jesus Christ *"not as servants on wages, but as slaves of love."* This demands some clarifications.

"I will explain myself":

*
* *

§ II. – THE SERVANT AND THE SLAVE

N° 69

The Saint gives, first of all, the *definition* of servitude and slavery (n° 69); then the *division* of slavery and its application to creatures with regard to God (n° 70); finally, the *differences* between the servant and the slave (n° 71).

1° DEFINITION

Here on earth there are two ways of belonging to another, and of depending on his authority, namely, simple service and slavery; what we mean by a servant, and what we mean by a slave.

a) **By** *common* **service** *amongst Christians a man engages himself to serve another during a certain time, at a certain rate of wages or of recompense.*

Man is free in his work. He can reserve it for himself or yield it to another, either by a purely free title, or by a contract. This contract will set both the work to be supplied by the servant and the sum payable in cash or the equivalent to be given in kind by the master. And, according to the nature of the work required by the master and the abilities required in the servant we shall have an employee, a worker, a domestic, a valet, a waiter, etc.... This is a terminology to which we have been accustomed for centuries, that is to say, since Christianity managed to abolish slavery.

b) **By slavery** *a man is entirely dependent on another for his whole life, and must serve his master without pretending to any wages or reward, just as one of his beasts, over which he has the right of life and death.*

It is not a question of telling whether the state of slavery is justifiable. Such an abdication of one man into the hands of another man, so that the will of the master becomes the only rule of what is just and unjust, good and evil, is totally repugnant to the dignity of the human person. The slave has no right to renounce to that extent a freedom which is the privilege of his nature. And the master has no right to exercise such a power over his fellow men. The state of slavery, such as it was practiced among the pagan peoples, is therefore totally reprehensible, and if the Jewish law allowed it, under certain conditions, it is because Yahweh reigned as much over the master as over the slave by His most holy laws.

Without asking, then, the question of legitimacy, Father de Montfort takes the fact, such as it was admitted and sanctioned by the civil laws, in the countries where slavery was in force. And it turns out that this state, which oversteps the rights of one man towards another man, expresses very exactly the rights of God towards the creature. It is, then, quite natural to try to discover in this human slavery the perfect model of what we must be towards God.

2° DIVISIONS OF SLAVERY

N° 70

...And its application to creatures with regard to God.

There are three sorts of slavery: a slavery of nature, *a slavery of* constraint, *and a slavery of the* will *or of love.*

a) **The slave of nature** is the one who is born in this condition, for example, in Roman law, all children who were born from a *slave mother.* "All creatures are slaves of God in the first sense: 'Domini est terra et plenitudo eius'." "The earth is the Lord's and the fullness of it."

No slave depends on his master as closely as we depend on the divine Majesty. God is the One Who created us. It is He Who maintains us in existence at every instant. In Him alone can we find the happiness that we lack, and that our will necessarily seeks in each of its acts, even the most free and the most spontaneous. His moral law is the only one which can lead us to our last end. Physically and morally, we are thus bound indeed with God by the ties of servitude and slavery.

Is this slavery dishonorable?

It would be for an intelligent and free creature, if God deprived it of the freedom to act as it pleases. But He disdains homage of this kind. Ecclesiasticus says: "God made man from the beginning, and left him in the hand of his own counsel" (Eccl. 15:14), free to recognize or not to recognize the divine dominion, reserving to Himself only to treat each according to his merit. The one who recognizes this dominion and who submits himself to it is therefore not more a slave than others. He does not give up his freedom; on the contrary, he accepts it as the supreme good, and immediately dedicates it to God, by making it carry out in complete freedom what God also wants it to carry out in complete freedom. The slightest infringement on the freedom of our homage deprives it of its value and merit.

b) **The slave of constraint** is the one who, not having wanted to recognize the
legitimate dominion of the master on whom he depended by nature, is held by force and against his will in submission to this master. We have an example of it in prison camps, but especially, with regard to God, in "*the demons and the damned.*" They did not want to carry out the divine will, when they were free to submit themselves or to rebel. Now the divine will is accomplished in them. This slavery, while glorifying the divine power and justice, is the height of dishonor for those who are forced to it, because it shows the folly of which they made themselves guilty, in despising the mercy of the One Whose justice they could not escape.

c) **The slave of love** is the one who not only submits himself wholeheartedly to the authority of his master, but would refuse to leave him, if the latter offered him freedom. That is how many Christian slaves acted after being freed by their masters who were also Christians. "*The just and the saints are slaves of God in this third manner.*"

Far from being this abject man, whose memory antiquity has passed on to us, the slave of love is the only one who is really free and worthy of his human condition. He reigns over his passions. He avoids any degradation. He tends toward his last end in each of his acts. In a word, he is the only one who is in the truth.

"*The slavery of the will*" is, then, indeed "*the most perfect.*" But it is also "*the most glorious to God,*" because the slave of love "*chose God and His service above all things*" to such an extent that, "*even when nature did not oblige him to it,*" he would submit himself no less to his sovereign power, by the simple inclination of his heart. And consequently for God "*Who looks at the heart,*" according to the word of God to Samuel about David: "Man seeth those things that appear, but the Lord beholdeth the heart" (1 Kgs. 16:7); for God "*Who asks for the heart*" with such insistence: "My son, give Me thy heart" (Prov. 23:26); for God "*Who is called the God of the heart*" and of the loving will, according to the saying of the Psalmist: "Thou art the God of my heart, and the God that is my portion for ever" (Ps. 72:26); nothing can be more pleasant than such spontaneous obedience.

3° THE DIFFERENCE BETWEEN THE SERVANT AND THE SLAVE

N° 71

There is an entire difference between a servant and a slave.

a) Because of **the extent of the donation**. "*A servant*" commits only his work, and even sometimes a part of his work only. He does not give to his master "*all he is and all he has and all he can acquire by himself or by another.*" Whereas the slave, in addition to his work, of all his work, "*gives himself whole and entire*" to his master; he also gives him "*all he has and all he can gain without any exception.*" This is what Roman law ruled on this subject: "The slave has no patrimony. All that he acquires, being in servitude, is acquired for the master; all the properties which he had before falling into slavery became the property of the master."

b) Because of **the gratuitousness of the donation**: "*the servant exacts wages* (in cash or in kind) *for the services which he performs for his master; but the slave can exact nothing, whatever assiduity, whatever industry, whatever energy, he may have at his work.* So many reasons nevertheless which would authorize the servant to demand a higher salary, or which would lead the master to grant it to him freely.

c) Because of **the irrevocability of the donation**: "*the servant can leave his master when he pleases,*" under certain conditions and for reasons which legitimize the break of the contract, for example, if clauses were not respected by the master; or at least he can leave him "*when the time of his service shall be expired,*" the contract usually having a limited duration fixed beforehand by mutual agreement. "*But the slave has no right to quit his master at his will.*" The master can get rid of him, sell him, dismiss him; the slave can neither abandon his post, nor ask for his change.

d) Because of **the extent of the lordly rights**. "*The master of the servant has no right of life and death over him*" neither directly by violence, nor indirectly by excess of compulsory work; "*so that if he kill him like one of the beasts of burden, he would commit an unjust homicide,*" which he would have to answer for before the law; even if it was proved that the servant died by excess of work. "*But the master of the slave has by the law a right of life and death over him, so that he may sell him to anybody he likes, or kill him as if he stood on the same level as one of his horses.*"

Certainly, the natural law and the Mosaic law do not recognize such a right outside of a special mandate of master of life and death. The fact is, however, that the civil law recognizes and sanctions it. For example, the Roman law: "The slave is not a person. Towards his master he has no right; the master has all rights over him. The power to which he is subjected, *potestas*, is absolutely unlimited. It is similar to the power which an owner has over the thing which belongs to him. The master can thus praise the services of the slave, alienate him, punish him, put him to death." Later some emperors, Antoninus Pius for example, tried to repress the cruelty of masters, by punishing anyone who may have killed his slave without just motives, but most of these protective laws went out of use almost as soon as they were promulgated.

It is, then, very true that the master possessed the right of life and death over the slave. Montfort does not approve this fact. He merely notes it, and he uses it to establish the difference between the servant and the slave. Nothing could be more normal.

e) Because of **the duration of the services to be rendered**. "*Lastly, the servant is only for a time in his master's service*," the duration of which the time is determined by mutual agreement in the contract of commitment: it can be for one year, one month, one week, and, at the expiration of every term, the contract must be renewed, otherwise the obligations cease on both sides. "*The slave*" is in the service of master "*for always*," at least as far as he is concerned. The master can get rid of him, but the slave cannot leave him on his own.

All these clarifications concerning slavery already serve to illustrate the true nature of our relations with God; but Father de Montfort does not make this application right here. He will speak about it a little in the following numbers. But he reserves the option of returning to it later with more details by explaining the perfect form of Marian devotion, that of the Holy Slavery.

*
* *

§ III. – THE SLAVES OF LOVE OF JESUS AND MARY
(72-77)

N° 72

After what he has just said in n° 71, Father de Montfort has the right to assert at the beginning of n° 72: "*There is nothing among men which makes us belong to another more than slavery.*"

He now adds this proposition, the proof of which will occupy all the rest of this paragraph:

There is nothing among Christians which makes us more absolutely belong to Jesus Christ and His holy Mother than **the slavery of the will**.

1° WITH RESPECT TO JESUS CHRIST

Our Saint proves by Holy Scripture, by the Council of Trent and by reason that we ought to be slaves of love of Our Lord.

a) In **Holy Scripture**: he finds four arguments:

1° *The example of Our Lord* Himself. Does not all Christian perfection consist in reproducing this divine model? Now it is in complete freedom and through love for us that the divine Word "*took the form of a servant: formam servi accipiens*" (Ph. 2:7). The prophet Isaiah had glimpsed Him under this form of slave, "Servus Yahweh," by which He rendered to His Father, in His humanity, reverence, love, submission and service. It is quite just that we take on, through love for Him, the same form as He.

2° *The example of the Blessed Virgin*. At the very moment when she was exalted to the supreme honor of the divine Maternity, she proclaimed herself "*the servant and the slave of the Lord*," happy to find, in the very exercise of her maternal functions, a unique means of showing her loving dependence towards her God Who had become her Son. Is not the mother a slave of her child, a slave of love of her child? What a beautiful model to imitate!

3° *The example of the Apostle St. Paul.* He "*is called by a title of honor*" at the beginning of his epistles: "*Servus Christi*," the slave of Jesus Christ. If he was not a slave freely and by love, he would not make of it one of his most beautiful titles of glory and nobility, the one which most justifies the liberty that he takes in writing to the faithful. Now, he recommends to his faithful to be imitators of him, as he is himself an imitator of Jesus Christ.

4° *The example of the first Christians. They are often called in the Holy Scriptures "Servi Christi,"* either in the Old Testament, especially in the Psalms, or in the New Testament, for example, when St. Paul recommends that slaves supernaturally obey their masters "as the servants of Christ doing the will of God from the heart" (Eph. 6:6).

Now the word "*servus*", used in every case about which we have just spoken, can have only one meaning.

As a great man has truly remarked, it signified in old times nothing but a slave, because there were no servants then like those of the present day. Masters were served only either by slaves or by freedman.

b) **The authority of the Council of Trent** comes also to support this interpretation, not by its decrees or its doctrinal chapters, but by the catechism which was drafted at its command, with the aid of St. Charles Borromeo, Cardinal Archbishop of Milan: "Aequum est... nos ipsos *non secus ac mancipia* Redemptori nostro et Domino in perpetuum addicere et consecrare. It is just that we give ourselves and consecrate ourselves *as slaves* to our Redeemer and Savior." Now the Latin term used by the catechism "mancipium" "*is unequivocal.*" It leaves "*no doubt about our being slaves of Jesus Christ.*" This expressive name, says Gaston May, means that the slave is, just like any spoil of war, a thing conquered, taken by force, *"manu captum, mancipium."* It thus connects very clearly our status of slave with the Redemption of Christ, with the right of conquest which Jesus has thus acquired over us.

N° 73

c) **Proof from reason**, which is at the same time the conclusion of the two previous reasons. It is based on baptism, as n° 68 told us. Baptism tore us away from the tyrannical empire of Satan, to put us back us under the legitimate dominion of our real owner, Jesus Christ. There is no possible middle for the Christian: either slave of Satan or slave of Jesus Christ.

But, anyway, our submission to Jesus must be without constraint. It has to lead us not only to recognize completely Jesus' rights over us, but to choose this good Master, even if nature and grace did not oblige us to do so. In other words, our baptism and our title of Christians commit us to be the slaves of love of Our Lord.

Having premised this, I say that we ought to be to Jesus Christ and to serve Him **not only** *as mercenary servants* (the desire of the heavenly reward is by no means to be excluded from our intentions and from our motives of acting), **but** *as loving slaves, who by an effect of great love* (of a thoughtful choice, a preference)*, give themselves* (to Jesus rather than to His enemy) *up to serve Him in the quality of slaves* (without any motive of personal interest, however legitimate it may be) *for the simple honour of belonging to Him.*

It is quite permitted to desire the reward, because, this also, is love: love of desire, given the nature of the heavenly reward: "I am thy reward exceeding great" (Gen. 15:1). But what is especially needed is pure love, disinterested love, the love of benevolence, which surrenders to Jesus for the sole honor of belonging to Him, and considers any remuneration not as due, but as an act of undeserved benevolence on the part of this good Master.

2° WITH RESPECT TO MARY

N° 74

The Saint then shows by three arguments that the expression 'slave of love' is the one which expresses most perfectly the nature of our relationships with the Mother of Jesus.

1° The close union of Jesus and Mary.

This union allows everything that is said about Jesus to be applied to Mary, for other motives, however. The divine will associating Mary with the Incarnation and the Redemption was purely free. God had many other means at His disposal. As a result, the actual choice of this means, in preference to all others, created in Mary a purely gratuitous title in homage of our servitude. It is neither by nature, nor by conquest, but by grace, that she is Mistress of all men: "Domina nostra," as Jesus Christ is Master and in the same measure: "Dominus noster."

Montfort expresses himself as follows:

What I say absolutely of Jesus Christ, I say relatively of our Blessed Lady.

That is to say, Jesus is entitled, personally, to all these tributes. Mary also has a right to them, but only because of her Son.

Jesus Christ, having chosen her for the inseparable companion of His life, of His death, of His glory, and of His power in heaven and upon earth, has given her by grace, relatively to His Majesty, all the same rights and privileges which He possesses by nature.

It is not about similarity, it is about identity. They are not similar rights, similar privileges; they are the same, numerically the same, that are fitting to Mary by grace and because of her Son. Hence the principle known well by Saints and theologians:

"*Quidquid Deo convenit per naturam, Mariae convenit per gratiam.* All that is fitting to God by nature is fitting to Mary by grace."

And so, we join the famous text, so frequently quoted, of *Arnaud of Chartres*, to which Fr. de Montfort alludes: "In sovereignty or power, the Mother cannot be separated from her Son, because Mary and Christ have only one flesh, one spirit and one love... Unity does not suffer division; it cannot be cut in pieces. If there were two elements to be merged together, they can no longer be separated now and, in my judgment, the glory of the Mother and that of the Son are as one common glory, as the same absolutely."

So that, says our Saint, *Mary and Jesus having but the same will and the same power, the two have the same subjects, servants, and slaves.*

And from this point of view, we cannot be a slave of Jesus, a slave of the love of Jesus, without also being that of Mary. (See n° 77.)

N° 75

2° Mary leads to Jesus.

Jesus and Mary have the same power. To submit oneself to one is to submit oneself to the other. Furthermore, Mary has only one purpose in using her maternal influence on us, by making use of the fact that we voluntarily accept her authority: to establish in souls the reign of her divine Son.

a) *Proof drawn from the conduct of the saints.*

We may, therefore, following the sentiments of the Saints and of many great men, call ourselves, and make ourselves, the loving slaves of the most holy Virgin, in order to be by that very means the more perfectly the slaves of Jesus Christ.

This was, indeed, the opinion of *St. Ildephonsus*, who said: "In order to be the devout slave of the Son, I aim to become the faithful slave of the Mother."

This was also the opinion of the entire French School. For example, Fr. Gibieuf: "Servitude is an unbearable yoke for the damned (slaves of constraint) but, on the contrary, to the saints it is for them a pleasant and honorable state, a glorious and delightful state, a state which disposes them to the honor of having Mary for Mother and to be able to be called her children, because what she is to Jesus in her capacity of Mother places her in a divine power and in a zeal equally great to give Him and appropriate everything which is His, and the more we depend on her, the more we belong to her Son, being given to Him by the hands of the Mother much more holily and worthily than we can belong to Him by ourselves."

b) *Proof drawn from the role which Mary played and still plays.*

Our Blessed Lady is the means our Lord made use of to come to us. She is also the means which we must make use of to go to Him.

This is very logical. *Contrariorum eadem est ratio.* Furthermore, we have already just heard Father Gibieuf say, and Montfort will repeat it later in many places: Mary

is not like all the rest of creatures, who, if we should attach ourselves to them, might rather draw us away from God than draw us near Him.

Why would they take away us from Him?

Because of the latent egoism, which is at the basis of the relations between creatures also subjected to the original corruption. Mary is purity itself; she is altogether relative to God (see n° 225). She does not seize for her advantage the honors which we attribute to her.

The strongest inclination of Mary is to unite us to Jesus Christ her Son; and the strongest inclination of the Son is that we should come to Him through His holy Mother. It is to honour and please Him, just as it would be to do honour and pleasure to a king, to become more perfectly his subject and his slave, by making ourselves the slave of the queen.

This is to *honor* Him, because we are given so "*much more holily and more worthily.*" It is to please Him, because it is "*to take Him by His weak side*" (n° 149) and to show that we recognize the value of His masterpiece.

It is on this account that the holy Fathers and St. Bonaventure after them said that our Lady was the way to go to our Lord. Via veniendi ad Christum est appropinquare ad illam.

N° 76

3° The universal sovereignty of Mary.

If Mary is truly sovereign of heaven and earth, as was proved in n° 28, "*she counts as many subjects and slaves as there are creatures.*" Is it not reasonable that among so many unwitting slaves, and even among so many slaves "*of constraint,*" there are also slaves of love, who, "*of their own good-will in the quality of slaves, should choose Mary for their mistress?*"

Then, laying the foundation of the two "a fortiori" arguments, he adds:

a) *What! are* **men** *and* **devils** (who by no means deserve it) *to have their voluntary slaves* (although this slavery is an ignominy for men) *and Mary* (who has a right to this homage) *to have none* (although this slavery is honorable for men)?

b) *What! shall a* **king** *hold it to be for his honour that the* **queen**, *his companion, should have slaves over whom she has the right of life and death* (which is nevertheless exaggerated, and he will insist on it), *because the honour and power of the one is the honour and power of the other* (the king does not, then, consider himself offended, but rather glorified by the tributes which these slaves render to the queen), *and yet are we to think that our Lord, Who, as the best of all sons, has divided His entire power with His holy Mother, shall take it ill that she too has her slaves? Has He less respect and love for His Mother than Ahasuerus had for Esther* (to whom he promised to grant all that she would ask, were it half of his kingdom), *or than Solomon for Bathsebee* (to whom he said he could refuse nothing)? *Who shall dare say so, or even to think of it?*

Undoubtedly no one!

N° 77

But Montfort corrects himself. It is not desired that Mary should have slaves; it is admitted, on the contrary, that Jesus has them. Let someone call himself a slave of Jesus, and he will be the slave of Mary herself! Does not the glory of the Son reflect on the Mother? It is useless, then, to delay any longer the proof of such an obvious truth!

And he ends by saying: "*It is this very thing which we do, by the devotion of which we are hereafter to speak.*" Every true devotion must recognize and realize the slavery of love; but the Perfect Devotion, the Holy Slavery, recognizes and realizes it essentially. It perfectly expresses, then, our relations with Jesus and Mary.

III. – Third Truth

We have to empty ourselves of what there is of evil in us
(78-82)

The formula "*slave of love of Jesus and Mary*" translates exactly our relationships with them. By our donation, Jesus and Mary again take up the domain which belonged to them, but which, from now on, belongs to them with an additional title.

This taking possession, however, does not deliver us from the terrible consequences of original sin. Nor is it a guarantee, permitting henceforth these consequences to develop without any danger for us. Presumptuous devotees believed this. The Protestants also, as regards faith in Christ. The *Avis salutaires* wrongly accused the true devotion to Mary of it.

Quite the contrary, this devotion furnishes us the means of emptying ourselves of the depth of corruption which we carry in ourselves, or at least to confine the disastrous effects of it. One could even say that the best among all the forms of Marian devotion will be the one which will protect us most effectively against all the digressions of an evil nature.

Montfort describes, first of all, our *misery and its effects* (n° 78). He then gives *three necessary conditions to emerge from them*:

1° To know oneself well (n°s 79 and 80).

2° To die to oneself every day (n° 81).

3° To choose a good devotion to Mary (n° 82).

It is useless to remark this is a very serious and in-depth work, showing one more time the insanity of the anti-Marian attacks.

1° OUR MISERY AND ITS EFFECTS

N° 78

Our nature was fundamentally vitiated by original sin, the concupiscence of which we have. This primitive imbalance and this tendency to evil have been further increased by our personal sins. There results three disastrous effects from it.

1° "**Our best actions are ordinarily stained and corrupted by the ground of evil, which is so deeply laid up in us.**"

Of themselves, they would divert the divine attention if we did not discover a means to remove these stains and to restore to our good works all the luster which they should have had. (See n°s 146-150.)

2° **The divine graces themselves**, the heavenly dews or the wine of the love of God, **are ordinarily spoilt by the bad leaven**, as the wine which is placed in a barrel which smells bad, is spoiled and easily assumes its unbearable smell. According to the proverb: "*Quidquid recipitur ad modum recipientis recipitur.*" Everything which is received in a subject, for example, some water in a receptacle, inevitably takes the form of this subject. The divine motion tended to push us to the good, but our bad disposition paralyzes this impetus.

3° If we do not empty ourselves of this ground of evil:

Our Lord, *Who is infinitely pure and hates infinitely the least stain upon our souls,* **will cast us out from His presence**, *and will not unite Himself to us.*

And leaving we shall be unable to reach perfection, because this latter is acquired only by union with this good Master.

We notice that in 1° it was about our works and in 3° it is about ourselves.

2° NECESSARY CONDITIONS TO EMERGE FROM THIS MISERY

They are three in number.

N° 79

1° **To know oneself well**. This was already the principle of ancient wisdom: γνῶθι σεατόν know yourself. To the principle of natural knowledge, which will already reveal to us many weak points in ourselves, in the simple light of reason and the voice of conscience, will come to be added a principle of supernatural knowledge, "*the light of the Holy Ghost*," the teachings which a lively, deep and enlightened faith bring us. (See n° 213.)

All this shows us, since it is the consequence of the sin of nature and our personal sins, whether mortal, or venial, even if they are forgiven:

Our inward corruption, our incapacity for every good thing useful for salvation, our weakness in all things, our inconstancy at all times (as a result of our increased concupiscence), (and consequently) *our indignity of every grace* (which would be corrupted in us, as dough is soured and corrupted by the yeast which is put in it), *and our iniquity in every position.*

Going into detail about our corruption, Father de Montfort indicates its effects in all the elements which compose our nature.

a) **Our bodies** *are so corrupted that they are called by the Holy Ghost bodies of sin,* corpus peccati, *because they have been conceived in sin, because they are also nourished in sin, that is to say, they are pleased only in sin and are capable of all sin.*

"*Caro enim concupiscit adversus animam,*" says St. Paul. The desires of the flesh are opposed to those of the soul. Furthermore, Montfort quotes the commentary of Origen verbatim: "Corpus peccati id est, corpus in peccato conceptum, nutritum et peccare solitum."

He then enumerates the other consequences of the loss of original integrity as regards the body itself:

Bodies subject to thousands of maladies, which go on corrupting from day to day, and which engender nothing but disease, vermin and corruption.

We do not see him tender-hearted toward our misery. Later, when he will explain the exercises in preparation for the consecration (1st week), he will again stress the shadows of its picture. (See n° 228).

b) "*Our soul,*" which is nevertheless spiritual, by the fact that it "*is united to our body, has become so carnal,*" that is to say, so accessible to the thoughts and desires of the flesh, "*that it is called flesh: all flesh having corrupted its way.*"

c) In *our spirit*: pride and blindness.

d) In *our hearts*: hardness.

In such a nature, seven deadly sins arrange to meet. Montfort expresses this by putting, next to sin, the animal which traditionally represents it:

We are naturally **prouder** *than peacocks, more groveling on the earth* (**miserly**) *than toads, more vile* (lewd) *than unclean animals, more* **envious** *than serpents, more* **gluttonous** *than hogs, more* **furious** *than tigers,* **lazier** *than tortoises.*

And he adds, with other comparisons taken from outside the animal kingdom:

Weaker than reeds, and more capricious than weathercocks.

Then, by way of recapitulation:

"*We have down in our own selves nothing but nothingness and sin.*" These words are verbatim from the Council of Orange: "Nemo habet de suo nisi mendacium et peccatum." No one has anything of himself except falsehood and sin" (Can. 22). St. Teresa also says: "It is a very great truth that nothingness and poverty are our lot" (Interior Castle, 6th mansion, ch. X). Indeed, without grace, we are capable of nothing, at least in the supernatural order. By acting in the direction of our perverse inclinations, "*we deserve nothing but the anger* (la colère) *of God and the everlasting hell.*"

N° 80

So, there is no reason to be surprised that Our Lord puts renunciation and hatred of self at the foundation of our spiritual life. He is infinite wisdom and mercy. He would not like to impose without reasons a precept the transgression of which would compromise salvation. If we must hate ourselves, it is because we are really worthy of hatred. In summary, nothing is so worthy of love as God, nothing is so worthy of hatred as ourselves.

N° 81

2° **To die to self every day**, according to the counsel of Our Lord and the practice of St. Paul. This is the negative side of Christian asceticism: to make empty, to renounce, to die. To obtain this result,

we must renounce the operations of the powers of our soul, and of the senses of our body. We must see as if we saw not, understand as if we understood not, and make use of the things of the world as if we made no use of them at all.

This is what *St. John of the Cross* calls the dark night of the senses, which can be active or passive, depending on whether it is produced by the soul itself, or by God. The holy Doctor thus explains the essence of this night and the procedure to be followed to obtain it: "Philosophers say that the soul is a blank when God first infuses it into the body, without knowledge of any kind whatever, and incapable of receiving knowledge, in the course of nature, in any other way than through the senses. Thus, while in the body, the soul is like a man in a dark prison, who has no knowledge of what passes without beyond what he can learn by looking through the window of his cell, and who if he did not so look could in no other way learn anything at all. Thus, then, the soul cannot naturally know anything but through the senses, which are the windows of its cell. If, then, the impressions and communications of sense be **rejected and denied**, we may well say that the soul is in **darkness and empty**, because according to this opinion there is no other natural way for light to enter in. It is true, indeed, that we cannot help hearing, seeing, smelling, tasting, and touching, but this is of no moment, and does not trouble the soul, when the objects of sense are repelled, any more than if we neither heard nor saw; for he who shuts his eyes is as much in darkness as a blind man who cannot see."

In a word, it is necessary to put oneself in the state of a man who would advance in the darkness of the night. Objects are there all around him. But they are capable of making an impression neither on his senses, nor on his soul, the light being lacking to establish the communication.

For lack of

...this necessary and useful death, we shall bring forth no fruit worth anything, and our devotions will become useless. All our justices (works of justice) *will be stained by self-love and our own will.*

Because, if it is not mortified, nature claims for itself and corrupts more or less all the good which we accomplish. And because, according to the principle: "Good from a sound cause, evil from whatever is defective."

God will hold in abomination the greatest sacrifices we can make, and the best actions we can do; so that at our death we shall find our hands empty of virtues and of merits, and we shall not have one spark of pure love.

Until the flames of Purgatory have consumed the dross which we had mixed with the materials of our spiritual edifice, the merits and virtues are neutralized, indeed, incapable of obtaining heavenly glory for us. Hence the advantage of purifying everything during this life.

But we arrive there only by renunciation, because the grace of pure love is:

...only communicated to souls dead to themselves, souls whose life is hidden with Jesus Christ in God.

N° 82

3° To choose a good devotion to Mary. The very one which will most lead us to this death to ourselves. This is the positive side of the work undertaken above, because it is necessary not to be deceived: we empty ourselves of one thing only by filling ourselves with something else. We shall by no means allow ourselves to be guided by the lights of the senses, if we are totally under the influence of the light of faith. This is the light which St. John of the Cross proposes, and, ultimately, everyone must arrive there: In order to obtain it itself, Montfort appeals to devotion to Mary. Even there, however, let us be careful not to deceive ourselves!

For we must not think that all that shines is gold, that all that tastes sweet is honey, or all that is easy to do and is done by the greatest number is sanctifying.

In other words, among the Marian devotions, some are true, others are false, and it is important not to be mistaken there. But if a good one is found, especially an excellent one, it will allow us to obtain easily and quickly the desired result:

As there are secrets of nature to do in a short time at little cost and with facility, natural operations, so also in like manner there are secrets in the order of grace to do in a short time with sweetness and facility, supernatural operations, such as emptying ourselves of self, filling ourselves with God, *and becoming perfect.*

Among these true devotions that are capable of producing this effect, Montfort wants to reveal one, that is

...one of these secrets of grace, unknown by the greater number of Christians, known even to few of the devout, and practiced and relished by a far less number still.

It is the resumption of the idea of secret, already describing this method in n° 21 of the *Treatise*, and especially in the entire *Secret of Mary*.

IV. – Fourth Truth

We need a mediator with the Mediator Himself Who is Jesus Christ
(83-86)

As Montfort remarks, this truth is based on the one which precedes, and it does so in two ways: 1° our corruption makes us unworthy to appear before God. That is why God Himself gave us mediators with His Majesty. The first and the most necessary of these mediators is Jesus Christ. But He is Himself the God of all holiness. Are we not unworthy of ourselves to approach Him? 2° Mary, the Mother of Jesus and ours, is good enough to love us in spite of our misery, and powerful enough to help us to emerge from it and to make us pleasing to her divine Son.

Montfort shows here: 1° The necessity of a mediator in general (n° 83); 2° Jesus Christ is our Mediator of redemption with His Father (n° 84); 3° Mary is our mediatrix of intercession with her Son (n° 85).

N° 83

1° **The necessity of a Mediator in general**. Always more perfect because more *humble*, this method is imperative for someone who is conscious of his very real *unworthiness*; at the risk of seeing himself rejected by the One before Whom he appears. God, moreover, in His great mercy, arranged between Him and us a long series of powerful mediators. To neglect these mediators, for us to approach His holiness directly, would be to lack humility and respect at the same time. This would be to have less esteem for this King of kings than we would for an earthly king, whom we would not dare to approach without being presented by some influential friend.

N° 84

2° **Jesus Christ, our Mediator of Redemption**. He is the only One Who is absolutely necessary, because He alone reconciled in His blood man with God. Through Him pass all the prayers of the Church triumphant and militant. Through Him we must pray for ourselves and we have access to the divine Majesty. We must appear before God only clothed in His merits.

N° 85

3° **Mary our mediatrix of intercession**. But is not Jesus God Himself, as deserving of respect as His Father? Therefore, is our purity great enough to unite us directly to Him? Would He, then, be entitled to less respect and fear, for having deigned to become our pledge and our mediator?

That is why we need a mediator with the Mediator Himself, and, Mary alone is capable of fulfilling this charitable office. She is our sister, because she belongs totally to our nature: in her there is nothing of the austere nor of the repulsive, nothing too sublime nor too brilliant. She is not the sun dazzling by its beams. She is rather the moon whose entire brightness comes from the sun, but which moderates its light and places it in our short reach. Through her Jesus Christ came to us, and through her we have to go to Him. In becoming the Mother of Jesus, she also became our Mother. We do not, then, have to be afraid of being rejected by her. She is so charitable, moreover, that she has never rejected anyone. She is so powerful that her requests have never been refused. She has only to appear before her Son: He immediately grants what she requests; He immediately receives the one whom she presents. Jesus *is always lovingly vanquished by the breasts, the yearnings and the prayers* of His most holy Mother.

N° 86

And thus we observe the gradation intended by St. Bernard and St. Bonaventure: Mary, Jesus Christ, God the Father. *"Now, it is by the devotion that I am about to bring forward that this order is guarded perfectly."*

V. – Fifth Truth

It is very difficult for us to preserve the graces and treasures received from God
(87-89)

This truth is also based on the third, because the major reason of our fears for the future is our weakness in the present. It is, however, this future which Montfort considers here especially, and the necessity of preserving, in spite of all difficulties, the treasures which, thanks to God, we were able to acquire and to show before God.

These treasures are sanctifying grace and the merits of our good works. The difficulties of preserving them come from a threefold source:

1° Our weakness (n° 87);

2° The mockery and guile of the demons (n° 88);

3° The corruption of the world (n° 89).

Each of these reasons will prove once more our present need to have recourse to Mary.

N° 87

1° Our weakness.

It sufficiently follows from what has been said above. We carry, consequently, very precious treasures in very fragile vessels.

N° 88

2° The mockery and guile of the demons.

They must frighten us all the more as our weakness is greater. If a mere nothing is enough to bring us down, what are we to say if we have against us a numerous, experienced, nasty and cunning army, relentlessly watching out for every occasion to surprise and rob us! This misfortune is that much more to be feared for us, as it happened to greater saints than we. "I saw cedars of Lebanon falling," said St. Augustine, "that is to say, men of consummate virtue, whose fall I no longer believed possible, than that of a Jerome and a John Chrysostom." How did this misfortune occur? It is not for lack of grace, which is lacking to nobody, but for lack of humility. They considered themselves strong enough to keep their treasures themselves, and because of this reliance, albeit imperceptible, which they had in themselves, the Lord allowed them to be robbed. It would not have happened to them *if they had known the devotion of the Holy Slavery*. They would have confided their treasure to a powerful and faithful Virgin, who would have kept it for them as her own property, and even taken it as an obligation of justice.

N° 89

3° **The corruption of the world**.

Taking inspiration from a beautiful passage of St. Leo, Montfort writes:

The world is now so corrupt that it seems to be inevitable that religious hearts should be soiled, if not by its mud, at least by its dust.

Then, accumulating images, he protests that almost a miracle would be needed not to be drawn in by this impetuous torrent, submerged by this stormy sea, plundered by this band of corsairs and suffocated by this pestilent air. But if a miracle is needed, the Virgin will work it in favor of all men and women who serve her *in the beautiful way*.

ARTICLE II

Essential marks of the true and false devotion to Mary

(90-114)

N° 90

The five fundamental truths must be found in any devotion to Mary. In explaining them, Montfort already had in mind "his dear devotion" and at the end of every paragraph, and sometimes even more often, he allows himself to note that all this will be perfectly fulfilled in the Holy Slavery.

Before following his attraction and confining himself to the study of this devotion, he thinks of the large number of those who are shipwrecked, and put their confidence in a devotion which Mary cannot bless, because it offends her divine Son and herself.

Hence comes the necessity of warning souls against the false devotions.

The demon is a subtle and experienced deceiver. Such a counterfeiter, who does not waste his time imitating mean metals, because they are not worth the trouble, the demon imitates only the devotion to the Eucharist and the devotion to the Blessed Virgin, because they are, among the other devotions, what gold and silver are among other metals. He knows that men are naturally led to have confidence in Mary. Never mind! He will multiply his efforts to lead this confidence astray and draw it to practices which have and can have no efficacy, and so he will maintain them in sin and will increase his chances of possessing them eternally.

N° 91

It is therefore very important: 1° to know the characteristics of false devotion in order to avoid them and those of true devotion in order to embrace them; 2° to know among so many practices of true devotion, the one which is the best in order to embrace it.

This second question will be the object of our article III, in keeping with the division which we adopted above. We thus have to see in this article II only the marks: 1° of *false* devotion to Mary (n°s 92-104); 2° of *true* devotion to Mary (n°s 105-111).

SECTION I

The marks of false devotion to Mary

(92-104)

N° 92

There is nothing impervious to corruption except what is totally good or totally evil. Now, the good is unadulterated only in heaven, and evil is complete only in hell. On earth, the good is necessarily corruptible. But corruption itself which hounds it is a proof of its goodness. Because, St. Thomas says, just as every privation relies on a foundation which is being, so too every evil is founded on some good, and every falsity on some truth. If there is a false devotion to the Blessed Virgin, there also has to be a true one, the corruption of which it is.

Furthermore, it is impossible that a devotion should be false from all points of view at the same time, as it is impossible for universal evil to exist here on earth without destroying itself. It is equally impossible that a man, however wicked he is, should wage war at the same time against all the virtues, because he must necessarily love some good.

As a result, instead of having a universal false devotion, in which nothing is good and everything is to be rejected, we encounter instead false devotions, distinguished according to the principle to which they are opposed, or according to the particular good of which they are the privation.

Father de Montfort enumerates seven of them. Father Crasset finds eight of them and does not give them in the same order. Nor are they absolutely the same in both authors. Fr. Tronson, in his "Particular Examinations," also gives seven, but in a slightly different order.

For Father Crasset, there are: 1° the superstitious devotees; 2° the hypocritical devotees; 3° the timid and scrupulous devotees; 4° the proud devotees; 5° the presumptuous devotees; 6° the inconstant devotees; 7° the scandalous devotees; 8° the sensual and unchaste devotees. He does not, moreover, stick to this order too much, because, after enumerating them in this way, he changes in the development and places the proud devotees in the next-to-last place.

For Fr. Tronson, there are: 1° the critical devotees; 2° the hypocritical devotees; 3° the timid and scrupulous devotees; 4° the presumptuous devotees; 5° the inconstant and frivolous devotees; 6° the self-interested devotees; 7° the scandalous devotees.

For Father de Montfort, there are: 1° the *critical* devotees through lack of judgment based on intellectual pride; 2° the *scrupulous* devotees through lack of judgment based on timidity and ignorance; 3° the *exterior* devotees due to the lack of application of the mind to the practices of devotion; 4° the *presumptuous* devotees by weakness of the will and attachment to passion, in spite of a very lively faith; 5° the *inconstant* devotees as a result of the natural instability of concupiscence; 6° the *hypocritical* devotees who are ashamed of their sins, do not want to abandon them, but want to cover themselves exteriorly under the mask of devotion to Mary; 7° the *self-interested* devotees who think of Mary only out of natural greed. The first three false devotions first are based, then, on a defect of the *intellect* and the other four on a defect of the *will*.

While probably depending on Crasset and Tronson, Montfort is at the same time more logical, more complete and more concise. The presumptuous, the scandalous and the unchaste make up only one for him. In speaking about critical devotees, he has the opportunity to include all that Crasset puts under the headings: superstitious and proud devotees. Like Tronson, he adds the self-interested devotees, about which Crasset does not speak. He brands, finally, the exterior devotees whom neither Crasset nor Tronson had included in their lists.

Let us quickly go through each category, without repeating what we said about the attacks of Port-Royal.

*
* *

§ I. – THE CRITICAL DEVOTEES
(93)

N° 93

This class of false devotees is composed most often of proud and self-important spirits who are very attached to their own judgment, incapable of understanding the simple and naïve confidence, which we can, without any superstition, have in Mary. They boast about their knowledge, true or feigned. They find fault in all the practices of devotion, because they do not suit their fancy. They reject all accounts about miracles and favors obtained, because these accounts are not authentic. They see obvious exaggerations in the praises which the Fathers attribute to Mary. Should you not know how to distinguish between the oratorical outbursts and the cold assertions of theologians?...

As Montfort says, "*they have at bottom some devotion to the holy Virgin,*" but they moan about "abuses" to which this devotion gives rise in those who are not sufficiently enlightened. And to eliminate these abuses more radically, they are of the opinion that the marks of devotion themselves must be suppressed.

We are already informed about the origin and reality of these recriminations. Here are a few more passages from the "Avis Salutaires" confirming the actual assertions of Father de Montfort:

"Do not honor me as a subordinate goddess. Do not mislead simple and ignorant persons. Do not scandalize and confirm in their errors those who are outside the Church; do not make dishonorable criticism fall again on the Church in honoring me in the same way as God." (VIII Avis.)

"Be careful not to grant me anything through hyperbole or excess of zeal. Let your praise be simple, unambiguous, not excessive, not hyperbolic... Do not allow yourselves to be moved by hyperboles, excessive phrases and the manners of speaking of some saints." (X Avis.)

And to give a completely modern and up-to-date proof of this monstrous idolatry, they are content to draw out of the dust of the grave the heresy of the Collyridians, dating from the IVth century. (X Avis.)

"Do not put your confidence in my images and statues, like the pagans do, *even if they are miraculous*: no power is attached to them. They are stones, wood, images or signs. Let those who put their confidence in them become like them." (XVII Avis.)

Obviously a work of serious criticism is imperative to distinguish the truth from the legendary in all the accounts of miracles attributed to Mary. We are not obliged to believe as Gospel truth all those which are contained, for example, in *The Golden Legend of Our Lady*. But this does not mean that we must not admit any of them, even those which are reported by reliable authors.

These attacks, says our Saint, "*do an infinite wrong to the devotion to our Lady; and they are but too successful in alienating people from it, under the pretext of destroying its abuses.*"

Shortly after the publication of the *Avis*, Pierre Grenier, in fact, was able to write in his *Apology for the devotees of the Virgin* (p. 11): "You know that everybody is not called to the contemplative life, and that most of the faithful show their devotion to the Mother of God only by reciting vocal prayers, by visiting her churches and adorning her statues, and I can tell you that, since this unfortunate book has become known, many people intended to abandon all these exercises of piety, because very learned persons assured them that they were only abuses... They became scrupulous about reciting the Rosary and Litanies, because the Blessed Virgin, in this book, forbade her devotees to pray to her longer than to God, and because in the Rosary there were ten *Hail Marys* to one *Our Father*."

*
* *

§ II. – THE SCRUPULOUS DEVOTEES
(94 and 95)

N° 94

As Father Crasset remarks, there are two sorts of scruples; some are innocent, the other bad and pernicious.

The first one is proper to excessively timid souls. They are afraid of gravely offending God where there is not even venial sin, and because of this they live in continual trouble of mind.

The second is the fact of certain souls whose judgment is completely false. They are scandalized by the trifles of others and allow themselves abominable things. They make the main part of religion consist in indifferent practices, and completely neglect their indispensable duties.

Among these latter scrupulous souls were the Pharisees in the time of Our Lord, and the devotees about whom speaks Montfort in this passage.

They object forcefully to devotion to the Blessed Virgin, under the pretext that Jesus Christ must be the only end of all our devotion.

"What they say is true in a certain sense," and we proved it ourselves at length, by establishing the first fundamental truth. *"But it is very dangerous, when, by the application they make of it, they hinder devotion to our Blessed Lady, and it is, under the pretext of a greater good, a subtle snare of the evil one."*

According to them, indeed, devotion to Mary is an obstacle to the devotion that is due to Our Lord. We dishonor the Son by honoring the Mother. We lower the one by raising the other. Hence, they find excessive the praises that are addressed to Mary, or the multitudes who hurry to her altar. They consider as wasted time and foolishness the traditional marks by which the Christian people have always expressed their devotion to Mary.

Such is by no means, we saw, the role of devotion to Mary. Does not the Virgin have as her purpose to lead souls to Jesus Himself?

There is no need, then, to be surprised to see more people at the altar of Mary than at the altar of Jesus. They are not opposed to one another. And to pray to one is to pray to the other.

N° 95

Is this not the method which the Church follows in reciting the *Ave Maria*? She blesses the Blessed Virgin, first of all, and then Jesus. Not that Mary is more worthy of her blessings than Jesus, nor even as worthy: "*That would be an intolerable heresy.*" But, after having blessed the Mother, the Church blesses the Son more perfectly, with her and through her. Mary is altogether relative to God (see n° 225). She keeps nothing for herself of the praises that we attribute to her: "*You never praise or honour Mary without Mary praising and honouring God.*" You bless her, first of all. She accepts, but, immediately after, she blesses Jesus with you. She renders Him all the glory which you give her. And so the blessings which you will make ascend to Jesus, multiplied a hundredfold by those which Mary will join to them, will supremely honor the divine Majesty of the Savior.

Hence comes the triumphal conclusion:

Let us, then, say with all the true clients of our Lady against these false scrupulous devotees, O Mary, thou art blessed amongst all women, and blessed is the fruit of thy womb, Jesus.

Also let us underline the fine irony with which Montfort reproaches the scrupulous devotees, so concerned, in theory, for the glory of Our Lord, and their lack of elementary practical respect in His regard. Professing such a devotion to Jesus, they should at least take off their hats when they pronounce His blessed name. To take off one's hat is not much, nevertheless. St. Paul wanted us to bend the knee: *In the name of Jesus every knee should bow* (Ph. 2:10).

*
* *

§ III. – THE EXTERNAL DEVOTEES
(96)

N° 96

Montfort will admit later that the exterior practices of devotion are necessary (n° 226 ss.). But they are precisely to arouse, sustain and develop the interior devotion. Whoever makes the devotion consist only in these exterior practices breaks this necessary unity and kills true devotion.

They only act, then, out of mechanical routine. It is necessary to say plenty of Rosaries, to hear a great number of Masses, to join all the confraternities, but without the soul having the slightest part in all these practices.

Exterior devotees enjoy only the sensible part of these devotions. They become attached to them as long as the sensible endures. As soon as it stops, they completely lose heart. "*They think they are doing nothing. They get all out of joint, throw everything up, or do everything at random.*"

If they labored only for them, we would still forgive them their great number ("*the world is full of these exterior devotees*") and their blindness. They would be the only ones to undergo the consequences. But in reality, they damage others a lot. They discourage them by their acerbic criticisms and the example of their laxity:

There are no people who are more critical of men of prayer, of those who foster an interior spirit as the essential thing, while they do not lightly account of that outward modesty which always accompanies true devotion.

*
* *

§ IV. – THE PRESUMPTUOUS DEVOTEES
(97-100)

N° 97

This class of false devotees is the least kind, the one that our Saint treats most harshly. It is not indeed about poor sinners, victims of their own weakness, or of the violence of the passions and the occasions, who regret their falls bitterly and, incapable of getting up by themselves, have recourse to Mary so as to leave that miserable state. For those, Montfort will have very tender, encouraging words, and he will point out to them in a true devotion to Mary, the means to recover very fast and to escape damnation. (The end of 99 and the beginning of 100.) – No! It is about sinners "*abandoned to their passions,*" indulging in unbridled "*pride, avarice, impurity, drunkenness, anger*" and probably the other capital sins, no less than "*swearing* (blasphemy), *detraction, injustice*" and other infractions of the commandments of God.

Not only do they passionately indulge in all sorts of excesses, but they aspire indeed to continue thus till the end of their life. They dread only one thing, because they are instructed and have faith: eternal damnation. And they ask of devotion, Marian devotion especially, only an assurance against this disaster. Mary is solely charged with obtaining for them a happy death. As she is very charitable and very faithful, she will not fail to give them what they desire. They can thus rely on her for that, sin at present in complete safety, and taste without danger all the forbidden fruits.

Montfort describes, with comic irony, all the false pretexts behind which they entrench this "*pernicious presumption.*"

a) First of all, the **divine goodness**. "*God has not made us to condemn us everlastingly.*" On the other hand, He knows our weakness very well. He knows "*that no man is without sin,*" and He is inclined to mercy. "*One good* **Peccavi** *at the hour of death is enough*" to erase all the faults of the past life. This assumption, which takes advantage of God's goodness to offend Him with more assurance, and which despises His justice so as to elevate His mercy, contains, says St. Thomas, a kind of sin against the Holy Ghost. It makes

God similar to this God of Marcion, who, according to Tertullian, delighted in all the vices by the protection that his government offered them, and made men more wicked by the impunity which it granted to their crimes.

b) Then **their devotion to Mary**. They complacently list all the practices: join her confraternities, that of the Rosary or the Scapular, and, in fact, to recite the Rosary, and wear the little habit (scapular); to recite sometimes the Office of the Blessed Virgin, and, every day, seven *Our Fathers* and *Hail Marys* in her honor, to fast on Saturdays, etc... So many very good things in themselves. But they no longer have any efficacy, since they are carried out in this state of mind: "*They sleep in peace in the midst of their bad habits, without doing any violence to themselves to correct their faults, under the pretext that they are devout to the Blessed Virgin; that they will not be allowed to die without confession.*" "*If Mary laid down a law to herself to save by her mercy this sort of people, she would be authorizing crime, and assisting to crucify and outrage her Son. Who would dare to think such a thought as that?*" (n° 98)

c) Finally the **innumerable stories** of protection of this kind granted by Mary. For this purpose, they collect everything that can be read or heard. They speak about persons who died in a state of mortal sin, whose judgment was supposedly delayed until Mary resuscitated them. They would thus have obtained the time to confess or even simply to make an act of contrition. And how would they have merited a favor so great? By similar practices of devotion which they would have shown to Mary! They speak about great sinners who allegedly obtained, through Mary and for the same reasons, the grace of contrition and the forgiveness of their sins at the time of death.

All the principal accusations then current against Marian devotion can be recognized in the case of these presumptuous devotees. The enemies of this devotion found it easy to ascribe to all those who loved the Virgin and served her, the sordid intentions of those. Generalizations of this kind were always in fashion against the Church.

N° 98

Therefore, Montfort protests energetically against such charges. Far from being the way of the Church herself or of true devotees, this conduct and this presumption are altogether harmful and most reprehensible. One cannot say sincerely that he loves and honors Mary if he continues to offend her divine Son – what am I saying? – if we take refuge under the mantle of the Mother, so as to be more sure of offending the Son with impunity.

N° 99

I say, that thus to abuse devotion to our Lady, which, after devotion to our Lord in the Blessed Sacrament, is the holiest and solidest of all devotions, is to be guilty of a horrible sacrilege, which, after the sacrilege of an unworthy Communion, is the greatest and the least pardonable.

N° 100

It was necessary to thunder against the diabolical presumption of those who count on being saved in spite of their sins because of Mary's protection. It is no less necessary to avoid the regrettable confusion committed by the author of the *Avis Salutaires*, in condemning any mark of devotion which would not start in a soul in a state of grace. It is to make this indispensable distinction that the Saint employs the rest of this paragraph. Let us reread on this subject n°s 40-42 of the present Commentary, which sufficiently explain this passage. One remark only: to all those who seek sincerely in devotion to Mary the means to get out of sin and to make their salvation sure, Montfort does not recommend any other practices of devotion than those of which the presumptuous devotees boast:

To enroll ourselves in confraternities, to say the Rosary or other prayers, to fast on Saturdays, etc...

so it is true that only the spirit with which they are inspired gives some value to these practices.

This is wonderfully useful to the **conversion** *of a sinner, however hardened...But on the condition that he will only practice these good works with the intention of obtaining from God, by the intercession of the Blessed Virgin, the grace of contrition and the pardon of his sins, to conquer his evil habits, and not to remain quietly in the state of sin, in spite of the remorse of his conscience, the example of Jesus Christ and the Saints, and the maxims of the holy Gospel.*

*
* *

§ V. – THE INCONSTANT DEVOTEES
(101)

N° 101

St. Jerome pronounced this judgment borne out by the experience of the centuries: "Many begin, few persevere." The earth is the kingdom of inconstancy and thoughtlessness. In it, perpetual change is necessary. That is why those who become attached to the world and dash into its movement can have no more stability than it does. The object which was pursued with so much ardor yesterday is a cause of disgust today and gives place to another tomorrow.

Ecclesiasticus puts this difference between the just man and the sinner, that "a holy man continueth in wisdom as the sun: but a fool is changed as the moon" (Eccli. 27:12).

The inconstant devotee is like the moon. The latter increases and decreases, appears and disappears, lives and dies almost at the same time. The same applies to inconstant devotees. Sometimes they are fervent, sometimes lukewarm. Sometimes they seem ready to undertake everything for the service of Mary; then shortly after, they are no longer the same. They join every confraternity, and follow the rules of none. Such devotees are unworthy to be numbered among the servants of the Virgin. Mary puts them under her feet, like the moon which they resemble. On the contrary, her true servants share her constancy and fidelity. They do not take on so many commitments, but keep them, in spite of the great causes of instability and battles: the devil, the world and the flesh.

*
* *

§ VI. – THE HYPOCRITICAL DEVOTEES
(102)

N° 102

This is the difference between the hypocritical devotees and the presumptuous devotees: the first are ashamed of their sins without having the courage to renounce them, whereas the others do not hide from them at all, and would easily be scandalous. Furthermore, the presumptuous knows very well the gravity of his state before God, and he hopes to get back into good graces with Him at the last moment of his life. The hypocrite, on the contrary, intends only to shield himself from the judgment of men. Some people go as far as to compromise their salvation, for fear of losing the esteem of their confessor, by sincerely admitting their sins at the time of death. While causing less damage to Christian society, the hypocritical devotees are more in danger of being personally lost. And they are accordingly held in horror before God, Who is essentially honesty and simplicity.

For these false devotees, Mary's mantle serves to cover their sins and bad habits, so that nobody can notice them. It also serves to make them pass for what they are not, that is to say, for true devotees of Mary, who put their private life in accord with their doctrine and their religious practices.

*
* *

§ VII. – THE SELF-INTERESTED DEVOTEES
(103)

N° 103

The last category of false devotees includes those who allow themselves to be guided only by the interest of the moment, and most often by *temporal* interest. They ask Mary only for graces of the material order, to win trials or important business, to preserve or to recover health, to avoid danger, etc.... And, outside of these cases, they never think of praying to Mary. These souls forget that devotion, like prayer itself, has three other purposes, as important as the request itself: veneration, gratitude and reparation. They also forget that spiritual graces have more value than temporal graces. Therefore they are not in favor in the sight of God and His holy Mother.

N° 104

Conclusion.

Let us, then, indeed beware of being numbered among all these false devotees: *critical, scrupulous, exterior, presumptuous, inconstant, hypocritical* and *self-interested*. Otherwise we shall think that we are walking on the royal road leading to salvation, and in reality we shall dash into an impasse, or even onto a path opening straight into the abyss.

SECTION II

The marks of true Devotion to Mary

(105-110)

N° 105

The false devotions, we said, are, from one or another point of view, the corruption of true devotion. To know the latter, it will be enough most of the time to take the opposite of the special defect identified and condemned in the former.

Father de Montfort follows this way, but reduces to five the number of the essential qualities of true devotion. Actually, the same quality can be opposed to several defects. Thus, **tender** devotion is opposed to *critical* and *scrupulous* devotion, and **holy** devotion is opposed to *presumptuous* and *hypocritical* devotion.

Let us also notice that the true devotion takes hold of the whole man, his mind as well as his will, his sensitive faculties interior as well as exterior. The foundation of the division will no longer, therefore, be exactly the same as previously. There were, indeed, several false devotions, based on partial defects. There is only one true devotion necessarily containing all the essential qualities of this true devotion. Each of these qualities only expresses more clearly an aspect already contained implicitly in the previous quality.

The fundamental quality, here, will be that devotion is *interior*, taking hold of the whole man. The rest will follow from that. If it is interior, it will necessarily be tender, because the heart will have given itself; it will necessarily be *holy*, because it will be expressed in all works; it will necessarily be *constant* because the faculties themselves have a stability against which concupiscence can fight, but which it does not remove; finally, it will necessarily be *disinterested*, showing itself on every occasion and by love.

Let us look "*in a few words*" at each of these qualities. I say "in a few words," because we are traveling more and more in familiar territory.

*
* *

§ I. – TRUE DEVOTION IS INTERIOR
(106)

N° 106

This quality requires that true devotion not limit itself to exterior practices (vocal prayers, pilgrimages, fasts, etc...), carried out automatically and without any application. These practices, let us note it well, are by no means excluded. But they originate from a completely different principle: they originate *"from the spirit and the heart"* **simultaneously**; *"from the esteem we have of the Blessed Virgin, the high idea we have formed of her greatness* (i.e., from the mind) *and the love which we have for her* (i.e., from the heart)." Because of this, this esteem and this love will be expressed in all sorts of ways. Every time it will be required, it will be carried out and spoken exteriorly. But these actions and these words will only be the reflection of interior convictions and profound love.

*
* *

§ II. – TRUE DEVOTION IS TENDER
(107)

N° 107

This word expresses the idea of absolute trust in Mary. Like the trust of a child in his good Mother. Moved by this trust, the soul has recourse to Mary, with much simplicity, in all its needs, those of the body as well as those of the spirit, those of the natural order as well as those of the supernatural order, without fear of bothering this good Mother or of displeasing Jesus Christ. The detailed specification of all these needs furnishes the Saint with the opportunity to paint a very beautiful picture, in the form of diptychs: on one side our miseries, on the other the efficacious and appropriate help which Mary brings to them.

In the first place a general assertion including all the details possible and set over both sides of the diptychs like a heading:

The soul implores the aid of its good Mother, at all times, in all places, and about all things.

Then the double series of the **evils** and the **remedies**:

In its doubts	=	*to be clarified* (enlightened)
In its wanderings	=	*to be brought into the right path* (returned into the way)
In its temptations	=	*to be supported* (and not to succumb)
In its weaknesses	=	*to be strengthened* (and avoid the fall)
In its falls (if they occur)	=	*to be lifted up*
In its discouragements (very often following the fall) (and resume the fight)	=	*to be encouraged*
In its scruples (excessive fears of offending God)	=	*that they may be taken away* (the ordinary effect of true devotion; see n°s 169 and 215)
In its crosses, toils, and disappointments of life (difficulties, trials, etc.)	=	*to be consoled* (not necessarily *delivered* from them; see n°s 153-154)

Finally, the general conclusion including everything again: "*In all its evils of body and mind, the soul's ordinary refuge is in Mary.*"

This is what can be called a tender devotion and childlike trust. Look at this little child: he hesitates between two paths to take: he is enlightened by his mother; he starts off down the wrong path since he was unable hesitate: he is returned by his mother to the right path; he is tempted, he is weak, he falls, he loses courage, and always his mother comes to his help! Sometimes also he is afraid of the dark, but his mother reassures him; or else he suffers, and his mother consoles him. Is this not at the same time very charming and very serious!

*
* *

§ III. – TRUE DEVOTION IS HOLY
(108)

N° 108

"Thirdly, true devotion to our Lady is holy, that is to say, it leads the soul to avoid sin (the negative side of holiness), *and to imitate the virtues of the Blessed Virgin"* (the positive side of holiness). The true way to honor the saints is, indeed, to imitate the examples which they have left us.

Father Gebhard tried an ingenious reconciliation between the Ascent of Carmel, as it is described by St. John of the Cross in his two books *The Ascent of Carmel* and the *Dark Night of the Soul*, and the enumeration of ten virtues of the Blessed Virgin, as it is found in n° 108. To come to God Who dwells on the summit of the mountain and Who is its all, the soul wants, like Mary, to despoil itself of everything, to realize its nothingness, and to walk by the arid and dark path leading all the way to Him. The first feeling produced in it by the consciousness of its nothingness and of the divine Majesty is a feeling of *profound humility*. It will try to establish itself in it. Then it will renounce the lights of its mind by a very great participation in the *lively faith* of Mary. It will renounce its own will by a *blind obedience*. Knowing that it can do nothing by itself, it will *pray continually* to obtain the divine help. It will distrust the creatures which surround it and will practice *universal mortification*, and, as if this active purification was not enough, it will ask for the help of the purifying action of God to obtain a *divine purity*, like Mary Immaculate. Thus purified actively and passively the soul will try to imitate the *ardent charity* of Mary. But having arrived at these heights it will no longer desire anything more, like John of the Cross, than to die and be despised for God, and it will practice the *heroic patience* of the Queen of Martyrs. And when it will have managed to suffer with a smile on its lips, it will reflect something of the *angelical sweetness* of Mary, and on the mystical Carmel will reign the divine silence described by John of the Cross: silence of the senses and the passions; silence of opinions and its own tastes; silence of personal cares and individual activity, even in spiritual things; silence, finally, of the world and every creature. And thus *divine wisdom* will be established in a soul beginning with this life. Above this, there is only the eternal marriage.

"*These are the ten principal virtues of the most holy Virgin.*" And their reproduction in a soul is the summary of the whole ascetical and mystical life. We shall soon find a proof of this in commenting on n° 119.

*
* *

§ IV. – TRUE DEVOTION IS CONSTANT
(109)

N° 109

True devotion is *constant*, that is to say, it strengthens a soul on the right path on which it has started out, and it leads it not to leave easily its practices of devotion. These practices being inspired, we said, by a profound interior conviction and not by a passing enthusiasm of sensible devotion, they are already by that very fact shielded from many sudden variations in the degrees of fervor.

True devotion also impels a soul to fight against all the obstacles opposed to this constancy; that is to say: a) against the *devil* and his infinitely varied temptations; b) against the *world* with its fashions and maxims, advocating perpetual change, so as to vary the pleasure; c) against the *flesh* with its troubles and passions, quickly becoming satisfied with its first object and moving violently towards another. In spite of these multiple sources of appeal to variety, the soul remains firm in its devotion. It is neither changeable, nor gloomy, nor scrupulous, nor timorous.

As the soul is, however, neither impeccable, nor pure spirit, it can sometimes fall into a more or less grave infidelity, or only experience sensible devotion more or less or even not at all. But, *"if he falls,"* he does not stay on the ground: *"he rises again"* promptly *"by stretching out his hand to his good Mother."* And *"if he loses the relish and taste of devotion, he does not disturb himself because of that."* The soul has only a political power over its sensible faculties, and it is not often possible to tame them to subject them to devotion. Besides, this is not necessary, because *"the just and faithful client of Mary lives on the faith of Jesus and Mary"* and not on feelings of the body.

*
* *

§ V. – TRUE DEVOTION IS DISINTERESTED
(110)

N° 110

The disinterestedness produced in a soul by the true devotion is universal. It does not simply lead this soul to prefer spiritual favors to temporal favors. It raises it above the desire for spiritual favors themselves. It inspires him, according to the saying of St. Bernard, to become attached to the God of consolations and not to the consolations of God. This is the most absolute indifference and the most complete abandonment to the divine will. Likewise with regard to Mary:

A true client of Mary does not serve that august Queen from a spirit of lucre and interest, nor for its own good, whether temporal, corporal, or spiritual, but exclusively because she merits to be served, and God alone in her. He does not love Mary precisely because she does him good, or because he hopes in her, but because she is so worthy of love.

This is the love of benevolence in its highest degree.

As a result of this disinterestedness, the true client of Mary will remain perfectly insensible to the presence or absence of sweetness or aridity, which, ordinarily, follow one another alternately in an indefinite series in the devout life in practice. He is no longer enthusiastic in moments of fervor. He is no longer depressed in the moments of drought. He loves Mary as much on Calvary as in the Wedding at Cana.

How such a devotee is pleasing to God and Mary! But also how rare he is! So that it may be less rare, Montfort took up his pen and tried to put on paper the principles of spiritual direction which were so successful for him for so many years.

*
* *

A DIGRESSION
PROPHETIC VIEWS ABOUT THE TREATISE AND THE DEVOTION

N°s 111-112

In the following numbers (111 and 114), Montfort gets carried away with the idea that he has just uttered, namely:

"the precious and efficacious help which his book will bring to the formation of true clients of Mary."

This book **can** contribute to it in spite of its imperfections. Our Saint says many things about Mary, but he passes over an infinity of others, either through ignorance, or through inability to express his thought, or through want of time. (Let us recall that the *Treatise* was written very quickly.) Nevertheless, not because of man's part in it, but because of divine grace, this little work, falling into the hands of a soul well-born, is capable of revealing to him the value and excellence of the true devotion. So, on the point of undertaking the composition of its second part, the one which especially concerns the devotion of Holy Slavery, he would like to write it with his blood, in the hope of giving more weight to the truths which he is going to teach.

N° 113

Not only will his book with the grace of the Holy Ghost be able to produce this effect, but the Saint **hopes** that it will be so:

Sooner or later the Blessed Virgin shall have more children, servants, and slaves of love than ever; and that, by this means, Jesus Christ shall reign more in hearts than ever.

N° 114

What transforms his hope into **certitude** are the diabolical *persecutions* which will be unleashed against this *little book*, against its *author* and against its *readers*.

We said previously that the future would bear out these prophetic views, at least as regards the relentlessness of the Jansenists against Father de Montfort, and the rage of the revolutionaries against his little writing. But persecutions are not wanting either against those who follow his doctrine and put it into practice. Far from demoralizing him, this thought rather excites him; far from deploring the fact, he is delighted at it:

But what matter? So much the better! This very foresight encourages me, and makes me hope for a great success!

Success of distribution, certainly! Very few devotional books count such a great number of editions. Interior success, moreover, by the multitude of slaves of Mary whom this book raised up in the world: a great success:

That is to say, a great squadron of brave and valiant soldiers of both sexes, to combat the world, the devil, and corrupted nature in those more than ever perilous times which are about to come!

Compared with the last sentence of n° 110, where Father de Montfort states that he has preached this devotion in public and in private for many years; compared also with n°s 99 and 100, where the holy missionary recommends his devotion even to sinners in order to leave their sad state, these words prove that no one is excluded "a priori" from the practice of this devotion, since he is inspired by goodwill and honestly seeks the best means to please God. Obviously, we shall see in n° 119 that the results obtained will be very different according to the generosity of the souls who will consecrate themselves to Mary. In a greater or lesser degree, however, all will be slaves of Mary.

ARTICLE III

Different practical forms of the true Devotion

(115-119)

Provided that the essential qualities of the true devotion are present, provided that they are all present, because *good comes from an integral cause, but evil from any defect,* several different forms are presented in the practice of this devotion, some good, others better, others perfect. Each will be free to choose the form which agrees with him the most. Similarly, in order to go to heaven, does everyone not have the power either to lead a Christian life simply, or to enter religious life, and among the different orders, to opt for the one which appears to him the most austere?

Freedom consists in deciding for one form or another. But it is inevitably necessary to accept one. It is, indeed, required to have practices of devotion, in the same way that it is required to have devotion. For devotion cannot exist without these practices. Montfort proves further on, in speaking about the Holy Slavery, the reason for the existence of these **practices** and the division into *exterior* practices and *interior* practices. All of them will play in the devotion the same role that, respectively, the body and soul play in the human composite.

He gives, first of all, *the practices common to every true devotion*. Then he announces simply *the perfect practice* with which the whole rest of the work will be occupied henceforth.

SECTION I

Practices common to every true Devotion

(115-117)

§ I. – INTERIOR PRATICES
(115)

N° 115

"Here are the principal of them stated compendiously":

1° "*To honour her as the worthy Mother of God, with the worship of hyperdulia, that is to say, to esteem her and honour her above all the other Saints; — a) as the masterpiece of grace* (which she possesses in fullness) and b) *as the first after Jesus Christ, true God and true Man*" (Whose Mother she is). These are the two principal reasons for the worship of hyperdulia.

2° "*To meditate on her virtues, her privileges, and her actions*," in order to conform our life to them, in the measure possible.

3° "*To contemplate her grandeurs*": the integral divine maternity and universal queenship.

4° "*To make to her acts of love, of praise, of gratitude.*"

5° "*To invoke her cordially*," and with trust.

6° "*To offer ourselves to her, and unite ourselves with her*," which is already a sketch of the consecration of the Holy Slavery.

7° "*To do all our actions with the view of pleasing her*," and especially:

8° "*To begin, to continue, and to finish all our actions* **through** *her,* **in** *her,* **with** *her and* **for** *her, in order that we may do them* **through** *Jesus Christ,* **in** *Jesus Christ,* **with** *Jesus Christ, and* **for** *Jesus Christ, our Last End.*"

Several of these practices overlap, and, furthermore, although being formally interior, or coming from the interior and from the use of the interior faculties, they are naturally expressed by exterior worship, either private or public, and inform our whole Christian life.

Most will be found entirely in the Holy Slavery, especially the 8th, as Father de Montfort himself remarks. "*We will presently explain this last practice.*"

*
* *

§ II. – EXTERIOR PRACTICES
(116-117)

N°s 116-117

They are very numerous. The Saint only enumerates a few of them, following the book of Rev. Fr. Paul Barry: *Le ciel ouvert à Philagie.*

Here are the principal ones (according to the *Treatise*):

1°, 2° and 5° To enter confraternities or Orders consecrated to Mary. To wear her liveries or scapulars.

4° To fast, practice mortification or give alms in honor of Mary.

6° To recite specifically Marian prayers with devotion: the Rosary, the chaplet, the Little Crown, the Little Office or the Little Psalter of the Virgin, the Marian antiphon of the season, and the *Magnificat.*

7° To sing or have sung in her honor spiritual canticles, and to publish her praises.

9° and 10° To adorn her churches and altars, to carry and have her images carried in procession.

11° To have her name and monogram carved or to place her statues over the entrances of cities, churches, and houses.

12° *To consecrate ourselves to her in a special and solemn manner*, as will also be prescribed for the Holy Slavery.

In concluding, the Saint says on which conditions these exterior practices will sanctify souls. They are the conditions which the Church demands for the recitation of the Divine Office, and which he himself inserted into his method of reciting the Rosary:

a) *A right intention* of honoring Jesus Christ and edifying our neighbor.

b) *Attention*, rejecting at least voluntary distractions.

c) *Devotion*, avoiding haste and slowness.

d) *Modesty*, consisting of a worthy and edifying posture.

SECTION II

The perfect practice

(118-119)

N° 118

Montfort cleared the ground. He spoke honestly and completely about the true devotion to Mary, such as it was known, practiced and recommended before him. It now remains for him to explain in every detail the form which he finds the most perfect, for which he is going to establish a complete method of spirituality, encompassing all the manifestations of life and subjecting them to the dominion of Mary.

This presentation will be the object of the whole second part of the *Treatise*.

Here, he is content to arrange the transition by remarking:

1° The indisputable fruitfulness of this practice in itself (n° 118).

2° The unequaled way in which it can be realized (n° 119).

*
* *

§ I. – THE INDISPUTABLE FRUITFULNESS OF THIS PRACTICE
(118)

But after all, I loudly protest that, having read nearly all the books which profess to treat of devotion to our Lady, and having conversed familiarly and holily with the best and wisest of men of these latter times, I have never known nor heard of any practice of devotion towards her at all equal to the one which I wish now to unfold…

At first sight, these words seem to announce a completely new method. This strangely contradicts what is expressed in n°s 159-163. Montfort begins to say there: "*The practice which I am teaching is not new. Fr. Boudon, who died a little while ago in the odour of sanctity, says* **in a book which he composed on this devotion** *that it is so ancient we cannot fix precisely the date of its commencement.*" Then the Saint draws there the history of the Holy Slavery in broad strokes.

To understand the true sense of n° 118, it is necessary to compare it to n° 219 of *The Love of Eternal Wisdom*.

Having said wherein this devotion essentially consists, Montfort adds: "*As there are several books which discuss this devotion,* it suffices for me to give assurance that I have never found a more solid practice of devotion to the Blessed Virgin, because it is supported by the example of Jesus Christ, *more glorious to God, more salutary to the soul,* and *more terrible to the enemies of salvation*; and, finally, *sweeter* and *easier"* (*Love of Eternal Wisdom*, #219).

This is also what is proved in n° 118.

To know what was taught in the past, Montfort consulted books; to know the sense of the Marian piety of his time, Montfort conversed with scholars. And he arrived at this conclusion: among all the forms of devotion honored by the Christian people, none can be compared to the Holy Slavery. This one is known and practiced by very few souls, but even so it is known and practiced, at least in each of its elements taken separately. He himself will only have to group these elements in order to compose a method of powerful spirituality, of which he can be called the author.

And he continues, declaring the prodigious fruitfulness of this method to lead one to true holiness. He does not know of another:

...exacting from the soul as it does more sacrifices for God, emptying the soul more of itself and of its self-love, keeping it more faithfully in grace, and grace more faithfully in it, uniting it more perfectly and more easily to Jesus Christ; and finally, being more glorious to God, (more) *sanctifying to the soul, and* (more) *useful to our neighbor.*

We find in this sentence a rapid summary of five fundamental truths, and we understand better the reason for the existence of the numerous anticipations indicated above. This one for example: "*It is this very thing which we do by the devotion of which we are hereafter to speak.*" (See n° 77.)

He asserted it several times. The time has come to prove it.

*
* *

§ II. – THE UNEQUALED WAY IN WHICH THIS VERY DEVOTION CAN BE FULFILLED
(119)

N° 119

This method, however, will not end in the same result for all. It is not comparable to a mold, imprinting inevitably and invariably the same form on all those who will pass through it. The method itself contains exterior and interior practices, the latter much more important than the former. Besides, souls will be more or less generous in the acceptance of the required sacrifices. We can thus count on a great variety in the classification of the results obtained.

As the essential of this devotion consists in the interior which it ought to form, it will not be equally comprehended by everybody. Some will stop at what is exterior in it, and will go no further, and these will be the greatest number.

They will have the perfect devotion, in this sense, that they will carry out perfectly these exterior practices, will submit themselves to the exercises of the preparatory month, will pronounce their act of consecration, will recite faithfully the recommended prayers, etc.... But, wanting to climb the mountain of Carmel, they have no courage to follow the arid and obscure path which leads straight to the Sovereign Good. They commit themselves in the way adorned by the goods of heaven. They thus make long detours and do not ascend fast.

Some, in small number, will enter into its interior, but will only ascend one degree there.

Who will mount to the **second** *step?*
Who will get as far as the **third**?
Lastly, who will so advance as to make this devotion **his habitual state**?

To what do these degrees correspond? It is rather difficult to determine, at least if we stay strictly in the perfect devotion. But the Holy Slavery is, on the whole, only a means of arriving more perfectly and more easily at union with Our Lord, union in which all Christian perfection is summarized. The diverse degrees of the spiritual life itself, by which this union is ordinarily realized, must, then, necessarily correspond with the degrees of the Holy Slavery. And so, it would be possible to enlighten them by one another. This is the way followed by Rev. Fr. Lhoumeau, and nothing proves that it is bad.

The first degree would be constituted in this case by all the exercises, but then rendered totally Marian, which are ordinarily fitting for the **purgative way**. As regards the past, the excesses of which it is necessary to repair:

> *Mary is my clear fountain*
> *In which I discover my ugliness.*

For what regards the future, the excellence of which it is necessary to prepare:

> *This is my arc in the deluge*
> *Where I am not drowned.*

The second degree would coincide with the exercises, likewise rendered Marian, of the **illuminative way**. The soul, cleansed of its faults, trains itself for the practice of the virtues. Coming to its help, Mary communicates to it her faith, her pure love of God, her trust in the divine goodness, her humility and all her other virtues. (See n°s 213-216.)

The third degree would contain all the characteristics of the **unitive way**. The soul is more under the action of the gifts than under the influence of the virtues. It is more prompted than acting, more passive than active. Mary will help her faithful slaves bear the painful trials of this way (See n°s 152-

154) and will communicate to them the grace of contemplation.

Finally, those who underwent the terrible purifications of the passive night of the senses and the spirit and arrived at **transforming union** or **spiritual marriage** become firmly established on such summits by their state. The presence of Mary will attract that of the divine Spouse, and will make His union with the soul supremely fruitful (n°s 20 and 36).

But who will reach this union?

"He alone to whom the Spirit of Jesus Christ shall have revealed the secret, the faultlessly faithful soul, whom He shall conduct there Himself, to advance from virtue to virtue, from grace to grace, from light to light, **until he arrives at the transformation of himself into Jesus Christ**, *and to the plenitude of His age on earth, and of His glory in heaven."*

Such is the radiant end proposed to those who embrace the perfect devotion. In this way of universal renunciation, all do not show the same courage. Some are content with the very first sacrifices. Others go up to the end of the divine requirements. And Mary reigns in everyone and establishes the reign of her Son there, in the measure in which they emptied themselves of self.

In this way the degrees of the ascetical and mystical life are scaled, from the first to the last, developing on a par with and more easily with the practice of the true devotion.

PART II

ON THE PERFECT DEVOTION

Montfort recalled, very briefly, we can say, the principal truths contained in the Marian domain. Most belong to common Mariology. But they already lead to this special form of devotion, which he proposes to teach. Let it suffice for us to mention again Mary's participation in the fruitfulness of the Father; her integral divine Maternity concerning Christ and His Mystical Body; the admirable dependence of Jesus on His Mother; Mary's maternal and royal power over the elect; her close collaboration with the Holy Ghost in the distribution of all graces and of each among them, etc. So many solid bases of the Perfect Devotion itself.

Finally, directly approaching his subject, Montfort is going to discuss it with all the desired fullness. This considerably reduces the work of the commentator. Rarely will the latter need to explain the text. He will often be content with a parallel step. Sometimes even, he will allow himself to summarize.

The *Perfect Devotion*, in other words, **the Holy Slavery**, is a *total consecration of oneself to Jesus Christ through the hands of Mary, as a slave of love*. In the supernatural order, this donation possesses the same extent as the donation of a slave in the natural order.

By this consecration, we understand, first of all, the act itself, then the state inaugurated by this act.

Following the Saint, we shall study in four chapters:

1° The **nature** of the Perfect Devotion (n°s 120-133).

2° The **motives** of the Perfect Devotion (n°s 135-212).

3° The **effects** of the Perfect Devotion (n°s 213-225).

4° The **practices** of the Perfect Devotion (n°s 226-273).

CHAPTER I

THE NATURE OF THE PERFECT DEVOTION

(120-133)

N° 120

Montfort himself summarizes thus the nature of this devotion:

All our perfection consists in being conformed, united, and consecrated to Jesus Christ; and therefore the most perfect of all devotions is, without any doubt, that which the most perfectly conforms, unites, and consecrates us to Jesus Christ.

Now, Mary being the most conformed of all creatures to Jesus Christ, it follows that of all devotions, that which most consecrates and conforms the soul to our Lord is devotion to His holy Mother, and that the more a soul is consecrated to Mary, the more is it consecrated to Jesus.

Hence it comes to pass that the most perfect consecration to Jesus Christ is nothing else but a perfect and entire consecration of ourselves to the Blessed Virgin, and this is the devotion which I teach.

What things are supposed in these few lines! The first fundamental truth as a whole: Jesus is the last end of all our devotions, and any formula of piety which would not have for its last end to lead to Him must be mercilessly pushed aside (n°s 61-67). The teaching of St. Paul: "For whom He foreknew, He also predestinated to be made conformable to the image of His Son" (Rom. 8:29) – "For all are yours; and you are Christ's; and Christ is God's" (1 Cor. 3:22-23). And even the teaching of Christ about the vine and the branches and that of St. Paul about the Mystical Body. We also find there a reminder of the role of the Virgin in our union with Our Lord (n° 75).

The idea is, then, very clear.

Let us apply ourselves rather to the conclusion.

Our Saint proposes it under a double form. The first responds exactly, as is fitting, to the two preceding propositions: this is the one that we gave above. The second explains, under absolutely different terms, an idea that Montfort asserts is the same. There would be, then, according to him, perfect equation among these diverse elements:

1° *Perfect consecration to Mary = Perfect consecration to Jesus.*

2° *Perfect consecration to Jesus = Perfect renewal of the vows of Baptism.*

And thus, by virtue of the principle: two quantities equal to a third are equal to each other:

Perfect consecration to Mary = Perfect renewal of the vows of Baptism.

The proof of the first two equations will provide him with the title and the material of the first two articles.

In the third, he answers some objections.

ARTICLE I

Perfect consecration to Mary equals perfect consecration to Jesus

(121-125)

N° 121

Montfort highlights, first of all, the extent of the donation constituting the Holy Slavery. Then he shows that it is the best way of consecrating oneself to Jesus Himself. *"This devotion consists, then, in giving ourselves entirely and altogether to our Lady, in order to belong entirely and altogether to Jesus through her."*

§ I. – THE EXTENT OF THE PERFECT CONSECRATION TO MARY

The second fundamental truth taught us the real nature of our relations with Our Lord and His holy Mother: they are the relations of a slave with his master or mistress (n°s 69-77). It insisted quite especially on the differences between the servant and the slave (n° 71). Just as the Saint had not made then the practical application to the Slavery of love (See n° 72, the end of 3°), similarly, he does not explicitly connect the current application with the theory which precedes. He supposes that his readers are capable of recognizing by themselves the link between the two passages.

In the light of this remark, let us see:

a) The detail of this consecration.

b) Some explanations concerning good works especially.

A. – DETAIL OF THE CONSECRATION
(121)

It is necessary to give to Mary:

1° "**Our body with all its senses** (external and internal) **and its members**," considered as principles of any operation belonging to the vegetative and sensory existence, and being of use to the intellectual life.

2° "**Our soul, with all its powers**," also considered as principles of all the operations belonging to our intellective and human nature, that is to say, coming from either the intelligence, or the will, and, for the latter, having issued from this very faculty or commanded by it, and executed by the other powers.

By these first two donations, our entire human nature is consecrated to Mary. This is the donation of the tree, not yet of the fruits.

3° "**The exterior goods**, *of fortune, whether present or to come.*" This is the realization of one of the sacrifices imposed on the slave: all the goods which belong to him or which he can acquire later are the possession of his master. Already a painful sacrifice, although it has exterior things as its object. And, furthermore, the quantity can be more or less great, the act of renunciation, from the subjective point of view, will be just as difficult and the merit will be just as great. Since these exterior goods, however, are added, so to speak, to the human personality, to continue it beyond its essential limits, the greater the quantity, the more considerable the objective value of the sacrifice will be.

4° "**Our interior and spiritual goods**, *which are our merits and our virtues, and our good works, past, present and future.*" Anther consequence of his position: the slave works only for his master. The fruit of his labors does not belong to him: it belongs to the one whose slave he is. A sacrifice so difficult, that no congregation or religious order dared to impose it on its members. (See n° 123.)

Montfort especially develops this fourth element, which is the characteristic of his devotion. "*In a word,*" he said, (it is necessary to give her) "*all we have in the order of nature and in the order of grace*": Grace, indeed, is in us at present a principle of supernatural actions and merits for heaven, either by itself, or by the infused virtues which accompany it. These actions and these merits must also be consecrated to Mary.

Then "*all that may become ours in future in the orders of nature, grace, and glory.*" Now our heavenly happiness itself constitutes, in advance, the object of this consecration, with the excellent actions of knowledge and love which will fill eternity. Nothing truly escapes from the reach of this act, which must be "*without any reserve of so much as one farthing (3°), one hair (1°), or one least good action (4°).*"

This offering, like that of the slave, will be:

a) *Unlimited in duration:* "*for all eternity.*" Since it involves the immortal soul and the gifts of grace and glory, natural death, which puts an end to human slavery, does not do so for the slavery of love. On the contrary, it stabilizes it in the immobility of the perpetual present.

b) *Absolutely gratuitous*: "*and without pretending to (as a right) or hoping for (as a mark of the goodness of the Queen, but brought about, nonetheless, by the donation of the slave), any other recompense for our offering and service, except the honour of belonging to Jesus Christ through Mary and in Mary, even though that sweet Mistress were not, as she always is, the most generous and the most grateful of creatures.*" The slave of love knows that he will be rewarded, but it is not for this that he consecrates himself. He would give himself with so much haste and so much love, if he did not foresee any remuneration.

B. — EXPLANATIONS CONCERNING GOOD WORKS
(122)

N° 122

Here we must remark that there are two things in the good work which we can do, namely, satisfaction and merit; in other words (he says), their satisfactory or impetratory value and their meritorious value. An important distinction, indeed, if we were to know what we can give to Mary and for which purpose we can give it to her.

1° Definition of each of these values.

a) *the* **satisfactory** *value of a good work is the good action, so far as it satisfies for the pain due to sin*, in whole or in part, for those who still live on earth, as well as for the souls in purgatory, in some by mode of remission, in others by mode of suffrage.

b) *the* **impetratory** *value of a good work is the same action so far as it obtains some fresh increase of grace.*

Impetratory value and impetration should not be confused. Value is attached to an *act* and requires remuneration, either in strict justice, or of simple suitability. Impetration is a potency ensuing from *prayer* and relying on God's goodness and promises. The first is never frustrated. The second does not always obtain the grace requested.

c) *the* **meritorious** *value, or the merit, is the good action, so far as it merits grace now and eternal glory hereafter.*

Every good work, indeed, carried out in a state of grace gives us the right to an increase of grace here on earth and of glory in heaven. It is a right of justice and, furthermore, strictly personal.

2° The meaning of the donation of our good works to Mary.

We give everything to Mary by our consecration of the Holy Slavery. A distinction, however, is imperative as regards the final purpose of our donation.

a) *Merits*, being strictly personal, are by that very fact incommunicable. Our Lord alone was able to communicate His merits to us, and to become our pledge with His Father in all justice, because, to carry out this application, it is necessary to possess a power not only over the person, but over nature itself. This is given only to God, and to Our Lord as God. If, then, we surrender to Mary our merits, graces and virtues, it is not so that she may communicate them to others, nor so that she may appropriate them, but so that she may preserve, increase and embellish them. (See the 5th fundamental truth, n°s 87-89.) That she really renders such services to us, n°s 146-150 will especially show.

b) *The satisfactory and impetratory value* of our good works can be applied either in our favor, or in favor of others. We leave it up to Mary, so that she may communicate it to whom it will seem good to her and for the greatest glory of God. And as we give to the Blessed Virgin, not only what we already have, but what we can have in *the future*, we include, it seems, even the satisfactory value of the prayers which will be offered for us after our death. We can only profit from them according to the will of Mary. It is as if we gave up an inheritance in favor of another, who would henceforth take care to provide for our needs. Besides, this clearly follows from the nature of slavery. Is not the master free to dispose of as he pleases the goods which his slave brings to him?...

*
* *

§ II. – THIS IS THE BEST WAY TO CONSECRATE ONESELF TO JESUS HIMSELF
(123-125)

N° 123

We have the proof of it, first of all, in the **extent** of the offering: "*All we can give.*" Absolutely no reserve. We have the proof of it thereafter in the **manner** of presenting this offering: "*through Mary's hands.*" This, if we consider the consecration of the Holy Slavery *in itself*.

If now it is **compared** to other devotions, these require only a part of our time, a part of our good works, a part of our satisfactions: the former abandons everything, including the right of disposing of the satisfactions gained by good works. Congregations and religious orders require the renunciation of worldly goods by the vow of poverty, of the goods of the body by the vow of chastity, of one's own will by the vow of obedience, sometimes also the freedom of the body by the vow of enclosure. But none obliges the religious to sacrifice the right which he has to his spiritual riches. This devotion requires the greatest possible detachment from what is most precious and dearest to the Christian: his merits and satisfactions.

So, in every way, this consecration to Jesus through Mary's hands is the most perfect of all consecrations of which the Savior can be the beneficiary.

N° 124

Remarks. – 1° This consecration makes it impossible for the slave of love to dispose of anything. He can, however, and *must fulfill of the obligations of his state*; the latter would contain the application of the satisfactory and impetratory value of his good works. A priest, for example, whether he was ordained before or after his consecration to Mary, is obliged by his office to apply the fruits of the Mass to those who expressed the request to him and gave him a stipend. He does not have to worry. This application is an act of his ministry. He is the only one who can formulate it. Does he say Mass for the intentions of the Blessed Virgin? He has to apply the fruits of it to the intentions that Mary herself desires to see accomplished. He cannot leave to the Virgin the care of making this application, under pain of invalidity. He thus carries out this offering, as Father de Montfort says, *"only according to the order of God and the duties of our state."*

N° 125

The consecration of the Holy Slavery is addressed *at one and the same time to the most holy Virgin and to Jesus Christ*; to the Most Blessed Virgin as to the perfect means chosen by Jesus Christ to unite Himself to us and to unite us to Him; to Our Lord as to our last end, our Redeemer and our God. It is not, then, required to pronounce two different acts of offering. The same includes both points of view. In reality, the formula composed by Montfort sufficiently highlights them both and with the hierarchy indicated right here. Even so, certain brief formulas are addressed to Mary alone, for example: "I am all yours, my good Mother, and all that I have belongs to you." They express exactly the same sense. Mary necessarily leads to Jesus those who abandon themselves to her.

ARTICLE II

The perfect consecration to Mary equals the perfect renewal of the vows of Baptism

(126-130)

N° 126

The second equation established in n° 120 concerns the identity which is revealed between the perfect consecration to Mary and the perfect renewal of the vows of baptism. *"I have said that this devotion may most justly be called a perfect renewal of the vows and promises of Baptism."*

Our Saint shows: 1° what is the relation between the vows of baptism and Marian consecration (n° 126); 2° the forgetfulness that men show of the commitments of their baptism (n° 127); 3° the necessity of reminding them about them by the renewal of these vows (n°s 128-129); 4° and consequently the opportuneness of Marian consecration (n° 130).

*
* *

§ I. – THE RELATION BETWEEN THE VOWS OF BAPTISM AND MARIAN CONSECRATION
(126)

This relation is expressed by an increase in value of the consecration. The latter eminently contains everything that the vows of baptism contain, and it adds very considerable elements to it.

"*Every Christian, before his Baptism, was the slave of the devil, seeing that he belonged to him.*" (See n° 68.) A tyrannical and de facto domination, but which constitutes no right for Satan.

"*He has in his Baptism, by his own mouth* (if he was an adult) *or by his godfather and godmother* (if he himself was incapable of this act), *solemnly renounced Satan, his pomps and his works; and he has taken Jesus Christ for his Master and Sovereign Lord, to depend upon Him in the quality of a slave of love.*" (See n° 68.)

This recognition of the real rights of Jesus over us is also in the Marian consecration, because "*we renounce, (as is expressed in the formula of consecration* [composed expressly by Fr. de Montfort]), *the devil, the world, sin, and self; and we give ourselves entirely to Jesus Christ,*" but all this "*through the hands of Mary.*"

Thus, in the consecration of the Holy Slavery, we have eminently all that is in the vows of baptism.

But, furthermore, the consecration offers three considerable advantages assuring the superiority of its importance and efficacy:

1° *It is not pronounced by proxy*, as the commitments of baptism are made most of the time. Someone who consecrates himself to Mary makes this donation in full knowledge of the matter, spontaneously and voluntarily. The commitments involved in this consecration, being made consciously and deliberately, have more chance of being more faithfully observed.

2° *It expressly assures the mediation of Mary*, with all the advantages attached to this mediation, concerning the glory of God, our protection against ourselves and our perseverance in our good sentiments. Now the consecration included in baptism takes place indeed, if we want, with the intervention of Mary, because Mary is universal Mediatrix, and there is no need to have recourse to her expressly, for her to intervene efficaciously. But explicit recourse makes her intervention more intimate and more fruitful. This is the advantage of Marian consecration. Furthermore, the use of the means established by God has its unequaled efficacy.

3° It gives to Jesus through Mary *even the satisfactory and impetratory value of our good works*, which the baptismal consecration does not achieve. After baptism, one remains free to apply to whom one wants the value of one's good works. After the consecration of the Holy Slavery, we no longer possess this freedom. The latter thus honors Our Lord more than the former.

*
* *

§ II. – THE FORGETFULNESS THAT MEN MANIFEST OF THE COMMITMENTS OF THEIR BAPTISM
(127)

1° THE EXTENT OF THESE COMMITMENTS

N° 127

They contain a negative point of view and a positive point of view.

a) **Negative point of view**. "*Men*," says St. Thomas, "*make a vow in holy baptism to renounce the devil and his pomps*," that is to say, the feasts, entertainments and other means which the demon organizes to ruin souls: "*In baptismo vovent homines abrenuntiare diabolo et pompis eius.*"

This text is drawn from an objection proposed by St. Thomas, but it expresses a truth: In order to save oneself it is necessary to renounce the devil and his pomps. How can this renunciation be the object of a vow in baptism? Does the vow not have for its object a work of supererogation?... And the holy doctor answers, after establishing all the distinctions in the article: "This renunciation is necessary for salvation, but it is no less voluntary and free of it, with the same freedom as salvation itself." And it is enough so that it can be the object of a vow, at least if we take the vow in the generic sense of spontaneous commitment.

b) **Positive point of view**. It is expressed by St. Thomas in the same passage following the previous text: "*Et fidem Christo servare,*" they also make a vow of fidelity to Christ.

Father de Montfort derives the same truth from a saying of St. Augustine: "*Votum maximum nostrum quo vovimus nos in Christo esse mansuros.*"

To renounce the devil is only preliminary. It is then necessary to give oneself to Jesus Christ. We empty ourselves of a thing only by filling ourselves with another thing. We empty ourselves of the spirit of the world only by filling ourselves with the spirit of Jesus Christ.

2° THE IMPORTANCE OF THESE COMMITMENTS

It is asserted by St. Augustine: "*Votum maximum nostrum*," our greatest vow, and by canonists: "*Praecipuum votum est quod in baptismate facimus*," the chief of vows is the one we make at baptism. This importance results from the impossibility of reaching our last end if we are not faithful to this vow. The subject of the other vows is mostly of supererogation. They aim at leading us more certainly and more perfectly to heavenly happiness. The subject of the vow of baptism is indissolubly linked to this happiness. To be able to enjoy it one day, it is necessary to accomplish at least this. And if salvation itself were not attained by the free effort of our will, the means which lead to it could not be said to be free and voluntary, so necessary is their connection with it. Whence comes the obligation in which we are to observe this vow, or at least to return to the right path, if we have had the misfortune to deviate from it.

3° THE FREQUENCY OF TRANSGRESSIONS

Yet who has kept this great vow? Who is it that faithfully performs the promises of holy baptism? Have not almost all Christians swerved from the loyalty which they promised Jesus in their baptism?

How few, indeed, do not give the priority to Satan over Jesus Christ, by committing mortal sin? And thus the vow of baptism is seriously broken. But how many others only have the name of Christian and live absolutely as if they had made no commitment?

4° THE CAUSES OF THESE TRANSGRESSIONS

Having noticed this distressing truth, the Saint informs us of the motive:

Whence can come this universal disobedience, except from our oblivion of the promises and engagements of holy baptism?

Are we seeking the reason for this forgetfulness?

Hardly anyone ratifies of himself the contract he made with God by those who stood sponsors for him.

The promise was given by proxy. The one who made the commitment was unaware of it. In His haste to grant him His benefactions, Our Lord contented Himself with the promise of fidelity pronounced on his behalf by another. But if the baptized person is not later instructed about his obligations, if he is unaware of them, he can neither ratify them, nor a fortiori observe them.

Let us note, however, the obligations exist, whether or not the contract is ratified by the baptized person. Baptism has the effect of placing us again under the authority of our true Head, Our Lord Jesus Christ. We belong to Him by natural right and by right of conquest. In dedicating ourselves to Him in the baptism received in our childhood, so that that baptism can entail obligations. And if the Saint sees in the non-ratification of these commitments the cause of this disorder, this is only as a result of the ignorance which results from it for the man or of the little importance that he assigns, mistakenly moreover, to the commitments made by others on his behalf.

The national Council of Sens, convened by Louis the Pious (814-840), also noted that the cause of the disorders of Christians was the forgetfulness and the ignorance in which they lived of the commitments of holy baptism.

*
* *

§ III. – THE NECESSITY OF REMINDING CHRISTIANS OF THESE COMMITMENTS BY THE RENEWAL OF THE VOWS OF BAPTISM
(128-129)

N° 128

To remedy such a great evil, the Council of Sens (Paris) prescribed the public and solemn renewal of the vows and promises of holy baptism. Thus, Christians would regain awareness of the personal obligations which they contracted by receiving this sacrament.

This took place in the ninth century.

N° 129

Seven centuries later, the catechism of the Council of Trent: *"faithful interpreter of the intentions of this holy Council"* exhorts priests *"to lead their people to remember and to believe that they are bound and dedicated to Our Lord Jesus Christ, as slaves to their Redeemer and Lord."* What means will help to obtain this result? The most effective will certainly be the renewal of the vows of baptism with all possible exterior splendor. This is the custom observed in many countries: either on the day of the solemn First Communion, or during the exercises of the mission, the children or the faithful are invited to take an oath themselves which others took for them on their entrance into life. These ceremonies, preceded by days of intense meditation, and prepared by passionate instructions, produce everywhere the best fruits and leave very long-lived memories in souls.

*
* *

§ IV. – CONSEQUENTLY, THE OPPORTUNENESS OF MARIAN CONSECRATION
(130)

N° 130

If such is, according to *"the Councils, the Fathers* (for instance, St. Augustine) *and experience,* the necessity for the faithful to remember the obligations of their baptism; if the best means to succeed in it is the renewal of the vows which they uttered, who does not see, then, the indisputable advantages and the absolute opportuneness of the consecration of the Holy Slavery? It is a perfect renewal of the vows of baptism: do not we consecrate ourselves more completely than at baptism, and do not we take the most perfect of all means to go to Jesus, the Most Blessed Virgin Mary?

This consecration, pronounced solemnly at least once a year, on the anniversary of one's entrance into the Confraternity, and renewed every day by the brief formula, constantly keeps the soul mindful of its commitments, and allows one to hope for the most beautiful results. It does not confer impeccability. The passions remain and falls are always possible. But the light with which the soul is filled will quickly arouse the voice of remorse and will make it find again, by prompt penitence and a sincere confession, peace of conscience and the joy of an irreproachable Christian life.

ARTICLE III

A response to some objections

(131-133)

N° 131

This article simply adds some complementary clarifications to the previous articles, in the form of answers to three objections.

First objection.

This devotion, such as it was explained by Montfort, is new in the Church or at least it is not imposed upon anyone as a necessity. Now, in the first case, it is dangerous to follow it; in the second case, we are not obliged to it. It is thus better to leave it aside: we do not run a risk there and we neglect nothing necessary for salvation.

Response.

a) *As for the novelty*: this total consecration to Mary is the equivalent of a total consecration to Jesus and a perfect renewal of the vows of baptism. We thus have as many witnesses testifying to the real antiquity of this devotion, as we have documents requiring the renewal of the vows of baptism, and showing this renewal as a practice held in honor by all Christians. Now, St. Augustine (IV-Vth centuries), the Council of Sens (IXth century) and the Council of Trent (XVIth century) speak about this consecration to Jesus, included in baptism, and of the necessity of renewing it, so that the disorders and corruption of morals among Christians disappear. What is new there is not the consecration itself; it is the perfect form of this consecration and the more explicit recourse to the means established by Jesus: the Most Blessed Virgin Mary. But there is a very justifiable novelty there. Nobody should complain about it, but much rather be delighted at it.

b) *As for its indifference*, we can have recourse to it or not: nothing is more false. A devotion, the negligence of which entails the gravest abuses, cannot be called an indifferent devotion. Now, according to the Council of Sens, the main source of all the disorders, and consequently the damnation of souls, comes from the forgetfulness and indifference of Christians towards this devotion. It cannot, then, be called an indifferent devotion. If we are not obliged to practice it in its perfect form with all the extent which Montfort gives it, it is at least necessary to have what corresponds to the renewal of the vows of baptism and to their perfect observation. And then, we shall quickly notice that the best way to succeed in it will be to accept the devotion of the Holy Slavery.

N° 132

Second objection.

If we relinquish to Jesus through the hands of Mary the satisfactory and impetratory value of our good works, as Montfort teaches, we shall make ourselves powerless to help the souls of our parents, friends and benefactors. Now, the obligations which we contracted in their regard compel us to help them. It is impossible, then, to pronounce his consecration of the Holy Slavery.

Response.

1° *This consecration does not entail any unfortunate consequence for our parents, friends, and benefactors.*

Even among humans, the one who gives up his fortune and the fruit of his work to another to show his benevolence can count on this other to meet his personal needs and the needs of all those toward whom he has real obligations. The recipient is free to accept or to refuse the donation or even to accept it without liability for debts exceeding the value. But, if he accepts, he takes under his care all the obligations of the donor, even if these obligations exceed in extent the objective value of the donation. If he did not satisfy these obligations, he would be lacking in justice and would act selfishly. Now, if this is true of a mere mortal, for stronger reason is it true of Jesus and Mary. It would thus be to offend their power and goodness to believe in the possibility of such neglect. They will, on the contrary, know well how to assist our parents, friends and benefactors, either by drawing from our little spiritual revenue (if it is sufficient), or by other ways (if it is not sufficient or if they do not find there what is required).

2° *This obligation in no way dispenses us from the obligation to pray for our parents, friends, and benefactors,* living or deceased.

Obviously, we give up by our consecration the right to apply by ourselves the satisfactory and impetratory value of our good works. Henceforth, this application depends on Mary. But it by no means follows that we can no longer pray to this good Mother to help such and such among those to whom we are indebted. There is nothing in this which contradicts our donation to Mary. On the contrary, it is to honor her by showing her our confidence. Let us suppose a rich person who would have given all his goods to a great prince, to honor him more. Would he not ask this prince with more confidence to give alms to any of his friends who might ask him for it? Not only would this confidence honor the prince, but it would please him. It would afford him the opportunity to show his gratitude to the one who despoiled himself in order to clothe him and who impoverished himself to honor him. If this is true of an earthly prince, it is much more so for Our Lord and the Blessed Virgin: they will never allow themselves to be outdone in gratitude.

3° *Our consecration assures the maximum efficacy to our prayers for our parents, friends, and benefactors.*

We shall prove it later, in n°s 171 and 172. Mary, purifying our good works of all imperfections, increases their satisfactory and impetratory value. They then become capable of obtaining much more. Then, Mary knows perfectly all the needs of the persons who are dear to us. It can happen that we ask for useless or harmful things for them. It can happen that we do not think either of praying for them, or of asking what they really need. Let us pray only that Mary act. Let us surrender ourselves to her will for them, for the choice of the persons to help and of graces to be granted. And everything will take place for the greatest glory of God and the greatest good of those who are dear to us.

It is important to note well this objection and the various answers which can be opposed to it, because it recurs very often against the Montfortian devotion.

N° 133

Third objection.

If I give to the Blessed Virgin all the value of my actions to apply it to whom she wills, there will be nothing more for me to apply to myself after my death, and, because of this, I shall perhaps have to suffer for a long time in purgatory.

Response.

1° This objection, says the Saint, *is inspired by self-love*. It is possible only thanks to our ignorance of the generosity of God and His holy Mother. It is not forbidden to think of oneself and to aim especially at sparing oneself the sufferings of purgatory. Ultimately, this could just as well be for the love of God, as out of the love of concupiscence. But to spare oneself effectively from these sufferings, the best thing is not to accumulate spiritual riches only for the purpose of being able to pay one's debts after death. The ideal is to try to contract no debt, by avoiding sin and by acting through love.

This is why this objection *demolishes itself*, according to the expression of Father de Montfort. Let us think of someone devoted totally to love. To prove this love better, he gives to God all that he can give, without reserving anything, either for himself, or for others. He yearns only for the glory and reign of God and His holy Mother, and sacrifices himself to bring it about. How could he be punished in the next life? How could he be treated more rigorously than another, who, seeking only his personal interests, did good things only for the love of himself? "For with the same measure that you shall mete withal, it shall be measured to you again" (Lk. 6:38). This soul was generous and selfless towards Jesus and Mary; Jesus and Mary will be generous towards him in this world and in the next, in the order of nature, grace and glory.

2° We shall also recall that Mary *can only dispose of our communicable goods*, that is to say, the satisfactory and impetratory value of our good works. With regard to our merits, she preserves and embellishes them, and she will hand them back to us entirely upon our arrival in heaven. There cannot, then, be a question of these merits in the fear which this third objection presupposes. But as merits have the proper effect of obtaining for us the light of glory on our entrance into heaven, they have no efficacy to protect us from purgatory. Similarly, they sustain no damage, because of a stay, even a prolonged one, in that place of expiation. Only our satisfactions can abbreviate our sufferings or protect us from them. The true response to this objection is the one, then, indeed, that Father de Montfort gave and that we explained in the first place.

CHAPTER II

MOTIVES FOR THE PERFECT DEVOTION

(134-212)

N° 134

In the **first section**, divided into eight articles, Montfort enumerates eight *"motives which ought to recommend this devotion of the Holy Slavery to us"* (n° 134).

In the **second section**, he explains the same truths and quite specially the IIIrd motive (n° 150), under the biblical figure of the good services of Rebecca to Jacob, and Jacob's devotion to Rebecca in order to win these good services.

SECTION I

The enumeration of the motives themselves

(135-182)

These motives are, in the order in which the Saint gives them:

1° The excellence of this consecration to Jesus through the hands of Mary (n°s 135-138).

2° The example of Jesus Christ and even of God, and the obligatory practice of humility (n°s 139-143).

3° The assurance of Mary's good offices (n°s 144-150).

4° The advantages resulting from Mary's intercession to obtain the greatest glory of God (n° 151).

5° The means which it places at our disposal to arrive at union with Our Lord (n°s 152-168).

6° The great interior liberty that this devotion gives us (n°s 169-170).

7° The great goods that it obtains for our neighbor (n°s 171-172).

8° The great matter of our perseverance, of which it is an admirable means (n°s 173-182).

We find here many ideas, which we have already encountered many times. And this is quite natural besides. Does not *perfect* devotion implement itself completely, which is the distinctive feature of all *true* devotion? We will, then, be allowed to go from now on much more quickly. We shall be content with highlighting, as much as it will be possible, the main thread of the thought of our Saint. We shall give real explanations only when these will be necessary and will include some new element. This will be the case especially for the Vth article.

Article I

First motive

The excellence of this consecration

(135-138)

N°s 135-136

The very nature of this act of consecration, embracing absolutely *all* that we are, all that we have and all that we can do, and consecrating it entirely to God's service, is the first motive which recommends it to us. The more valuable a thing is, the harder we have to try to obtain it. Let us recall the Gospel parable of the precious stone.

In this case, the argumentation of the *Treatise* is simple. It is reduced to the two following syllogisms:

1º There is nothing more worthy here on earth than the service of God: *To serve God is to reign*. The more someone is dedicated to the service of God, the more he will be raised in dignity.

Now, no act of consecration influences a subject in the service of God more than that of the Holy Slavery. It is not a question, indeed, of reserving for God a definite time or a category of special actions. By virtue of this offering, and unless it is expressly retracted, every action, from the smallest to the greatest, belongs to Jesus, through the hands of Mary, whether we think of it or not.

Thus, nothing more establishes man in dignity than this act of consecration, and nothing is more capable of stimulating its noble emulation.

N°s 137-138

Jesus promised to reward a hundredfold, even on earth, the sacrifice of worldly goods granted for His love.

Now, the sacrifice of spiritual goods has incomparably more value. It denotes, in a supreme degree, the delicacy of a soul. Wanting to belong entirely to its Savior, as its Savior lived entirely for it, this soul would be afraid of seeing a spirit of ownership creep in with regard to these spiritual goods, and prevent it from belonging completely to Jesus.

How would Our Lord not be infinitely generous in time and eternity towards such a generous soul? *Cum liberati, liberalis erit*.

Is this not, here again, a powerful stimulant to accept this devotion?

Article II

Second motive

The divine examples and the obligatory practice of humility

(139-143)

1° OUR LORD'S EXAMPLE

N° 139

It is indisputable that, to come into the world, the Son of God had the choice of a great number of means. He could have descended from heaven to earth with a human body in the fullness of life and maturity. He could have fashioned a body for Himself, as He had molded that of Adam or formed that of Eve at the beginning of the world. He would have had at least this advantage of being able to show, from the beginning of His earthly life, the treasures of grace and knowledge contained in His human soul as a result of its union with His divinity.

So of course the divine Word chose the way which would seem to our way of thinking the least indicated. He agreed to be conceived in the womb of a woman, imprisoned for nine months in strict and constant dependence. He followed all the vicissitudes of childhood, without another visible concern than eating and sleeping, receiving caresses and lavishing them. For thirty years of His life out of thirty-three, Mary seemed to monopolize all His affections and concerns. In all this, there must be a reason.

That infinite Wisdom, Who had a boundless desire to glorify God His Father, and to save men; and yet He found no more perfect means, no shorter way to do it, than to submit Himself in all things to the Blessed Virgin, not only during the first eight, ten, or fifteen years of His life, like other children, but for thirty years.

This reason is that Jesus thus obtained the greatest glory for God.

And He (the divine Wisdom) *gave more glory to God His Father during all that time of submission and dependence to our Blessed Lady than He would have given Him if He had employed those thirty years in working miracles, in preaching to the whole earth, and in converting all men.*

What does this prove to us? This little sentence:

Otherwise, He would have done it.

Otherwise, He would have chosen this other way, because Jesus is perfection itself, and all that He said, all that He did led most certainly to the purpose which He proposed to attain.

And the Saint concludes:

Having, then, before our eyes an example so plain and so well-known to the whole world, are we so senseless as to imagine that we can find a more perfect or a shorter means of glorifying God than that of submitting ourselves to Mary, after the example of her Son?

Jesus is our model in everything and everywhere, and Christian perfection consists in imitating the examples that He gave us. Only one of His actions, only one of His words, revealed to certain souls the way of holiness. What do we say then of the splendid light which will manifest itself to us, when it will no longer be just a word in passing, nor one transitory action of Jesus which will offer itself for our meditation, but a life of thirty years, intentionally lived to serve as an example for us and inspire our imitation?

And it is on this way that Montfort wants to launch souls, by asking them to model their devotion on the model of that of Jesus for His Mother. And however much we shall do, never shall we love, never shall we honor, never shall we serve Mary as much as Jesus loved, honored and served her before us. What an encouragement and also what a pledge of security in our Marian devotion!

2° THE EXAMPLE OF THE THREE DIVINE PERSONS

N°s 140-142

The Saint summarizes here what he said in complete detail in n°s 14-39. Namely: **God** willed to make use of Mary *before, during* and *after* the Incarnation. So, he showed us how far we ourselves must go in our dependence on this good Mother. Each of the three divine Persons willed to act only through Mary. Can we without an extreme blindness do without her to go to God and sacrifice ourselves to God?... The reason for this conduct is given to us by St. Bernard: "Qui indignus eras cui daretur, datum est Mariae ut per eam acciperes quidquid haberes. *God, seeing that we are unworthy to receive His graces immediately from His hand, gives them to Mary, so that we may have through her all that He wants to give u*s." Is it not just, St. Bernard also says, that grace returns its author, in the form of gratitude, respect and love, by the same channel which brought it to us? This is pleasing to God, because this is to imitate His conduct. Other texts quoted by Father de Montfort, n° 141, are already familiar to us. (See above, n° 32.)

3° THE OBLIGATORY PRACTICE OF HUMILITY

N° 143

Besides the necessity for us to imitate the divine examples, another no less urgent motive obliges us to have recourse to Mary: it is the consciousness that we ought to have of our unworthiness. We are such miserable sinners!

To want to approach God by ourselves, without the help of any mediator, would be an act of great pride and a foolish presumption. Now, God resists the proud and gives His grace only to the humble. To practice this humility by having recourse to Mary's intercession is therefore the best means to be assured of the divine favors. (See 4° fundamental truth, n°s 83-86.)

Article III

Third motive

The assurance of Mary's good offices

(144-150)

These good offices can be grouped under two different headings: 1° Mary gives herself to her slave of love (n°s 144-145) and 2° Mary purifies our good works, embellishes them and makes them agreeable to her Son (n°s 146-150). So, thanks to this devotion, not only shall we not be unworthy to appear before God, but all that we offer will be truly agreeable to His divine majesty.

1° MARY GIVES HERSELF TO HER SLAVE OF LOVE
(144-145)

N°s 144-145

The Virgin does not allow herself to be outdone in generosity. Like her divine Son Himself, she gives herself completely to the one who has given himself to her. She adorns him with her merits, supports him with her prestige, communicates to him her virtues, and makes herself his guarantee with Our Lord. As a result of this exchange, the slave of love no longer puts his trust in himself and in his good works. He puts it solely in Mary. He no longer has any fear of approaching Jesus. Is he not equipped with the merits and intercession of Mary? As much as he dreaded this confrontation with the divine Master when he had to count on himself alone, so much does he desire it since he took, like St. John, Mary for all his riches. (See the text of "the learned Abbot Rupert", quoted by Montfort in n° 145. P.L. CLXVIII, 837-838.)

2° MARY PURIFIES OUR GOOD WORKS, EMBELLISHES THEM AND MAKES THEM BE ACCEPTED BY HER SON
(146-150)

N°s 146-150

Mary does not keep for herself the merit of the good works which the slave of love gives up to her by his consecration. Poor merit, moreover, diminished by so many stains! To try to offer this to such a powerful God, as the sole homage of our dependence towards Him, would this not be to imitate a poor peasant who has to present to the king as the cost of his rent only one miserable apple? This is precisely the comparison that our Saint uses to shed light on the role of Mary. What, indeed, would this poor peasant do in order to win the friendship and benevolence of the king?

He would go to find the queen. He would hand her the apple and ask her to present it to the king. The queen, having accepted the poor little present of the farmer, would put this apple on a beautiful golden dish and would present it herself to her royal spouse, on behalf of the farmer, with all the love which she would be able to put into it. In truth, this present, although unworthy in itself to be presented to the king, would become a present worthy of his majesty, in consideration of the beautiful golden dish on which it is and the loved one who passes it on.

In the same way, our works, soiled in so many ways, are purified and embellished as soon as they touch the very pure and very fruitful hands of Mary. Not only do they lose what they have of the imperfect, but they are positively adorned with the merits and virtues of Mary. This good

Mother then presents them herself to her Son on our behalf, with all the love which she knows how to put there. And Jesus no longer sees the basic poverty of the offering, but His Mother who presents it, and He accepts eagerly.

To try to present one's merits to Jesus by oneself is to risk being rejected, because Jesus will examine the offering and often He will reject it because of the stain contracted by it.

This rejection, sometimes for light motives, could seem hard on the part of the Savior. But let us reflect a little. A work deserves supernatural reward only if it is entirely ordered towards God. Any depraved intention intervening to divert it, even partially, from this end, by that very fact deprives it of a part of its meritorious value, if not of the totality, because, even if there is merit, it is ineffective until the order of charity is perfectly restored, and the consequences of the fault removed. It can be said, then, that Jesus examines the offering and rejects it because of its stains.

And how does it happen that Mary: 1° purifies this work of its stains; 2° embellishes it and causes it to be accepted?

1° *She purifies it*, by inspiring in her slave the intention of consecrating himself to her, and by using the act of charity which he then produces. Is there not, indeed, in this filial request of her maternal intervention, a formal recognition and an implicit retraction of the bad intentions which had soiled the good works? Once these intentions are retracted, the order of charity has been restored, nothing prevents the meritorious value from producing its effect.

2° *She embellishes it* by adding to our personal merits some of her own. That is to say, she takes advantage of this request for intervention made by us to renew the offering of her own merits. In the same way, does not the ministerial offering of the Priest at the altar allow Jesus to offer again to His Father the sufferings which He endured on the Cross? The little offering of the slave of love ends up eliciting the offering of Mary, which is supremely pleasing to the divine Majesty. As Montfort says, to present one's offering to Jesus "through the pure and virginal hands of His beloved is to take Him by His weak side" and to be assured of a favorable welcome.

Is this not the counsel which St. Bernard gave (De aqueductu, n° 18, towards the end. P.L. CLXXXIII, 448)?

"*Modicum qui offere desideras, gratissimis illis et omni exceptione dignissimis Mariae manibus offerendum tradere cura, si non vis sustinere repulsam.*" *When you want to offer something to God, take care to offer it through the very pleasing and very worthy hands of Mary*, **unless you want to be rejected**.

Besides, is this not the process which nature inspires in children towards adults? Our advocate possesses all the qualities required to inspire trust in us. She is so *powerful* that she is never refused. She is so *full of inventions* that she knows all the secret ways of gaining the heart of God. She is so *good* and so *charitable* that she repels no one, however little and wretched he may be. We can thus everywhere and always have recourse to her intercession. And she will always win our case.

Is this not yet another powerful motive recommending the perfect devotion to Mary?

Article IV

Fourth motive

The greatest glory of God obtained by this devotion

(151)

N° 151

In all our actions, we ought to seek not only the glory of God, but the greatest glory of God. Now Mary alone:

1° *Knows perfectly* the greatest glory of God, hidden from most of us.

2° *Always acts* in the direction of this greatest glory, for which many of us have no courage.

Thus the slave of Mary has surrendered everything to this good Mother. But he is sure that everything will be used for the greatest glory of God. There is only one exception: namely, if he expressly revokes his offering, thus himself preventing Mary from obtaining this end for him.

Is there any consolation equal to this for a soul who loves God with a pure and disinterested love, and who prizes the glory and interest of God far beyond his own?

Let us allow ourselves to be guided by this luminous knowledge of the Virgin. Let us surrender blindly to her care. Let us subject the special intentions which we may have to hers, and they will tend toward the greatest glory of God. Let us say, for example: "Only if what I ask for is for the greatest glory of God do I wish to be heard, because this is also the will of Mary. Otherwise, I conform myself to the desires of my Queen, because the greatest glory of God is there, and there only."

Article V

Fifth motive

A quick way of arriving at union with Our Lord

(152-168)

N° 152

We know the teaching of Our Lord about the vine and the branches: He Himself is the vine and we are the branches. We know the teaching of St. Paul about the Mystical Body. The Christian life consists, then, in being united with Our Lord, as a vine shoot is united with the vine stock, and as a member of the body is united with the head. The closer this union, the more perfect the Christian life will be. If we can even arrive at the transforming union, the Christian life will attain its highest degree of perfection.

As a result, the spirituality which will lead most quickly to this union will be the most advantageous for the soul, the one which most deserves to be accepted.

Now, such is the devotion of the Holy Slavery. And Montfort proves it in showing that this way is: 1° **easy**; 2° **short**; 3° **perfect**; 4° **secure**, to arrive at the union with the divine Master.

Each of these modifiers goes further than the preceding and adds its special mark. An *easy* way is easily traveled. But is it about a high summit? This way can well be also the longest, because it will have to multiply circuits in order to reach the summit. Here, while being the easiest, it is also the *shortest*. It turns neither to the right nor to the left. There is no danger of being lost on it and we walk on it more readily. It is a *perfect* way: it was cleared by Jesus Himself in his great and admirable voyage to come to us. Now the road which leads perfectly from Rennes to Paris is also the one which leads perfectly from Paris to Rennes. Jesus was God; He became incarnate. Man must be divinized. The means which was of use to one will equally be of use to another. Finally, the same way is a *secure* way: most of the greatest saints followed it. Furthermore, it leads only to Jesus. There is, then, no fear of taking the wrong road. There is no fear either of being attacked during the journey: Mary is the immaculate way where the devil has no access.

Let us speak about these four different aspects of the Marian Montfortian way.

§ I. – THIS DEVOTION IS AN EASY WAY
(152-154)

The major reason for this ease is because Jesus, in passing through this way, leveled all the obstacles. Let us not delude ourselves, however. It is a question of arriving high, very high, at the summit of perfection. This end will not be reached without great efforts on our part. Therefore, do not see all the difficulties on one side and no difficulty on the other. Place yourself in the presence of the situation, and see how it is more bearable.

Now, asserts our Saint, we can, in truth, arrive at divine union by other ways. But this will be by many more crosses, combats and dark nights. Whereas, by the way of Mary, we pass *"more gently and more tranquilly."* This good Mother helps her slaves of love to carry their crosses. She supports them in their battles: she enlightens them in the darkness. So that, while involving essentially the same difficulties, the way of Mary is a way of roses and honey compared with other ways.

Therefore, some saints needed a singular grace to know the sweetness of this way. Others, while having a very great devotion to the Most Blessed Virgin, did not enter this way, or only a little. That is why they passed through rougher and more dangerous trials.

This allows Montfort to resolve an objection against his teaching in general, and against the ease of the Marian way in particular.

N° 153

Objection:

If the Marian way is so sweet, why do those most devoted to Mary have more occasions to suffer? They are contradicted, persecuted, libeled, and cannot be tolerated; or they walk in darkness without any interior consolation. All this does not seem to confirm the sweetness of the Marian way.

N° 154

Response:

The servants of the Virgin, being her greatest favorites, receive from her the greatest graces and favors of heaven, which are crosses. For the same reason, it is possible that their crosses are **objectively** heavier than those of others.

Nevertheless, **subjectively**, the servants of Mary are the ones who carry them with more ease, merit and glory. The reason for this is that Mary preserves all the crosses "*in the sugar of her maternal sweetness and in unction through pure love.*" This strength which it gives them makes them **capable** of carrying *great* crosses and of carrying them *joyously and perseveringly*.

Montfort uses here the graceful comparison of Mary as a "*confection of crosses.*" This comparison is drawn from the treatment to which the exterior covering of the walnut is subjected. Of itself, it is very green and very bitter, and it could not be taken without an extreme violence being imposed. But, having been preserved in sugar, it becomes sweeter and passes easily. Thus the cross, very bitter in itself, becomes sweet and acceptable thanks to devotion to Mary.

Rev. Fr. Lhoumeau, paraphrasing this article, explains this ease of the Marian way according to the method of the pedagogy employed: that of **maternal education**. It is the sweetest and the easiest method: it is inspired by love, supported by love and it has recourse voluntarily to the means most proportioned to the weakness and ignorance of the child. The mother has almost all the work, and the child – ease.

Farther on, alluding to the sacrifices inherent to the Holy Slavery, which Mary does not remove, but which she helps to accept, he associates two apparently opposite expressions: "**easy way and narrow way**." And he thus proves the compatibility of these two features. "With their rails, only a few centimeters wide, and from which the wheels cannot deviate at all, our railroads are undoubtedly narrow ways, if we compare them with our beautiful highways. Who will deny that they are an easy way, thanks to the considerable suppression of the frictions and other advantages? This narrow way is thus easy, and in a sense, a wide way, that is to say, where we feel at ease."

These ideas depart somewhat from the actual framework of the *Treatise*. They are, however, inspired by the whole Montfortian spirituality. That is why, it seemed to us good to note them, to cast a little more light on the true character of this ease, attributed to the Marian way.

*
* *

§ II. – THIS DEVOTION IS A SHORT WAY
(155-156)

N° 155

Montfort assigns two causes to this brevity:

N° 156

1° We do not get lost there;

2° Walking there with more joy and ease, we also walk there more quickly.

It is especially 1° which is developed here. **We do not get lost in Mary**. She is not, indeed, as other creatures often are, an obstacle hindering or delaying our union with God. On the contrary, she moves us closer to Jesus Christ and shortens the distance which separated us from Him. There is no place where the creature can find God closer to it and more proportioned to its weakness. That is why Jesus descended there. Therefore, one risks long and painful searches when one does not go to ask for Him directly from Mary. The example of the Magi is a striking proof. How much easier it would have been for them to find the Savior if they had known beforehand that He was the Son of Mary!

Furthermore, Mary did not know personally the tortuous ways of sin, where one travels so quickly the slopes which lead away from God, but where the distance seems infinitely great, when one wants to return to his starting point. In the same way, those who will live resolutely in submission and dependence on her will have nothing to fear from the attempts of their enemies to prevent them from walking, or to make them retreat, or to make them fall. With the support, help and guidance of the Virgin, they will advance in giant steps to Jesus Christ, as Jesus, by the same way, came in giant steps to us: "*He hath rejoiced as a giant to run the way*" (Ps. 18:6). The man obeying Mary will win signal victories over all his enemies: "*An obedient man shall speak of victory*" (Prov. 21:28).

Thanks to the rapidity of this Marian way, Jesus, Whose life on earth was only thirty-three years, lived longer than Adam, whose fault He came to repair: "*Being made perfect in a short space, he fulfilled a long time*" (Wis. 4:13). He lived longer, because He lived subject to Mary, because the one who honors his Mother amasses treasures every day: "*He that honoureth his mother is as one that layeth up a treasure*" (Eccli. 3:5); and those who live, as it were, enclosed in the womb of Mary (which is, we shall see, the characteristic feature of this devotion) quickly become old men in light, holiness, experience and wisdom. This is a mystical interpretation of these words of Psalm 91:11: "*Senectus mea in misericordia uberi*, my old age in plentiful mercy."

Even there, however, let us not be deceived. Everything will not be done in one day. Many souls lose courage because they did not obtain in a few weeks (much less in a few days), the results about which they had dreamed. Let us remember that here on earth, every life, begun in time, needs time to develop. That is why, "in speaking of the wonderful fruits of the Perfect Devotion, St. Louis-Marie de Montfort insists "on its faithful and persevering practice." To this tree of life which is Mary, it is necessary to apply the word of the Psalm: "*Which shall bring forth its fruit in due season*" (1:3). The time of fruits is preceded by the summer when they mature, of the spring when the flowers appear, finally the winter when everything seems dead."

*
* *

§ III. – THIS DEVOTION IS A PERFECT WAY
(157-158)

N° 157

The reason for this perfection is again twofold:

N° 158

1° Mary is the most perfect of creatures, the one who is the most capable of conforming us to Jesus Christ (n° 158).

2° By passing through her, Jesus was formed on our model. "Contrariorum eadem est ratio."[1] By passing through her, we will be formed on the model of Jesus (n° 157).

---

[1] A philosophical adage: opposite effects can proceed from the same cause. For example: to create and to annihilate both require the divine omnipotence.

It will be noticed that, to make things easier, we invert in the commentary the order of n°s 157 and 158 of the *Treatise*.

1° Mary is **the immaculate way**, where there is neither sin, nor shadow, nor darkness. Furthermore, this way is enlightened by all the natural and supernatural lights possible for a creature, more brilliant in them alone than the lights of all the Angels and Saints together. On the other hand, Mary is more powerful to support and defend those who will walk on her way, than all the Angels and Saints carrying out the same office towards those who would walk on theirs. Therefore, Montfort can exclaim enthusiastically:

Make for me a new road to go to Jesus, and pave it with all the merits of the Blessed, adorn it with all their heroic virtues, illuminate and embellish it with all the lights and beauties of the Angels, and let all the Angels and Saints be there themselves to escort, defend, and sustain those who are ready to walk there; and yet in truth, in simple truth, I say boldly, and I repeat that I say truly, I would prefer to this new perfect path the immaculate way of Mary.

Returning to the idea of educator, *Fr. Lhoumeau* reasons thus: the education of a child is all the more easy, all the more rapid and all the more perfect, the more enlightened, more skillful, more correct in their manners, their language, and their pronunciation the master and mistress are. Now can we imagine a teacher more learned, more skillful, and more impeccable than Mary? It is thus impossible to place oneself in a better school. With her, the studies will be easy, progress rapid and the education excellent.

2° Mary is not only (an) immaculate way and (a) perfect educator. St. Augustine calls her and our Saint calls her after him **the Mold of God**, *Formam Dei* (n° 219), the one in whom God was formed on our model and where we are formed on the model of God. In Mary, the *Most-High* humbled Himself even to us, so that, through her, we may rise up to Him. The

Incomprehensible allowed Himself to be taken in and contained in Mary, so that, through her, we may be taken hold of and led to God. In Mary, the *Inaccessible* approached us and united Himself personally to our nature, so that, through her, we may approach God, and unite ourselves closely with Him. In Mary, "He Who is" became "He Who is not," so that, through her, we who are nothing, can become like to God, by grace and glory.

It is through Mary that Jesus came the first time, and this arrival was perfect and glorious, although hidden and secret. It is through her that He will also come at the end of the world, in all His splendor and majesty. He could not, then, choose another way for His journey than holy Mary, by whom He so surely and so perfectly arrived the first time. For us, therefore, as for Jesus, not only on earth and during this life, but at the end of the world, and during eternity, we shall never find a more excellent way to go to Jesus than the immaculate way of Mary. The mold is absolutely perfect. If the material that is cast in it is liquefied just in time, the reproduction will be ideal. (See the *Secret of Mary*, n°s 16, 17, 18.)

"*Alas*," Montfort groans as he concludes, "*here is a mystery which is not understood: Hic taceat omnis lingua.*" It does no good to be surprised that, if this way, which is yet so perfect, is not more commonly followed. But is this not yet another reason, for those who know, to become passionately attached to it?

*
* *

§ IV. – THIS DEVOTION IS A SECURE WAY
(159-168)

"There is no more precious advantage than that of walking in security on the way of perfection! To go without getting lost on the arduous and difficult paths, finding a precious guide in the midst of events of the interior life as grave as they are delicate, is undoubtedly a pledge of Paradise, and like a deposit of the repose of the homeland."

Now Montfort asserts: *"This devotion is a secure way to go to Jesus, and to acquire perfection by uniting us to Him."*

He proves it:
1° *By the voice of authority*, basing his arguments on the teachings and examples of a large number of holy personages. On this occasion, he gives a beautiful historic outline of this form of devotion (n°s 159-163).

2° *By the voice reason*, basing his arguments on the providential role of Mary (n°s 164-165).

1° THE VOICE OF AUTHORITY
(159-163)

N° 159

The Church, in proposing the saints for our veneration, also aims at showing us, in their examples, the way to follow so as to arrive at salvation. If, then, the Holy Slavery was practiced, taught and strongly recommended by men whom the Church canonized or beatified, or whose authority it admits, this kind of devotion is a secure way to go to heaven.

Now Father de Montfort, relying on Fr. Boudon's authority, gives the names of the saints and illustrious persons who formally practiced the devotion of the Holy Slavery. Boudon himself draws this historical survey from a little anonymous book, entitled: *La devotion de l'esclavage* [The devotion of the slavery]. And he entitled his chapter III: *De l'origine et du progrès de la devotion de l'esclavage de la sainte Mère de Dieu* [On the origin and progress of the devotion of the slavery of the holy Mother of God].

This historical survey begins with St. Odilon, the third Abbot of Cluny, who lived in the middle of the XIth century

(962-1049). We could also quote older cases; for example: holy king **Dagobert II** (652-679), who had consecrated himself to Mary, in the quality of a slave, and Pope **John VII** (701-707), who, in an inscription on the ambo of the church Santa-Maria-Antiqua, calls himself: "†ΙΩΑΝΝΟΥ ΔΟΥΛΟΥ ΤΗΣ ΘΕΟΤΟΚΟΥ", slave of the Mother of God. In the epitaph which he had prepared for himself, he also said: "Ioannes, indignus episcopus, fecit. Beatae Dei Genitricis servus." Made by John, unworthy bishop, slave of the Mother of God. (See Dom Leclerc: *Dictionnaire d'Archéologie chrétienne et de liturgie*, tome V, col. 2016-2018.)

1° For **St. Odilon**, the fact is very exact. He was supernaturally cured by Mary in his youth. So he preserved a tender devotion to her, which incited him to offer himself to Mary in the quality of a slave. Here is the text of his consecration:

"O most pious Virgin and Mother of the Savior of all the ages, from this day and from now on, take me to your service and be my most merciful advocate in all my affairs. After God, I hold nothing more dear than you, and it is of my own free will that forever I am completely delivered to your service *as your slave.*"

2° St. Peter Damian, cardinal, bishop of Ostia and Doctor of the Church, having related the vision with which his brother, **Blessed Marin**, was consoled at his last moments, relates the testimony of his director, an old and venerable priest, by the name of Severus. This testimony is summarized by Montfort, citing Boudon, in n° 159. It can be read in full in Migne (P.L. CXLV, 566 and 567). The essential passage is this one: "Altari se Beatae Dei Genitricis *velut servile mancipium tradidit*, mox se *quasi servum malum*, coram Domina sua fecit verberibus affici," etc.... It is, then, indeed, a matter of the Holy Slavery. And this took place in 1016.

3° **Cesarius Bollandus** or **d'Heisterback** mentions an illustrious knight **Vautier** or **Gauthier of Birback**, close relative of the dukes of Louvain, who, having offered himself to the Mother of God in the quality of a slave, in approximately the year 1300, was then favored by extraordinary gifts and supernatural graces.

N° 160

4° **Fr. Simon de Rojas** (1552-1624), of the Order of the Most Holy Trinity for the redemption of captives, preacher of the Catholic King Philip III and confessor of Queen Margaret, made this devotion fashionable in Spain and the Netherlands, then reunited with the Spanish crown.

He had, and he inspired around him, the custom of greeting using the words *Ave Maria*. The queen herself greeted the king in this way. Now, one day, she was struck all at once with apoplexy, which deprived her completely of the use of her faculties. They ran to look for Father Rojas. The latter, according to his custom, said upon entering: "Ave Maria, Señora." The queen immediately returned to herself and answered: "Gratia plena, Padre Rojas." She then received the sacraments and died a holy death.

Touched by this miracle, the king promised Fr. Rojas to grant him all that he would ask for himself. But the man of God forgot his own interests and even those of his Order. He thought only of the interests of his good Mother, and only asked the king to obtain indulgences from Gregory XV (1612) for the slaves of Our Lady. He had set up, indeed, a pious association, with the authorization of Paul V.

5° Fr. Bartholomew de Los Rios (1580-1652), of the Order of St. Augustine, was a preacher of the Court, under King Philip IV and Princess Isabella Clara. In this capacity, he accompanied the princess, when she was appointed governess of the Netherlands. His friend, Fr. Rojas, took advantage of it to entrust to him the propagation of the Holy Slavery in Belgium. He successively established confraternities in Brussels, where the princess and all her court consecrated themselves solemnly, on August 15th, 1626, at Malines, Louvain, and then in Germany, Poland and Italy.

The emperor of Germany, Ferdinand II, made his consecration of the Holy Slavery with all his court, in 1640, encouraged too by the preaching of Fr. de Los Rios.

The latter propagated the Holy Slavery, not only by his words, but also by his writings. He composed several small treatises, which were soon translated into diverse languages. But his principal work, the one which makes him one of the precursors and teachers of Fr. de Montfort, is his book **Hierarchia mariana**, published in Antwerp in 1641. *"He treats with as much piety as learning of the antiquity, excellence, and solidity of this devotion."*

In ending the enumeration of the colossal works which this holy religious had undertaken for the glory of Mary and to win slaves for her, Boudon writes: "His zeal for the interests of the Mother of God deserves the praise of Angels and men, and this beloved of God deserves that his memory be held in benediction for all ages to come."

6° We find in the history of the Clerks Regular (**Theatine Fathers**) the confirmation of what the Saint said about them. In 1601, in one of their chapels, near Naples, they enlisted the faithful who came in very large numbers to venerate a miraculous image of the Virgin: "That they might *dedicate* themselves completely to the *service of this illustrious Mother*, and this not perfunctorily and in name only, but by a strict bond and a formal promise. So they subjected their will to her and they were called her slaves by a special title." And as a sign of their dependence, they wore little chains.

From Naples, this devotion passed into *Sicily*, especially in Palermo. The slaves have their chapel in St. Joseph's church there, staffed by the Theatine Fathers.

Finally, in Turin, the zeal of these religious was seen to triumph, when Charles-Emmanuel, Duke of Savoy, with all his children, and Cardinal Maurice, solemnly took their glorious chains, thus giving a wonderful example to all their subjects.

N° 161

7° The King of Poland, **Wadislas IV**, having been enrolled in Louvain, wanted all his subjects to be ranked among the slaves of Mary. He charged the Fathers of the Society of Jesus and in particular **Fr. Phalacius** to preach this devotion in his whole kingdom. The latter had the little works of Fr. de Los Rios translated and printed.

On the occasion of the apostolate of Fr. Phalacius in Poland, **Rev. Fr. Cornelius a Lapide**, as much to be commended for his piety as for his profound erudition, received the commission of several bishops and theologians, to examine this doctrine and this devotion. He gave it his entire approval. Many distinguished persons have followed his example.

And the **Jesuit Fathers**, always zealous in the service of the Most Blessed Virgin, presented in the name of their sodalists to the Archbishop of Cologne, Ferdinand de Bavière, a small book by Fr. de Los Rios entitled: *Mancipium Virginis*, The Slavery of the Virgin, to obtain approval for it. The archbishop allowed it to be printed and recommended all the religious and parish priests of his diocese to propagate this solid devotion as much as they could.

The **bishops** of *Malines*, *Cambrai* and *Ghent* had already approved it at the request of Fr. Rios. The latter reports the names of the princes, princesses, dukes and cardinals of various kingdoms who embraced this devotion. This is what historical documents (coat of arms, numismatics, genealogies) also demonstrate, showing frequently the little chains of the Holy Slavery on the blazons of the great families.

"The Spirit of God urged so strongly all sorts of persons to embrace (this devotion) that sometimes, as happened in Brussels in 1626, there were hardly enough workers to make the chains, with which these glorious captives loaded themselves."

N° 162

8° In France, this devotion was especially propagated by **Cardinal de Bérulle**, in spite of the calumnies and persecutions which this apostolate started. To the calumnies, the Cardinal only opposed patience at first. Then, on the advice of friends, he answered triumphantly to the attacks of novelty and superstition. He showed that this devotion is based on the example of Jesus Christ. Its obligatory character derives from the vows of baptism, of which this consecration is a perfect renewal.

N° 163

9° For this devotion, practiced by the faithful, examined by theologians, encouraged by bishops, all that was still lacking was **the approval of the Holy See**. It came in the form of the concession of indulgences. Pope *Gregory XV* gave it at first, at the request of Philip III of Spain (1613). *Urban VIII*, having been consulted about the little chains which the slaves wore, approved this custom and issued, on July 20, 1651, the Bull *Cum sicut accepimus*. He granted it great indulgences for these captives of the Blessed Virgin. The Discalced Augustinian Fathers of Provence, wanting to establish in Marseille an association of slaves of Our Lady, addressed Pope *Alexander VII*, who approved their project (on June 23, 1658), confirmed the indulgences given by Urban VIII and granted in addition all those with which the confraternity of Our Lady of the Pilar, in Saragossa, is enriched.

Conclusion. This study, although very abbreviated, shows that the devotion of the Holy Slavery is not an unsound and untrustworthy novelty, as some tried to say. It contains the very foundations of Christianity, and a blow cannot be struck at it without touching these foundations. It is, therefore, a secure way to go to God, and, if this devotion is not more common, it is because it is too precious to be enjoyed and practiced by everybody.

2° THE WAY OF REASON
(164-168)

N°s 164-168

Besides the example and teaching of the saints and other devout persons, led to holiness by this practice and recommending it to the faithful, the providential role of Mary in the economy of our redemption also proves to us that devotion to her is the most secure way to arrive at her divine Son.

Mary is not, indeed, as other creatures too often are, an obstacle to our union with God. Far from taking advantage of the devotion which she inspires in her children, she has no greater desire than to present to her Son all those who entrust themselves to her. It is proper to Mary to lead us to Jesus, as it is proper to Jesus to lead us to the eternal Father. She found grace before God for herself and for the whole world. How would devotion to her be an obstacle to grace? It is indeed rather the lack of devotion to her which explains why so few souls arrive at perfect union with Our Lord. If Jesus is everywhere and always the fruit of Mary, how could we have the fruit, without possessing the tree that produces it?

Let us, then, be firmly persuaded: the more we are united with Mary, the more we shall be united with Jesus, and the more Jesus will be active in us. This union with Mary must be accomplished in faith. We have to look at her in everything and always, if not with a distinct and deliberate view (that is to say, precise and conscious), at least by a general and imperceptible view (that is to say, implicit and underlying). In return, she will fill us with the thought of God, and will chase away any foreign thought, especially any thought that is erroneous, heretical or inspired by the malicious spirit. Let us remember that true devotion to Mary is an infallible sign of the true Church, the devotion to this good Mother being in itself a purely negative mark of the Church of Christ. We can thus assert with our Saint: the slave of the love of Mary could not be heretical, at least formally. The two terms are mutually exclusive. And furthermore, if he happened to be so materially, he would not persist when he would be enlightened. Otherwise, he would stop being a slave of the love of Mary. And if he died in his material heresy, his good faith would save him. It would be the means which Mary would use to lead her slave to Jesus and unite him to Him for all eternity.

If that is how it is in hopeless cases, what is to be said, then, about normal cases or of enlightened and faithful Christians who put themselves on the Marian way? Their salvation is assured as well as it can be here on earth. If, then, someone wants to realize great progress along the way of perfection and to find Jesus Christ surely and perfectly, let him set out on the Marian way. It is the path cleared by Jesus Christ, our Head; the member, in following it, could not make a mistake.

Article VI

Sixth motive

This devotion procures a great interior liberty

(169-170)

N° 169

This is what should recommend the Holy Slavery to timorous souls, wishing ardently to serve God with all their heart, but dreading to offend Him for the most pointless reasons. This fear can cause real torments and totally paralyzes the impulses of the soul towards God.

Now, one of the effects of the Holy Slavery is to free souls from these *servile fears*, to assure them of a great interior liberty, *the liberty of the children of God* and, by opening their heart to trust, to launch them in the ways of perfection.

In spite of what he says at the beginning of n° 170: "*without stopping to prove these truths by arguments,*" Montfort summarizes these reasons very felicitously, before proving the same truth by the example of Mother Agnes de Langéac.

1° Reasons establishing this liberty. By this devotion, we are voluntarily established in a loving captivity with respect to Jesus, a slave of Jesus in Mary. As recompense, this good Master:

a) frees the soul from the servile fear which captivated and confused it, reducing it thus to a constrained and humiliating state of servitude;

b) enlarges the heart by a holy confidence, by bringing the soul to look at God, not as a severe and demanding judge, but as a benevolent and merciful Father;

c) inspires a tender and filial love that is incompatible with the apprehensions of an anguished heart: "*Perfect charity casteth out fear*" (1 Jn. 4:18).

N° 170

2° The example of Mother Agnes of Langéac. We can point out in support of this interior liberty obtained by the Holy Slavery the experience of the nun as well as the special promise of Mary.

a) *The nun's experience.* Agnes Galand, in religion, Sister Agnes of Jesus, was born in Puy, on November 17,

1602. Her father, a simple cutler, was a rough man, and several times Agnes felt weighing, on her face or tender shoulders, a hand that was more accustomed to striking an anvil than to lavishing caresses. At the age of 7, she saw the body of a tortured victim. She experienced such an impression that she did not sleep the next night. These various causes perhaps increased the tendencies of a slightly worried nature. The next day, she went to the church of Notre-Dame to ask for the protection of the Virgin. After the Elevation, she heard clearly in the depth of her heart: "Make yourself a slave of the Most Blessed Virgin, and she will protect you against your enemies." – "Blessed Virgin," Agnes responded, "because you deign to will that I belong to you, from this moment *I consecrate to you all that I am*, and promise *to serve* you all my life *as a slave*."

It is to be noted that nobody then had spoken about the Holy Slavery in France. The first book on this subject was published only six years later. Nothing, therefore, humanly speaking, could give this thought to a child of this age.

So, having returned to the home of her father, she looked for an iron chain, which Providence allowed her to find immediately, and she put it on her flesh around the lower part of her back, as testimony of her servitude.

After this action, all her troubles and scruples ceased, and she was in great peace and expansion of heart. This committed her to teach this practice to the nuns of Langéac, whose prioress she became, to her confessors, and especially to Fr. Olier, founder of Saint-Sulpice, whose conversion she obtained by her prayers and tears. She is justly called the spiritual Mother of Saint-Sulpice, and she has a major role in the Marian devotion of this institute. All this, thanks to her delivery from scruples, obtained by the Holy Slavery.

b) *The special promise of Mary*. Agnes lived in great intimacy with the heavenly court. She spoke familiarly with her Guardian Angel, and often had apparitions either of the Blessed Virgin, or of one or the other of her favorite saints: Catherine of Siena, Mary-Magdalene, Cecilia, Teresa…

In one of these apparitions, the Virgin put round her neck a chain of gold, while saying: "I accept you again for my slave." And when, on the day of the Assumption, Agnes renewed her offering, according to a custom which was dear to her, Mary affirmed to her again that she accepted, and St. Cecilia, who accompanied her, added, in the name of the Virgin: "Happy are the faithful salves of the Queen of heaven, *for they shall enjoy true liberty.*"

Agnes died at Langéac, on October 19, 1634, scarcely 32 years old. Her cause was introduced long since at the court of Rome (by the cardinal of Noailles in 1703). The decree of heroic virtue was pronounced by Pius VII, on March 19, 1808.

Article VII

Seventh motive

This devotion obtains great goods for our neighbor

(171-172)

N°s 171-172

One of the principal objections formulated against the total donation of the Holy Slavery is the inability to help our parents, friends and benefactors afterwards. We have already resolved the question as regards the negative side (this is not an obstacle). Montfort now considers the positive side: the great goods which will result from it for all those whom we love. Indeed, thanks to this devotion, we give more in quantity, we give more in value, and we obtain more considerable goods for our neighbor.

1° *We give more in quantity*. We abandon into the hands of Mary the satisfactory and impetratory value of all our past, present and future good works, without excepting the slightest good thought, the slightest little suffering. Is this not to practice charity in an eminent degree, and to show by this charity that we are followers of Jesus Christ? Normally, already by the extent of this donation, we ought to obtain more.

2° *We give more in value*. Often, in reality, it concerns very ordinary works. We would be obliged to accomplish them even apart from the Holy Slavery, because they make up the daily duty of our state in life. To offer the value of them to Mary so that she may apply it herself for the greatest good of our neighbor is to protect oneself from vanity, because nature easily delights when its good works are noticed. This value thus has less risk of being diminished. But above all, these good works, passing through the hands of Mary, receive an increase of purity and richness. They thus acquire greater value, and become more capable of softening the anger of God, or of attracting His mercy.

3° *We obtain more considerable goods*. These goods are: the conversion of sinners, or the deliverance of souls from Purgatory. Now, to convert a sinner is to make him a sharer in the divine nature, a child of God and an heir of heaven. Nothing equals the greatness of these goods. To deliver a soul from Purgatory is to put it in possession of God, Whom she will love and glorify for all eternity. This is more than to create heaven and earth. And we can obtain these two goods by doing nothing more than our duty of state, without even the knowing it before the hour of death, simply because we left it entirely to Mary's mediation.

Is there any more powerful reason to commit a truly charitable man to embrace this practice? What joy at his judgment to make such a discovery! What glory during eternity!

Article VIII

Eighth motive

This devotion is an admirable means of perseverance

(173-182)

N°s 173-182

Is there any more powerful reason, did we say just now, to commit a man to embrace this practice? Father de Montfort answers: yes! And this motive concerns a most alarming question: that of our eternal salvation, that of our predestination. Now, the devotion of the Holy Slavery is an admirable means of perseverance. How would this special efficacy succeed in winning for it the sympathy of everyone?

It is not a question of repeating what was said either about the 5th fundamental truth, or even previously about true devotion to Mary as sign of predestination.

Whoever trusts in himself after his conversion will fall again into sin: this is certain. Whoever wants to guard his treasures himself, will be the prey of numerous and experienced thieves: we see this every day. But by this devotion: 1° we entrust all that we possess to Mary; 2° we rely only on her help to keep standing. It is impossible for this double confidence to be disappointed.

1° *The fidelity of the trustee.* What we gave to Mary by our consecration had no great value. Moreover, Mary was not obliged to receive it. She received it, however, out of pure charity, as she always does in such cases. She, then, has thus become the trustee of our little spiritual goods. Now, the trustee is obliged in justice, in virtue of the contract of deposit, to guard what was entrusted to him. If he came to lose it by negligence, he would be responsible for it. Let us not be afraid that this may happen with Mary. She is the faithful

Virgin, who repairs, by her fidelity, the losses which were incurred or caused the unfaithful Eve, by her infidelity.

Let us not hesitate, then, to entrust to her the gold of our charity, the silver of our purity, the waters of heavenly graces and the wines of our merits and virtues. Let us pour into Mary's lap all our treasures, all our graces, all our virtues. Since God enclosed Himself with all His perfections there, Mary's womb became a completely spiritual vessel, and the spiritual dwelling of the most spiritual souls. In spite of the world, the devil and the flesh, not only will Mary preserve, but she will increase our virtues and our merits.

2° *Power of the protector.* Poor children of Mary, our weakness is extreme. But let this not discourage us! In the turbulent sea of this world, Mary was given to us as a firm anchor, to which we can attach ourselves and which will prevent us from shipwreck. This good Mother loves those who love her: "Ego diligentes me diligo" (Prov. 8:17). She loves them not only with an affectionate love, but an actual and efficacious love, preventing them, by a great abundance of graces, from backsliding in virtue or from falling into sin. She keeps the saints in their fullness, as St. Bonaventure says, so that the latter does not diminish. She prevents their virtues from dissipating, their merits from perishing, their graces from being lost, the devils from harming them; and if they happened to fall all the same, she prevents Our Lord from chastising them, obtaining for them the time and the strength to get up and to do penance.

How, indeed, would she measure her favors to the one who gave everything to her? Being the most generous of all creatures, she will never allow herself to be outdone in love and generosity. However little we give her, she will return the abundance that she possesses, putting all her credit with God in the service of her slave of love. On one condition, however: it is that while abandoning himself completely to her and by entrusting himself to her help, he is not given to presumption, because the protection of Mary exempts no one from working to acquire the virtues and to tame his passions. Is this not rather an encouragement to make him be assured of success?

These are the principal ideas which Montfort develops on the same level with prodigious lyricism in the course of this article. The reader feels that he is sure of attacking the last bastion of criticism (n° 180), and of attracting the supreme adherence of the servants of Mary. He appeals to quotations of Scripture, passages from the Fathers, invocations of litanies, and familiar comparisons in order to force the last uprootings of them, and to bring all souls who have their heart set on being saved to embrace the devotion which he preaches to them.

Recalling these pages so complete, in which we found so many things, even while examining them so quickly, we arrive at this conclusion: Montfort splendidly kept the promise he made at the beginning: the *motives* which he gave us truly make the devotion of the Holy Slavery *commendable*.

SECTION II

Rebecca and Jacob
Biblical figures of this Perfect Devotion

(183-212)

N° 183

Montfort minutely explained the advantages of total consecration to Mary: God, our neighbor, and we ourselves derive considerable profit from it. He is not content, however, with this development, in spite of its great richness. The theory always benefits, when it can be proposed in a concrete form. It is thus more accessible, more likeable, more convincing. It is more easily accepted and put into practice. Let us not forget that this is the purpose pursued by our Saint in this 2nd chapter: to cause a large number of souls to set out on this Marian way.

To obtain this result, he does not ask the lives of the saints to supply him with one of these exact cases, perfectly in connection with his plan, which he can then exploit in every detail.

He does not even ask the Gospel to obtain for him what he seeks, and what he could find there, even if it be in the example of St. John. Besides, all this was sufficiently outlined in the previous section.

This time, he ascends higher. Relying on the secondary sense of Sacred Scripture, the *spiritual* or *mystical sense*, he will study, in the light of later revelations, what the Holy Ghost Himself wanted to teach us in the wonderful story of Rebecca and Jacob, told in chapter 27 of Genesis.

The Holy Ghost Himself wanted to give us the teaching which Montfort is going to derive from this story. For the spiritual sense is truly a sense of Scripture, willed and ordained by God. It is expressed, not directly through words, but indirectly through persons or things. These persons or things which have a figurative character are called "Types". The future fulfillment will be called "Antitype". It is up to God alone to choose and to arrange a biblical type in view of its signification, because only He directs men and things as He pleases and knows that events will happen as He foresees them. Furthermore, He is the only One Who knows of the existence of these figures until their fulfillment. And, even then, a simple resemblance between certain events and certain persons of the Old and New Testaments would not be enough to establish the existence of the spiritual sense in such or such passage of our holy Books. It is necessary for God Himself to have revealed the relationship which exists between these events and these persons. And this revelation, like all the others, will be contained in Sacred Scripture and Tradition. And it must be proposed to us by the Church in order to reach the highest degree of certainty and acquire a demonstrative value.

Now, after *Malachy* and *St. Paul*, *"all the holy Fathers and the interpreters of Scripture" have seen in* **Jacob** *the figure of Jesus Christ and the predestined, and in* **Esau***, that of the reprobate* (N° 185). St. Paul, wanting to establish the doctrine of gratuitous predestination, relying by no means on foreseen good works, but only on the divine good pleasure, quotes as examples Esau and Jacob. Of them it was said, even before their birth, and consequently before all merit or demerit: "the elder shall serve the younger" (Gn. 25:23) and "Jacob I have loved, but Esau I have hated" (Rom. 9:13). This divine preference had the effect only of granting to Jacob and to his offspring earthly predominance. It is not, for Esau and Jacob, about exclusion from heavenly glory or from admission to the same glory. It is even likely that Esau personally, or at least some of his descendants, of whom the most famous was Job, were saved. But, as often happens in Sacred Scripture, the granting or the refusal of worldly goods, in the Old Testament, are taken as a figure of the granting or the refusal of eternal goods in the New Testament.

And this is enough to establish the parallel. Jacob obtains, thanks to the industry of his mother, Rebecca, the paternal blessing. The latter establishes him as the owner of his father's goods, and gives him the ascendancy over his brother, who is excluded from the same inheritance. In all this, he prefigures the elect. Thanks to the love and protection of Mary, the latter enter into possession of their heavenly kingdom, from which the reprobate, represented by Esau, are excluded.

Such is the teaching of St. Paul. Such is the teaching of Tradition, whose principal witnesses are St. Augustine and St. Bernard. Such is the teaching of the interpreters of Sacred Scripture, the two principal representatives being Cornelius a Lapide and Rev. Fr. Lagrange.

It is, then, indeed the Holy Ghost Himself Who gives us, in the history of Rebecca and Jacob, an admirable figure of the devotion of the elect to Mary and of Mary's care for the elect.

Following the Saint:

1° We shall explain *the story of Jacob and Esau*:

2° We shall see:
    a) *in Esau, the figure of the reprobate*;
    b) *in Jacob, the figure of the predestined*.

The feelings of the one and the other towards Rebecca are the perfect image of the feelings which the reprobate and the predestined cultivate respectively towards Mary. (*The literal sense and the spiritual sense* of this story).

3° We shall see what *Mary's devotion is for her slaves of love*, a devotion prefigured by that of Rebecca towards Jacob.

Article I

The story of Jacob and Esau

(184)

N° 184

The Book of Genesis tells how Esau sold to his twin brother, Jacob, the birthright that he possessed by the fact that he had been born the first of the two. Rebecca, mother of the two brothers, tenderly loved Jacob. She resolved to secure for the latter the advantages that the title of elder brother entailed. The purpose was legitimate: due to the bargain decided on between the two brothers, these advantages must henceforth fall to Jacob. The whole question was to obtain, for Jacob, the blessing which Isaac reserved for Esau, because, in the eyes of Isaac, Esau was still the elder son, and thus the favorite. The good old man was far from suspecting the little importance that his son had ascribed to all his privileges.

In order that this blessing might return to Jacob, Rebecca employed "*an address most holy but most full of mystery.*"

Montfort quotes the famous remark of St. Augustine: "*Non est mendacium sed mysterium.*" Several Fathers think as St. Augustine does. Others, with Saint Jerome, admit that there is a lie there, but they excuse it. St. Thomas takes up again St. Augustine's argumentation under another form. For St. Augustine, Jacob did not lie by saying: "I am Esau, your first-born son"; no more than we, when we say of Christ: "Rock, Lion, Lamb" etc. Jacob was not Esau personally, but he was Esau by birthright. For St. Thomas, moreover, he thus spoke prophetically, to indicate that the youngest people, that of the gentiles, would one day take the place of the first-born people, that is to say, the Jews.

The moderns are less likely to consider as good and praiseworthy all the actions attributed to biblical personalities. Moreover, the intention of the sacred writers is by no means to approve everything that they relate. It is admitted, however, that in the East these sorts of procedures are rather considered as strokes of skill than as frauds.

These difficulties which we experience in explaining the role of Jacob and especially that of Rebecca must by no means disturb us as regards the application to Mary. This series of deceits was perhaps capable of misleading the old and almost blind Isaac. Do we imagine that God could also allow Himself to be fooled? If the end to be obtained is appreciably the same, the means are inevitably different in the sense of perfect honesty, while being just as effective in their application.

This being said once for all, let us continue the story of Jacob and Esau.

Several years after this barter between the two brothers, Isaac felt himself aging and wanted to bless his children before dying. He called Esau near him and commanded him to go hunting and to bring back a fine piece of game, so that, in having eaten, he might bless him afterwards.

Rebecca was present at this scene and heard Isaac's words. She quickly warned Jacob of what was brewing and ordered him to go take two kids from the herd and bring them to her. When she had received them, she killed them, and skinned them; with the flesh, she prepared a delicious dish, in keeping with the taste of Isaac which she knew perfectly; she dressed Jacob in Esau's clothes; she covered his hands and neck with the skin of the kids, so that he might be able to offer by touch, apart from the voice, the appearances of his elder brother. All this took place very quickly, because it was a question of anticipating Esau, who was a skillful hunter and would not delay in finding prey. So, when Jacob appeared before his father, carrying the dish which his mother had prepared, Isaac marveled at the speed of the capture. But what he noticed at first was the voice of the one who spoke. The latter appeared to be Esau, and nevertheless, it seemed to him that he heard the voice of Jacob. Like all blind persons, he wanted to touch the one that he could not see. When he felt these hairy hands, so much like those of Esau, so different from those of Jacob, he exclaimed: "The voice indeed is the voice of Jacob; but the hands are the hands of Esau" (Gn. 27:22). He was, however, only half reassured, because he asked Jacob if he was indeed Esau. On his affirmative answer, he agreed to eat and did not hide the satisfaction he took in such well-prepared dishes.

Then, having drawn his son to him to kiss him, he smelt the odor of his perfumed clothes. Transported by joy, he granted the blessing which he reserved for his elder son. He wished him the dew of heaven and the fruitfulness of the earth, established him heir of all his goods and master of his brothers, covering beforehand with curses the one who would curse him and with blessings the one who would bless him.

Isaac had hardly finished these words, when Esau entered, proudly bringing the fruits of his hunt. Isaac was surprised beyond all words by what had just taken place. He retracted nothing, however, of what he had done, seeing there too evidently the hand of God. Esau uttered true howls, accused his brother of cheating and asked his father if he had only one blessing. In this there was the image of those who want to ally God and the world, and to enjoy at the same time the consolations of heaven and those of earth.

Touched by the cries of Esau, Isaac finally blessed him, but with an earthly blessing, and subjected him to his brother. Esau harbored an embittered hatred against his younger sibling. He waited only for the death of his father to kill him, and Jacob could not have avoided death, unless, here again, Rebecca, who had already earned him the blessings of his father, had not protected him by her pious diligence and good advice. On the pretext of making him seek a wife at the home of his uncle Laban, she sent him to Mesopotamia, where he remained until Esau's anger was calmed.

Article II

The literal sense and the spiritual sense of the story of Jacob and Esau

(185-200)

N° 185

Jacob is, then, the figure of the predestined, and Esau the figure of the reprobate. What is said in the literal sense of the two sons of Isaac, must be understood in the spiritual sense of the two major categories into which men will be divided for eternity. It is sufficient, consequently, to examine in detail the conduct of the one and the other towards Rebecca to know what is the conduct of the predestined and the reprobates towards Mary. This study will bring us to imitate the conduct of Jacob and the predestined and to condemn that of Esau and the reprobates.

*
* *

§ I. – ESAU, FIGURE OF THE REPROBATE
(185-190)

Father de Montfort returns to the five different characteristics of the temperament and conduct of Esau.

This is only one panel of the diptych. The other side will follow shortly, which will reproduce the first, point by point, in the temperament and conduct of the reprobate. One could pass from "first" of the type to "first" of the antitype, etc. Let us follow rather the method of the Saint.

Another remark. In studying later the character of Jacob and the predestined, we shall find that in each of the five successive reflections, it is a question of Rebecca in Jacob's case and of Mary in the case of the predestined. The reason for this is that all goods have come to the one through Rebecca and to the others through Mary. For Esau, on the contrary, it is a question of Rebecca only in the third place. And also of Mary for the reprobate. And it is a question about one or the other only in order to separate them. But once this negative result is obtained, Esau and the reprobate found themselves and the outside world again. This provokes different reactions which are analyzed minutely in 1°, 2°, 4° and 5°.

A. – A PRESENTATION OF THE LITERAL SENSE
(185)

1° **Esau was satisfied with himself**. Strong and robust in body, skillful and industrious with a bow, capable of taking much game in the hunt, he was made to succeed in great temporal enterprises. Form this point of view, understandably, he was more pleasing than Jacob in the eyes of his father Isaac. But if Isaac was proud of his elder son, the latter was also proud of himself.

2° **Esau was led towards the exterior**. So many qualities did not have to remain hidden. Because Esau had strength, it was necessary to display it; because he had skill, it was necessary to use it. He would thus have the opportunity to make an impression, to have influence. In brief, he lived more willingly outside than in the family home. Another tendency which could not displease Isaac.

3° **Esau was indifferent towards Rebecca**. A creature as sweet as his mother could have no hold on a nature so violent and so full of itself. That is why Esau went to no trouble at all to please his mother, to help her in her labors, to take her advice. On the contrary, he displeased her formally, by marrying two Hittite girls, who were a cause of continual bitterness for Rebecca.

4° **Esau was incapable of ruling his passions**. The first reaction of an unbridled nature in the presence of earthly goods. It wants to possess them all and at all costs. Hunger exists. The appetite is violent. The thin gruel which is presented has no great value, but Esau wants it and wants it right now. To get it for himself, he unhesitatingly renounces his birthright and the fortune which this right assures him.

5° **Esau was jealous of his brother's happiness**. He nevertheless renounced it voluntarily. But he cannot bear it that his brother is happy by the use of the means which he himself despised. He hates him. He persecutes him. He thinks about killing him. He wants to snatch his happiness away from him, without any hope of regaining it for him, because he knows that he irreparably lost it.

The picture is not flattering, but it is exact. It is indeed thus that Esau shows himself in Sacred Scripture. Let us see now how in all this he is the figure of the reprobate.

B. – A PRESENTATION OF THE SPIRITUAL SENSE
(186-190)

This is the second panel of the diptych, corresponding point by point to the first one, because the reprobate give every day proof that they are animated by the same feelings as Esau.

N° 186

1° The reprobate are satisfied with themselves. Nothing equals their skill in temporal affairs, their resistance to the fatigue that these affairs cause them, the successes which crown their efforts, the light with which they are enlightened and the opportunities of which they take advantage. But since the earth is enough for them, they neglect heaven. They who are so strong, so skillful and so enlightened in earthly business, are very weak and very ignorant, in reality, in heavenly things. *In terrenis fortes, in caelestibus debiles.*

N° 187

2° The reprobate are enemies of the interior life. Being naturally inclined to show their feelings, to parade, to gain the esteem of others, they do not understand the happiness which is found in staying at home and shutting themselves up there, like God Who never leaves home. Personally, they loathe solitude, spirituality, and interior devotion. They cannot bear it in others either. They treat as small-minded, religious zealots, and savages, those who gladly flee the company of the world in order to devote themselves to the attractions of the interior life.

N° 188

3° **The reprobate are indifferent towards Mary**. They do not hate her formally. They sometimes praise her, and they pretend to have some practices of devotion in her honor. But they cannot tolerate the fact that others love her tenderly, serve her faithfully, try to win her affection and good graces. They protest that such devotion is by no means necessary for salvation, that it is even exaggerated. Is it not enough, to be servants of the Virgin, to mumble some prayer in her honor, without tenderness for her nor amendment for oneself?

N° 189

4° **The reprobate are slaves of their passions**. In this exterior, fickle life, there is nothing that matters except pleasure. The reprobates rush to it with gluttonous avidity. They are incapable of mastering their passions. For a coarse plate of lentils (that is to say, for the false pleasures of the earth), they sell their birthright (that is to say, their right of entry into heaven). To gain for themselves one vile pleasure of the moment (concupiscence of the flesh), the empty smoke of honor (pride of life), or a yellow or white coin (desire of wealth), they will not hesitate to sacrifice the grace of baptism, or at least their robe of innocence (their state of grace) and even their heavenly inheritance. Thus life is joyful. They laugh, drink, eat, amuse themselves, play, dance, etc., without going to any trouble, like Esau, to make themselves worthy of the blessing of the heavenly Father, while making themselves even positively unworthy.

N° 190

5° **The reprobate are persecutors of the predestined**. Not content to live at their ease and to taste all pleasures, the reprobate resent the predestined for savoring in peace a happiness which they themselves renounced and which they know is irreparably lost for them. That is why they hate and persecute them, openly or in secret, but in either case so inexorably. They laugh at them, mimic them, criticize or scold them. Or else they rob them, deceive them, ruin them and cover them with ignominy. And to make yet more depressing for them the poverty to which they reduced them, they take care to display complacently the spectacle of their rude fortune, hoping thus to spoil their happiness or to bring them to renounce it.

But he who laughs last laughs best. In all things, it is necessary to consider the end. The reprobate seem happy here on earth. Like Esau, they received the earthly blessing. As he also, they try to overturn the order established by God by escaping from the rule of the predestined. It is in the distant descendants of Jacob and Esau that Isaac's prophetic blessing was completely fulfilled, when, after the advent of the Messiah in the race of Jacob, the people that he established were formerly heathen people, to the exclusion of the Jewish people. It is also in the other life that the effects of predestination will be manifested in their fullness. Then, like Esau, the reprobate will roar with pain and vainly demand a share in the happiness of the elect. And their powerless hatred will no longer be of use except to torment the reprobate themselves.

Would anybody like to imitate their madness, so as to end in the same eternal disaster?

*
* *

§ II. – JACOB, THE FIGURE OF THE PREDESTINED
(191-200)

Another diptych, no longer in somber colors, but in bright reflections. The first picture shows us five different aspects of Jacob's love for Rebecca. The second analysis, in the same way, shows the love of the predestined for Mary.

Let us also notice, in order to highlight the train of thought, that this love, calling for and obtaining reciprocity, is considered at present only from Jacob to Rebecca, and from the predestined to Mary. The following article will draw more especially our attention to Rebecca's love for Jacob and Mary's love for the predestined.

Let us study, like our Saint, first according to the literal sense, then according to the spiritual sense, this wonderful biblical figure of the perfect devotion.

A. — A PRESENTATION OF THE LITERAL SENSE
(191-195)

N° 191

1° **Jacob seeking the company of Rebecca**. Being of a mild and peaceful nature, which contrasted singularly with that of Esau, of a less herculean constitution, without being for this reason weak or sick (at least nothing allows us to suppose it), Jacob usually remained at home. This is not because he feared going out. But he wished to gain the good graces of his mother, whom he loved tenderly. He wanted to lose nothing of the charms which he enjoyed in her company. So, when he went out, it was not by his own will, nor by the confidence which he would have had in his skill, like Esau. It was only to obey his mother and to encounter her also in the faithful fulfillment of the orders that she gave him.

N° 192

2° **Jacob loving and honoring Rebecca**. This love led Jacob to remain near his mother. He was never happier than when he saw her. He, however, did not remain inactive, even when he remained at home. He was not content with contemplating blissfully the object of his love. He sought to please her in every way, and he carefully avoided displeasing her in anything. In particular, he took much care not to marry, like Esau, a woman who would have been a cause of annoyance to his mother. These first two qualities won him over to Rebecca's love in the highest degree.

N° 193

3° **Jacob was subject to Rebecca**. This was even for him the most practical way to show his love for his mother. He obeyed her completely and in all things, carrying out everything that she commanded and as she commanded it. He obeyed her promptly without delaying or looking for excuses. He obeyed her lovingly, without complaining or showing ill-humor. He did not even wait for formal orders. At the slightest sign of her will or even simply her good pleasure, little Jacob ran and worked. We have proof that he carried out all that she said to him, without arguing or discussing the orders received. Thus she ordered him to fetch two kids and to bring them to her, so that she might prepare them for his father Isaac to eat. Jacob did not answer, as had been possible, that one kid was enough to prepare a meal for a single man. Without arguing or discussing, he executed what she had said.

N° 194

4° **Jacob trusting in Rebecca**. Far from putting his trust in himself and in his know-how, like Esau, Jacob relied only on the care and protection of his mother. This is a habit which he had formed of calling for her help in all his difficulties and of consulting her in all his doubts, which led his mother to take his interests in this circumstance so magnificently. Here too he is reassured in his concerns by the answer, so full of care, which his mother gave him: anxious, he had asked her if, instead of his blessing, he would not receive the curse of his father. He believed her and had confidence in her, when she had said to him that she took this curse on herself.

N° 195

5° **Jacob at the school of Rebecca**. For Jacob, the consummate model of all perfection was his mother. So he tried to imitate the virtues which he saw her practicing. He did not need to go far in search of examples to be reproduced. He knew that nowhere would he find more beautiful ones than in the paternal home. So he escaped the temptation and danger of bad company which corrupts common decency, and he made himself worthy of receiving the double blessing of his dear father: innocence preserved, virtues developed, nothing prepared him better for this supreme happiness, on which so many things were to depend in the future.

We have here a truly beautiful picture of filial devotion that the Saint painted in these few lines. If the letter is already so beautiful, what shall we say about the spirit which is enclosed therein?

B. – A PRESENTATION OF THE SPIRITUAL SENSE
(196-200)

Jacob is the figure of Jesus Christ as well as of the predestined. Our Lord is the leader of the predestined, and these are predestined only in the measure in which they are conformed to this divine model. Because of this resemblance, Jesus is constituted as the first-born of many brothers. From this point of view, Jacob and the predestined can be considered as the younger children of the divine family, and no longer Esau, but Our Lord as the eldest, the One Whose merits Mary communicates to us. This remark has its importance in understanding the consequence of this biblical figure. We take, henceforth, Jacob as the figure of the predestined, and of none but the predestined, that is to say, of those who want to receive the divine blessing to which only Our Lord is entitled.

To attain this purpose, they place themselves in the hands of Mary, and here is the rule which they keep every day towards her, reproducing point by point the conduct of Jacob towards Rebecca.

N° 196

1° Like Mary, the predestined love the interior life.
"They are sedentary, and home-keepers, with their Mother," that is to say, they love solitude and gladly give themselves to prayer, but always following the example and in the company of Mary. This good mother, indeed, always loved and practiced solitude and prayer. She esteemed much more the hidden work of her personal perfection, than exterior work, even of the apostolate. And when to obey the divine will, she had to collaborate in the salvation of the world, she did so without leaving her habitual recollection, nor seeking for the respect or the approval of the world. In the same way, she teaches her slaves of love to put the care of their own salvation above every exterior preoccupation. This work is more important than to perform by oneself miracles of nature and grace in the world to the detriment of this unique affair, like Esau and the reprobate.

So, are the slaves of love charged, by the will of God and that of Mary, with appearing in the world, to carry out the duties of their state, to be in contact with the souls which they have to evangelize? They will acquit themselves of these duties without losing anything of their habitual recollection, without looking for praise or the applause of men, without overturning, either in theory or in practice, the hierarchy of values. Exterior works are good and even necessary, but they should not distract from the work of one's own sanctification, nor take priority over this work. All other works compared with the latter are only children's games.

Not only do the predestined remain at home with Mary, but they also remain in Mary's house. Not only are they subject to Mary like Jesus in the house of Nazareth, but they live, like Jesus before His birth, in the beautiful interior of Mary. To sing the happiness of this divine dwelling where man is enriched with merits by going from virtue to virtue, Montfort borrows the words of Psalm 83:

"*Quam dilecta tabernacula tua, Domine virtutum:* Lord Jesus, how lovely are Thy tabernacles." "*Passer invenit sibi domum et turtur nidum ubi reponat pullos suos.* The sparrow (that is to say, man passing over this earth) hath found herself a house (that is to say, Mary), and the turtle (that is to say, the exile sighing for his homeland) a nest for herself where she may lay her young ones (also Mary)." "*Beati qui habitant in domo* **tua** *Domine*", Oh! Blessed is the man who dwells in *Thy* house, that is to say, the house of Mary, where You first established Your home!" "*Beatus vir cuius est auxilium abs te! Ascensiones in corde suo disposuit in valle lacrimarum in loco quem posuit!* It is in this house of the predestined (where he has chosen to dwell) that he receives his help from You alone (without counting, like Esau and the reprobate on his own skill), and that he has arranged, by ascents and degrees, all the virtues in his heart, to raise himself to perfection in this valley of tears. (See the interior practice: to act *in* Mary.)

N° 197

2° **The predestined love and honor Mary**. Mary is for them a "*good Mother and Mistress*," an association of words which is found in the correlative "children and slaves." Mary is rightly, indeed, Mistress: "Lady", but because of her maternity. And we are her slaves, but because of our filiation towards her. Dominion and servitude are quite particular, leading the slaves as much to love as to honor their Queen. In reality, they love her not only in words, but in deed; they honor her not only outwardly, but in the bottom of their hearts.

In order to prove their love, like Jacob:

A) They carefully avoid everything which can displease her and practice with fervor whatever they think will make them find favor with her. This, *in general*, is in its negative aspect and in its positive aspect.

B) They bring her *in particular* no longer two kids, but **their body and their soul**, represented by these two kids, so that Mary:

a) *may receive* them as a thing which belongs to her and over which we freely recognize her right, allowing her to exercise it as she pleases;

b) *may kill* and *make* them *die* to themselves and to sin, *strip* them of self-love and bad inclinations, thus enabling them to please Jesus; the latter wants as disciples only men dead to themselves.

c) *may prepare* them to suit the taste of the heavenly Father and for His greatest glory; doesn't Mary know it better than any other creature?

d) may make them thus a delicate dish, worthy of the *mouth* and the *blessing* of the heavenly Father.

It is in this way, indeed, that those who practice the perfect consecration to Jesus Christ through the hands of Mary want to show their effective and courageous love. A sacrifice which leads far and strikes deep in our affections and even our substance. That is why it frightens the reprobate. These content themselves with fine words or with purely outward veneration.

N° 198

3° **The predestined subject themselves to Mary**. Jesus Christ spent thirty out of the thirty-three years of His life in submission to Mary, and He thus obtained more glory for His Father than if He had used the same time to travel the world, to preach the Gospel and to work miracles (n° 139). Through His example, the predestined are subject and obedient to Mary, as to their good Mother. They know that she can only give them good counsels, and they follow them very exactly, as Jacob followed the counsels of Rebecca, and as the servants of Cana complied with the instruction of Mary: "Whatsoever He shall say to you, do ye" (Jn. 2:5). The consequences of this submission were that Jacob received as if by a miracle the blessing reserved for Esau, and that the guests of Cana were honored with the first miracle of Jesus Christ. In the same way those who will be subject to Mary will receive the blessing of the heavenly Father and will be honored with the marvels of God, and nobody will enjoy this double favor, if he does not show a perfect docility to Mary. That is why Esau loses the blessing, for lack of obedience to this good Mother.

N° 199

4° **The predestined have confidence in Mary**. They know her great power and her indefatigable goodness. They have recourse to her in all their difficulties. They consider her as their polar star, capable of guiding their march through the ocean of this world. They reveal to her their pains and their needs with much openness of heart. They attach themselves to her merciful bosom, to seek pardon of their sins there, and to her bosom of sweetness, to draw there consolation in their trials. They even cast themselves, hide and lose themselves in her virginal bosom, to be remade there on the model of Jesus, and to find there Jesus Who resides there as on His most glorious throne. Ah! What happiness! "Think not," says abbot Guerric, "that it is happier to dwell in Abraham's bosom than in Mary's, for it is in this last that our Lord placed His throne." The whole joy of paradise is the presence of God which is manifested there entirely. Is it not also the privilege of Mary's womb to have contained the divinity completely in one of its most loving manifestations?

All these things are incomprehensible to the reprobate. Putting their confidence in themselves, they cram themselves with earthly and vulgar consolations, which maintain their hunger instead of calming it. Besides, far from complaining about this hunger, they love it miserably and flee horrified from everything that could calm it, particularly from devotion to

Mary. They consider as illusory the help that the predestined attribute to their heavenly Queen.

N° 200

5° **The predestined imitate Mary**. The little child finds perfect and tries to imitate everything that his mother does in his sight. In the same way, the predestined look at Mary as the finished model of all perfection. With all the ardor of their soul, they try to reproduce her virtues. This is what makes them truly happy and devout, and constitutes the infallible mark of their predestination, because Mary said by the mouth of Eternal Wisdom: "*Blessed are they that keep my ways*" (Prov. 8:32), that is to say, blessed are those who practice the same virtues as I, blessed are those who walk in my footsteps, all this with the help of divine grace. They are blessed *in this world* during their life, by the abundance of graces and sweetness which Mary communicates to them from her fullness; this good Mother does not treat with the same generosity those who do not imitate her so closely. They are blessed *in their death*, which is sweet and tranquil, usually consoled by the sensible presence of Mary; the latter is anxious to assist her child in this painful moment and to lead him herself into the joys of paradise. Finally, they are blessed *in eternity*, because never was a good servant of Mary, who imitated her virtues during his life, lost after his death. It would be a contradiction impossible to realize. Both terms of the equation cannot be true at the same time: either we truly imitated Mary, and then we shall not be damned, or we are damned, because we have not imitated Mary.

And this is indeed what happens to the reprobate. They will not have kept Mary's ways. They did not imitate her virtues. And if they have some devotion to her, it is a purely outward devotion, incapable of sanctifying and saving them. That is why they are unhappy in their life, in their death and during eternity. They are cursed, because, abusing devotion to Mary, they believed, that with the protection of the Mother, they could violate with impunity the commands of the Son:

"They are cursed who decline from thy commandments" (Ps. 118:21). They could not make a more disastrous error!

In the face of the observation of such a disaster and its cause, we understand the enthusiastic exclamation of our Saint:

O holy Virgin, my good Mother, how happy are those (I repeat it with the transports of my heart) – how happy are those who, not letting themselves be seduced by a false devotion towards you, faithfully keep your ways, your counsels, and your orders!

They are infallibly of the number of the predestined! Who would not like to be counted among those?...

Article III

The Blessed Virgin and her slaves of love

(201-212)

Having come to this point of his explanation, the Saint no longer discusses separately the case of Rebecca and that of Mary. He merges one into the other. Just as above we could have united the literal sense and the spiritual sense, here we could separate them and consider them each in its turn. Here again, let us follow rather the method of Father de Montfort. It will certainly have its advantages.

The devotion of the predestined to Mary, represented by Jacob's devotion to Rebecca, elicits infallibly on the part of Mary, who never allows herself to be outdone in generosity, a whole series of charitable services, represented by the aid of Rebecca towards Jacob.

To prove to her their love, her slaves consecrated themselves totally to her, and put in her hands the merit and value of their good deeds. In her turn, Mary, as the best of all mothers:

1° *loves* those who love her, and proves this love for them in various ways (n°s 201-207);

2° completely *looks after* those who abandoned themselves totally to her (n° 208);

3° *conducts* in the ways of salvation those who ask for her good advice (n° 209);

4° *defends* and protects those who have recourse to her to escape their enemies (n° 210);

5° *intercedes* for them so that they obtain the blessing of the heavenly Father (n°s 211-212).

*
* *

§ I. – MARY LOVES HER SLAVES OF LOVE
(201-207)

N° 201

Mary resembles Eternal Wisdom and possesses to an eminently perfect degree all the qualities contained in human nature. One of these qualities, an obvious reflection of the divine perfection itself, is that love calls forth love: "Ego diligentes me diligo. I love them that love me" (Prov. 8:17). Supposing that her love for her slaves does not precede the love of her slaves for her, which is no more true for her than for God, for Rebecca and for any mother, it must be elicited at least by the love of her slaves. A human heart does not refuse its love to the one who gives it his.

Montfort studies the reasons and the qualities of this love, then its various manifestations.

1° THE REASONS AND QUALITIES OF THE LOVE OF MARY FOR HER SLAVES
(201-202)

A) **The reasons** are four in number.

Mary loves her slaves:

a) *"Because she is their true Mother."* She is Queen because she is Mother, and she exercises in heaven and on earth the rights of her sovereignty, only because she fulfills in heaven and on earth, the responsibilities of her maternity. Thus all her slaves are her slaves only because they are her children and they are even her children before being her slaves. It is she who gave them and preserves the supernatural life of grace in them. *"Now, a mother always loves her child, the fruit of her womb."* From this point of view, Mary's love precedes that of her children and is independent of it.

b) Because *"they love her as their good Mother."* This love of gratitude multiplies in the mother the strength and sweetness of her own love; while the latter becomes rather an agony, when the child is ungrateful and rejects the love of his mother.

c) Because *"God loves them,"* and because the will of Mary is identical to that of God. And God loves them, because He predestined them. Predestination is, indeed, the result of an absolutely free choice, by pure benevolence. "Jacob I have loved, but Esau I have hated" (Rom. 9:13).

d) *"Because they are all consecrated to her,"* adding to the bond of their natural slavery the bonds of their slavery of will, and declaring themselves so disposed that, even if they were not otherwise obliged to it, they would take upon themselves of their own volition the chains of their slavery. Thus, they have become, they especially, the portion and inheritance of Mary. "In Israel, take root" (Eccli. 24:13). (See n° 31.)

N° 202

B) **The qualities** of this love are two in number.

Mary loves her slaves:

a) *Tenderly:* a comparison will give a suggestive idea of the tenderness of this love:

Throw, if you can, all the natural love which all the mothers of the world have for their children into the one heart of one mother for one only child. Surely that mother will love that child immensely. Nevertheless, it is true that Mary loves her children yet more tenderly than that mother would love that child of hers.

For the perfection of an act depends on the perfection of nature and its powers, in the natural order, and of the perfection of grace and the infused virtues, in the supernatural order. Now, from this twofold point of view, Mary exceeds in perfection, not only the most perfect of creatures, but all creatures combined. When she performs an act of charity, it is, then, this whole magnificent apparatus which comes into play, and there results from it an exquisite fineness, an incomparable tenderness, an invincible strength and a fullness that lacks nothing.

b) *Efficaciously.* Mary's love does not limit itself to fine words or affectionate feelings; they were very real and very considerable. It is love which wants and produces the good of the one that it loves, like that and infinitely more than that of Rebecca for Jacob.

2° THE MANIFESTATION OF THIS LOVE
(203-207)

The purpose of Mary, like that of Rebecca, is to obtain for her slaves of love the blessing of the heavenly Father which Jesus merited for them. In these conditions, everything that Rebecca did to draw the blessing of Isaac upon Jacob, becomes the figure of what Mary undertakes to draw down upon her children the supreme benefaction of the divine blessing.

N° 203

A) **She, like Rebecca, keeps an eye out for the opportunity to do good to them**.

Knowing, henceforth, all things in God through the beatific vision, she arranges everything from afar to exempt her servants from troubles which would not be salutary, and to obtain for them the goods which will lead them to salvation. It is even certain that, if there is good fortune to be realized in God by the fidelity of a creature in some high employment, Mary will reserve this good fortune for some one of her faithful servants, assuring him at the same time the grace to acquit himself of it promptly.

N° 204

B) **She gives them good advice**. "My son, follow my counsel" (Gen. 27:8), either by herself, by enlightening the intelligence of her slaves and by moving their will, by means of the actual graces whose distributor she is, or by the ministry of the Angels, who are only too happy to fly, at her command, to the aid of one or another of her children. These counsels can concern multiple objects in connection with the state of their soul or their actual needs. But she especially gives them, like Rebecca, the counsel to bring to her, not two kids now, but their body and their soul, and to consecrate them to her with everything which depends on them; or, as she herself did formerly at Cana, she advises them to carry out faithfully all that Jesus Christ, her Son, taught by His words and examples.

N° 205

C) Having received from her slaves the offering of their body and their soul, symbolized by the two kids, **this good Mother hastens**, like Rebecca:

a) *to kill them* and make them die to the life of the old man, by inspiring in them the will and by granting them the strength to break with sin and to live henceforth a virtuous life;

b) *to strip them* of their self-love and their natural inclinations by leading them to renounce their personal dispositions, to adopt hers and allow themselves to be guided by them;

c) *to purify them* of their spots, vilenesses and sins, by helping them to produce acts of sincere penance and fervent love, which will place them again in the order willed by God;

d) *to dress them* to suit God's taste and for His greatest glory, which only she knows perfectly, and according to which she acts surely (n° 151). Thus no one but Rebecca knew the taste of Isaac and could prepare dishes capable of pleasing him. For this purpose, Mary obtains for her slaves, because of their consecration itself, a great abundance of grace, and this grace makes them pleasing in God's sight. Then, she obtains that all their works should be more informed by the virtue of charity.

N° 206

D) So that we may be even more worthy to appear before our Father, Mary **is not content to strip us** of the rags of sin, and to wash from us the stains contracted:

a) *She clothes us* "as Rebecca clothed Jacob" in the clean, new, precious and perfumed garments of Esau, the elder, that is to say, of Jesus Christ.

These garments represent the infinite merits of the divine Savior, of which Mary was constituted the treasurer and dispenser. For her part, Mary guards these merits as Rebecca guarded the garments of Esau, and she communicates them, very fairly and not by fraud, to whom she wills, when she wills, as she wills and as much as she wills.

These clothes are *clean*, because no stain came to diminish the beauty of them; they are *new*, because the merits of Christ being of unlimited value, each can participate in them in fullness, as if he were alone, and without any prejudice to others; they are *precious* because of the infinite price which the hypostatic union gives them; they are *perfumed* because the sacrifice offered by Jesus on the cross was the only sacrifice of pleasant odor capable of appeasing the divine wrath and of drawing down the Father's blessings.

b) *She covers the neck and hands* of her servants with the skins of the kids she killed and skinned, that is to say, she adorns them with the merits and value of her own actions.

This point was variously interpreted by those who see in Jacob the figure not of the predestined, but of Jesus Christ Himself. Among many others were *St. Augustine* and *St. Bernard*. For them, Jacob covered with the skins of kids thus represents Jesus Christ, burdened before His Father with all the sins of the world.

We understand, however, that Montfort looked for another explanation, because, far from diverting from Jacob the blessings of his Father, as this would have to have been according to the first explanation, this hairy appearance helped to assure him of them. Montfort saw in Jacob the figure of the predestined and interpreted the offering of the two kids in the sense of the consecration of their body and their soul to Mary. He considers it necessary to seek along the same lines the solution of the present question. Mary killed and mortified what there was of evil or of the imperfect in the predestined. But she was indeed careful not to dissipate the good which grace had produced in them. She reserved this good very carefully. She further increases it by the removal of any impure alloy. By the influx of actual charity which animates her children and which she skillfully cultivates, she restores to this good all the perfection which it should have had at the moment in which it was carried out. And she makes of them the ornament and the strength of the neck and the hands. She thus shows to the Lord the results which they have already obtained, and which they are capable of obtaining still, that is to say, to carry on their neck the yoke of the Lord, and to do with their hands great things for the glory of God and the salvation of their poor brothers.

c) "*She bestows a new perfume and a new grace upon their garments* (coming from her Son) *and adornments* (coming from us), *in communicating to them her own garments*," that is to say, by giving them part of her merits and virtues.

Father de Montfort even goes so far as to say that Mary "*bequeathed to them by her testament her merits and virtues.*" And he quotes in support of this the authority "*of a holy religious of the last century, who died in the odour of sanctity, and learnt this by revelation.*"

This nun is doubtless Maria of Agreda (1602-1665). The *Revue des Prêtres de Marie, Reine des Coeurs* gives the complete text of this testament, to which Montfort seems to refer. The main passage is this one: "Of all my merits and treasures which I acquired with your divine grace and by my works and sufferings, I make universal heiress the holy Church, my Mother and my Mistress, and, with your permission, I testify in wishing that there were many more of them... I shall apply them to the spiritual good of my devout clients who call upon me and will call me to their help, with the aim of obtaining for them your grace and protection, and then eternal life."

Be that as it may of this testament, it is certain that Mary merited for us *by suitability* all that her Son merited in strict justice. She can thus request the application of these merits to her slaves of love. As for her virtues, we have already spoken on the subject in n°s 33-34-35, and we shall soon see on the subject of faith (n° 214), in what sense she communicates them to us. She produces likenesses of them in us, so that God, Who was well-pleased in her, can be well-pleased also in all her children.

Thus, concludes Montfort, quoting the book of Proverbs, *all her domestics*, "that is to say, all the people of her house, all her faithful servants and slaves" *are clothed with double garments:* "*Omnes domestici eius vestiti sunt duplicibus*" (Prov. 31:21). And so they do not have to be afraid that Jesus Christ, white as the snow, and seeking the brightness of this snow in souls, looks at it with coldness and freezes them with fright. Those that He will so look at will be the reprobate. Naked and stripped of the merits of Jesus Christ and of the Blessed Virgin, they cannot bear the rigor of the icy look of the supreme Judge. The predestined, on the contrary, dressed in the double coat which Mary prepared for them, will present to the tender looks of the divine Master the spectacle which He loves above all: His own holiness and that of His Mother reproduced in souls.

N° 207

E) Having thus prepared her children, **Mary obtains for them the blessing of the heavenly Father**, to which, alone, Our Lord is entitled, because He is the only Son of God by nature and alone worthy of this blessing.

Then is fulfilled point by point the whole figure contained in Jacob. With these garments all new, most precious and of most fragrant odor, established by the merits of Jesus and Mary; with their body and soul well-prepared and dressed by Mary; with their neck and hands well-protected by the skins of kids, that is to say, by the merits of their good deeds, they draw near with confidence to the heavenly Father's bed of repose.

The latter hears and recognizes their voices, which is that of a sinner, as the voice of Jacob was that of Jacob and not that of Esau. But He touches the hands covered with skins and loaded with merits, and He finds that these hands are those of virtuous and active men. He smells the good odor of their clothes, and He distinguishes there clearly the perfume of His Son and His Mother, whose lives were so full and merits so abundant. He eats with joy what Mary, their Mother, prepared for Him, finding that this body and this soul, which are presented to Him, are adorned as He wishes with His life-giving grace, and they obtain for Him indeed this exterior glory which He had desired to receive from them.

Then, recognizing that all this came to them through the merits of His Son and the holy Mother, and finding perfectly in them the twofold object of His divine kindness, symbolized by this good smell emanating from their double clothes:

a) *He gives them His double benediction*, that is to say, the *benediction of the dew of heaven*; the pledge of divine grace for this earth, itself the seed of glory for the next life; and the *benediction of the fat of the earth*, the pledge of the daily bread and the sufficient abundance of the goods of this world so as to practice virtue.

b) *He makes them masters of their other brethren*, the reprobate: true primacy, although not always apparent. It will be manifested fully only in the next world and for eternity.

c) Not content with blessing them in their person, *He blesses also those who shall bless them* and curses those who shall curse and persecute them.

This efficacious love is the principal way for Mary to respond to the love of her slaves. It can even be said that it already contains in itself all the other marks of benevolence which are going to follow. The only reason for dwelling on it, with the Saint, is because they concern rather the life of the slave of love after his consecration. It is interesting to know how Mary will behave towards them in the subsequent development of their earthly life.

*
* *

§ II. – MARY SUPPPLIES EVERYTHING TO THOSE WHO HAVE ABANDONED THEMSELVES TOTALLY TO HER
(208)

N° 208

Just as love calls for love, trust also calls for devotion, and absolute trust for unlimited devotion. The slaves of love abandoned themselves completely to Mary, gave themselves to her body and soul for time and eternity. In return, Mary supports them with everything, for the body as well as for the soul, for the natural life as well as for the supernatural life.

Not only does she double clothe them, but she presents to them the most delicious dishes from God's table to eat. That is to say, she offers them the Eucharistic bread, over which she has full power. Is not Jesus, there as everywhere, the fruit of life which she brought into the world? So, she multiplies her invitations to bring all her children to sit down at her holy table, to eat the bread that she kneaded for them, and to drink the wine which she mixed for them.

Then, as she is the Treasurer and Dispenser of all the graces of the Most High, she reserves a good portion of them, and the best, to support her children and slaves; they are really nourished at the breast, according to the word of the prophet Isaiah. Mary gives them such a sweetness in carrying the yoke of the Lord that they almost do not feel the gravity of it. The oil of devotion and the fervor in which it bathes him, decreases the harshness and the weight of it, until persuaded, according to the word of the same prophet, that the wood of this yoke is putrid: *"The yoke shall putrify at the presence of the oil"* (Isa. 10:27).

Moreover, is this not the way Rebecca acted towards Jacob? All that she had of the best, either by way of clothes, or by way of food, was reserved for her child of predilection. And she was not afraid of placing at his disposal even the animals of the paternal fold, to help him obtain his father's good graces.

*
* *

§ III. – MARY LEADS AND DIRECTS HER SLAVES OF LOVE
(209)

N° 209

Personal conduct is a thing in which a mother can interfere with difficulty when the child has reached a certain age, if the child himself does not spontaneously request his mother's advice. We have an example of it in the case of Esau and Jacob. Whereas Esau trusted in himself only, and asked advice from no one, thus running the risk of displeasing his parents outright, Jacob gladly had recourse to the lights of Rebecca. And this confidence of her son in a matter so delicate made Rebecca free to intervene, even without having been specially asked to do so. It made her industrious in the discovery of the means capable of obtaining the good and of warding off evil.

The same spontaneous and confident recourse of the slaves of love to their Queen and Mother puts the latter at ease towards them, and elicits her intervention at every good moment. From time to time Rebecca gave good advice to Jacob, either to draw down on him the blessing of his father, or to avoid the hatred and persecution of his brother. These counsels, followed well, led Jacob to the desired end. Likewise Mary directs in the ways of salvation those who request her good advice. Star of the sea, she does not simply show them the way; she brings them into it, makes them walk there, prevents them from deviating from it; she supports them, if they are close to falling; raises them, if they have fallen; takes them back as a charitable mother, when they fail, and sometimes even chastises them lovingly. A child obeying Mary, his enlightened director, cannot get lost on the paths of eternity. He cannot be allowed to be taken either in the illusions of the malignant spirit, nor in the subtleties of the heretics. Mary will dissipate the shadows and prevent the disorder: *"Following her you will not stray. Holding her you will not fall"* (St. Bernard).

Is not this result worth the trouble of entrusting ourselves to Mary?

*
* *

§ IV. – MARY DEFENDS AND PROTECTS HER SLAVES OF LOVE
(210)

N° 210

Often, here on earth, the predestined are exposed to hatred and persecution on the part of the reprobate. The slaves of Mary are no exception to this rule. But they find in this great Queen a powerful protector against their enemies.

As skillful as Rebecca in uncovering the plots contrived by the Esaus of all times against the Jacobs favored by heaven, she is incomparably more capable of annihilating their projects and shielding their victims from their blows. Rebecca only found one way to deliver Jacob from the death that his brother wanted to inflict on him, that of separating the two brothers, as long as the anger of Esau would last. Mary has thousands of means at her disposal.

Sometimes she proceeds **directly** and **personally**, hiding her slaves under the wings of her protection, as a hen does her chicks. To protect them from the sparrow hawk and the vulture, she puts herself around them and surrounds them as an army in battle array: *as an army set in array* (Cant. 6:3). What could a man fear from his enemies, if he was surrounded with an army of a hundred thousand well-trained, well-disciplined soldiers? A faithful servant of Mary, surrounded with the protection and imperial power of his sweet Queen, has less still to fear.

Sometimes **she delegates the angels in their service**. By herself she has the power to bring down all hell and to annihilate all the evil which is here on earth. She has, then, the possibility of shielding her slaves from any sorts of pitfalls. She does not disdain, however, to arrange for this purpose a whole sequence of movements of intermediate causes. In the first rank of beings who are in her service to carry out her merciful designs for the benefit of the elect come the angels of the heavenly militia. They are all very honored, and St. Michael more than all the others, to receive and to execute her beneficent orders (see n° 8). She even shows the importance of the goal to be attained and the price which she attaches to the result obtained. Because she:

would rather dispatch battalions of millions of angels to succor one of her servants than that it should ever be said that a faithful servant of Mary, who trusted in her, had had to succumb to the malice, the number, and the vehemence of his enemies.

Here is also what is capable of increasing our desire to be ranked among the faithful servants of Mary.

*
* *

§ V. – MARY INTERCEDES FOR HER SLAVES OF LOVE
(211-212)

N° 211

This is the fifth and supreme benefit which Mary obtains for her faithful devotees. She intercedes for them. And the purpose of her intercession is to obtain for them the blessing of the heavenly Father, not only at the very moment when they pronounce their consecration, but at every moment of their earthly life, and for all eternity. Is this not, indeed, the real extent of their act of donation? The future is involved in its unlimited expanse, as well as the present and the past.

Mary purifies and embellishes our good works. She mortifies and eliminates from our body and soul everything which is not in conformity with the taste of the heavenly Father, and adorns them with sanctifying grace, so that they are pleasing in His sight. She clothes us in the double perfumed coat of the merits of her divine Son and with her own merits. Thus prepared, we receive the divine blessing, just as Jacob received Isaac's blessing.

Very well; but all this must not be limited to a fleeting moment. The same effect has to occur continually. And such is indeed the purpose pursued by Mary.

Having obtained for her children the blessing of the heavenly Father and union with Jesus Christ, she preserves them in Jesus Christ and Jesus Christ in them. She guards them and watches over them, lest they lose the grace of God and fall into the traps of their enemies. She keeps the saints in their plenitude so that it does not decrease: "*In plenitudine sanctos detinet, ne plenitudo minuatur.*" This supposes that Mary helps her servants to behave always according to supernatural motives and under the influence (at least virtual) of charity. Besides, if she truly communicated her own virtues to us, or, at least, if she produces in us virtues similar to hers, we do not see why this influx of charity would not be always possible and always in the highest degree.

N° 212

Experience shows us, however, that there are fluctuations in our Marian life as in our spiritual life. Suppose that there are no mortal falls, which is not always true. Suppose even that there are no fully deliberate venial sins, which is infinitely rarer still. Nevertheless all our acts are not always as fervent as the others.

How can we explain the fact that, in every case, Mary presents us to God and makes obtain His blessing?

1° For the one who *gets up again from a mortal fall*, Mary can use, for the salvation of her child, the cry of an anguished and confident appeal, which he directed towards her. According to the measure of his dispositions, which she will complete and perfect in a motherly way, she will obtain for him from God justifying grace, and the latter will make him pleasing again to the eyes of the heavenly Father and will obtain for him His blessing.

2° *For the one who has committed deliberate venial sins*, she will inspire in him, first of all, an act of fervent love, accompanying, for example, the renewal of his consecration and coming to restore perfectly the order of charity. And it is at this moment that she will present her servant to God and will draw down upon him the divine blessing.

3° Finally, for the one who, without committing deliberate venial sins, is often *lukewarm and lax in his fervor*, nothing obliges Mary to present his good works to God immediately. The Thomistic doctrine is known, according to which only the acts of the more fervent virtues produce in us an increase of grace. The intermediate lax acts only contribute to this increase indirectly, by preparing an act of more fervent charity. But in reality, when it comes, the new infusion of grace will be the reward both of the final act of charity and of those which preceded. Why would Mary not also wait to be able to obtain this more fervent act to present to God the works of her slave of love and make them pleasing to Him? The act of burning love by which she leads her child to renew so frequently his self-donation as a slave will be what she will use to restore to previous works this supplement of beauty which laxity had stolen from them. And God will accept the offering and will bless her slave.

Such is the explanation of this beautiful figure, in which, to encourage us to walk in the Marian way, the Holy Ghost Himself willed to depict a long time in advance the multiple fruits of this devotion. Although very great and very old, this figure of predestination and reprobation was, before Father de Montfort, "unknown and full of mystery." His explanations showed the precision and charm of them. They succeeded in producing the conviction in those who honestly look for proportionate motives, in order to decide to pronounce and to live out their consecration of the Holy Slavery.

CHAPTER III

THE EFFECTS OF THE PERFECT DEVOTION

(213-225)

N° 213

Having seen *"as briefly as we can"* (n° 134) the motives which make this devotion commendable, our Saint now studies the *"wonderful effects which this produces in faithful souls."* This is another aspect of the advantages that it obtains. But, here, it is no longer immediately God or Mary who spare no effort because of this unconditional consecration. It is the devotion of the Holy Slavery that is efficient cause, and which, by the very strength contained in its nature, produces the seven effects which Montfort analyzes in this chapter. Thus the habit of prayer leads spontaneously to the interior life, and the practice of the exercises of piety arouses, maintains and develops piety itself.

My dear brother, be sure that, if you are faithful to the interior and exterior practices of this devotion, which I will point out, the following effects will take place in your soul (see the following chapter),

1° You will know and despise yourself (n° 213);

2° You will share in Mary's faith (n° 214);

3° Your heart will open to the grace of pure love (n° 215);

4° You will have great confidence in God and in Mary (n° 216);

5° You will be animated by the spirit of Mary (n° 217);

6° Your soul will be transformed into the image of Jesus (n°s 218-221);

7° You will procure the greatest glory of Jesus Christ (n°s 222-225).

These effects are linked to one another with an admirable logic. Having been led by this devotion to renounce our natural lights (1st effect), we allow ourselves to be guided by the lights of faith, and not any faith, but that of Mary (2nd effect). The intelligence, enlightened by faith, draws with it the will, which itself is raised on high by the grace of pure love (3rd effect). This produces the blossoming of the soul in an absolute confidence (4th effect). But it is little for the soul, growing more and more in the practice of its slavery, to be guided by Mary's distinct gifts. Like the gifts of the Holy Ghost themselves, these gifts are only a means for Mary to take possession of this soul and subject it directly to her action (5th effect). And so what will Mary do in the soul where she is mistress and where her spirit animates? What she did formerly, which is the purpose of her mission: she will form Jesus in it, she will transform it into Jesus (6th effect). And so we shall obtain, thanks to Mary, what should be the last end of our whole life, as it is the last end of our creation and sanctification: the greatest glory of Jesus Christ and, through Jesus Christ, God (7th effect).

Let us enter into the detail of this enumeration.

Article I

Knowledge and contempt of oneself

(213)

This first effect is of the order of those which the philosophers call "*Removentes prohibens*". The definitive result is rather negative: the destruction of all trust in oneself. But, it is already a considerable merit of the perfect devotion to obtain so quickly such a necessary thing. Since these obstacles are profoundly rooted in our nature, it is necessary, in order to overthrow them, that the perfect devotion possess a powerful causality, capable, at one stroke, of purifying and renewing nature.

How does it arrive at this purpose?

1° By giving us the light of the Holy Ghost **in order to know ourselves**. This light will mercilessly reveal all creases and folds, destroying any illusion and showing such as they are:

a) our *evil heart* and vitiated nature;

b) our original corruption, increased still *by our personal falls*;

c) our *incapacity for any good*, not only in the order of salvation – which is then absolute – but also in the order of nature with a few exceptions.

2° This knowledge, which Mary will thus produce in us, will not bring us to accept ourselves as we are, philosophically, **but to despise ourselves** and to think of ourselves only with horror. This judgment, which we shall feel about ourselves bluntly, is very well highlighted by the following three comparisons:

You will regard yourself:
a) *as a* **snail** *that spoils everything with its slime;*
b) *as a* **toad** *that poisons everything with its venom;*
c) *as a spiteful* **serpent**, *only seeking to deceive.*

Is this not, in reality, the conduct of man, if he follows the instincts of his fallen nature? The best things will be for him an occasion of sin, and he will always try to abuse them.

3° To increase further this feeling of contempt of ourselves which Mary will arouse in our heart, **she will communicate to us her profound humility**. That is to say, she will lead us to judge ourselves as she judged herself, by setting as a point of comparison no longer ourselves, but God. The contrast will then be more sharply noticed. And we shall obtain as though naturally such surprising results as these:

a) "*You will despise yourself,*" which already is not an easy thing.

b) "*You will despise nobody else,*" which is so contrary to our natural tendencies; as much as we are inclined to exalt ourselves, we are as quick to disparage others.

c) "*You will love contempt,*" oh! This is the last thing to which we resign ourselves naturally; we can seemingly despise ourselves, and speak unfavorable words about ourselves. But, if the humility is not sincere, we shall be extremely offended to see others truly judging us as we pretend to judge ourselves!

To despise oneself truly, to despise nobody sincerely and to love contempt without any pretense, this is the mark of an authentic humility that is difficult to achieve.

If Mary produces it in a soul, nothing will hinder her maternal action in this soul any longer. The ground is cleared. Self-love is annihilated. And Montfort asserts that this is the first effect of perfect devotion to her.

Article II

Participation in the faith of Mary

(214)

N° 214

Humility is necessary as a foundation. But of itself it never built anything. If it were alone, the feeling of mistrust of oneself which it excites would paralyze our activity. That's why true humility is always accompanied by a very lively faith, and the feeling of mistrust of oneself is counterbalanced by the feeling of trust in God. The saints were humble, but they were also men of faith, and, because of this, fearless, enterprising, and daring.

Having produced humility in us, the perfect devotion to Mary will therefore produce faith in us. Having led us to renounce our natural lights, it will lead us to allow ourselves to be guided more and more by the lights of faith. In the moral order, there is no such thing as a vacuum. We are emptied only of what we replace.

But, just as Mary had granted to us, not just any humility, but her humility, in the same way, she communicates to us, not faith pure and simple, but her own faith.

Repeatedly already, we have seen Father de Montfort return to this idea: Mary communicates her virtues to us. Mary bequeaths (as though by legacy) her virtues to us. A theological question arises here, and it is all the more difficult for us to avoid it, as it is singularly complicated, when it concerns the permanence of faith in the beatific vision.

Now that she is reigning in the heavens, she has no longer this faith, because she sees all things clearly in God by the light of glory. Nevertheless, with the consent of the Most High, in entering into glory she has not lost her faith. She has kept it, in order that she may keep it in the Church Militant for her faithful servants.

The explanation of this sentence troubles the commentators of the Montfortian doctrine. How could Mary, without having personally preserved the virtue of faith, which is incompatible with the permanent beatific vision, preserve it so as to make her slaves of love share in it?

To give an answer to this problem, let us see, first of all, what St. Thomas teaches about the permanence of the virtues and the gifts in general, and of faith in particular, in heaven; then let us see the Bérullian teaching on the perseverance of conditions and virtues in Jesus and Mary; finally, let us see, in the light of these teachings and of the whole of Theology, how to resolve the present difficulty.

1° What St. Thomas teaches.

The Angelic Doctor speaks expressly of the perseverance of the virtues and the gifts after this life. (See I^a-II^{ae}, question LXVII for what concerns the virtues and question LXVIII, art. 6, for what concerns the gifts.)

a) *Is it about the moral virtues and the gifts of the Holy Ghost?* These have, here on earth, a twofold purpose. First of all, to tame the opposite inclinations, either of the sensory part (virtues), or of the soul itself, but because of its union with the body (gifts). In this sense, the moral virtues and the gifts will no longer exist in the next life, because all opposition on the part of the sensitive elements will cease. But virtues and gifts have a nobler purpose to fulfill: to maintain in the whole human being a constant inclination towards the good (virtues), or to render man always docile to the promptings of Holy Ghost (gifts). From this point of view, the moral virtues and the gifts of the Holy Ghost will never be more perfect than in heaven. No contrary force will delay the movement toward God that they will impress on our nature.

b) *Is it about the theological virtue of faith?* St. Thomas says clearly (art. 3) that it is excluded by the beatific vision. We cannot have a knowledge at the same time perfect and imperfect of the same object under the same aspects. Vision and faith do meet in the general element of *knowledge* (art. 5). But this knowledge relies on *different principles* for each of the two. In faith, we admit the truth because of the indisputable authority of the one who teaches it. In vision, we admit it because the obvious fact is there, and because there is no means to fight reasonably against it. It is not, then, the same knowledge which, here on earth, is obscure, and, in heaven, very clear. And nothing of what is strictly speaking in faith, is found again in the beatific vision.

2° The Berullian teaching.

For Cardinal de Bérulle, the acts of Jesus, although passing and temporary, have been crystallized in acquired states for all eternity. Or else the acts, themselves emanating from predetermined states, for example from the state of childhood, slipped into time without drawing in their rapid flow the imperishable "solid", made up of the dispositions in which Jesus was, when He worked this mystery or these acts. These dispositions are still as lively, actual, and effective as at that moment. "In such a manner that if it were necessary for us or if it were pleasing to God His Father, He would still be ready both to leave and to carry out all over again this work, this action, this mystery."

This obliges us to discuss the things and mysteries of Jesus, "not as things past and lifeless, but as things living and present and even eternal, whose fruit we also have to gather, present and eternal."

Thus, in all the mysteries of Jesus, "there is something divine which persists in heaven and which brings about a similar manner of grace in the souls which are on earth."

It seems that, relatively speaking, we can apply the same reasoning to the dispositions in which Mary was when she practiced such or such virtue. These dispositions remain eternally, and, "*with the consent of the Most High*", they still preserve an actual efficacy to operate "a similar manner of grace in souls" for the faithful servants of Mary.

3° An attempt at an answer to the problem.

In the reality of her physical being, the virtue of faith does not remain, and cannot remain in Mary. Furthermore, it cannon subsist outside of Mary. It cannot pass further into another subject without losing its previous identity and becoming another faith than that of Mary. In no way, consequently, can we participate *physically* in Mary's faith.

But the *dispositions* in which Mary was, when she allowed herself to be guided by faith, remain eternally. The glory that she possesses crowns all her merits, particularly those which she acquired by her faith, which was so lively and so full of abandonment. Because of this past faith, which honored Him so much; because of Mary's current dispositions, which are so pleasing to Him; to draw the consequences of the responsibility which He entrusted to her, to be the Mediatrix in the acquisition and distribution of graces, God allows Mary to produce in the souls of her servants a faith similar to hers. This faith reproduces such or such detail of that of Mary, as every created being reproduces such or such perfection of the supreme Being Himself. Thus Mary "*keeps the faith in the Church militant*", "*makes her most faithful servants and handmaidens participate in her faith.*" She had, she alone, more faith than "*all the Patriarchs, Prophets, Apostles and saints*" combined. She is capable of communicating to each of her slaves of love a faith which will be fragmentarily hers, or at least, an imperfect copy of hers.

*
* *

Having established the *fact* and the *mode* of this communication, let us see now what the **qualities** of this communicated faith are.

The more you gain the favour of that august Princess and faithful Virgin, the more you will go by pure faith in all your conduct.

A general assertion, which is then taken up in every detail.

This faith will be:

1° *Pure*, that is to say, it will be content with the certainties on which it depends. It will firmly believe revealed truths because it is God Who revealed them. It will not care about the sensible and the extraordinary. It will believe as firmly in aridity and spiritual desolation, as in the most enjoyable consolations.

2° *Lively*, that is to say, animated by perfect charity, which urges to action and always, from the motive of pure love. For, the First Vatican Council says, in quoting St. Paul: "Living faith is that which shines in charity" (cf. Gal. 5:6), whereas "faith without works is a dead faith" (cf. Jas. 2:17).

3° *Firm and immovable*, in spite of all the storms and hurricanes, of all bad examples and of all apostasies.

4° *Active and piercing*: "faith seeking understanding," as St. Anselm says. That is to say, a faith which, while remaining in its own limits, will seek to know explicitly all the mysteries that it must acknowledge, and, like a mysterious pass-key, will seek to penetrate into all the elements thereof that are accessible to our intelligence, in everything which touches God, Jesus Christ and man.

5° *Courageous*, that is to say, leading us to undertake and carry out great things for the glory of God and the salvation of souls.

It is understood that such a faith will be, for all those who will participate in it, a blazing torch, a principle of life, a treasure of wisdom and an all-powerful weapon. As a *blazing torch*, it will serve us, either to enlighten those who sit in darkness and the shadow of death, or to inflame those who are lukewarm, and to bring them to true charity. As a *principle of divine life*, it will serve us to restore to grace those who died there by sin. As a *hidden treasure of divine wisdom*, it will inspire in us sweet and persuasive, powerful and irresistible words, by which we shall touch hearts exalted in their pride, like cedars of Lebanon. Finally, as an *all-powerful weapon*, it will allow us to resist effectively the demon and all the enemies of salvation.

Article III

The grace of pure love

(215)

N° 215

Normally, the intelligence enlightened by the gift of such a lively faith must draw after it the will of the slave of love. So does divine grace not have the power to enlighten the understanding and act indirectly on the will? But it can also move the will itself directly, without impairing freedom. In the same way, the slavery of love, having communicated to us the faith of Mary, will produce in us the grace of pure love.

The soul, stripped of all trust in itself and enlightened by Mary's faith, is freed little by little from all servile fear and scrupulous preoccupation.

The humility in which it is established showed it what it is capable of by itself. It no longer, then, seeks a perfection which is above its strengths and which is fitting rather for the angelic nature. It knows that God is a good God, full of condescension, desiring especially the love of His children. Mary, the Mother of Fair Love, will teach it to allow itself to be guided by love, to imitate the conduct of a child towards his good father, to converse familiarly with him and to try to please him in all things without any contention.

And if, despite everything, fallen nature recaptures the upper hand, it does not lose courage, as less perfect and prouder souls do. It is humbled by its fall. It recognizes that it is indeed its work. It asks God very simply for forgiveness of them and lovingly extends its hand to Him so that He may help it to get up. And it starts its march again without trouble or anxiety, quite persuaded that God pardoned its fault entirely.

In this way, Mary opens and expands the hearts of her children, so that they can run in the way of the commandments of her Son with the holy freedom of the children of God and the unction of pure love.

Article IV

Great confidence in God and in Mary

(216)

N° 216

The link is obvious between this effect and the ones preceding, especially with the last one. Here, however, the object of confidence is no longer simply God by means of Mary, but simultaneously God and Mary. This does not prevent this confidence from being produced by Mary, and by means of the perfect devotion. To be convinced of this, it is enough to consider four reasons given by Montfort:

1° *One no longer approaches Jesus by himself* and supported by his own merits, but only by Mary and presented by this good Mother. This is already sufficient reason not to fear being rejected. (See 3rd motive, n°s 144-145.)

2° Mary, in order to compensate for the merits, graces and satisfactions which he gave up to her, *communicates her virtues* to her slave of love and clothes him with her own merits. He himself can say to God, in all truth and with complete confidence: "Behold Mary, Thy handmaid: be it done unto me according to Thy word."

3° Mary not only communicates her virtues and merits, but *she gives herself* entirely to those who gave themselves completely to her. For never will it be said that she will allow herself to be outdone in generosity. Such an exchange, so advantageous for us, is the foundation of our confidence. Mary will be our *riches*: "He took her to his own" (Jn. 19:27), our *strength*: "You are my strength and my praise in the Lord" (cf. Isa. 12:2), *the pledge of our fidelity*: "I will put you as a seal upon my heart," the *bosom* where, like a child weaned from the pleasures of earth, we shall draw heavenly consolations: "As a child that is weaned is towards his mother, so reward in my soul" (130:2).

4° We handed over everything to Mary, either for her to guard it (meritorious value of good works), or for her to apply it for the greatest glory of God (impetratory and satisfactory value of the same good works). *This good Mother will thus become the only treasure* whom we shall trust.

But, while being our treasure, Mary is also the treasure of the Lord: "Ipsa est thesaurus Domini." This great God enclosed there all of His most precious possessions, including His own Son (n° 23), so that men might be enriched with her fullness. Who does not see thenceforth what reason for confidence and consolation this exchange will bring us?...

Article V

Communication of Mary's soul and spirit

(217)

N° 217

Growing more and more in the faithful practice of this devotion, the soul will end up being totally under the influence of Mary herself and no longer only of her gifts

The soul of Mary will communicate itself to us.

This will not come true, however, by a kind of substantial derivation. That would be an absurdity. The soul is only where it animates, especially when it is united to a body. Nor will it be a sort of communion analogous to Eucharistic communion. The possibility of this communion rests on the miracle of transubstantiation. And the case is absolutely unique. It is not, then, along these two lines that we must look for the explanation of this wonderful effect. The latter appears much simpler in reality.

By the emptying of self and the grace of humility, by the gift of such a lively and penetrating faith, by the birth in it of pure love and filial abandonment, the soul is endowed with a supernatural armature, which makes it extremely capable of perceiving the motions of Mary, and extremely docile to follow them. The case is comparable to that of the gifts of the Holy Ghost, allowing the soul to catch the slightest breath of the Spirit, when the latter will deign to pass over it.

From then on, the soul of Mary can communicate to her slave of love the vibrations which she herself experiences. Or simply, she produces similar things of them in it. And as Mary said of herself in her sublime *Magnificat*: "My soul glorifies the Lord and my spirit rejoices in God my Savior," she will produce these two effects in us. **Her soul** will teach us *to glorify the Lord* and **her spirit** will teach us to *rejoice in God*. When two lyres are perfectly tuned and placed very close by one another, it is enough to play one so that the other begins immediately to vibrate. Similarly, the soul and the spirit of Mary will communicate their vibrations to the soul and the spirit of her slaves of love. This caused St. Ambrose to say: "May the soul of Mary be in each so that it magnifies the Lord; may the spirit of Mary be in each so that it rejoices in God."

Such a mystery of assimilation inspires a beautiful lyrical passage in the Saint. He expresses the same wish as a holy man of his time (whose name, however, is unknown to us): "*Ah! when will the happy time come when the divine Mary will be established mistress and queen of hearts*" not to keep them for herself, but "*to subject them to the empire of her great and only Jesus? When will souls breathe Mary as the body breathes air?*" St. Germanus of Constantinople had said: "As breath is the sign of life of bodies, in the same way devotion to Mary is the sign of life of souls." Here we go farther. It is no longer only devotion to Mary which regulates the breath of the soul; the soul devoted to Mary breathes Mary, as the body breathes air. The thought of Mary, the love of Mary gives it life, as air purifies, renews and gives life to the body in which it is breathed.

"*For then* (that is to say, when this will be realized), *wonderful things will happen in these lowly places where the Holy Ghost, finding His dear Spouse* **as it were** *reproduced in souls* (similarity and not identity), *shall come in with abundance* (as occurred in Mary on the day of the Annunciation), *and fill them with His gifts, particularly with the gift of wisdom, to work the miracles of grace.*"

According to the Saint, indeed, the perfect devotion to Mary is the best means of acquiring and the only means of preserving divine Wisdom.

In all this, we see realized the doctrine on the necessity of the union of souls with Mary, so that the Holy Ghost may work wonders there. When this union will grow to the supreme degree, the action of the Holy Ghost will be supremely effective, and this is the case in the Holy Slavery.

Finally, getting back to his question, so as to give, this time, an answer to it: "*My dear Brother, when will that happy time, that age of Mary, come, when souls* (several in the sense of "plures": a great number of souls and not only a few), *losing themselves in the abyss of her interior, shall become living copies of Mary* (according to the principle: "filii matrizant", children resemble their mother), *to love and glorify Jesus Christ* (as Mary loved and glorified Him herself!).

"*That time will not come* **until** *men shall know and practice this devotion which I am teaching. Ut adveniat regnum tuum, adveniat regnum Mariae.*" We deliberately highlighted the exclusive formula "*not…until*". It is not about one means among many others. It is the only one which can truly produce such an effect. It informs us about the necessity of the perfect devotion, for all those who want to establish the reign of Jesus in its fullness in themselves and in the world. But how this also exalts the prodigious efficacy of this form of Marian devotion!...

Article VI

Transformation of souls into the image of Jesus

(218-221)

N°s 218-221

We come to see that the soul, losing itself in Mary, takes on the resemblance of its good Mother. But the womb of Mary only ever formed Jesus corporally, and spiritually only souls resembling Jesus. That's why all those who will enclose themselves there will be assured of putting on there this divine resemblance. Mary is always and everywhere the tree of life, which produces its fruit wherever it is planted, and this fruit is none other than Jesus. If, then, by the fidelity to the practices of this devotion, we cultivate Mary in our soul, we are assured of reaping Jesus at the appropriate time, that is to say, when the time of the harvest will have come.

Here Montfort introduces a comparison which is fundamental in his method: **that of the mold.** This comparison is exact and suggestive, from the point of view where our Saint stands.

There are two ways to produce a statue. One consists in *sculpturing it* in a block of marble, stone or wood. The other consists *in using a mold*. The first way is extremely difficult and slow. It is necessary to strike countless of blows; the slightest clumsiness can spoil the whole work; and to reproduce perfectly the image of the one that we want to represent, consummate skill is necessary, which is rare even among artists. The mold, in contrast, if it is itself conformed to the model, allows anyone to obtain a statue that is a perfect likeness, if the material which is cast in it is liquefied just in time. Those are the elements of comparison that will be used and very exactly.

But we must be careful not to push the comparison too far. A sculptured statue has much more value than a molded statue, especially when the material used is exactly the same. We must be formed on Jesus' model: our resemblance with the divine Master would have to be appreciated more if it was the fruit of a slow work of sculpture than if it resulted from a rapid molding.

Montfort does not dwell on this consideration. What matters for him is the perfection and the speed of the result obtained: resemblance with Jesus. The quantity of efforts supplied and the length of time employed matter little, if, in spite of everything, we obtain only a grimacing form, or even if we obtain a beautiful form, but have nothing in common with that of Jesus.

That's why the Saint is allowed to joke pleasantly about the disappointment of certain pious persons or spiritual directors. They trusted their skill. They wanted to accomplish the work themselves. But they notice the insignificance of the fruit of their labor.

How many devout souls do I see who seek Jesus Christ, some by one way or by one practice, and others by other ways and other practices; and after they have toiled much throughout the night, (that is to say, without consolation), *they say:* "Per totam noctem laborantes, nihil cepimus (Lk. 5:5). *We have toiled all night, and have taken nothing."* *We may say to them:* "Laborastis multum (the text of Haggai 1:6 reads Seminastis multum, but the meaning is identical) et intulistis parum. *You have labored* (sown) *much and gained* (reaped) *little."* *Jesus Christ is yet feeble in you* (N° 218).

Here is the cause of their failure:

It seems to me that I can very aptly compare directors and devout persons, who wish to form Jesus Christ in themselves or others by different practices from this, to sculptors who trust in their own professional skill, ingenuity or art.

This art may be real. But it is necessarily disproportionate with the purpose to be attained. They "*give an infinity of hammering and chiselings to a hard stone or a piece of badly polished wood,*" what we all are supernaturally, "*to make an image of Jesus Christ out of it.*" The purpose is legitimate and noble. It is the one that all have to pursue.

But "*sometimes, they do not succeed in giving anything like the natural expression of Jesus, either from having no knowledge* (speculative) *or experience* (practical) *of the Person of Jesus, or from some blow awkwardly given* (through distraction, clumsiness or fatigue), *which has spoiled the work* (n° 220)."

It is not easy, indeed, it is even impossible for a mere mortal to possess a perfect knowledge of Our Lord, to have experienced all the ways which lead to Him, and to be shielded from the slightest failure of nature. We would thus admire the result, even if it were small, obtained by these devout persons and directors, and we would understand their mishaps, if they had not had, as we all have, a much simpler means of doing real miracles.

This means is Mary, the mold of God, a mold fit to form gods, according to the phrase attributed to St. Augustine: "*Si formam Dei te appellem, digna existis.* If I call you the mold of God, it is because you deserve this title."

This mold is perfect, because it underwent no deformation, and because it gave to Jesus a flawless humanity. All those who are cast in this divine mold are soon formed and molded into Jesus Christ, and Jesus Christ in them. At little cost and in a short time, they will become gods, because they are cast in the same mold which formed a God (n° 219).

That's why the greatest saints are molded in Mary. They recognized the value of this beautiful mold where Jesus Christ was naturally and divinely formed. They do not trust their own industry which, nevertheless, is very real. They cast themselves and lose themselves in Mary, to become the ungarnished portrait of Jesus Christ (n° 220).

Let us not believe, however, that there is nothing left to do for someone who thus casts himself into the Marian mold. If he wants truly to take all the forms which Mary will imprint on him, he must become like a well-molten and very liquid metal, capable of penetrating into all the details of the mold. He must destroy and dissolve in himself the old man with all his depraved inclinations, or, at least, reduce as much as possible the effects of these inclinations. And this is no small task (n° 221). But this work itself is accomplished in Mary and with Mary. It is developed in a brilliant light, in broad daylight, because there is nothing of the night in Mary. Everything in her is bright, exempt from sin and even from imperfection (n° 218).

This is, then, truly **a secret of grace** which Montfort presents to the slaves of Mary. It is a means suited to their ignorance and inexperience. And it is capable of leading them quickly to holiness, which, St. Paul asserts, consists in resembling the Son of God.

The mold of God! *"Oh! Beautiful and true comparison! But who will comprehend it? I desire that you may, my dear brother!* (n° 221)"

Article VII

The greatest glory of God

(222-225)

This last effect is the consequence of all the others. It has, however, itself its special reasons, which give it a very distinct identity and allow it to be distinguished and studied separately. Besides, is this not the purpose of our creation and sanctification: to obtain the greatest glory of Jesus Christ, and through Him, the greatest glory of God? The method of sanctification proclaimed by Montfort would not be more commendable than others if it were not a better means to render glory to God.

But, by its very nature, the perfect devotion possesses this special efficacy:

By this practice, faithfully observed, you will give Jesus more glory in a month than by any other practice, however difficult, in many years.

Indeed, it is not the difficulty which increases the merit. It is the fullness of charity, with which we act. Now, the total donation of the Holy Slavery supposes a superior degree of true charity. On the other hand, charity needs only a moment in order to accomplish or inspire the most meritorious acts.

Consequently, from this point of view, the assertion of the Saint is already fully justified.

Even so, by basing his arguments on the very nature of the perfect devotion, he finds four reasons which he advances.

1° You act by following *Mary's intentions* and not yours (n° 222).

2° You rely on *Mary's dispositions* and not on yours (n° 223).

3° Mary offers to God your actions *purified and embellished by her care* (n° 224).

4° It is no longer you who praise God, but *Mary who praises Him in your place* (n° 225).

Each of these reasons throws a magnificent light on the sentence which we quoted a short time ago.

N° 222

1° You act by following Mary's intentions and not yours.

Everyone knows the importance of the intention in determining the value of an action for better or worse. So, actions that are quite indifferent in themselves, like eating, drinking, sleeping, can become eminently meritorious, and obtain much glory for God, if they are carried out with the right intentions and from the motive of pure love.

Now, our best intentions are always marred by some imperfection: vanity, self-love, vain complacence, self-seeking, to speak only of the most subtle stains, capable of creeping in everywhere. On the contrary, the intentions of Mary are always pure and upright, without any search for a particular interest, with the constant preoccupation for the greatest glory of God.

To renounce one's personal intentions, as good as they may be, to take Mary's and let oneself be guided by them, is to share in the sublimity of these intentions. And this is quite easy to see. Because, by the least of her actions, for example, by spinning her distaff or needlepoint, Mary obtained more glory for God than all other saints by the most striking actions, e.g., like St. Lawrence on his grill, undergoing the cruelest martyrdom. More than this even: Mary alone gave more glory to God than all Angels and saints combined for eternity. Montfort is fond of repeating it, so as to exalt once again this masterpiece of grace. Likewise, the one who is willing to lose himself in Mary and to be blindly guided by her intentions, will work wonders, accumulate riches of grace and render to his Creator all the glory which is due to Him.

N° 223

2° You rely on *Mary's dispositions* and not on yours.

For us to approach so great a Master and offer Him the tribute of our homage, we need a dignity of which we can be conscious. This dignity may truly exist, because it is enough to be in the state of grace and to know that we are. But do not all have to dread the searching look of the One Who probes hearts and depths and finds stains even in His Angels? And, anyway, to rely solely on one's own dignity, can one go without a feeling of imperceptible complacence in oneself? If this method is followed, do we have a sufficient idea of the greatness and holiness of God? Are we as capable of glorifying Him?

On the contrary, not to count on one's own dispositions for anything, to rely only on Mary's, is resolutely to commit oneself to the path of humility. This is to glorify more highly this God Who loves only the praise of the meek and humble of heart. This is to allow the eminent holiness of Mary to sing the hymn of glory that God always loves hearing.

N° 224

3° **Mary offers to God your actions** *purified and embellished by her care.*

Mary accepts with great charity the poor little present of our actions, as the queen accepts the apple, the price of the farm rent of the insolvent farmer. She cleanses these actions from the stains which they contracted by our imperfections. She embellishes them by adding to them the merit of her personal actions. By now the gift is more presentable. But she especially offers it herself to her divine Son with all the love which she knows how to put in it. Undoubtedly, Jesus is more glorified than if we offered ourselves to Him with our own criminal hands.

N° 225

4. **It is no longer you who praise God, but** *Mary who praises Him in your place.*

The adage is known: *Honor est in honorante*. Honor is measured by the person who honors. It is more honorific for a king to be greeted by another king than by a subject of his kingdom. That is why only a divine person was capable of glorifying God perfectly.

After the praise of His Son, God appreciates nothing more than the praise of His Mother, and the one who can appropriate this praise to send it back to God will be assured of being supremely pleasing to Him.

Now, this is possible in this form of devotion, because Mary is altogether relative to God. She exists only with regard to God, and she immediately refers back to her Creator the praise that we address to her personally. An **echo**, but an echo of a special kind, which says and repeats only "God", even when we ourselves say and repeat "Mary!" St. Elisabeth praised Mary and congratulated her for having believed; Mary, the faithful echo of God, intoned *Magnificat anima mea Dominum*: My soul glorifies the Lord.

Do we, then, want to make sure that Mary will glorify God in our place, and as she herself knows how to do it? It is enough to think of her, to praise her and to honor her. She cannot keep for herself the honor which we refer to her. She immediately refers it back to God. And God holds this substitution as supremely pleasing. He is infinitely more honored by Mary's praise than by ours. And there is truly the best means of obtaining His greatest glory.

*
* *

Thus ends chapter III on the wonderful effects of the perfect devotion. Having come out from the depth of the abyss by the knowledge and contempt of ourselves, we have been brought by the Holy Slavery up to the foot of the throne of the Most Holy Trinity, and we become capable of singing His glory already in this life. An obvious anticipation for the life hereafter, because devotion to Mary will not be absent in it, our slavery towards this good Mother extending in time and eternity.

CHAPTER IV

THE PRACTICES OF THE PERFECT DEVOTION

(221-273)

The consecration of the Holy Slavery introduces us into a **state** similar to the religious state. Even without his knowing it, the virtuous acts of a member of a religious order gain an additional value, resulting from the virtue of religion. Thus, whether he thinks of it or not, the slave of love is consecrated to Mary, and all his actions proclaim the glory of his Queen as long as they are good and since the donation is not retracted.

But this state itself would be more imaginary than real, if everything were restricted to the act of initial consecration. Our memory is so easily forgetful, that soon it would no longer retain any memory thereof. Then, there would no longer be any difference between the slave of love and the other faithful.

To prevent this drawback, and so that the consecration preserves, all the time and in all our actions, its maximum efficacy, it is necessary to add another element to the consecration, if not equally essential, at least equally necessary: **the practices of the Holy Slavery**.

In the *Secret of Mary*, n° 28, Father de Montfort distinguishes these two conditions very clearly. The Perfect Devotion, he says, "*consists in giving oneself entirely, as slave, to Mary and to Jesus through her; then to do everything with Mary, in Mary, through Mary and for Mary.*"

Similarly, in n°ˢ 115, 8°, and 116, 12°, of the *Treatise*, where obviously the topic is the Holy Slavery, Montfort indicates an **exterior practice**: "*To consecrate ourselves to her in a special and solemn manner,*" and an **interior practice**: "*To begin, to continue, and to finish all our actions through her, in her, with her, and for her.*"

Clarifying now, therefore, this state of dependence described in the 1st chapter of this 2nd part, Montfort asserts that his devotion requires a certain number of practices, either exterior, or interior. In one way or another, these practices belong to the Holy Slavery and guarantee the efficacy of it. In explaining them, the Saint provides a perfect overview of his spirituality.

The subdivisions of this chapter will be those of the *Treatise* itself:

Article I: **Exterior practices of the Perfect Devotion** (nos 226-256).

Article II: **Interior practices of the Perfect Devotion** (nos 257-265).

Supplement: *Communion with Mary* (nos 266-273).

Article I

Exterior practices of the perfect devotion

(226-256)

N° 226

Although what is **essential** *in this devotion consists* **in the interior**, *we must not fail to unite to the inward practice certain external observances.*

The interior under discussion here is not established by the interior practices. It is about the interior of the soul, which the perfect devotion has to inform, consecrate and establish in a state of total belonging to Mary (see n° 119).

Montfort begins by giving reasons why, while caring especially for the interior, the exterior must not be neglected either. *"These things you ought to have done, and not to leave those undone"* (Mt. 23:23).

These reasons are three in number. They are based on the very nature of man:

1° **The exterior practices well-performed aid the inward ones and almost infallibly lead to them**. It is enough, in many cases, to take hold of the exterior of piety, to be soon drawn by real feelings of interior piety. Antonin Eymieux demonstrated in his book: *Le gouvernement de soi-même*, the influence of a simple position on a whole series of acts. Hardly does someone give an hypnotic an order to kneel, join his hands and tilt his head slightly to the left, immediately and without further order, he begins to pray fervently. Is this not spontaneous proof of the natural connection that exists in us between the exterior and the interior?

2° The reason for this connection is because man is composed of a body and a soul. As long as these two elements are united on this earth, the soul needs the body to carry out its actions, even the most elevated ones. It can manage to know, and consequently to want and to desire only what has passed through the senses beforehand: *"Nothing reaches the intelligence without having passed beforehand through the senses."* From this point of view, **the exterior practices of devotion will be necessary to elicit, maintain and develop** the interior sentiments of the soul toward Mary, to help it to wish for this consecration, to pronounce it, and to remember it.

3° **Finally, man has to live in society, and communication with his fellow men is established only by means of external signs**. When these are lacking, man remains a closed, impenetrable, mysterious being. If he shows no exterior devotion, he will be considered as not having it, and the effect on others can be disastrous.

Let us not go so far, then, as to criticize these exterior practices, by proclaiming that they are a hypocrisy or a cause of vanity and that one must hide his devotion! The answer to these attacks was given by the good Master Himself: "*That they may see your good works, and glorify your Father Who is in heaven*" (Mt. 5:16).

This does not mean, as *St. Gregory the Great* remarks, that one must devote himself to his activity and external devotions to please men and draw some praises from them, because that would be vanity.

But one sometimes carries them out *before men* in order "**to please God**" and "**cause Him to be glorified**", without caring for the contempt or praises which this conduct will attract.

Finally, it is good to note, these practices are not called exterior because they are carried out without an interior spirit. This would be grotesque play-acting and would have no value. But they contain an exterior element. This distinguishes them from purely interior practices.

The exterior practices enumerated by Montfort are seven:

1° The consecration itself, preceded by preparatory exercises (n°s 227-233);

2° The recitation of the Little Crown (n°s 234-235);

3° The wearing of little iron chains (n°s 236-243);

4° Devotion to the mystery of the Incarnation and to the feast of March 25th (n°s 243-248);

5° Devotion to the *Ave Maria* and the Rosary (n°s 249-254);

6° The recitation of the *Magnificat* (n° 255);

7° Contempt of the world (n° 256).

It will be very useful to review each of these practices, because, in discussing several of them, Montfort gives precious additional information on his form of devotion.

§ I. – PREPARATORY EXERCISES AND CONSECRATION
(227-233)

N° 227

Let us leave aside two small questions raised by the beginning of this paragraph: the establishment, wished by Montfort and realized now, of the association of the slaves of Mary in a regular confraternity; and the exact determination of what he calls *"the first part of this preparation for the reign of Jesus Christ."* Let us take simply what directly concerns this first and more necessary practice of the perfect devotion.

An act of great importance, an act which commits the whole life and even eternity, is not carried out thoughtlessly. The Church imposes a one-year novitiate on the one who wants to take religious vows. In the same way, Montfort prescribes a one-month preparation for the one who wants to make his consecration of the Holy Slavery.

I. – PREPARATORY MONTH
(227-230)

The plan drawn up for this month gives us the veritable standard for the Montfortian spiritual exercises and makes Montfort the emulator of St. Ignatius of Loyola.

"Month" is taken in a special sense, because of the number of days allowed for each week: $12 + 6 + 6 + 6 = 30$. We could also take three weeks of 7 days; which brings the total to 33. But besides the figure of 12, allowed to the first period, it seems rather a minimum: "having employed *at least* 12 days."

In this month, the general division is thus designed: 12 days to empty oneself of the spirit of the world: then three consecutive weeks, one in order to know oneself, the second in order to know the Most Blessed Virgin, the last in order to know Our Lord.

1° To empty oneself of the spirit of world.

The Saint spoke in another book, which has not come down to us, about the world, its spirit and the ways of emptying oneself of it. He does not return to this subject, and is content with saying briefly: "*The spirit of the world, which is contrary to the spirit of Jesus Christ.*" We understand that it is necessary to empty ourselves of it.

If it was a matter of defining it, the **world** is made up of all those who profess a doctrine, accept principles, advocate methods, and practice a way of life absolutely opposed to those of the Gospel. Worldly men "*have a doctrine as opposed to that of Wisdom incarnate* (Jesus Christ) *as darkness is to light, and death to life*" (Love of Eternal Wisdom, n° 199). Sometimes, they display it openly and blatantly. More often "*they disguise their lies under the appearance of truth.*" (Ibid.)

In order to manage to commit sin themselves or to lead others to commit it, "*they discuss it either as a virtue, or as honesty, or as an indifferent thing and of little consequence*" (Ibid.). Furthermore, the world exercises its tyranny over souls by means of three concupiscences: the concupiscence of the eyes or desire for the goods of the earth; the concupiscence of the flesh or the desire for sensual pleasures, and the pride of life or the desire for human glory.

To have the spirit of the world is, then, to be guided by its false maxims, to believe that evil is no longer evil, that

God has no right to forbid it, that it can be committed with impunity, even if it means going to confess afterwards in order to calm the divine sensitivities. He will also take care for this to choose a confessor "*the least scrupulous (thus are called the lax confessors who do not carry out their duty), to have from him, cheaply, peace in a soft and effeminate life*" (See Love of Eternal Wisdom, n° 81.).

To empty oneself of the spirit of the world, it is necessary to fill oneself with the spirit of Jesus Christ, because, in the moral life, a vacuum does not exist. We are emptied only of what we replace.

A good method of knowing if we are animated by the spirit of Jesus Christ is to benefit from the Gospel warning: "Every good tree bringeth forth good fruit, and the evil tree bringeth forth evil fruit. A good tree cannot bring forth evil fruit, neither can an evil tree bring forth good fruit" (Mt. 7:17-18). We shall thus examine which fruits are in our soul and we shall thus know by which spirit it is animated.

Now, St. Paul, in his Epistle to the Galatians, enumerates twelve fruits of the Holy Ghost (one for each of the days of this period). They are: *the love of God, joy, peace, patience* in adversities, *benignity* and *goodness*, in which our charity towards our neighbor is manifested, *longanimity*, or the firm expectation of the goods that God has promised, *mildness, faith, modesty, continency*, understood in the sense of moderation of disordered desires. If these last are focused on the goods of this world, we shall have the *spirit of poverty*; if they are focused on the pleasures of the senses, we shall have *chastity*.

To cultivate these fruits in our souls, so that they fill the whole space and do not allow the tree of death (which is not in our power to uproot) to develop its pernicious fruits. To fill oneself thus with the spirit of Jesus Christ in order to empty oneself of the spirit of the world. The spirit of world is not the thing that, by leaving, will call the spirit of Jesus Christ to take over for it. Rather, it is the spirit of Jesus Christ, which, by coming to take possession of its domain, will chase away all prowlers from it.

In order to Marianize this period, consider every fruit realized in its perfection in Mary, then, see the opposite fruit completely spread throughout the world, from the hatred of God to impurity in all its forms; finally, to examine oneself to draw the conclusion.

There are no special prayers indicated for this period; one can recite, as for the other periods: the *Veni Creator*, the litanies of the Holy Ghost and the *Ave Maris Stella*.

Normally, these 12 days must end by the preliminary act of choice of the divine Wisdom. (See the hymn: *O Wisdom, come*, and the little work: *Preparation for consecration*, 1929.)

N° 228

2° To know oneself.

This is the object of the first week. This knowledge has to concern our evil nature. This latter arises either from depraved inclinations left in us by original sin, or from personal sins committed since the age of reason. As this whole question was already discussed previously, we can be content with referring back to it, as Father de Montfort does.

Let us note only that here there is no more fundamental opposition between the spirit of Jesus and ours. There is only a miserable state, caused by sin. The world had dealings in place. It could easily reign there by its three concupiscences. Jesus finds obstacles there. He has to begin by eliminating them. And it is necessary for us to be well persuaded of the presence of these obstacles and of the necessity of removing them. Otherwise, we shall not arrive at perfect union with the divine Master or at the establishment of His reign in us.

As for the *method to follow*, Montfort suggests two:

A) *To consider oneself* during each of the six days as one or the other of the following animals, obviously because of the symbolism which it embodies:

1) as *snails*, lazy and selfish; 2) as *crawling things*, soiling everything with their slime and corrupting the best things; 3) as *toads*, stuck to the ground and venomous; 4) as *swine*, greedy and dirty; 5) as *serpents*, nasty and envious; 6) as *unclean animals*, lewd and scandalous. We could add to this miniature zoo, in order to complete the number seven and the allusion to each of the deadly sins: the *peacock*, proud and self-important.

B) *To reflect on this consideration* attributed to St. Bernard:

1° "*Think of what you were: rotten seed.*" An allusion to our physical origin, which, certainly, has nothing glorious and explains already many weaknesses: "Think of what you were: rotten seed."

2° "*Think of what you are: a vessel of dung.*" An allusion to the necessities of our vegetative life, which are indeed such as to humble us: "Think of what you are: a vessel filled with excrement."

3° "*Think of what you will be: the food of worms.*" An allusion to what our body will become after our death and while awaiting the resurrection: "Think of what you will be one day: the food of worms."

These two methods are excellent for showing us what we are of ourselves and as a result of sin. They sharply reveal all the shadows of the picture. But they do not accentuate so well what grace does or can do with beings so miserable.

That's why a third method could be offered. It would even have the advantage of being able to be applied identically in the course of the three weeks. Consider each of the seven days of the week what each of *the seven gifts* of the Holy Ghost manifests in us. The gift of *wisdom* (that is to say, the knowledge of things through their highest causes), teaches us our divine origin. The gift of *understanding* brings us its lights so as understand divine truth. The gift of *knowledge* helps us to grasp in creation what is the work of God. The gift of *counsel* protects us from shadows of doubt and moral uncertainty. The gift of *piety* urges us to return to God. The gift of *fortitude* comes to our help so as to overcome obstacles. The gift of *fear* inspires us with regret for our sins and the horror of falling into them again.

Emphasize, indeed, starting from the beginning or even further back, the end to which we must come in the light of each of these gifts. We can thus acquire a perfect and complete knowledge of self.

The prayers recommended for this period are, first of all, frequent aspirations of this kind: "*Domine ut videam, Lord, that I may see!*" my unworthiness, my weakness, my powerlessness to do any good. Or also: "*Noverim me! That I may know myself!*" (St. Augustine) in order to despise in me what is my work, so as to exalt and develop on the contrary what is Your work. Then we shall recite, as in the preparatory period, the litanies of the Holy Ghost and the *Veni Creator*, to ask for the light of the Holy Ghost and the *Ave Maris Stella*, as well as the Litany of Loreto to ask for the help of the Most Blessed Virgin.

N° 229

3° To know the Most Blessed Virgin.

This is the purpose pursued during the 2nd week. In order to lead us to it, Montfort recommends that we read and meditate on what he himself wrote in his *Treatise* and his other works. There is there, indeed, as we were readily convinced of it, a whole mine to be exploited; and there is not one page on which an ardent prayer and a profound reflection cannot draw a special light to enlighten one of the vast panoramas of this "*world of God.*" (See n° 6).

The reason for this study of Mary, placed between the study of ourselves and the study of Our Lord, is clearly indicated by the Saint. "*If, then, as is certain, the kingdom of Jesus Christ is to come into the world, it will be but a necessary consequence of the knowledge of the kingdom of the most holy Virgin Mary*" (n° 13). Let us learn, then, to know her in order to know Jesus better. Let us subject ourselves to her reign, in order to be more subject to that of Jesus. Let us pursue this twofold purpose in each of our prayers, and even in each of our works, by already carrying them out them in the spirit of the Holy Slavery.

To establish the frame of this meditation, we can decide to read and meditate on a certain number of pages every day. We can also consider Mary's principal privileges. Finally, we can seek in her what each of the seven gifts of the Holy Ghost makes us discover there, by following the same plan as above. In the light of the gift of *Wisdom*, we discover the marvels of her predestination. The gift of *Understanding* makes us penetrate into the immense impact of her divine maternity. *Knowledge* shows us the chain of the causes and effects in Mary, and in the world thanks to Mary. *Counsel* highlights the magnificent intellectual and moral balance of Mary. *Piety* shows her to us lost in God. *Fortitude* shows itself especially on Calvary and the *Fear of God*, in the infinite delicateness of her conscience.

Besides the litanies of the Holy Ghost or the *Ave Maris Stella*, already recommended for the previous periods, we shall recite every day of this week the whole Rosary or at least a chaplet, so that the dew of prayer and meditation on the mysteries may obtain for us this knowledge which is so necessary.

A useful conclusion will be an act of contemplation on Mary, like hymn n° 56 on the beauties of Mary: *O holy and divine Mary.*

N° 230

4° To know Our Lord.

The last step of this ascent, the last stage of this preparation. The same program as the previous week. Read and meditate on what has been written, either in the *Treatise*, or in *The Love of Eternal Wisdom*. If it was necessary to point out some passages in particular, we would select the first and second fundamental truths in their entirety. They establish that Jesus alone is the final end of all our devotions, including devotion to Mary, and that we belong to Him as slaves. Then the ardent passages on the necessity of His reign and on His admirable dependence on His Mother. We can finish by studying the mystery of the Incarnation, which gives us a God-Man, full of grace and truth; the mystery of the Redemption, which gives us a Savior, so loving and devoted; the mystery of the Eucharist in which Jesus becomes our food and our companion in exile, etc....

So many truths of which it is necessary for us to be well-persuaded, if we want to love Jesus Christ and give ourselves to Him with all the fervor that He is capable of inspiring.

Here again, the plan given for the other weeks applies magnificently. Moreover, it is of the Incarnate Word that the prophet Isaiah prophesied the fullness of these gifts. Consequently, it is easy to study them in Him and to study Him in their light.

Wisdom, which governs everything "fortiter et suaviter"; *Understanding* which reads the depth of hearts and is never baffled; *Knowledge* which knows everything and is subject to no error; *Counsel* which He possesses perfectly and communicates to His servants; *Piety* which devotes Him totally to the worship of His Father; *Fortitude* which allows Him to endure for us torments so cruel and *Fear of God*, completely filial, in virtue of which he accepts so lovingly the will of His Father.

Recite during this week the prayer of St. Augustine: *Tu es Christus*, given in n° 67, the litanies of the Holy Ghost and the *Ave Maris Stella*, as usual, but furthermore: the litanies of the Holy Name of Jesus and the aspirations: "*Noverim te, That I may know You, Lord*" in order to love You (St. Augustine) and "*Domine ut videam, Lord, that I may see Who You are.*"

End with an act of desire for Communion, which, the next day, must immediately precede your consecration. (See hymn n° 38: *Mille fois, mon coeur vous désire*, either one or the other of the hymns on the love of Jesus, 115, 115a and 115b.)

II. – THE CONSECRATION
(231-232)

This ceremony will be, preferably, a feast day dedicated to Mary or to her great servant, St. Louis-Marie Grignion de Montfort. It will be clothed in the most possible solemnity, to fix profoundly the remembrance of it in the memory. For this purpose, certain prescriptions concern the day of the consecration itself. Others envisage the periodic renewal of this consecration. The first few aim at impressing the spirit, the others at preserving the memory.

A. – THE DAY OF THE CONSECRATION

We shall notice there:
    a) the *preliminaries* of the consecration;

b) the *consecration* itself;
c) the *accessories* of the consecration.

N° 231

a) **The preliminaries of the consecration.**

They shall confess and communicate with the intention of giving themselves to Jesus Christ in the quality of slaves of love.

There is no truly Christian feast without confession and Communion. How could these two great acts of piety be absent from this solemnity? We shall thus confess expressly for this feast, even if we had already confessed during the preparatory month, especially, which would be normal, at the end of the first week. One or the other of these two confessions can be general, if the confessor considers it appropriate. Is it not a question, indeed, of breaking definitively with a perhaps very turbulent past?

Then they shall approach the Holy Altar with the greatest recollection possible and by calling upon Mary's help, so that her divine Son may be better received, "*they shall try to make this Communion*" according to the Montfortian method, explained in the appendix of this chapter.

*
* *

b) **The consecration itself.**

Montfort supposes it is pronounced immediately, or shortly after Communion. Thus the initiation into the Holy Slavery resembles, as much as possible, the rite observed in certain religious professions. It is always the moment which is the best chosen in order to consecrate oneself in private. But, if this act coincides with admission into the Confraternity of Mary Queen of Hearts, and if a meeting along with instruction and admission of new associates must be held on the same day, one can wait until the evening to pronounce his consecration.

The formula of consecration was composed by the Saint himself. He had originally put it in the appendix to his *Treatise*, as we are informed by the reference: "*Which they will find afterwards.*" These pages have been lost. Thank God the book on *The Love of Eternal Wisdom* also contains an act of consecration. Why would it not be the one to which Montfort alludes here?

The formula is divided into three principal parts: 1° preparatory prayers to divine Wisdom and Mary Immaculate; 2° the consecration properly so-called; 3° a final prayer to Mary.

1° PREPARATORY PRAYERS

The future slave of love addresses himself, first of all, by a *solemn invocation*, to Jesus, *eternal and incarnate Wisdom*.

O eternal and incarnate Wisdom! O sweetest and most adorable Jesus, true God and true Man, only Son of the eternal Father and of Mary always Virgin!

This is followed by four preparatory acts for the great sacrifice of the consecration, assigning to it the same purposes as for the sacrifice of the Mass.

An act of *adoration*:

I adore Thee profoundly in the bosom and splendours of Thy Father during eternity and **in the virginal bosom of Mary**, *Thy most worthy Mother,* **in the time of Thine Incarnation**.

The Holy Slavery strives especially to imitate Jesus living in the womb of Mary. This is affirmed from the beginning by this act of consecration.

An act of *thanksgiving*:

I give Thee thanks for that Thou hast annihilated Thyself, in taking the form of a slave, **in order to rescue me from the cruel slavery of the devil**.

I praise and glorify Thee for that Thou hast been pleased to submit Thyself to Mary, in all things, **in order to make me Thy faithful slave through her**.

Jesus snatches us from the tyranny of Satan to put us back under His legitimate dominion. By the right of war, we are His slaves, but He Himself gives us the model of this slavery and indicates to us the means to acquit ourselves of it perfectly.

An act of *reparation*:

But, alas! ungrateful and faithless as I have been, I have not kept the promises which I made so solemnly to Thee in my Baptism; I have not fulfilled my obligations; I do not deserve to be called Thy son, nor yet Thy slave; and as there is nothing in me which does not merit Thine anger and Thy repulse, I dare no more come by myself before Thy Most Holy and August Majesty.

Here we have, highly condensed, the teaching on the cause of all the breaches of trust of men: the forgetting of the vows of baptism; on our fallen nature, corrupted and the cause of corruption; on the necessity of a mediator with the Mediator Himself.

An act of *supplication*:

It is on this account that I have recourse to the intercession of Thy most holy Mother, whom Thou hast given me for a mediatrix with Thee. It is by her means that I hope to obtain of Thee contrition, and the pardon of my sins, the acquisition and the preservation of wisdom.

Summarized in the whole Montfortian doctrine on the role freely entrusted to Mary by God in the whole economy of our salvation. Mary Mediatrix will obtain for us, first of all, the removal of the obstacles to the reign of her divine Son by the grace of contrition and the forgiveness of our sins; then she will establish the reign of Jesus by granting us the signal favor of the acquisition and preservation of Wisdom.

At this moment, the future slave turns to *Mary*, and greets her as having a *threefold crown*:

A crown of *grandeur and excellence*, resulting especially from her divine Maternity:

I salute Thee, then, O immaculate Mary, **living tabernacle** *of the Divinity, where the eternal Wisdom willed to be hidden, and to be adored by Angels and by men.*

The divine Maternity is indeed taken on at the moment when it came about, and when Mary exercised an incomparable power over her divine Son.

A crown *of power*, resulting from her dominion over heaven and earth:

I hail Thee, **O Queen of heaven and earth**, *to whose empire* **everything is subject** *which is under God.*

Marvelous power, the purpose of which was shown in n°s 27-28. Mary exercises it in order to lead to heaven those whom God has marked with the mysterious sign of predestination.

A crown *of goodness*, resulting from her mercy towards sinners:

I salute Thee, **O sure Refuge of sinners**, *whose mercy fails no one.*

Encouraged by this great goodness, of which he must not be the first one to doubt, he asks to Mary to grant him the supreme purpose of his desires: divine Wisdom:

Hear the desires *which I have of* **the divine Wisdom**.

And in order to enlist her to grant him the object of his prayer, which, for him, as for Solomon, will assure him all the rest: "*All good things came to me together with her*" (Wis. 7:11), he abandons into her hands all that he is and all that he possesses.

And receive the vows and offerings which my lowness presents to Thee.

2° The consecration itself

Even there, however, the slave of love goes there gradually and with a perfect logic.

Recalling to himself that the cause of the infidelity of so many Christians and his personal infidelities was the forgetting of the promises of baptism (he has even just repeated it a short time ago), he renews and ratifies them with full awareness of the cause:

I, N., a faithless sinner – I renew and ratify today in thy hands **the vows of my Baptism**. *I* **renounce** *for ever Satan, his pomps and works; and* **I give myself entirely to Jesus Christ**, *the incarnate Wisdom, to carry my cross after Him all the days of my life, and to be more faithful to Him than I have ever been before.*

Was it not previously proved that perfect consecration to Jesus equals the perfect renewal of the vows of baptism?

The phrase: "*To carry my cross after Him all the days of my life*", shows us the purpose of our donation to Jesus: it is not to enjoy His favors; it is not in order to ascend on Tabor; it is to carry His cross. "If any man will come after Me, let him deny himself, and take up his cross, and follow Me" (Mt. 16:24).

In the past, editors connected the last words with the following sentence. This gave: "*And to be more faithful to Him than I have ever been before, I choose thee this day, O Mary*", etc. Some people would still prefer this way of reading it.

The manuscript of the Saint reproduced in the typical-edition of *The Love of Eternal Wisdom*, between pages 302 and 303, by no means authorizes this claim. There is a period between "*ever been before*" and "*I choose Thee.*" Since the other paragraphs are not all marked (e.g. the preceding one. "*I, N., a faithless sinner...*"); since all the punctuation marks are not indicated either. This period had to have in the mind of Father de Montfort a special importance. It is also at "*I choose Thee...*" that he begins to underline.

The new meaning created by this way of reading would be objectively acceptable. But it no longer corresponds to the explanations supplied by Montfort in the chapter on the *Nature of the Perfect Devotion*. The forgetting or non-ratification of the vows of baptism were the cause of the infidelities of those who renounce Jesus so as not to have to carry His cross. We cannot absolutely disregard, then, the purpose pursued by the renewal or ratification: perfect fidelity to Jesus in the acceptance of the daily cross.

It has also been established that perfect consecration to Mary equals perfect consecration to Jesus. That is why total and absolute donation is going to be made to Mary, so as to come, through her, to her divine Son. These words are extremely important. There is not a word to be changed, and, besides, these words are clear, after what was said to explain them:

In the presence of all the heavenly court I choose thee this day for my MOTHER AND MISTRESS. I deliver and consecrate to thee, as thy slave, my body and soul, my goods, both interior and exterior, and even the value of all my good actions, past, present, and future, leaving to thee the entire and full right of *disposing of me, and all that belongs to me*, **without exception, according to thy good pleasure, to the greatest glory of God, in time and in eternity.**

Note in this truly essential formula that summarizes in a few words the whole Montfortian doctrine.

a) The association of the words "*Mother and Mistress*", titles of Mary which allow us to call ourselves her "*children and slaves.*"

b) The association of the words: "*I deliver and consecrate to thee*". We deliver to Mary what she is entitled to and from which we are completely separated (e.g. the value of good works). We consecrate to her, on the contrary, what also belongs to her but from which we cannot be separated (e.g. our body with all its senses, our soul with all its powers). We remain the trustee thereof; but everything must be used to honor Mary.

c) The expression: "*as thy slave*", a slave of love, because this donation results from a free choice. This donation ascribes to the master or mistress a fullness of ownership and a freedom of disposal, including not only earthly life, but eternal life.

3º FINAL PRAYER TO MARY

After this consecration, the new slave of love begs Mary to *approve his offering*, and *promises fidelity* to her. The latter addresses the *benignant Virgin*, because the offering is little and weakness is great.

Offering of the present consecration:

Receive, O benignant Virgin, this little offering of my slavery, in the honour of, and in union with, that subjection which the eternal Wisdom deigned to have to thy Maternity, in homage to the power which both of you have over this little worm and miserable sinner, and in thanksgiving for the privileges with which the Holy Trinity hath favoured thee.

Promise of fidelity:

I protest that I wish henceforth, as thy true slave, to seek thy honour, and to obey thee in all things.

He then expresses three burning wishes:

– he asks the *admirable Mother* to present him to her divine Son as an eternal slave:

O admirable Mother, present me to thy dear Son as His eternal slave, so that as He hath redeemed me by thee, by thee He may receive me.

– he asks the *Mother of mercy* to be always treated as her *child* and her *slave*, in order to obtain the true wisdom of God:

O Mother of mercy, get me the grace to obtain the true Wisdom of God; and for that end put me in the number of those whom thou lovest, whom thou teachest, whom thou conductest, and whom thou nourishest and protectest, as thy children and thy slaves.

They are at the same time maternal and regal duties: to love, to teach, to guide, to nourish and to protect, that Mary will perform with regard to her children and slaves.

– finally, he asks the *faithful Virgin* to make him the perfect disciple of Jesus Christ, so that he can arrive at the fullness of His age on earth and His glory in the heavens.

O faithful Virgin, make me in all things so perfect a disciple, imitator, and slave of the incarnate Wisdom, Jesus Christ thy Son, that I may attain, by thy intercession and by thy example, to the fullness of His age on earth, and of His glory in the heavens.

N° 232

c) **Accessories of the consecration.**

Having pronounced his consecration, the new slave will take care to submit his name to the *Confraternity of Mary Queen of Hearts*. Thus, he will participate in all the privileges granted by the Supreme Pontiffs to this association. If he is a priest, he should also request his admission as a *Priest of Mary*. It is on the register of these groupings that he will affix the *signature* required by Montfort. But he can be content with signing the small enrollment form, giving evidence that he was received on such date into the Confraternity or Association.

The text of the Consecration is entirely reproduced on this diploma. It is useless, then, *to write* it. This would be required only if we had no printed text (the end of n° 231).

On this day also, imitating Blessed Marin, brother of St. Peter Damian, whose history we recalled in n° 159, each *will offer* a tribute to Jesus Christ and to His holy Mother. By this tribute, the slaves of love intend to impose on themselves a penance for their past infidelity to their baptismal vows, and to manifest their dependence on Jesus and Mary, even as regards the use of worldly goods.

It must be proportioned to the devotion and resources of each. Those who possess nothing, like the members of a religious order and the destitute, content themselves with a fast day or a mortification. Those who can dispose of their goods will give an alms, or will have a wax candle burned at the altar of Mary.

But what one gives spiritually or materially, a little or a lot, let each give wholeheartedly what he intends to offer to satisfy this obligation of his slavery. Even if it was only a pin, it is enough for Jesus; because this good Master looks only at the goodwill. This slight offering will be enough to acknowledge Mary's dominion over their goods, and will allow them to make use of them afterward without any scruple, in spite of their consecration.

B. – PERIODIC RENEWAL OF THE CONSECRATION

N° 233

In spite of the solemnity given to this first consecration, the memory of it would fade inevitably in the long run, especially for those who are continually absorbed by daily duties. And soon there would no longer be a great difference between the slaves of love and the other faithful.

To avoid this disintegration of our Marian life, Montfort asks that, every year, on the anniversary of our first consecration, we renew it with the same solemnity. It would be good even to prepare for this renewal by three weeks of spiritual exercises. They are the three weeks prescribed above, with the same program. We begin them again every year, because it is always possible to grow in the knowledge of Jesus, Mary and oneself. On the contrary, we do not renew the twelve days in order to empty ourselves of the spirit of the world, because the true slave of love can no longer be moved by it. It is up to each one to see whether he realized this ideal, and whether there are not certain areas of backsliding to be remedied.

But, no more than the first time, even less than the first time, are these exercises an obstacle to ordinary occupations. It is thus necessary to know how to reconcile one with the other.

The confessor will supply on this point all the information and will say what the penitent has to carry out, precisely and in his particular case, in order to acquit himself of this duty.

As the year is still very long, however, it is better to follow the counsel of the Saint: "(The slaves of love) *might also once a month, or even once a day* (and we can add: several times a day) *renew what they have done by these few words: Tuus totus ego sum, et omnia mea tua sunt. I am all for Thee, and all I have belongs to Thee, O my sweet Jesus, through Mary, Thy holy Mother.*" It is not even required to pronounce the words, unless it is to gain the 300 days indulgence attached to the recitation of this formula. To reach the purpose aimed at by this practice, a quick raising of the thought "by one glance of the mind" suffices, as the Saint will say further on (see n° 259). Indeed, the first interior practice *"through Mary"* agrees on this point with the first exterior practice.

Thus, without fatigue, without prolonged effort of the mind, by the simple spontaneous movement of a loving heart, he shall arrive there, by frequently recalling his consecration. And, by the faithful observation of this practice, which is by far the most important, he will already attain a very high summit of Marian life.

With greater reason it will be the same, if other practices are joined to that one.

§ I. – RECITATION OF THE LITTLE CROWN
(234-235)

N° 234

This second practice inaugurates the series of vocal prayers recommended every day in honor of Mary so that memory of her does not go away, or as little as possible, from our thought.

Certain Third-Orders impose on their members the daily recitation of the Little Office of the Blessed Virgin. Franciscan religious or their affiliates have to recite the Franciscan Crown in honor of Mary. Similarly, Father de Montfort desires that the slaves of love recite "*every day of their life, without, however, making any burden of it,*" the Little Crown of the Blessed Virgin.

1° The origin of the Little Crown.

Already the Fathers of the Church, such as St. Epiphanius, St. Ambrose, St. Augustine and St. Methodius, and other saints as St. Bernard, St. Bernardine of Siena, St. Antoninus and Denys the Chartreux (Carthusian monk) had seen in the woman of the Apocalypse a figure of Mary. This woman, among other remarkable things, had her head surrounded with a *crown of twelve stars*. This inspired in the faithful the custom of offering Mary a prayer composed of as many *Hail Marys* as stars counted in her crown. This prayer bore the name of "Little Crown", to distinguish it from other crowns (Rosary, crown of seven joys, crown of seven sorrows), which were also very esteemed.

2° Meaning of the Little Crown

As rubies alternate with diamonds in a royal crown, so too, in the Little Crown the *Hail Marys* are divided into three series, each preceded by an *Our Father* and ended by the *Glory be*.

And as *"there are many ways of saying this Crown well"*, we also find several meanings attributed to this prayer. Some people see, in this division into three series, an allusion to the Holy Trinity. The first series would be recited in honor of the eternal Father, the second in honor of the coeternal Son, and the third in honor of the Holy Ghost, Who is equal to the other two Persons. And, in every Hail Mary, one of the most distinguished virtues of the Blessed Virgin would be honored, and we would implore her help to imitate her and make progress in this virtue. Others, like Fr. Poiré, see in this tripartite division an allusion to three sorts of perfections that Mary possesses in a sovereign degree: the first series represents her grandeurs of *excellence*, the second her grandeurs of *power* and the third her grandeurs of *mercy*. Her excellence comes to her from privileges which belong exclusively to her, and ensue from her divine maternity. Her power extends over the whole Church, the Mystical Body of Christ: she maintains it and causes it to make progress. Her mercy is exercised more particularly towards her devout servants: she supports them during life and at the hour of death. The brief formulas of prayers and praises which Montfort placed after every *Hail Mary* authorize this second meaning.

N° 235

3° The way of reciting the Little Crown.

One can be content with simply saying twelve *Hail Marys*, while thinking either of the virtues or privileges of Mary. One can adapt his recitation and meditation to the first explanation which we gave above. But the best way is to follow the method recommended by the Saint.

First of all, we entreat Mary to approve our praises and to give us the strength to overcome her enemies. And we proclaim our faith by reciting the *Creed*. We then go through the three series mentioned above, while giving them the sense analyzed in the second place. A fervent prayer, containing the renewal of the consecration, concludes this Little Crown. But before taking leave of Mary, we address a *Sub tuum* to her.

A few minutes are enough to recite this prayer. It will hardly encroach on the day of the slave of love. Furthermore, it is required to use a formula of morning prayer every day: the latter is particularly suitable for those who have made their consecration. This is the practice in both congregations founded by our Saint, and it is necessary to admit that they are the most faithful guardians of his spirit. In this case, this second exterior practice brings no overload, and goes straight to the point in an ordinary Christian life.

§ III. – THE WEARING OF LITTLE IRON CHAINS
(236-242)

N° 236

This prescription seemed to put Father de Montfort in contradiction with the Holy Office and to cast shadows on the orthodoxy of his doctrine and the heroicity of his prudence. In a word, here is the problem: Montfort recommended the wearing of little chains and the Church condemned it.

To solve the problem, it will be necessary to establish the precise meaning both of the condemnation of the Church and of the recommendation of the Saint.

1° MEANING OF THE CONDEMNATION

Blessed Marin, the brother of St. Peter Damian, loaded himself with chains in front of the altar of the Blessed Virgin, in order to take on himself an exterior sign of his slavery. Through his example, the slaves of love of Naples, Sicily, Savoy and the Netherlands liked to wear little chains having the same purpose. Their eagerness was such, sometimes, that there were not enough workers to make these little chains, as happened in Brussels in 1626.

But a thing, excellent in its principle, was then spoiled in a twofold way:

First of all, some slaves of Mary, ill-informed as to the meaning of their donation, sincerely believed that *they gave up their freedom* into the hands of Mary. Thus, neither merit nor responsibility would have been left for them. It is easy to see what disastrous conclusions may follow from these principles.

Then, many turned the chains away from their first meaning, a symbol of the Holy Slavery. They applied them to profane love, or transformed them *into ornaments of vanity and into the business of gallantry*. Instead of little iron chains, of rather crude workmanship, they took golden necklaces, finely chiseled, and wore them ostentatiously, for the obvious purpose of catching the eyes of the creature rather than those of the Creator.

It is understood that Rome did not remain insensible to such a profanation. By a decree of the Holy Office (July 5, 1673) and by the apostolic brief *Pastoralis officii* (December 15, 1675), *Clement X* abolished certain confraternities of the Most Blessed Sacrament, of the Blessed and Immaculate Virgin Mary, of St. Joseph and the Flock of the Good Shepherd, in which they made use of chains. And he also banned the images and the medals bearing figures of chained slaves. *Benedict XIV*, by a decree of the Index, confirmed the same condemnation in 1758.

But these condemnations aim at the abuses and not at the substance of this devotion. This is clear from the indulgences granted to the Confraternity of the Slaves of Mary by Gregory XV, Urban VIII, Innocent X and Alexander VII. A brief of Urban VIII (December 18, 1631) approved even the constitutions of the canonesses of the Holy Sepulcher, and it spoke expressly about the slavery of Jesus and Mary as being proper and particular to the Order. According to these constitutions, little chains of various colors with their handcuffs (rings) must be worn on the neck and arm, and kissed in the morning and evening, while saying: "Here is the poor slave of your Grandeur." And these chains were always and are still worn in the Congregation of the Holy Sepulcher. Now the infallible Church cannot approve one day what will be condemned a few years later, nor condemn today what it had approved in the past.

Besides, Fr. Olier wore the chains of the Holy Slavery before their condemnation by Clement X, and his memory is not tarnished as a result. Father de Montfort himself made use of them and recommended them after their condemnation, and this did not prevent him from being canonized. Father Simon de Rojas, who made this devotion fashionable in Spain, was beatified in 1765. And countless persons of both sexes and every condition have been sanctified by this practice.

Let us conclude, then, with the Saint: *"We cannot see how the Holy Slavery of Jesus through Mary, which is in reality only the renewal of the vows of baptism could be condemned without overturning the very foundations of Christianity"* (cf. T.D., #163).

2° THE MEANING OF THE SAINT'S RECOMMENDATION

Montfort by no means imposes this practice. He even declares: *"These external badges are not essential, and a person who has embraced this devotion may very well go without them."* He proclaims, however: *"It is a most glorious and praiseworthy thing, and very useful to those who have thus made themselves slaves of Jesus in Mary, that they should wear, as a badge of their loving slavery, little iron chains, blessed with the proper benedictions."*

All the rest of this section, from n° 236 to n° 242, tends to demonstrate the advisability of this recommendation. It seems that the Saint's argumentation can be reduced to four main heads:

The wearing of iron chains is commendable:
  a) because of what they signify (n°s 236-237);
  b) because of what they effect (n°s 238-239);
  c) because of the pressing exhortations of the Holy Ghost (numbers 240-241);
  d) because of the examples of holy persons (n° 242).

a) Because of what the little chains signify.

They signify that we have renounced the shameful chains of the slavery of Satan, in which original sin and perhaps personal sins had involved us, and that we have enrolled ourselves voluntarily into the glorious slavery of Jesus Christ.

N° 237

That is why these chains, although of iron and dull, are a thousand times more precious than all the golden necklaces of all the emperors. We can say about them what we say of the cross: formerly, they were a sign of ignominy, when they bound a slave to his pagan master; now, they are a sign of glory, when they bind by love to Jesus and Mary: "*Traham eos in vinculis caritatis*, I will draw them to Me," God says by the mouth of the prophet Osee, "with the cords of charity" (Osee 11:4). Bonds forged by love and as long-lasting as love. Thus they will endure beyond death. The corruption which destroys the body will have no grip on them.

Perhaps, at the day of the resurrection of the body, the grand last judgment, these chains shall still be round their bones, and shall make a part of their glory, and be transmuted into chains of light and splendour. Happy then, a thousand times happy, the illustrious slaves of Jesus who wear their chains even to the tomb.

N° 238

b) **Because of what they effect.**

Man allows himself to be led more by the senses than by pure faith. So these chains have a great efficacy for him. He would forget too easily his dependence on God if something exterior did not remind him of it. Little chains recall to him the vows and promises of his baptism and the ratification which he gave them by pronouncing his consecration. Every time he strikes against this chain or every time he notices the hindrance that it brings, he is brought to remember his commitments, and even to renew them. And if all Christians resorted to this means to help their memory, perhaps they would not live with so much dissoluteness like the pagans.

In short, little chains effect what they signify. They signify the slavery of love towards Jesus and Mary, and they effect this slavery in the soul of the one who wears them. The chains of ancient slaves were marked with the name of the master to whom these slaves belonged. Not only did they thus furnish proof of the condition and of the possessor of the one who was wearing them, but they also constituted slavery itself, by the obstacles which they effectively placed to freedom. In the same way the chains of the slave of love give evidence of his voluntary dependence and the name of his two venerated masters. Furthermore, they effect this dependence by the memory which they continually maintain of them.

N° 239

In the past also, the slaves of constraint were often proud to wear the liveries of a powerful master. Now again, and for greater reason, the slave of love considers it a badge of honor to show off external witness of his belonging to Jesus and His Mother.

Finally, here on earth, there is no possible middle course between two masters who fight for rule over the world. It is necessary, then, for us to accept either the slavery of

Satan, or the slavery of Jesus Christ, and that we bear the marks of the one or the other.

N° 240

c) Because of the pressing exhortations of the Holy Ghost.

Our Saint multiplies the texts of Scripture, where God presses us either to break the chains of sin: "*Let us break their bonds asunder: and let us cast away their yoke from us*" (Ps. 2:3), that is to accept the chains of Jesus Christ: "*Injice pedem tuum in compedes illius, et in torques illius collum tuum.* Put thy feel into her fetters, and thy neck into her chains" (Eccli. 6:25). "*Bow down thy shoulder, and bear her, and be not grieved with her bands*" (Eccli. 6:26).

N° 241

The Holy Ghost, however, takes care to say it only after having prepared the soul to receive His counsel, so important it is: "Give ear, My son, and take wise counsel, and cast not away My advice" (Eccli. 6:24). It is not at all surprising that Montfort joins his pressing exhortations to those of the Holy Ghost to persuade souls to take upon themselves the bonds of the slavery of love: they are salutary bonds: "*alligatura salutaris*" (Eccli. 6:31), bonds of charity: "*vinculis caritatis*" (Osee 11:4), bonds which will chain and draw especially the predestined, whereas the reprobate will be bound and drawn as convicts, by the avenging justice of God. The mystery of universal attraction: "*I will draw all things to Myself*" (Jn. 12:32), but which will be applied in a twofold sense, according to the sentence pronounced at the judgment.

N° 242

d) Because of the examples of holy persons.

Montfort applies to all the slaves of love this term of honor that St. Paul attributes to himself, *"Vinctus Christi"*, "the Prisoner of Christ" (Eph. 3:1; Philem. 9). And he concludes that they can indeed show off these sacred chains on their neck or arms, around their loins or on their ankles, because noble examples have preceded them in this way. *Fr. Vincent Caraffa*, seventh superior of the Society of Jesus, who died in the odor of sanctity in 1643, had put *an iron circle on his ankles* as a sign of servitude. His pain was so lively, that, of his own confession, he could not drag the chain publicly. *Mother Agnes of Jesus* (see n° 170) put an iron chain around her loins. Some suspended it from their neck, as penance for the pearl necklaces which they had worn in the world. Others surrounded their arms with it, in order to remember in the works of their hands that they are slaves of Jesus Christ.

§ IV. – SPECIAL DEVOTION TO THE MYSTERY OF THE INCARNATION
(243-248)

N° 243

In this paragraph, we really achieve the peak of the Marian life, such as Montfort desires it. And this point is directly connected with the third interior practice: to live and act *in* Mary. It is precisely here, in reality, that we have the explanation of this mysterious term: *in* Mary.

In this connection, Montfort betrays his ties with the French school and more especially with Fr. Olier and Saint-Sulpice. He relies even expressly on information supplied by Fr. Tronson, the former superior of the famous Seminary and the whole Association of Saint-Sulpice (1622-1700). He quotes the prayer of Fr. de Condren, modified by Fr. Olier: *O Jesus living in Mary*. He preaches devotion to the incarnate Word, etc...

Since all Christian perfection consists in being conformed to Jesus-Christ, the best among all devotions will be the one which will conform us more to this divine Model (n° 120). That is why it is not necessary to seek elsewhere than in Him the perfect ideal of true devotion to Mary. Now, of all the mysteries of the life of Jesus, the one which best shows His devotion to Mary is the mystery of the Incarnation. It is on this day, indeed, that Jesus, the Son of God, made Himself, for the glory of His Father and for our salvation, a voluntary prisoner and slave of love in the womb of holy Mary, and that He began to depend on her in everything. It is on this day as well that He raised Mary to the highest dignity possible: the divine Maternity.

So the mystery of the Incarnation will be especially venerated by the slaves of love, and the feast of March 25th will be the principal feast of this devotion.

For that reason Montfort wants all the predestined to consider themselves as enclosed in the womb of Mary, in order to be conformed to the image of the Son of God. There, they will be "*guarded*" against everything which could compromise their divine life; "*nourished*" with grace in all its forms; "*brought up*" so that the natural decrease of their spiritual forces is constantly repaired and "*made to grow*" by the increase of this supernatural life, "*by that good Mother until she has brought them forth to glory after death, which is probably the day of their birth, as the Church calls the death of the just* (n° 33)."

And such is indeed the entire scope of the act of consecration of the slaves of love. It tends to establish them in a close and constant dependence on Mary, like that of a child on his mother. It also tends to give to Mary a right of propriety and absolute dominion over her slaves of love, as a mother over the child whom she carries in her womb. This dominion on Mary's part and this dependence on our part are totally conscious and completely voluntary. In this, perhaps, the predestined will differ from the ordinary child. But he will perfectly resemble Jesus, Who perfectly realized His dependence and submitted Himself at every instant of His own free will.

The imitation of the life of Jesus in Mary, practical recognition of the grandeur of the divine Maternity, such is, then, indeed the essence of the slavery of love of Jesus in Mary. By recalling it every year on a very solemn feast, by thinking of it frequently by devotion to these mysteries, one perfects his life of a slave. We become more and more conscious of it.

*
* *

N°s 244-245

But a formula was used which is going to make its appearance in multiple commentaries. It was said: *"the slave of Jesus in Mary, the slavery of Jesus in Mary."* A very happy expression, because it indicates in a few words the great Mystery about which we spoke just now. It is, then, a matter of putting it in full light, and, first of all, of distinguishing it from other similar formulas.

1° **Other formulas.** We can say, in truth, either *slave of Jesus Christ*, or *slave of Mary*. The first of these formulas would please even more these critical and proud devotees, who were discussed in the first fundamental truth. In their opinion, Jesus being the last end of our devotion to Mary, it is He and not she who has to give His name to the devotion. This scruple has no reason for existing. Is not Mary the direct way leading to Jesus? And does not devotion to her have the unique purpose of leading us more directly to Jesus? We can thus say either slavery of Mary or slavery of Jesus, just as a traveler going from Orléans to Tours by Amboise can say equally: I am going to Amboise or I am going to Tours, obviously supposing that he is indeed going to Tours and is content with passing through Amboise.

2° It is better, however, to call ourselves: "**slave of Jesus in Mary**."

N°s 246-247

a) *Proof from authority*. It is drawn from the advice which Fr. Tronson, "renowned for his rare prudence and consummate piety", gave to an ecclesiastic who consulted him on this subject. This formula, indeed, lends itself to no criticism (caution) and expresses very well the mystery of Jesus living in Mary (piety).

b) *Proofs from reason*. The *first* is drawn from the mystery of Jesus living in Mary. Is it not the main purpose of this devotion to reproduce Him as perfectly as possible? It is, therefore, better rather to use the formula which expresses this mystery most perfectly. And this formula, immortalized by the beautiful Sulpician prayer: *O Jesus living in Mary*, is the slavery of Jesus in Mary.

The *second* is because this formula shows more the close union existing between Jesus and Mary. They are so closely united to one another, so completely merged in one another, that one could rather separate light from the sun than separate Jesus from Mary, and Mary from Jesus. We can, then, call Our Lord: *Jesus of Mary*, and the Blessed Virgin: *Mary of Jesus*, as is the practice in religious names.

*
* *

N° 248

Montfort then returns to the contemplation of the mystery of the Incarnation or of Jesus living in Mary. He apologizes for being unable, for lack of time, to explain all the grandeurs and excellences of it. What he says, however, is quite capable of completely exalting the prodigious fruitfulness of this life of Jesus in Mary's womb.

1° This mystery is at the same time the most **hidden** and the most **exalted** of all the mysteries of Jesus Christ. Because of this, it seems a mystery of annihilation. In reality, it is a mystery of glory. Mystery of annihilation, yes! The dignity of Jesus is so completely veiled there that nobody in His circle of acquaintances will discover it without a special revelation. But a mystery of glory also in which the human nature was supremely ennobled and where the divine nature was supremely honored.

2° It is in this mystery, during His night prayer, that, together with Mary, **He chose and determined all His elect**, as later, on the mountain, during His night prayer, He chose and determined all His apostles, so as to summon them to their vocation on the following morning. That is why the womb of Mary is called by the saints *Aula sacramentorum*, the room of the secrets of God.

3° This mystery is already the **fulfillment**, and consequently it is the **summary** of all the other mysteries of the life of Christ, by the solemn acceptance which Jesus made of it: "*When He cometh into the world, He saith: behold, I come to do Thy will, O God*" (Heb. 10:5, 9). It contains, therefore, in itself alone the grace of all the other mysteries, as it contains the intention of them.

4° Finally, this mystery is **for us the throne of mercy, for Mary the throne of generosity, for God the throne of glory**.

a) *For us, it is the throne of mercy.* There truly we can approach Jesus only through Mary. We cannot express our prayers to Him either, except through Mary. And Jesus is always eager to grant the prayers of His Mother, or the prayers presented and supported by His Mother. He always grants His grace and mercy to poor sinners. The womb of

Mary is, then, indeed, in this case, a throne of mercy, which we can approach in all confidence: *"Let us go therefore with confidence to the throne of grace"* (Heb. 4:16).

b) *For Mary, it is the throne of generosity.* The first Adam had been placed in the earthly Paradise, to cultivate it by diligent work. The new Adam, living in Mary's womb as though in the true and authentic earthly Paradise, did not leave it uncultivated. He even worked there in secret so many marvels, that neither angels nor men can understand them. That is why the saints call Mary the magnificence of God, *magnificentia Dei*, that is to say, the work of the divine magnificence and the grandiose designs of the Lord. We could truly say that God is magnificent only in Mary, according to the word of Isaiah applied to Sion: *Because only there our Lord is magnificent* (Isa. 33:21).

c) *For God, it is the throne of glory.* While resting in Mary's womb, as though on the altar of sacrifices, Jesus sacrificed His will and His entire self to His Father. And thus He perfectly appeased His anger against men; He perfectly repaired the glory which sin had stolen from Him. By this same sacrifice, He gave Him more glory than all the sacrifices of the Old Law ever would have given Him; He has even given Him an infinite glory, which He had never yet received from man.

These are fruitful, rich, and even new ideas, in spite of the already considerable number of years that the *Treatise* has been printed. There are nevertheless here outlines for numerous instructions about this ineffable mystery. It is a pity they are not utilized more often...

Thus, the Holy Slavery is only a more comprehensive form of spiritual childhood. Our Lord, by proposing to His disciples the child as the ideal of the virtues and simplicity, placed before their eyes a child already rather tall, as is clear from the Gospel narrative. Likewise St. Thérèse of the Child Jesus. For her, the model of the kind seems to be a child between three and five years old, having his little spiritual and roguish replies, joined to charming virtues and unlimited trust. For Montfort, to be a child, is not to have been born yet. Never, indeed, will the dependence of the child on his mother be closer than during this period. This is what allows the words "child" and "slave" to be paired up so often as well as their correlatives "mother" and "mistress." (See The interior Practice: in Mary.)

§ V. – GREAT DEVOTION TO THE "HAIL MARY" AND THE ROSARY
(249-254)

Some of the previous practices suppose a certain formation, at least in order to be relished fully. It is not the same with this latter one. Devotion to the *Hail Mary* and to the Rosary is a popular devotion *par excellence*, and, thanks to it, the humblest of Christians can aspire to the practice of the Holy Slavery. In reality, there are few Christians, especially among the ignorant, who, for lack of other more learned and more complicated prayers, do not often repeat the *Hail Mary* or even say the Rosary often. This prayer fulfills, then, the general purpose assigned to exterior practices. To one who cannot offer better, it is sufficient to maintain in the slave of love the memory of his Queen, and the dependence which he professed towards her.

Fidelity to this practice does not entail the obligation to say two Rosaries a day when someone was used to reciting one before his consecration. The same Rosary, recited in a new spirit, will satisfy all the obligations as well as all the needs of the heart. This fifth prescription thus brings no excessive burden in an ordinary Christian life.

To persuade us to recite often, and even daily, not only the *Hail Mary*, but a chaplet and even, if we have time for it, the Rosary, Montfort multiplies the proofs of the excellence and necessity of this prayer.

The excellence of this prayer is based:

1° On the testimony of the Most Blessed Virgin herself (n°s 249-250);

2° On the testimonies of the saints (*ibid.*);

3° On the testimonies of heretics and bad Christians (n°s 250-251);

4° On the intrinsic value of this prayer (numbers 250-251).

N°s 249-250

1° The witness of the Most Blessed Virgin herself.

The Church always knew, commented on and used, in the angelic Salutation, the very words of the Angel, and those of Elizabeth. We have proof of it in the innumerable homilies which the Fathers left us on these two words. The ancient liturgy of St. James even united them, as the offertory of the votive Mass of the Blessed Virgin, attributed to Alcuin, did later. The final invocation, constituting the third part of the prayer, is said to have been, according to a tradition admitted by Cardinals Baronius and Bona, composed by the faithful on the occasion of the Council of Ephesus (431); but it is certain that the pious custom did not become widespread, even in this period. And it even fell out of use soon. It is necessary to wait until the fifteenth century to find our complete invocation, and, consequently the *Hail Mary* such as we possess. It is St. Bernardine of Siena who provided it to us first. Its introduction into the Little Office and soon into the Breviary goes back to the late XVth century and to the beginning of the XVIth century.

Thus the devotion to the *Hail Mary* took time to become established. This explains the words of our Saint: until the Virgin taught it to us, very few Christians, even educated and enlightened, knew *"the price, merit, excellence and necessity"* of this devotion.

The same goes for the Rosary. The custom of reciting the *Hail Mary* a definite number of times so as to weave, after a fashion, a crown for Mary, is generally attributed to Peter the Hermit (XIth century). This was not yet the Rosary. The latter received its definitive form only two centuries later. But this was already the outline of it.

So that the Rosary might be known, it was necessary for the Most Blessed Virgin to appear several times, to St. Dominic, St. John of Capistrano and Blessed Alan de la Roche.

St. Dominic was, in 1214, the first confidant of this heavenly message. He despaired of converting the Albigensians of the region of Toulouse. But the Virgin appeared to him, and indicated to him, in her Psalter (that is to say, her Rosary, composed of 150 *Hail Marys*, as the Davidic psalter is composed of 150 psalms) the all-powerful weapon for vanquishing heretics.

St. John of Capistrano, a disciple of St. Bernardine of Siena, inherited from his master a great devotion to Mary, and several times, he was delighted by her apparitions. One time in particular, the Queen of Angels presented him a chalice full of a celestial liqueur, whose sweetness filled his whole heart with an unspeakable joy. Is this what Father de Montfort interprets as a recommendation for the *Hail Mary*, *"this chalice of divine ambrosial nectar which we hold to Mary?"* The fact is that St. John of Capistrano was an ardent promoter of the Rosary; this allows us to suspect, on the basis of this apostolate, Mary's direct action to encourage him to it.

Blessed Alan de la Roche, a Dominican of the convent of Dinan, received at first from Our Lord, then from the Virgin herself, the order to preach the Rosary and to revive the confraternity of the same name. This good Mother taught him, among others things, that after the holy Sacrifice of the Mass, the holy Rosary is the best representation of the life and Passion of Jesus. And she added, in order to commit him more effectively to spread this devotion: "*Know, my son, and make all others know, that it is a probable and proximate sign of eternal damnation to have an aversion, a lukewarmness or a negligence in saying the Angelical Salutation, which has repaired the whole world.*"

2° The witness of the Saints.

Many saints, but especially the three that we have just named, "*have composed entire works on the wonders and efficacy of that prayer for converting souls. They have loudly published and openly preached that, salvation having begun with the* Hail Mary, *the salvation of each one of us in particular is attached to that prayer.*" "*It is that prayer which made the dry and barren earth bring forth the fruit of life.*" "*Well said it makes the word of God germinate in our souls.*" This is "*the heavenly dew for watering the soul, to make it bring forth its fruit in season, and that a soul which is not watered by that prayer, brings forth only thorns and brambles, and is ready to be cursed.*"

N°s 250-251

3° The witness of heretics and bad Christians.

Let us recall the words of the Virgin to Blessed Alan de la Roche. They are at the same time "*very consoling and very terrible.*" *Very consoling* for the good, who love reciting the *Hail Mary*. They already have, moreover, great marks of predestination. But the last is not the least. And, in general, the more they belong to God, the more they like this prayer. This is what the Virgin said, following the words which we have just quoted. Besides, it is a fact of experience. *Very terrible* are these words for all those who do not like this prayer. And if we did not have Alan de la Roche and St. Dominic as guarantors of this truth, we would have difficulty believing it. But the experience of several centuries is there to prove it: All those who already bear, moreover, the mark of reprobation, like the heretics, the godless, the proud and the worldly, hate or despise the *Hail Mary* and the Rosary. The *heretics* (and this is especially true of the Protestants) still learn and recite the *Our Father*. But they do not want either the *Hail Mary* or the Rosary. They loathe them. And they *would rather wear a serpent than a Rosary*. The *proud*, even if they are Catholic, have only contempt or indifference for these prayers. Therein they share in the same inclinations and same aversion as the devil, their father. They look at the Rosary as a devotion of a weakling, good at most for the ignorant and those who do not know how to read.

So these two prayers, thanks to the sentiments that they inspire, will become an excellent criterion to know whether a soul is of God or of Satan. If he likes reciting the *Hail Mary* or the Rosary, he is of God unmistakably. I say "*if he likes reciting*", because it can happen *that a person may be under some natural inability* (occupations, illnesses, etc.) or even supernatural (obsession of the demon, for example) to say it. But he still loves them and *always inspires the same liking into others*.

N°s 252-254

4° Intrinsic value of the "Hail Mary".

In a pressing exhortation, Montfort encourages the predestined souls, the slaves of Jesus in Mary, to recite the *Hail Mary*.

a) It is, first of all, the most beautiful of all prayers, after the *Our Father*. Nobody will dispute it.

b) *It is the most perfect compliment which you can make to Mary*. This compliment comes from God by the mouth of the archangel Gabriel, and it won so well the heart of the Virgin by the secret charms of which it is full, that she gave, in spite of her profound humility, her consent to the Incarnation of the Word and to the supreme honor of the divine Maternity. It is also by this compliment that you will infallibly win Mary's heart, if you say it as you should, that is to say, with attention, devotion and modesty.

c) It is, for the *devil*, the enemy which puts him to flight and the hammer which crushes him; for the *good*, it is *the sanctification of the soul, the joy of the angels, the melody of the predestined, the canticle of the New Testament, the pleasure of Mary and the glory of the Most Holy Trinity*. Suggestive expressions gleaned from the writings of the Saints and lending themselves to limitless commentaries.

d) It is the *heavenly dew which fertilizes the soul; it is the chaste and loving kiss which we give to Mary; it is a vermilion rose which we present to her; a precious pearl which we offer her; a chalice of divine ambrosial nectar which we hold to her which we bring to her lips. All these are comparisons of the Saints.* And, if it did not take us too far afield, it would be interesting to prove it.

So Montfort begs the slaves of love not to be content with reciting the Little Crown of the Blessed Virgin every day, but to join to it also the chaplet, and even, if they have time for it, the Rosary. And they will bless, at the hour of their death, the day and the hour when they will have believed him. Having sown in benedictions (that is to say, by blessing Jesus and Mary in the *Hail Mary*), they will reap eternal benedictions in heaven: *He who soweth in blessings, shall also reap blessings* (2 Cor. 9:6).

§ VI. – RECITATION OF THE "MAGNIFICAT"
(255)

N° 255

Another vocal prayer is also recommended. We shall say it often, like Blessed Mary d'Oignies (1177-1213), so called because of her burial place in Belgium. She showed her ardent devotion to Mary by multiplying genuflections in her honor day and night, by inserting a *Hail Mary* into every psalm of David or also, according to the testimony of Montfort, by frequently reciting the *Magnificat*.

But like this Blessed and several other saints, the slaves of love will recite this prayer, not so much to thank God for the graces from which they themselves have benefited, as to thank Him *for the graces granted to Mary*. They forget themselves in order to think only of their Queen, to whom, besides, they have given everything. They glory only in her glory, and ask only to carry out the divine will, by increasing this glory by their humble servitude.

In order to obtain for the slaves of love a great devotion to this prayer, Montfort suggests three thoughts to them:

1° *It is the only prayer composed by Mary*. This humble Virgin has never personally written any work. The influence of her accounts of the whole history of the childhood of the Savior is obvious, however. But under the pressure of the magnificent benefits that she had received from God, and which began to be known exteriorly, her poetic soul at length could no longer contain the feelings of gratitude which filled her heart. She spoke enthusiastically, under the inspiration of the Holy Ghost, and even, Montfort said, under the inspiration of the divine fruit Whom she carried in her womb. This spontaneous explosion was not a temporary impulse in Mary's soul. The surety with which she dictated her hymn to St. Luke shows that it had remained very much alive in her memory. Gerson, in his *Commentary on the "Magnificat"*, even goes so far to say that she recited it often, especially as thanksgiving after Communion. They are assertions difficult to verify, but one can piously believe them and draw from them an encouragement frequently to recite it oneself.

2° *It is the greatest sacrifice of praise, which God received in the law of grace*. Because this sacrifice had the aim of thanking God for the Savior granted to the world, it relied on the infinite merit of this same Savior, and it was offered to God by the creature whom He loved best in heaven and on earth. That is why in the Office of Vespers, replacing the sacrifice of praise which, in the Old Law, was celebrated in the evening, the *"Magnificat" occupies the highest point*. All stand in order to sing it, and it is during this time when the celebrant offers to God the incense, formerly the material of the sacrifice of praise.

3° This hymn is *on the one hand the most humble and grateful, and on the other hand, the most sublime and exalted of all canticles.* Mary considers herself as nothingness, upon whom God deigned to lower His eyes. But moreover she recognizes, in all its extent, the greatness of the privilege with which she was favored. Far from taking any personal advantage of it, she refers all the glory to God. And this was by nature infinitely pleasing to God, because, if He loves to shower us with benefits, He also loves for us to recognize the value of them and attribute the merit of them to Him.

There are some great and hidden mysteries in this canticle. *The Angels do not know them* and, on earth, those who know the most about divine things consent to speak of them only with fear. Among those, Montfort quotes the pious and learned *Gerson*. He had composed numerous works of moral or mystical theology, where he discussed the most difficult questions with erudition and devotion. But he undertook only with trembling, at the end of his life, his *Tractatus super Magnificat*. He wanted this volume to be the crown of all his works. And, in fact, he wrote admirable things on this beautiful and divine canticle.

Another testimony, that of the learned *Benzonius*. In explaining the same *Magnificat*, he reports several miracles worked by its power. The devils tremble and run away, he says, when they hear these words: "He hath shewed might in His arm: He hath scattered the proud in the conceit of their heart. *Fecit potentiam in brachio suo, dispersit superbos mente cordis sui*" (Lk. 1:51).

§ VII. – CONTEMPT OF THE WORLD
(256)

N° 256

It is surprising that Montfort assigns to contempt of the world the role of the seventh and last *exterior* practice of the Holy Slavery. He had already recommended, in the first practice, the employment of twelve days, to empty oneself of the spirit of the world. Also, in *The Love of Eternal Wisdom*, n°s 198-199, he shows that one cannot possess divine Wisdom if he conforms himself to the maxims of the world.

Here, he requires the faithful servants of Mary "*to despise, to hate, and to eschew the corrupted world.*" In order for this conduct, which is obligatory, moreover, to be able to be raised to the dignity of an exterior practice of the Holy Slavery, it is necessary for it to be expressed exteriorly in one way or another. For example: one must strive not to have the manner of speaking of the worldly, the manner of dressing of the worldly, etc.

This is what he said in n° 198 of the aforementioned book:

You should not conform to the exterior fashions of the worldly, either in clothes, or in houses, or in meals and other practices and actions of life.

On the other hand, Montfort composed a treatise on contempt of the world, containing more than 2,500 verses (Hymns, n°s 77–82 F). It is divided into two parts: 1° the *misfortunes*; 2° the *traps* of the world. He enumerates five traps: worldly games, dances, spectacles, luxury with its fashions, and human respect. The latter, he says, is only an illusion, but it leads us to the most shameful actions. Let us also note that, in the eyes of our Saint, fashion is an implacable enemy; against its follies, he has justly severe words. Does it not deserve the same condemnation nowadays?...

The slaves of love will, then, carry out this program, in order to be faithful to their consecration. This last practice will perhaps require real sacrifices. It will impose a life very different from the one that some had led until then. At least it will save them a lot of time and a lot of money. Is not this motive sufficient for us to follow it wholeheartedly?

Article II

Interior practices of the Perfect Devotion

(257-265)

N° 257

The exterior practices already include an interior element, that is to say, the part that the intellect and the will must take in these acts, so that they are *human* acts. Furthermore, the exterior practices have to proceed from the interior spirit and be a faithful expression of them, at the risk of not being sincere and of dishonoring Mary.

Other practices are confined exclusively to the interior faculties of man (intellect, will, imagination, memory). They constitute rather a general state of mind than a set of particular practices. This state of mind can and must resonate in the exterior actions, infusing in them, so to speak, a new life. But these actions themselves will not take on thereby a special appearance. The work of a slave of love will not be distinguished from that of another believer. All its beauty, all its additional riches are interior and in the realm of faith.

Such practices are our topic now. Montfort calls them "*very sanctifying*". And he recommends them "*for those who*

wish *to be perfect*" (the title) or even (is it more, is it less)? The mystery of the divine vocation and the free cooperation of man!...: "*for those whom the Holy Ghost* **calls** *to high perfection*" (n° 257). It is not, however, the difficulty attached to these practices, which will make the distinction between those who will follow them and those who will not follow them. In themselves, they are not more difficult; perhaps they are even less so than certain exterior practices. But although very easy in themselves, they require from the one who wants to be faithful to them a more total renunciation of his whole personality, a more complete obedience to all the motions of the Holy Ghost. There is there, then, perhaps the opportunity, more than ever, to repeat with St. Paul: "*So then it is not of him that willeth, nor of him that runneth, but of God that sheweth mercy*" (Rom. 9:16): This does not depend either on the will, or the efforts, but on God, Who is inclined to mercy.

These interior practices are summed up in a formula of a remarkable conciseness, applying either to Our Lord, or to the Most Blessed Virgin, or better, applying to both at the same time, to the one as to the last end of our devotion, to the other as to the perfect way to reach this last end. They consist *in doing all our actions* **through** *Mary,* **with** *Mary,* **in** *Mary and* **for** *Mary, so that we may do them all the more perfectly through Jesus, with Jesus, in Jesus and for Jesus.*

Before entering into the explanation of these practices, it is good to ask ourselves where Montfort got the idea. It seems that he borrowed from two sources, from the contemporary authors of the French school, and from the Liturgy.

I° **Borrowing from the French School.** Several authors use a formula identical to that of Fr. de Montfort. Almost contemporarily we have:

1° *Fr. Olier.* He placed in the foundations of the physical building of Saint-Sulpice some medals on which the **Virgin was depicted covering the house with her**

protection. We read this inscription there: "Cum ipsa et in ipsa et per ipsam omnis aedificatio crescit in laudem Dei. It is *with* her, *in* her, and *through* her that any building is raised into a temple of God."

The same Fr. Olier had placed in the chapel of the Virgin, in the church of Saint-Sulpice, a picture representing the mystery of Pentecost and bearing engraved all around: "With her, through her and in her."

2° *St. John Eudes*. He wrote: "Man having miserably lost himself, and the Father of the mercies looking for the means to save him, behold the name of Mary which appears in the treasures of divine Wisdom, and which presents itself to the eyes of His infinite goodness, at the sight of which this God of all consolation makes a decree, in His divine counsel, that this great work of the Redemption of men and the reparation of the world will be done *through* Mary, *in* Mary, *of* Mary, and *with* Mary, so that, as nothing was made without the Word incarnate, nothing may be repaired without the Mother of the Word incarnate."

3° *Marie of St. Teresa*, Flemish mystic. She thus described the Marian life: "This life *in* Mary, *for* her and *with* her." And farther: "The supernatural life of the soul *in* Mary, *for* her, *with* her and *through* her, continues and grows in a greater perfection and stability."

Already previously, the pious *Idiot* had said: "*Per* ipsam et *cum* ipsa, et *in* ipsa, et *ab* ipsa habet mundus et habiturus est omne bonum. Through her, with her, in her and of her the world has and will always have every kind of good."

None of these authors, however, gave to this formula a more precise sense and more amply explained it than Father de Montfort. Here again consequently, while being solidly traditional, he is also wisely personal.

II° **Borrowing from the Liturgy.** This seems to be the most direct influence which Montfort underwent, at least if we consider these practices as they are enumerated and explained in the *Treatise on the True Devotion*.

At the end of the Canon of the Mass, the priest says, while tracing signs of the cross with the consecrated host, over the chalice, which likewise has been consecrated, and with the awareness of expressing, not a wish whose realization would be uncertain, but a result actually obtained: "*Per* ipsum, et *cum* ipso, et *in* ipso est *tibi* Deo Patri omnipotenti in unitate Spiritus Sancti omnis honor et Gloria." *Through* Him, *with* Him, and *in* Him, we render to *You*, O almighty Father, in the unity of Your Holy Spirit all honor and glory.

Montfort returns to the liturgical formula and applies it to Mary. And thus he obtains: *Through* her, *with* her, *in* her and *for* her. In this formula, *through* indicates the union of intentions; *with*, the association in the work; *in*, an incomparably close union of persons; *for*, the final goal of the efforts.

In the *Secret of Mary*, the Saint does not follow the same order. He puts at the head: *with* Mary, then *in* Mary and finally *through* and *for* Mary. He puts the imitation of Mary (with) as a fundamental principle. But this imitation does not apply to Mary as to an ordinary model which the slave of love would simply have before his eyes. By an ardent love, which spiritually transports the lover into the beloved, a close union is realized, in virtue of which the model forms its copy (*in*). And so, only after having thus indicated these two movements "to Act *with* and *in* Mary" does he speak of the two other conditions of a slave: "to *Act* through *Mary* and *for* Mary."

Obviously, we shall keep ourselves, as always, to the order of the "*Treatise*": *through, with, in* and *for*. This is the best established and the easiest to explain. And, in the end, the particular commentaries on each member hardly change, depending on the place which this member occupies in the formula as a whole. Each preposition keeps its precise and bounded sense, whether it is at the head, in the middle or at the end.

Quite naturally, this article will be divided into four paragraphs. Each of them will show how exact the formula of the Holy Slavery is, that is to say, with what profound truth Mary reigns totally over her slaves of love, and her slaves are completely subjected to her rule over them.

*
* *

§ I. – TO ACT THROUGH MARY
(258-259)

In some substantial pages, Montfort defines *what it is* to act through Mary, and recalls *what this entails*.

1° WHAT IT IS TO ACT THROUGH MARY

N° 258

This means to say: obey Mary in everything; be guided by her spirit in everything. Imitate the good Jesuit brother coadjutor, Alphonsus Rodriguez (†1616), canonized by Leo XIII on January 15, 1888: be possessed and governed by the spirit of Mary. Be in the hands of Mary like a musical instrument in the hands of a good player. It does not resist. It executes all the tunes, adopts all the rhythms and all the movements which the artist wants to impress on it. Thus is the slave of love in the hands of his Queen. He espouses all her intentions, yields to all her impulses, offers no resistance to her action.

Having thus defined what action through Mary is in itself, the Saint enumerates **its advantages**.

First of all, those who are *led by the spirit of Mary* are also *led by the Spirit of God*, because the Spirit of God and the spirit of Mary are one.

This calls for an explanation. It is honestly given.

I have said that the spirit of Mary was the Spirit of God, because she was never led by her own spirit, but always by the Holy Ghost, Who has rendered Himself so completely master of her, that He has become her own proper spirit.

Indeed, Mary herself was and still is guided only by the Spirit of God. To place ourselves under her guidance is nothing other than to place ourselves under the guidance of the Spirit of God. The latter by reigning directly over her, reigns indirectly over us.

Subsequently, those who are led by the Spirit of God are, according to St. Paul, the children of God. In the same way, those who *are led by the spirit of Mary are the children of Mary* and also the children of God, because it is the same spirit. Those are the true and faithful devotees of Mary. This good Mother lends them her soul to glorify the Lord, and her spirit to rejoice in God. They are happy to be totally under the influence of this spirit. Is this not a spirit sweet and strong, zealous and prudent, humble and courageous, pure and fruitful? Surprising antitheses, which show well the riches of this new state, capable of reconciling in a single person such contrasting qualities.

2° WHAT ACTION THROUGH MARY ENTAILS

N° 259

Two conditions are absolutely required in order for the soul to be thus led by the spirit of Mary: the complete *renunciation* of its own intentions and the blind *acceptance* of Mary's intentions.

a) **Complete renunciation of one's own intentions.**

It is necessary to realize beforehand the emptiness of all that is one's own spirit, one's own proper lights, and will. It is required, then, to renounce one's dispositions and personal intentions, however good they may be, for example before one's prayers, before saying or hearing holy Mass, before receiving Communion, because our spirit is filled with darkness, even when it seems bright to us. Our will is filled with malice, even when it seems very upright to us. Our actions are always soiled by some stains, as imperceptible as they may be, even when they seem excellent to us. All these obstacles would prevent the spirit of Mary from leading us as it pleases.

b) **Blind acceptance of Mary's intentions.**

These intentions are unknown to us. But we know that they are always very holy, exempt from any search for personal gain, conformed to the greatest glory of God. We know also, therefore, that by accepting Mary's intentions and allowing ourselves to be guided by them, we shall please God and work for His glory.

To obtain this result in practice, it is necessary:

a) *To make a general act* of donation to Mary. By this act, we deliver ourselves to her spirit to be moved and guided by her in the way that she desires. To place ourselves again in her virginal hands, as a tool in the hands of the worker, as a lute in the hands of a good player. To abandon ourselves to her as a stone that is cast into the sea.

Of all these comparisons, the one which best seems to indicate the exercise to be carried out is the comparison of the instrument. Let us take the musical instrument. This is what, materially, produces the sound, and the latter will already have a different quality depending on the quality of the instrument which emits it. What matters especially, however, is the skill of the artist handling the instrument. If he has complete mastery of it, he will draw magnificent sounds from it, even if the instrument itself is fairly defective. But also, the one to whom all the merit of the streams of harmony will return is the artist and only to him. It is necessary to be this way in the hands of Mary: the least defective instrument possible, but having at least one quality, that of being completely under the impulse of Mary, to execute nothing by oneself, but to carry out exactly what Mary suggests. If she finds in us this complete obedience, this good Mother will produce, in us and by us, marvels of which she alone will have the merit. We shall have the praiseworthy title, (and this will already be a lot) of having allowed ourselves to be led, not to have placed an obstacle to Mary, to have cooperated in her action. This is exactly, from the Marian point of view, the application of the doctrine touching the action of the Holy Ghost in the just, thanks to the gifts which He poured out there: "*They are led by the Spirit of God*" (Rom. 8:14), they are under the impulse, not of their will, but of the Holy Ghost Himself.

This donation is not difficult. It suffices for an instant, "*by one glance of the* mind", that is to say, by a rapid elevation of thought, to say to Mary, without words or with words: "*I renounce myself, I give myself to thee, my dear Mother.*" We shall not necessarily have then the impression that everything is changed. Here we are in the domain of pure faith. This act of union, then, does not cease to be true, even if we feel no sensible sweetness while carrying it out or after having carried it out. Its effect is as real as would be, in the inverse sense, the effect of the following sentence, pronounced with sincerity: "*I give myself to the devil.*" No sensible change!... And nevertheless we would really belong to the devil.

b) *Frequently repeat this act of donation.* From time to time, either during the action, or even after the action, we ought to renew the same act of offering and union. The more we repeat it, the sooner we shall sanctify ourselves, and the sooner we shall arrive at union with Jesus Christ. Because an ever-closer union with Mary, the direct object of this donation, leads always and necessarily to union with Jesus. And the spirit of Mary, animating, in this case, the slaves of love, is none other than the Spirit of Jesus, the one with Whom the Savior Himself was filled and by Whom He was led.

There is, then, a perfect equation between all these formulas: Spirit of God, Spirit of Christ, spirit of Mary, as there is equation between these formulas: be moved by the Spirit of God, by the Spirit of Christ, or by the spirit of Mary. It is always the same supreme principal cause. And the intermediate causes serve only to accentuate more and to place within our reach the supremely efficacious action of the divine Spirit. To act through Mary is, then, indeed to act through Christ. This is to recognize the order established by God. This is to follow the way which He Himself walked, to reach His infinite Majesty: *ad Patrem per Iesum, et ad Iesum per Mariam.* Let us go to the Father through Jesus; let us go to Jesus through Mary.

§ II. – TO ACT WITH MARY
(260)

N° 260

This practice is called by Montfort (*Secret of Mary*, n° 145) *essential* in this devotion. Then he gives an explanation corresponding exactly to what he says in n° 260 of the *True Devotion*. It consists in looking at Mary, in taking her as the accomplished model of every virtue and perfection, and in imitating her according to our limited capacity.

After that, in n° 46 of the *Secret*, the Saint develops at greater length what this practice entails. But the explanations which he places there under the heading "*with*" are exactly the ones that he placed in the *Treatise* under the title "*through*". Perhaps he considered only these two conditions (to renounce one's very self and to lose oneself in Mary) as prerequisites, and, as such, indicated them on the occasion of the first expression of his fourfold formula. We shall also note that the word "*through*" in the *Secret* takes only the sense of "*through the intercession of Mary*", by relying on her influence and authority. This does not contradict what we said in the previous paragraph. But it is much less profound. Nothing, then, obliges us to turn away from the sense given to "*through*" and "*with*" in the *True Devotion*.

And there, it is not "*with*" which seems essential, but rather "*through*" and "*in*."

"*With*" entails two elements: 1° *imitation of Mary on our part*, and the most perfect reproduction possible of the virtues which she herself practiced; 2° *association with our efforts on Mary's part*, in virtue of which the final result will depend more on Mary than on us.

1° **Imitation of Mary's virtues.** It is natural for someone who is not capable himself of creating a masterpiece to act under the inspiration of a model, to copy it faithfully. It is no less natural for a child to find his mother perfect and to try to imitate her in everything. This twofold tendency of our nature is satisfied by devotion to Mary. *First of all*, the Holy Ghost formed in her the highest model which can be found in a pure creature: whoever is inspired by this model in the practice of every virtue is assured: 1° of carrying out the divine will; 2° of reaching perfection. *Secondly*, Mary is our Mother, our beloved Mother, our admirable Mother. She is capable of stirring in us, much more perfectly than an ordinary mother stirs in her child, this feeling of admiration which leads him to imitate her in everything. We shall try to look at, in every action, how Mary carried it out, if, historically, she had the opportunity, or how, given what we know about her grandeurs and holiness, she would carry it out, if she was in our place. We shall try to put into it the same supernatural views, the same purity of intention, the same ardent love, the same dedication to the glory of God, etc.

We shall thus imitate all the virtues of Mary, but especially three of them:

a) *Her lively faith*. Because our supernatural activity is at present in the domain of faith. The light of a lively faith is, then, absolutely necessary in order to lead us, in order to teach us to appreciate everything at its just value. That is why we shall try to imitate, and Mary on her part will communicate to us, her lively faith, that is to say, this faith by which she believed unhesitatingly in the word of the Angel, in spite of the natural impossibility of the event announced; this faith by which she believed in the divinity of her Son, first of all, during the whole time of His hidden life, in which, when nothing of such a dignity showed through exteriorly; then and especially at the foot of the cross when everything seemed to sink amid ridicule and dishonor. In the same way our faith will not allow itself to be upset neither by the opposite appearances, nor by the disasters of life.

b) *Her profound humility*. This humility led Mary to hide herself, to keep silent, to submit herself to everything, and to put herself last. It is easy to prove it by her life, either before the Incarnation, or during the whole life of her Son here on earth, or after the Ascension. To practice the renunciation required previously, it is necessary for us to have humble sentiments about ourselves, to love silence, obscurity, and submission. This humility is also an effect of the perfect devotion. But nothing prevents us from trying especially to obtain what Mary wants to communicate to us.

c) *Her divine purity*. Mary's purity has never had and will never be equaled in heaven and on earth. It began through the splendors of the Immaculate Conception, which already placed her above all the Angels and saints. Then, it kept increasing at every moment and in incalculable proportions. The imitation of Mary's purity will help us to avoid backsliding and to be always flexible and docile under the motion of the divine Spirit.

2° The association of Mary in the efforts which we produce.

The Maternity of Mary with regard to us and our filiation with regard to her are fully conscious and entirely free and spontaneous (n° 243). The likeness which it will imprint in us and which we shall receive will, therefore, be the fruit of her enlightened and deliberate activity, and our conscious and willed passivity. The situation is different in ordinary maternities. The likeness is imprinted unbeknownst to the mother and the child, and therefore also without real collaboration. Mary works in us and on us; and we submit ourselves lovingly to her action. She is the divine mold, proper to form gods in a short time and at little cost. We are the material liquefied adequately, which, of itself, casts itself into this mold to be wedded to all the forms thereof. The work of Mary consists in putting the finishing touches on us, so that we may take on the likeness of her Son. Our work consists in allowing ourselves to be remade on this divine model.

The practical realization of this collaboration is very well described by *Rev. Fr. Lhoumeau*: "Look how the mother proceeds with her child, when she teaches him to walk, to pray. Not only does she imitate and encourage him by gesture and voice, but she acts with him, by giving example, by helping his weakness and inexperience. On his part, the child acts with his mother; because he looks at her and continues to be docile to her guidance; he does not part from her. In order to act with Mary, therefore, after having obeyed her impulse to live under her guidance and influence, I must keep my look fixed on her so as to imitate her, and, if necessary, to get back up; finally, I have to follow her without anticipating her nor delaying."

And thus, we have the connection between "*through*" and "*with*": "*we must deliver ourselves to the spirit of Mary to be moved* (at the beginning of the action: **through**) *and influenced* (in the course of the action: **with**) *by it in the manner she chooses*" (n° 259).

§ III. – TO ACT IN MARY

(261-264)

Nº 261

Several times already, we have spoken incidentally about the predominant role which this practice plays in Montfortian spirituality as a whole. The key to its explanation consists in this life of Jesus in Mary, of which our slavery tends to be the voluntary reproduction. Just as Jesus lived and worked in the womb of His mother, so too, we ought to live and work in the womb of Mary.

But as this blessed womb was the earthly Paradise of the new Adam, all the explanations of Montfort, at least in the *Treatise*, are inspired by this basic idea. This helps to give a figurative sense to this passage. We would be tempted to take it in a purely symbolic sense. In reality, everything must be taken literally, although, it goes without saying, in the spiritual and mystical sense, at least in what concerns us ourselves.

We have already previously spoken (nos 243-248) about the main part of this life in Mary.

St. Thomas (Iª IIae qu. XXVIII art. 2) suggests to us another explanation of this same mystery that is more philosophical, but no less fruitful:

We said in nº 20 how Mary makes herself present to her devout slave as an object of knowledge and love. A completely spiritual presence, but which already in certain cases, can attain even the mystical order.

The converse is also true. The slave of Mary is, in the same way, present in his Queen. For she has a perfect knowledge of him and loves him profoundly. This reciprocity causes an infinitely sweet mutual presence, quite to the advantage of the slave of love. The latter is not less honored by Mary's presence in him than by his admission into the spirit and heart of his good Mother.

Love, however, is not necessarily mutual. The feelings of one are not always shared by the other. But this by no means prevents the one who loves from being present in the object of his love. It is even so in a twofold way.

First of all, the one who truly loves is not content with a superficial knowledge of the one loved. He wants to know in great detail, and I would say almost, from inside, everything which can relate to him. That's why he tries to get deep inside and make himself comfortable with him. Is it not the need for light that seizes the slave of love, never sufficiently instructed about the mystery of Mary?

Then, the one who truly loves does not stop at just any possession, exterior and superficial. He requires perfect possession and absolute enjoyment of the beloved. He wants to be admitted to his most complete intimacy. And thus he gives way to the first tendency of his love: to possess so as to enjoy. But furthermore he is generous and disinterested. He considers as his everything which affects the object of his love. He adopts his intentions. He is delighted at his happiness. He suffers from his sorrows. In brief, he has for him the purest benevolence. And if such a love is shared, it is not only union, it is fusion, almost identification. Is this not again what characterizes the love of the slave for his heavenly Mistress and justifies once more his presence in Mary?

But let us return to the ideas expressed by Montfort, either in the *Treatise on the True Devotion,* or in n° 47 of the *Secret of Mary*.

According to the various effects that the life in Mary produces in us, this good Mother is compared either to the earthly Paradise where the new Adam reposes, or to the *sanctuary* where God lives and is honored, or to the *oratory* where we enclose ourselves to pray to God, or to the *Tower of David* where we are safe against our enemies.

Let us see, first of all, the *truth* of these comparisons, then the *consequences* which follow from them for the one who wishes to live in Mary.

1° THE TRUTH OF THESE COMPARISONS

Let us take up again the four principal comparisons enumerated above.

a) **Mary, the earthly Paradise of the new Adam.** This comparison is developed at length in the *Treatise*. And the Saint applies to this new earthly Paradise everything which is said about the old one in Scripture. First of all, this place consists of a *virgin* and spotless earth, from which the new Adam was formed and nourished, without any spot or stain, by the operation of the Holy Ghost: thus the body of the first Adam had been formed by God with the earth of the earthly Paradise. And the Holy Ghost dwells in Mary better than God formerly dwelt in this garden, because there He walked only from time to time. Besides, everything is such as to please Him in this place of delights. We see trees *planted* by the hand of God and watered with His divine unction there, which bore and bear every day fruits of a divine taste: an image of the wonderful powers of the Virgin, whose acts are so perfect and so pleasing to God. We see there flowerbeds adorned with beautiful and varied *flowers* the smell of which perfumes even the angels: an image of Mary's virtues, superior to those of the blessed spirits. We see there *meadows* green with hope, impregnable *towers* of strength, *houses* full of charm and security: images of what the souls who take refuge there find in Mary. We breathe there air without stench: Mary's purity; we enjoy *day* there without night: the holy humanity of the Word incarnate; we are enlightened there by a *sun* without shadows: the divinity of Christ; we are warmed there by a burning *furnace*, capable of setting ablaze the base metal which is cast into it, and of transforming it into the charity of

Mary. A deep *river* springs from the earth and, dividing into four branches, waters this whole enchanted place: they are the four cardinal virtues springing from Mary's humility and making her whole life fruitful. Finally, concluding the resemblance with Eden, a tree is planted in the middle of this earthly Paradise; it is at the same time the *tree of life* that gives the fruit of life, Our Lord Jesus Christ, and the tree of the *knowledge of good and evil*, which gave the light to the world, also Our Lord Jesus Christ. This tree is the womb of Mary.

Moreover, the Holy Ghost alone can reveal the truth hidden under these figures. We have only given the most general indications, capable of guiding more detailed searches. But we already understand what charms, what security and what vitality will be drawn from Mary by the souls who will be admitted to enclose themselves there.

N° 262

b) **Mary, the sanctuary where God lives and is honored**. The Saint heaps up the expressions to reinforce this idea: Mary is not only the sanctuary where God resides, she is the room where He reposes, the throne where He sits, the city where He lives, the altar where He receives sacrifices, the temple where He is adored, the world which sings His glory. So many allusions to the marvels of grace which God carried out in Mary. But also so many encouragements to enter and remain in Mary to find God there and honor Him there perfectly. It is in Mary Immaculate that "*the hidden eternal Wisdom* **wants** *to be adored by angels and men.*" And, having made His sojourn in her, Jesus, our high priest, goes out from her as from the Eastern Gate, to come to consummate His sacrifice and to save us. If we want to find Him, now that He has gone away from us, it is through the same gate that we must pass.

c) **Mary, the oratory where we enclose ourselves to pray**. In this very holy place, the noises of the earth have no access. Recollection is more profound; fewer distractions to dread. No place is, then, more favorable to prayer. But, furthermore, nowhere are we more sure of being heard, not only because we always find Jesus there, but because Jesus is always inclined to listen to us there. (See n° 248.)

d) **Mary, the Tower of David where we are safe**. The Litany of Loreto applies to Mary this name of Tower of David which is encountered several times in Holy Scripture. Montfort has recourse to it also in the *Secret*, n° 47, and a little bit also in the *Treatise*, n° 261. The idea connected with this expression is that Mary is this powerful and impregnable Tower, shielding from their adversaries all those who will come to seek refuge there. Because it is a question of imitating and of reproducing the life of Jesus in Mary, shall we not be protected, as He Himself was, on all sides, by our Mother? In reality, no blow could reach the child in the womb of his mother without reaching the mother herself; and, if the mother is assumed to be out of reach of the blows of the opponent, the child will be in perfect safety. Such is indeed the case of Mary and such is the protection which she confers on her slaves of love.

2° CONSEQUENCES RESULTING FROM THESE COMPARISONS

N° 263

These consequences aim, first of all, at the conditions required to be admitted to remain in such a holy place; then the advantages that the soul derives from this divine sojourn.

A) **Conditions of admission and dwelling**. Adam and Eve, guilty of having transgressed the divine law, were chased away from the earthly Paradise, and a cherub, armed with a blazing sword, was placed at the entrance to forbid sinful humanity access. Even this figure has its realization in Mary. It is of her especially that it is said in the Canticle of Canticles: "*My sister, my spouse, is a garden enclosed, a garden enclosed, a fountain sealed up*" (Cant. 4:12): Mary is for the Holy Ghost, her divine Spouse, a garden enclosed, a sealed fountain. The Holy Ghost Himself guards the entrance of it. Nobody can enter this garden or draw from this fountain without receiving from the Holy Ghost: 1° the permission to try such an approach; 2° the capacity to lead it to good purposes; 3° the light guiding its steps towards such a mysterious and secret place. This supposes, then, a very special grace, a grace which can be called "*illustrious*" (n° 264). The Holy Ghost will refuse it to no one. But He will not give it free of charge. In order to receive it, it is necessary to merit it. And one merits it by one's fidelity in following the inspirations of grace, and particularly by one's fidelity to the practices of the Marian life. It is obvious, indeed, that, to enjoy such an intimacy with Mary, it is necessary to be absolutely pure of any fault, at least perfectly deliberate, and to have given sufficient proofs of one's love for her.

N° 264

B) **Advantages that the soul derives from its dwelling in Mary**. Nothing is worth the feeling of peace and security which takes hold of the soul dwelling spiritually in Mary. Obviously, there is and there always will be a great difference between the child living really and physically in his mother's womb and the slave of love living only morally and spiritually in Mary's womb. The advantages which ensue from it for the child have a physical certainty. For the slave of love, they have only a moral certainty and also assuming the continuation of a dependence from which it is very easy for him to escape at any time.

But, this dependence being certain, the soul ought to remain complacently in the beautiful interior of Mary, repose there in peace, rely on it confidently, hide itself there assuredly and lose itself there unreservedly. There, however, more than anywhere else, we are in the domain of faith. A soul could very well realize perfectly the state of dependence described previously without feeling any of the sentiments enumerated by our Saint. At least it will try to acquire them, as the verbal forms used here indicate: "*Remain, lean, hide ourselves, lose ourselves.*" This comes much more from an active abandonment of the soul than from the direct infusion of a feeling originating from Mary or from grace. As a matter of fact, this interior peace of the soul, the consequence of its dwelling in Mary, can be either acquired or infused. And also, to this security resulting from the filial abandonment of the slave of love can be added an incomparable serenity, originating from the direct action of the Virgin.

More important, besides, than sentiment, are the effects really produced in the soul by this dwelling in Mary. These effects are four in number. We have already met them several times.

a) The soul is *nourished by Mary* with the milk of her grace and her maternal mercy, as the child receives from his mother the food and the blood necessary for his life and development. This grace is the divine grace which Mary receives to give to us and put in our reach.

b) The soul is *delivered from its troubles*, fears and scruples there more efficaciously even than was said in n°s 169 and 170 and 216, because all this is absolutely incompatible with the state of childhood thus understood.

c) The soul is *in safety* there against all its enemies, the devil, the world and sin, which have never had and never will have entrance in Mary. That is why she says herself by the mouth of divine Wisdom: "*They that work by me shall not sin*" (Eccli. 24:30). We cannot, indeed, be and act in Mary, and commit sin, unless it is a sin of sheer frailty. Whoever deliberately commits sin abandons by himself this divine dwelling and freely places an obstacle to the graces which Mary had prepared for him.

d) There the soul is *formed in Jesus Christ*, and Jesus Christ in it (n°s 218-221), because the womb of Mary is, St. Ambrose says: "*Aula sacramentorum*", the room of secrets or the divine sacraments. Jesus Christ was formed there first, and all the elect are formed there after Him: "Homo et homo natus in ea (Ps. 86:5), This man and that man is born in her."

§ IV. – TO ACT FOR MARY
(265)

N° 265

To understand this practice, let us recall the doctrine on the slavery. The slave no longer belongs to himself; he belongs to his master or mistress. All the goods of fortune which he possessed before falling into slavery, all those which may accrue to him afterwards are the property of his master or mistress. In the same way, all the fruit of his labor is for the benefit of his master or mistress.

On the other hand, it was proved in the same place that we are slaves of Jesus and Mary, and of Mary in order to be perfectly the slave of Jesus. This is what also returns in this short paragraph.

1° **As slaves of Mary**. We have freely acknowledged the bonds of slaves which bind us to Mary. We are so disposed towards her, that, even if God had not granted her this right of dominion over us, we ourselves would grant it to her out of love. It is just that we should carry out all our natural and supernatural actions for her. Are they not the fruit of our activity? And does not this activity have to bear fruit for our good Mistress?

This thought, that nothing belongs to us any longer of what we acquire by our works, must by no means daunt us. On the contrary. Like good servants and slaves, we shall not remain idle. Counting on Mary's protection, we shall undertake great things for this august sovereign. Particularly, we shall defend her privileges, when they are disputed; we shall stand up for her glory, when it is attacked; we shall try to entice everybody to her service, and we shall even try to win all hearts to this true and solid devotion. On the one hand, we shall speak and cry out against those who abuse her devotion to outrage her divine Son; on the other hand, we shall be no less ardent in order to establish the true devotion, especially that of the Holy Slavery.

And, after that, like true slaves, we shall only claim from our queen, as reward for these meager services, the honor of belonging to such a lovable princess, and the happiness of being united by her, to Jesus, her Son, by an indissoluble bond, in time and eternity.

And this brings us to our second consideration.

2° **As slaves of Mary to belong perfectly to Jesus**. Mary is not the last end of our devotion. Jesus alone deserves thus to be the end of our acts. Any devotion which would not lead to Him would have to be mercilessly pushed aside.

If, therefore, we call on Mary to lead us to Jesus, it is so that she may serve us as a mysterious environment and easy means to go to Him. These works, which we offer to this good Mother, will undergo in her hands the transformation which we know, and thanks to it, will be more worthy of the One for Whom they are intended.

Moreover, would somebody, in his ignorance, believe he acted only for Mary? This Virgin, the faithful echo of God, would be all the more eager to restore the unconsciously violated order. She would refer to her divine Son, and, through Him, to her Creator, the untimely honor that her child would attribute to her. See this little child. He wants to prove his love to his mother. He seizes everything which is in his reach, and comes to offer it to her in tribute. The mother benevolently accepts the present of her child. But she takes advantage of his first moment of distraction to restore to its owner, or put back in its place, the object which he had seized to carry out this offering.

To conform ourselves to this practice, we must, asserts the *Secret of Mary* (n° 49), in all that we do, renounce our self-love, which almost always takes itself as an end imperceptibly, and to repeat often from the bottom of the heart: *"O my dear mistress, it is for you that I go here or there, that I do this or that, that I suffer this pain or this insult."*

In another form, we return, then, to the twofold condition of renunciation and donation, which was spoken about in speaking of *"through"* and *"with"*.

The actions of which Montfort speaks in this article are not extraordinary, exaggerated, heroic actions, which rarely occur, and which we should seek and undertake in order to be faithful to the Holy Slavery. These are ordinary actions, those which make up our daily duties. Thus, the practice of the perfect devotion fits of itself and without difficulties into all states and manners of life. It does not consist in these very actions, but in the spirit which drives them, and which gives to them, if we want, a new value, a greater richness.

And this spirit is none other than the spirit of Mary, Queen of heaven and earth, specially the Queen of the elect, more specially still the Queen of the heart of the elect. It invades the slaves of love of this great Queen, and subjects them completely and spontaneously to all the requirements of Mary's domain, to all the delicate touches of her gentle and maternal direction.

Mary accepts this empire without false humility. She exercises it unfailingly, conscious of fulfilling thus the mission which God entrusted to her, and to lead to their sovereign happiness the souls which abandon themselves to her. She does not draw vanity from them. She does not attach to herself the souls over which she reigns. She seeks only to lead them to her divine Son, and does so with a love that is as admirable as its disinterestedness; the two would not exist simultaneously in a woman's heart, if Mary was not the

Immaculate Virgin, all relative to God, without any shadow of personal interest.

A question arises here:

WHAT IS THE DEGREE OF OBLIGATION OF ALL THESE PRACTICES?

Two things are to be considered:

1° The consecration of the Holy Slavery is itself perfectly free. The practices which result from it cannot be obligatory under pain of sin, whether mortal, or even venial. They are means of perfection, intended to safeguard the fulfillment of the precepts necessary for salvation.

2° But, for the one who has pronounced his consecration, the practices are imposed by virtue of fidelity to the given word, and under pain of deriving no fruit from this form of devotion. All are not required, however, at the same time, nor all in the same degree. Some are even left by our saint to the free choice of each. (e.g. n°s 234, 236.) What matters especially is to stir and maintain in ourselves the spirit of Marian dependence. Since this result is obtained, there is nothing to worry about if some practice was omitted, even if we did promise to be faithful to it, because all interior practices, and the principal exterior practices coincide necessarily with this spirit of Marian dependence.

Souls more eager for perfection wondered if they could not impose on themselves, by vow, an obligation which Father de Montfort does not impose, at least under pain of sin. To this question, we could answer affirmatively. But on a twofold condition:

1° *Determine rightly what we are committing to do.* The Holy Slavery, in general, embraces all the manifestations of human life, in all orders and kinds of activity. It would be imprudent, it seems, to make a commitment by vow to observe absolutely all the details of them. On the contrary, one or another clearly specified prescription can become the matter of a vow.

2° *Determine rightly the extent of its obligation.* One can only commit himself under pain of grave fault to do or avoid an objectively grave thing. It is better only to commit oneself under pain of venial sin to do or avoid things which objectively are material for venial sin.

Any other vow, for example, to avoid simple imperfections, to aim always at the most perfect, etc., would be especially difficult and could be expressed only with the permission of the confessor, with the proviso that it would always be revocable by him, and for a determined time.

SUPPLEMENT TO CHAPTER IV

The practical realization of this devotion: COMMUNION WITH MARY

(266-273)

The Saint established in every detail the form of devotion which he considers perfect and of which he was the ardent promoter for all his life. Before putting down his pen, he wishes to give an example of the practical realization of this devotion.

Certainly, the examples must have swarmed in his mind, and appeared of themselves to his imagination. In all truth, he had only the difficulty of choosing among them.

But this choice hardly embarrasses Fr. de Montfort. Accustomed, as a missionary, to the direction of souls of all categories, he knows what importance the great act of Communion has for each of them. Apostle of frequent and daily communion, at the height of the age of Jansenism, he is anxious to offer to all those who see in the Eucharist the ordinary nourishment of our divine life, an excellent method of profiting from this sacred banquet and approaching it worthily. He will, then, set aside all other matters, where his devotion, well-practiced, can also produce marvels, and he will choose Communion with Mary. He will thus prove one more time that the perfect devotion is the best means of going to Our Lord, and to Our Lord not only in heaven, where He will be the reward of all our good works, but also among us, in the Eucharist, where He is at present our fellow traveler and our support in the practice of good.

This method is divided quite naturally into three parts: 1° *before* Communion; 2° *during* Communion; 3° *after* Communion. We do not intend to propose in these pages a series of acts before or after Communion. We simply want to highlight, as we have always done until now, the ideas expressed by Montfort. We especially want to show that his method is truly an example of the practical realization of his dear devotion.

*
* *

§ I. – BEFORE COMMUNION
(266)

N° 266

Montfort suggests a series of four very sound reflections that produce many insights.

1° **You will humble yourselves profoundly before God**. This is only a preliminary disposition, but how essential in the presence of such a mystery! Jesus, infinite greatness, but greatness exteriorly hidden and humbled. We, true nothingness, but nothingness which would still try to glory in what it received... Is not one of the prerequisites of the Holy Slavery to know oneself, to know Jesus?... And, besides, does not the perfect devotion have as its first effect to obtain for souls the knowledge and contempt of their fallen nature, the gift of a profound humility, a participation in the very humility of Mary, by the similarity of sentiments produced by this good Mother in her slaves of love?

2° **You will renounce your corrupt interior and your dispositions, however good your own self-love may make them look**.

If Mary truly gives us a share in her humility, we shall easily be convinced of the obligation to renounce our fallen nature, because it is in reality this interior of poverty and corruption, so sensible in our heart and in all our being, which makes us powerless to prepare for Jesus a suitable dwelling in our soul. If, then, our dispositions are much too obviously *soiled* by this fallen nature, it will not be difficult to renounce it.

The sacrifice will be more painful, if our dispositions seem to us *excellent*, for example if our heart longs to receive Jesus, if our fervor is uplifted at this thought alone. Even then, however, it is necessary to renounce it; because, as good are, they always sin in certain ways.

By these two acts, we try to produce an emptiness, so as to conquer ourselves. But this is still only negative. The positive will come with the following two acts.

3° **You will renew your consecration**, by saying: "*Tuus totus ego sum, et omnia mea tua sunt, I am all thine, my dear Mistress, with all I have.*" Mary gives herself completely to the one who gives himself completely to her. We see the opportunity for the renewal of the consecration at the moment in which we approach the Holy Altar. This is, equivalently, to invite Mary to come into us, to receive her divine Son herself. And that will lead to the two major ideas, contained in the following paragraph.

4° **You will implore this good Mother to lend you her heart to receive her Son there with the same dispositions**.

First idea. Jesus will be received by His Mother with the same eagerness as on the day of His Incarnation. He will enjoy the same joys and find the same happiness. In order to obtain for Him this maternal hospitality one more time, "*you will represent to Mary that it touches her Son's glory to be put into a heart so sullied and so inconstant as yours.*" This impure heart would not fail to deprive Him of His external glory, and would soon lose Him. It is entirely up to her, on the contrary, to come to dwell with you to receive her Son. She can do it, by the dominion which she has over hearts. Her Son will be well-received by her, without stain, without danger of being offended or lost. "*God is in the midst thereof; He shall not be moved*" (Ps. 45:6). We can, then, without fear, renounce our personal dispositions, however good they are, if they are replaced by those of Mary. Jesus will no more hesitate to come to us than He did to be born in the poor stable of Bethlehem, because His Mother was there, and because her presence alone transformed this miserable hovel into a luxurious palace.

Second idea. You will say confidently to Mary that everything that you gave her by your consecration is indeed nothing much in reality. Furthermore, she was already entitled to it due to her Immaculate Conception, her divine Maternity and her Co-redemption. We only acknowledged this right by our consecration. We were, however, so disposed, in pronouncing it, that, even if God had not granted her this right, we would have given it to her ourselves out of pure love. And this is very substantial. But finally, our gift has no more value than we ourselves have. Whereas *by the Holy Communion you wish to make her the same present as the eternal Father gave her* on March 25th. And she will more be honored with it than if you offered her all the goods of the world. A mother worthy of this name will always prefer her child to all goods of fortune, and, if the life of this child came to be threatened, and if such a sacrifice could make it safe, she would gladly abandon all her goods in order to preserve her child. For greater reason it will be so of Mary. She is the ideal Mother and she has, furthermore, reasons for preferring her Son to all the rest of creation. Is not her Son at the same time her God?

In this connection, we shall recite fruitfully the prayer of St. Gertrude: *O Maria, Virgo et Mater sanctissima...*, which is in the Breviary, among the prayers of thanksgiving after Mass. It expresses splendidly these two ideas, especially the second.

With such dispositions, we can confidently approach the Holy Altar. Our Communion will be pleasing to Jesus. This sweet Savior always loves to descend into our heart in spite of its misery, and He also desires to take His delight and repose in Mary. It will also be pleasing to Mary. This good Mother will be happy to welcome her divine Son in our place. Let us repeat, then, these sweet words to bind her to it more: "*Accipio te in mea omnia*, I take you for my all", like the beloved disciple, and "*Praebe mihi cor tuum, O Maria*, Lend me your heart, O Mary."

*
* *

§ II. – IN COMMUNION
(267-269)

N° 267

Having recited the *Our Father*, with the Eucharistic and Marian sentiments that this prayer supposes, you will say three times: "**Domine, non sum dignus**."

1° The first time, you will address **God the Father**, and you will say to Him: "Lord, I am unworthy to receive Jesus, your only Son, because of my *bad thoughts* and *ingratitude* towards You, Who are so good a Father."

In order to understand the two key thoughts of this paragraph, it is necessary to think of the special attributions of each of the divine Persons, either towards the other two, or towards the rest of creation.

Thus the Father is the principle of the second Person of the Most Holy Trinity. The latter proceeds from Him according to the operation of the intelligence. God the Son is thus the result of the Father's thought, an immense thought, like the divine substance which it expresses perfectly, but thought of an infinite purity and holiness. Whereas our thoughts are very often soiled by the sad concupiscence and are the most frequent cause of our fears of receiving Jesus badly. Let us not attach too much importance to what does not depend on our will and is incapable of depriving us of divine grace. But let us be happy to be able to say to God the Father: See Mary, the Immaculate Virgin, who will receive Jesus in my place. In her, nothing will offend His divine eyes, and the palace where He will be accommodated will shine with a brightness without shadow. It is she who gives me confidence with Your divine Majesty. "*Quoniam singulariter in spe constituisti me*" (Ps. 4:9). It is there that You established me in great security.

God the Father is also considered as the Creator of the world and the Benefactor of humanity, although these external works are common to the three divine Persons. From this point of view, He is thus entitled to the gratitude of all His creatures. Instead of this, we have accumulated marks of ingratitude. Fortunately, Mary is there, submitting herself perfectly to the divine power and proclaiming humbly: "I am the handmaid of the Lord", before singing her *Magnificat*. Her conduct will repair our past ingratitude.

N° 268

2° The second time, you will address **God the Son**, and you will say to Him: "Lord, I am not worthy to receive You because of my *useless* and bad *words* and my *infidelity* in Your service."

God the Son is also called *the Word*, that is to say, the purely mental word, by which the Father expresses interiorly His divine substance and by which He also created the world. A powerful, efficacious and very holy word, with which our words, so often useless or contrary to charity or to modesty, clash pitifully.

Subsequently, Jesus was essentially a servant of His Father. It is under this special aspect that the Prophet Isaiah liked envisaging Him. We know to what extremes this divine service drove Him. How many times, on the contrary, have we not avoided it?

But in order to win His clemency, in either case, you will introduce Him into the house of His Mother and yours, and you will not allow Him to go as He came to live with her. "*I held him, and I will not let him go, till I bring him into my mother's house, and into the chamber of her that bore me*"

(Cant. 3:4). Of yourselves, you are Esaus and sinners. You do not put, however, like him, your confidence in your merits, strength and preparations. You rely only on the preparations of Mary, your dear Mother, like little Jacob surrendered himself totally to Rebecca's care. If you dare to approach His holiness, it is because you are adorned with Mary's virtues.

N° 269

3° The third time, you will address **God the Holy Ghost**, and you will say to Him: "Lord, I am not worthy to receive the masterpiece of Your charity, because of the lukewarmness and injustice of my *actions* and my *resistance* to Your inspirations."

God the Holy Ghost is the result of the mutual love of the Father and the Son. Next to this consuming fire what are our poor actions, which are so tepid and often so blameworthy?

Furthermore, God the Holy Ghost is considered as the author of holiness in souls and the instigator of all good promptings. Alas! We have often resisted His inspirations, and we are quite far from having reached the degree of holiness to which He would have wanted to lead us.

But all your confidence is in Mary: "*Haec mea maxima fiducia est; haec tota ratio spei meae.*" She is the faithful and indissoluble Spouse of the Holy Ghost. Her womb is still so pure, and her heart as ardent as ever. He can, then, come there unexpectedly, as for the mystery of the Incarnation. Because, without His descent in your soul, Jesus and Mary will not be in you, nor divinely formed, nor worthily accommodated.

*
* *

§ III. – AFTER COMMUNION

(270-273)

N° 270

These delightful moments which follow Communion will also gain in sweetness, if we apply the Montfortian method to them. The latter contains, first of all, a preliminary act consisting in introducing Jesus into the heart of Mary, then a series of several kinds of thanksgivings: 1° thanksgiving of contemplation; 2° thanksgiving of praise; 3° thanksgiving of zeal; 4° thanksgiving of amends.

Preliminary act.

After Holy Communion, while you are inwardly recollected and holding your eyes shut, you will introduce Jesus into the heart of Mary. You will give Him to His Mother, who will receive *Him lovingly, will* place *Him honourably, will* adore *Him profoundly, will* love *Him perfectly, will* embrace *Him closely, and will render to Him, in spirit and in truth, many homages which are unknown to us in our thick darkness.*

What marvels are stored up in these few words! This is the protocol of a reception both supremely royal and maternally affectionate.

N° 271

1. **Thanksgiving of contemplation.** "*You will keep yourself profoundly humbled in your heart, in the presence of Jesus residing in Mary.*" What can we say, indeed, that would be on a par with mysteries like these? You could only disturb this ineffable concert of praises inspired by love, by blending your weak voice in it. Your praise is silence, gratitude, the confession of your nothingness: "*Tibi silentium laus…*" or still: "*You will sit like a slave at the gate of the King's palace, where He is speaking with the Queen.*" You do not have to intervene in their conversation. Remain there, however, to receive their orders, if necessary.

2. **Thanksgiving of praise.** *"While they talk one to the other without need of you, you will go in spirit to heaven and over all the earth, praying all creatures to thank, adore, and love Jesus and Mary in your place. Venite adoremus, venite…"* This is the example which the priest gives in descending from the altar. He invites all creatures, from the highest of the heavens to the depths of the oceans, to come join him in order to thank worthily Jesus and Mary for such a condescension towards him. Let all nature, from the rising of the dawn to the setting of sun, raise a solemn chant of blessings and praises. The Lord, Who reigns over all nations and Whose glory illumines the heavens, is infinitely worthy of them. Who, then, is as high as He is, and who knows as He does, from the heart of His greatness, to regard with love the humble and the poor man, and to lift him up from the dust in order to give him a place in the midst of the princes of His court?...

N° 272

3. **Thanksgiving of zeal.** *"You shall ask of Jesus, in union with Mary, the coming of His kingdom on earth, through His holy Mother, or you will sue for the divine Wisdom, or for divine love… or for some other grace, but always through Mary and in Mary."* Because how can one remain unmoved by the observation that Jesus is not adored and loved by all men, and that whole peoples still live in ignorance of His laws? How can one not be saddened to see His divine Name blasphemed and despised even by those who know Him?... Pray so that apostles, ever more numerous and ever holier, may extend further and further the limits of the reign of God. And, because this must happen only through Mary, pray that these apostles may receive a more intimate and deeper knowledge of this glorious Virgin, and of the wonderful connections which unite them to Jesus.

4. **Thanksgiving of amends**. *"You will ask from Jesus in union with Mary… pardon for your sins."* Speak while

admitting the innumerable quantity of sins committed, remorse stifled, of graces rejected, etc.: "*Ne respicias, Domine, peccata mea*, Lord, look not at my sins." And, by casting your eyes on Mary, you will add: "*Sed oculi tui videant aequitates Mariae.* But let your eyes look at nothing in me but the virtues and merits of Mary." These sins were committed by the hostile man that each carries in himself: "*An enemy hath done this*" (Mt. 13:28). To ward off relapses, it is necessary for Jesus to tear us away from this depraved nature, whose deceptive solicitations leave us no rest: "*Deliver me from the unjust and deceitful man*" (Ps. 42:1). And this will come true only if Jesus and Mary increase in us. Let us, then, say to Jesus: "*Te oportet crescere, me autem minui*, My Jesus, it is necessary for You to increase in my soul and for me to decrease" (cf. Jn. 3:30). And to Mary: "Mary, it is necessary for you to increase in me, and that I be less than I was." And to both of them: "*Crescite et multiplicamini.*" O Jesus and Mary, increase in me, and multiply yourselves outwardly in others.

*
* *

N° 273

Such is the method of Father de Montfort for receiving Communion with Mary. It is not an exclusive method. The Saint even says:

There are an infinity of other thoughts which the Holy Ghost furnishes, and will furnish you, if you are thoroughly interior, mortified, and faithful to this grand and sublime devotion which I have been teaching you.

We can thus be inspired by everything which was said in the course of the *Treatise* and its *Commentary* in order to renew its treasure of ideas and have a discussion about its sources of good inspirations.

But always remember that the more you leave Mary to act in your Communion, the more Jesus will be glorified.

On certain days, you will be so helpless that you will just have the strength to call Mary to your help. But this will also suffice, provided that it is not a pretext to cover your laziness. If, even in your periods of fervor, Mary acquits herself better than you of your duties to Jesus, all the more reason will it be so in your hours of spiritual aridity.

Anyway, you will abandon yourself to Mary, and you will let her act for Jesus, and you will let Jesus act in her for the glory of His Father, for the honor of His Mother, for your good and that of the whole world. And they will carry out this office all the more perfectly the more profoundly you humble yourselves and the more peacefully and silently you will listen to them.

You will not, then, go to any trouble to see, taste or feel Jesus present in you, or to measure the progress which you realize in every Communion. You will not be upset either to remain always the same, in spite of even daily or frequent Communions. For Communion is a mystery of faith. Nothing, neither the presence of Jesus, nor the effects it produces, must show through to the eyes of the body, nor fall under the senses, in any way whatsoever. And, besides, this is not necessary: the just man in all things, but especially here, lives by faith and contents himself with it: "*My just man liveth by faith*" (Heb. 10:38). Furthermore, this small degree of virtue, as minimal as it is, that we have preserved, are we indeed sure that we would still have it, if we had not received Communion frequently? We are under the continuous influence of the Eucharist. We perhaps notice less the changes than those who rarely receive Communion. But it does not mean that our Communions are less fervent, nor especially that they act less in us.

Let us, then, follow the counsel of Fr. de Montfort. Communions through Mary, without concerning ourselves with the sensible or the extraordinary, and our Communions will be good, fruitful, and, be it only in the obscurity of faith, the foretaste of the happiness of heaven.

General conclusion

Those who will have studied the *Treatise on the True Devotion* by means of this *Commentary* will admit without any difficulty that we have a grand work there, standing out less by the number of its pages than by their indisputable value.

Montfort is not only an apostle, but a doctor of the perfect devotion to Mary. No one emphasized as much as he the extent of Mary's power, and the way she exercises her royalty. We know now all that it contains, and how it is realized. No royal power can be compared with that of Mary. It rules everything for her slaves of love, the spiritual as the material; the natural as the supernatural. And in order to give an exact idea of this power, we would return gladly to the word which we used about Brother Rodriguez: it is really a possession. It is no longer only a physical possession, where a foreign power seizes the body and governs it as it pleases, independently of the soul and contrary to the soul, as occurs in diabolical possessions. It is a possession of the whole human person, without any violence and without any downfall, where, consciously and freely, the man eagerly carries out everything that his Sovereign commands him and everything to which she inclines him.

The Holy Slavery does not constitute a special degree of the spiritual life. It can be found in beginners, in the proficient and in the perfect. Depending on whether the slave of love acts more by himself or is more urged on by Mary, we have in its practice either the ascetical or the mystical life. Joined to the other graces that Mary will obtain for her most faithful servants, the slavery of love is capable of leading souls to the highest summits of spirituality. It is capable of introducing them and of stabilizing them in the unitive life, while giving to them, as we saw at the appropriate time, very special help to bear the trials inherent to this way.

May this powerful teaching be understood and put into practice by a very large number of souls. It is for no other purpose that this modest *Commentary* was undertaken and carried out.

Made in United States
North Haven, CT
17 September 2022